Bitter Harvest

Bitter Harvest

Antecedents and Consequences of Property Reforms in Post-Socialist Poland

Suava Zbierski-Salameh

LEXINGTON BOOKS
Lanham • Boulder • New York • Toronto • Plymouth, UK

Published by Lexington Books
A wholly owned subsidiary of The Rowman & Littlefield Publishing Group, Inc.
4501 Forbes Boulevard, Suite 200, Lanham, Maryland 20706
www.rowman.com

10 Thornbury Road, Plymouth PL6 7PP, United Kingdom

British Library Cataloguing in Publication Information Available

Library of Congress Cataloging-in-Publication Data

Zbierski-Salameh, Suava, 1955–
Bitter harvest : antecedents and consequences of property reforms in post-socialist Poland / Suava Zbierski-Salameh.
p. cm.
Includes bibliographical references and index.
Summary: "This book links political and economic sociology examining how postsocialist property changes are rooted in the socialist past and how they relate to the meaning and practices of transition states and their capacity for sustainable economic development. It raises the issue of the applicability of Western institutions in the Eastern European context and the implications for the contemporary politics of European integration in which EU politics aim to smooth over the many divergences of its members"— Provided by publisher.
ISBN 978-0-7391-6513-3 (hardback)—ISBN 978-0-7391-6514-0 (paper)—ISBN 978-0-7391-6515-7 (electronic)
1. Privatization—Poland. 2. Right of property—Poland. 3. Post-communism—Poland. I. Title.
HD4215.7.Z35 2012
333.3'1438—dc23
2012000743

∞™ The paper used in this publication meets the minimum requirements of American National Standard for Information Sciences Permanence of Paper for Printed Library Materials, ANSI/NISO Z39.48-1992.

Printed in the United States of America

In memory of my brother, Wlodzimierz, Adam

Contents

Preface

At the twenty-year anniversary of the 1989 fall of socialism, previously disjointed discourses regarding East European societies have converged upon the same conclusion: These societies are no longer in transition; the massive, state-directed rebuilding projects are complete, even if the expected objectives were not fully realized; and, despite ongoing reforms, post-socialist societies have undergone little further transformation from the dramatic changes produced by the earlier wave of reforms (OECD 1996, Greskovits 2004, Kis 1996, Carothers 2002).

This conclusion has eroded the post-socialism transition discourse centered on examining the nature, direction, and pivotal points of these societies' transitions away from socialism. The transition debate focused on the *internal* process, the effect of the past of these societies on their present, either understood as a defiant repudiation of socialism that was then channeled into the construction of its alternative, or as an inescapable shadow cast by the socialist past on the present. Given the widespread conclusion that these societies have completed their post-socialist transition, the transition discourse has been eclipsed by a new capitalism-centric discourse among scholars both inside and outside of those societies (Amin, Ash, and Tomaney 1995; Dunford and Smith 1998; Kagarlitsky 1995; Pickles and Smith 1998; Bradshaw and Stenning 2004). The latter discourse asserts that the internal dynamics of the East European societies, now integrated into the institutional framework of the European Union and no longer exhibiting transitory characteristics, are the outcome of the powerful forces of capitalism in its global spread. In other words, the focus is on *external* agents of change. With this broad shift in discourse and the acknowledged passage of over twenty years since the fall of socialism, why should we revisit the early post-socialist period? What does an ethnographic study of Polish agriculture during such period have to offer?

First, I believe there is good cause to resurrect the transition analysis. My findings suggest that the transition in Poland and other Eastern European countries is not complete. Rather, these are societies still in the process of creation, being shaped by evolving internal interactions between state and individual, as well as external global forces. A better understanding of the transformations, including why the reform outcomes differed from those predicted, can inform the ongoing development of these countries. In the process, we will also gain insight into social action in Western societies by examining the limits of its universality and the feasibility of replicating Western institutions in other contexts, as was attempted in Eastern Europe. Second, and more broadly, my findings highlight the importance of a more dynamic understanding of property than has been present in the post-socialist discourse to date. Given the centrality of property in the post-socialist reforms, it is imperative that property is defined properly—not just as an economic construct but as a bundle of rights and obligations that figures prominently in negotiated interactions between individuals and states.

An Incomplete Transformation

Scholars have identified significant deficits in the economic and political results of the 1989 revolutions and the ensuing reforms aimed at "joining the West." Oberschall (1996), among many others, fears the post-socialist economies will detour to a stagnant mode. As evidence, he points to their growing national debts, large budget deficits, persistent two-digit-level unemployment (particularly high among young work-seekers), level of poverty among the unemployed and elderly, underinvestment in education, health, and social welfare, inefficient tax base, and threat of inflation. He concludes, all these ills could make for an economic foundation unable to sustain a nascent democratic civil society.

Further, the democracy promoters widely attest to disappointing political outcomes. A deepening distrust between the Eastern European states and their citizens has steadily replaced the initial euphoria surrounding the installation of the post-socialist regimes following the peaceful 1989 revolutions (Sztompka 2000; Ost 2005; Podemski 2011; Drozdowski 2009; Wozniak 2009). Scholars refer to an "unfinished transformation," expressing their concern over anemic democratic institutions, an absence of clear political platforms differentiating parties, and a weak participation of the citizenry in the political process. They fear the erosion of democracy, a disappointing outcome in itself, but more so because of its negative impact on the capacity of these societies to further implement necessary measures for sustainable economic performance. They attribute this political decline to the recent institutional integration into, and dependence on, their Western counterparts, resulting in insufficient attention paid to the needs of internal constituencies.

Although there is agreement that the post-socialist outcomes have fallen short of their Western ideals, there have not been satisfying answers as to why these deficits occurred or why seemingly uniform members of the old Soviet bloc experienced vastly different post-socialist trajectories (Csaba 2006; Greskovits 2004). Transition discourse withered away before resolving these puzzles. The capitalism-centered debate picks up the unresolved questions left by transition discourse not as matters to be explained but rather as "given conditions," and also emphasizes the new contextual dimension, situating Eastern European societies within the capitalist system. It derives their present internal changes from their *external* relations with the West. It explains the chasm between the earlier projections of "joining the West" and Eastern Europe's real political and economic outcomes by centering on capitalism's propensity to produce global unevenness as it penetrates new terrains, with those late Eastern European entrants relegated to the periphery.

In this book I seek to connect the otherwise disjointed transition- and capitalism-centric discourses on the development of post-socialist societies. Instead of treating the unanticipated outcomes of post-socialism as "given conditions," my analysis restores these outcomes to genuine puzzles that challenge us for answers. Without disputing the global forces increasingly at play in Eastern European societies, I call for redrawing attention to the internally generated processes, set early in the transition and thus preceding the economic, political, and institutional integration of those societies into global capitalism. In shifting the focus temporally and conceptually, I demonstrate that the transition discourse has not exhausted its usefulness. By incorporating advances in neoinstitutional theory and legal scholars' perspectives, it can provide a conceptual reassessment of the transformation processes, recasting them in a new light and facilitating a more comprehensive understanding of those processes and their effect on current development.

The Centrality of Property

The shaky economic foundations of these post-socialist societies and the disconnect between the governing and the governed reveal an ambiguous legitimacy basis for the regimes. The roots of the present economic woes and political discord can be traced back to the initial measures for constructing the new social order, more specifically, to the pillar of reform: the early privatization drive. The privatization drive, undertaken as an economic imperative, was a government-led project of destatization of production assets designed to dislodge the state from exercising ownership rights over national production resources in order to vest those rights in individuals. The post-socialist privatization drives rested on a binary conception of property, with state-owned property under socialism defined as opposite to private property under capitalism. The state property signified a negative, homogeneous category connoting in essence the absence of real (that is, private) property.

I submit that, in the course of implementation, the privatization drive, instead of maximizing the economic self-interest of individuals, as intended, set off an *interaction crisis* between the government and those affected by the reform. The attempted change in property arrangements spurred a deep contestation over far broader prerogatives than the narrow economic objectives pursued by the post-socialist regime. I argue that the privatization drive produced unanticipated outcomes in the early phase of the transition because its theoretical underpinnings were erroneous; its underlying dichotomous model of transition from state to private property had obscured the very objects of the reform: the nature, complexity, and dynamics of property arrangements under socialism. This interaction crisis over the privatization drive early in the transition had effects on the further course of post-socialist development and contributed to the corrosion of trust in the post-socialist regime.

Curiously, despite the fact that privatization drives were the centerfold of post-socialist regimes' reform programs, property proved to be an enigmatic subject for analysis. The economist Kowalik (2009), surveying Polish literature to date, marveled about the plethora of studies of post-socialist privatization drives, and the relative dearth of analysis of property in post-socialism. Yet, a process of property change cannot be taken as a given; a change in property arrangements in East European societies is not synonymous with a directed-from-above privatization drive or a transition from state to private ownership (Walder 1995; Stark 1996; Verdery 1999; Hann 2003). Hence in this book I reexamine property change in the Eastern European societies by moving away from rendering socialist property as a homogenous negative of capitalistic private property. Instead, I aim to construct a positive content of property under socialism. I propose the category of *conjoint property* in an attempt to capture conceptually the shared characteristics of the multiform property arrangements existing under socialism. Further, I detail the constraints such conjoint property created on the span of feasible property rearrangements in post-socialism and in turn their effect on the state's capacity for continued guidance of post-socialist change.

Contrary to the prevailing rendition of socialist property where the state is viewed as the sole ownership claimant, effectively preempting any ownership rights of its citizens, conjoint property is conceived as a duality of distinct property subjects. It refers to the shared claims—legal or physical—to discrete productive resources by both the state and diverse groups of entities. This subject duality characterized all forms of ownership existing under socialism—state, cooperative, and private. I posit that these property claims were not limited to the economic behavior of the actors on the ground regarding extraction and allocation of resources for production purposes, but also pertained directly to the social redistribution of economic rewards. As such, I posit, in accordance with neoinstitutional theory, that these property claims reflected underlying ideological values and normative, nonmaterial expectations as to what was socially just in the economic conduct of individuals and in the mode of state governance. These shared ownership claims were therefore a part of a broader social contract of rights *and* obligations bonding the state with its citizens. The state was a coclaimant in conjoint property relations as an actor-owner and as an institutional structure erected under socialism for governing the exercise of ownership claims. This institutional structure was designed to perform as much for economic as social and political goals.

The post-socialist transition should be understood in turn as an evolution of *conjoint-property* in its multiforms into *incomplete exclusive property* in post-socialism, in which the formal ceding of ownership claims by the state in favor of exclusive private ownership was short-circuited by changes in the institutional structure governing the exercise of exclusive property rights and by the long-established and deeply engrained normative expectations associated with property held by the newly vested exclusive owners.

A View from the Ground

In the early 1990s, the first Polish post-socialist government of Tadeusz Mazowiecki introduced a shock therapy of privatization, liberalization, and marketization. The reforms first targeted agriculture, an economic sector considered best suited for a faster implementation of reforms due to its unique ownership structure. This book originated with my fieldwork in a western province of Poland, a primarily advanced agricultural region called Greater Poland (Wielkopolska), conducted in the aftermath of such shock therapy.

Polish agriculture's ownership structure did not align with the general image of a socialist society based on homogeneous state property. While other agricultural systems in Eastern Europe were fully collectivized early on in socialism, the Polish socialist regime managed to convert only a small segment of agriculture into cooperative and state farms. A vast majority of land, by default, remained privately owned, a condition that emerged out of years of contestation of power between the socialist state and the peasants. Therefore, for the post-socialist reformers, the central and, at the same time, daunting reform objective to establish private ownership appeared far simplified in the context of the vast, already private subsector of Polish agriculture. The program amounted to strengthening already existing private owners in the exercise of their property rights and a full-scale privatization drive only for the relatively small state and cooperative agricultural segments.

I conducted field interviews over several months during a four-year period with agricultural producers in the private, cooperative, and state sectors of agriculture, during which I began to perceive Polish agriculture as the key to providing deeper insight into the nature of social change in not just post-socialist Poland, but also broader socialist societies and post-socialist transformation. Although the multiform property structure dominated by private ownership in Polish agriculture and the historical circumstances of its formation were atypical, Polish agriculture, nonetheless, reflected a far more general trend in the dynamics of socialist property arrangements *predating* the 1989 post-socialist revolutions. These earlier property arrangements impacted the outcome of the post-socialist reform efforts, as well as the perceptions of such reforms, as illustrated by two diametrically different interviews I conducted in 1991, one with the minister of agriculture and the other with a recipient of those reforms, an individual peasant.

In the spirit of Western-style utilitarian economic theory, the minister confidently predicted that shock therapy reforms would achieve sustainable economic growth in agriculture. The lifting of all governmental constraints, together with the cancellation of extensive agrarian subsidies under the former socialist government, and introduction of "real" prices for agricultural goods were meant to lead producers to a careful production resource allocation and an efficient and competitive level of production. Under his rendition, those producers who were guided by economic rationality would develop modern, commodified farms, while those who did not heed such market lessons would have to find a different line of work. This natural selection process was to result in the long-awaited consolidation of fragmented land plots into efficiently sized farms, at last rationalizing the land distribution structure in Polish agriculture. Those growth-oriented private farms focused on expansion of land and production would in turn serve as the engine for the speedy privatization of state farms.

Yet, early into the reform implementation, I encountered a deep cleavage between this veteran politician's confidence in constructing a new social reality from the top down and the assessments of the reform effects by the agricultural producers. One particular encounter gave me a glimpse of the complexity and intensity of peasants' assessments of the lessons spoken of by the former minister of agriculture. A proud-looking man in his sixties, an owner of a large farm with modern-looking and well-maintained buildings in a village in the Greater Poland (Wielkopolska) region, displaying a visible anger, commented on the privatization reforms.

He charged that the post-socialist reform program was a conspiracy inflicted on Eastern Europe by the Western establishment in order to replace

Soviet dominance over its societies and markets. As an owner of his land for the last forty years, he proclaimed himself a proud challenger of the failed state socialist collectivization drives, turned successful farmer over the last twenty years of socialism, with a thriving specialized agricultural production. While he always approached the socialist regime's agrarian policies relating to private ownership with suspicion and uncertainty, he counted on the post-socialist Solidarity-based government to unequivocally support private agriculture. Instead, as an agricultural producer, he believed the post-socialist policy ruined his specialized farm and forced him to retreat from markets. He referred to his declining economic production from the standpoint of reduced incomes, but even more so from that of the degradation of his social standing—from a modernizing specialist in herbal seed production on contract with the Agricultural Academy to an inefficient subsistence producer, cut off from his earlier connection to the national economy. He expressed a deep indignation over the impending collapse of domestic food production under the post-socialist reforms, which would threaten Polish sovereignty, replacing Poland's former dependence on the Soviet Union with dependence on the West. These and many other similar sentiments expressed by members of all segments of agriculture left three lasting impressions on me.

I saw a disconnect in the perception of the scope and nature of the reform-triggered outcomes. The intended change for the minister resided narrowly within the economic domain, confined to eliciting an enhanced production performance from the actors on the ground. On the other hand, the peasant's assessment of the reform's economic impact not only sharply challenged the minister's evaluations, but also used broader measures to evaluate reform outcomes, invoking civic values and a consideration of public good. Instead of strengthening his property rights, he saw the post-socialist government as betraying him by, in effect, attenuating the production rights so steadfastly and effectively defended earlier in the contestation with the socialist regime. He felt debased and constrained in his production activities, removed from his earlier career opportunities, and cut off from the material proceeds of commodity production. More importantly, he focused on unwelcome changes in other domains of his life. He referred to his lesser social status, following the end of his contract with the state-run Agricultural Academy. Further, he defended his individual rights while also calling upon the post-socialist regime to show a sense of responsibility toward the welfare of society at large.

Furthermore, I was struck by the discord in expectations of the state. The post-socialist regime equated protection of private property rights with liberating the owners from the constraints of the state, whereas the peasants viewed the state's withdrawal from the coordination of economic matters as an abdication of its obligations.

Thirdly, there was a deep chasm in how the two sides understood the socialist past and its constitutive events. For the minister, the electoral defeat of the Communist Party in 1989 created a point of political extrication from socialism, an unexpected yet desirable constitutive event, which provided a political will and space to denounce partial and ineffective socialist economic measures. This political revolution created unprecedented opportunity both to spearhead an economic revolution, and to establish the predominance of private property rights as an indispensible mechanism for economic growth. In the peasant's rendition, the periodization of the changes in property arrangements looked different; he believed the greatest gains in the consolidation of his ownership rights were accomplished in the struggle with the socialist regime, thus preceding, by a decade, the political demise of the regime in 1989.

The contentious nature of the exchange revealed that the post-socialist government's intentions with respect to property rearrangements could not be taken as stipulations that had been heeded or bought into by agents on the ground. The peasant revealed he is not a passive object of reforms. In place of expected conformity, his defiance showed he did not apply these stipulations. Instead, he subjected the reform meanings to his own interpretations, filtered by his assessment of his own purposeful past activities. This exchange showed me that the dominant teleological approaches within the transition debate[1] have overlooked the importance of the intentions and strategic responses of the actors on the ground and their influence on the actual changes in property arrangements.

Weaving a New Future

As these exchanges illustrate, privatization reform should be reconsidered as interactive, operating not only from the top down as a purposeful strategy by the post-socialist government to bring about systemic structural change but also operating bottom-up with important inputs from the actors on the ground (Hausner and Tilbury 1995). The actual, rather than government-projected, outcomes of the privatization reform stem from the purposeful actions of the aggregate of actors aiming to influence the privatization process in order to accomplish their ends. And, as we have seen from the peasant's account, those ends, bounded by context, are not limited to economic ones.

This approach thus presents the structural change as having a process-like nature. Norbert Elias captured this unfolding of social reality within a constant process of purposive actions in his notion of "interweaving," where out of "innumerable individual interests and intentions . . . something eventually emerges that, as it turns out, has neither been planned nor intended by any single individual. . . . And this is actually the whole secret of social interweaving . . . ; this is the secret of socio-genesis and social dynamics" (1994: 221).

The post-socialist privatization drive spearheaded an interactive process of change in property arrangements that was marked by conflict and bargaining instead of conformity, revealing clearly its political nature. Despite the reformers' intentions, post-socialist property change did not merely affect microlevel economic activities related to the extraction and allocation of production resources, but also dislodged a complex constellation of social and political relations imbedded in these microlevel economic activities and revealed a deep clash of expectations as to the strategies and desired end of the changes. Already, the early stage of post-socialist transition problematized the generally accepted conception of property as a purely economic institution with universal and stable characteristics and thus with predictable outcomes. The question remained then—how should property be properly conceived?

* * *

In summary, with the benefit of these twenty years since the collapse of socialism, this book seeks to apply anew transition theory, as it has evolved with recent developments in neoinstitutional theory. I will refocus the debate on the specific historic context, particularly with respect to property arrangements both pre- and post-reform, so as to more aptly identify the pivot points in the post-socialist transformation on which the debate should be focused. In so doing, I will demonstrate that the failure of post-socialist outcomes to align with expectations was not due to failures in reform implementation, but rather stemmed from flaws in the theoretical underpinnings of the reforms and the subsequent assessment of their effects, including, generally, a disconnect between Western-style capitalism and lingering socialist values and, specifically, an incomplete understanding of property arrangements under socialism and the effects of such arrangements on expectations of the parties subjected to the reforms. Further, in examining the latter issue, I will expose the shortcomings of common conceptions of "property" as solely an economic construct and endeavor to better answer the question "What *is* property?" Finally, having sought to answer the questions that earlier forms of transition theory left unanswered by exposing the dynamic and interactive nature of property and related economic, political, and social arrangements, I hope to demonstrate that, in fact, the transition is not complete. The gap between transition- and capitalism-centric discourses is bridged when we recognize that the transition is not a unidirectional, top down reform process but, rather, a dynamic process influenced by the interweaving and constantly changing relations between internal actors and state *and* state and global forces.

Note

1. For a comprehensive outline of a transition debate, see Ivan Szelenyi and Eric Kostello, 1996, "The Market Transition Debate: Toward a Synthesis?" *American Journal of Sociology* 101 (4): 1082–1096.

References

Amin, Ash, and John Tomaney. 1995. *Behind the Myth of European Union: Prospects for Cohesion*. London: Routledge.

Bradshaw, Michael, and Allison Stenning. 2004. *East Central Europe and the Former Soviet Union: The Post-Socialist States*. Harlow, Essex: Pearson Education Limited.

Carothers, Thomas. 2002. "The End of the Transition Paradigm." *Journal of Democracy* 13 (1): 5–21.

Csaba, László. 2006. *Social Change in Central and Eastern Europe: General Trends and National Patterns*. Warsaw: Tiger. Working Paper no. 98.

Drozdowski, Rafal. 2009. "Polska w polowie drogi miedzy pierwszym a drugim skokiem modernizacyjnym." *Ruch Prawniczy, Ekonomiczny i Socjologiczny* 2: 423–438.

Dunford, Michael, and Adrian Smith. 1998. "Uneven Development in Europe." In *The New Europe: Economy, Society and Environment*, edited by D. Pinder, 203–222. Chichester: Wiley.

Elias, Norbert. 1994. *The Civilizing Process*. Oxford: Blackwell.

Greskovits, Bela. 2004. "Beyond Transition: The Variety of Post-Socialist Development." In *From Liberal Values to Democratic Transition*, edited by R. Dworkin, 201–226. Budapest: CEU Press.

Hann, Chris. 2003. "Introduction: Decollectivization and the Moral Economy." In *The Postsocialist Agrarian Question: Property Relations and the Rural Condition*, Chris Hann and the "Property Relations" Group, 1–46. Munster: LIT Verlag.

Hausner, Jerzy, and Jasper Tilbury. 1995. "Imperative vs. Interactive Strategy of Systemic Change in Central and Eastern Europe." *Review of International Political Economy* 2 (2): 249–266.

Kagarlitsky, Boris. 1995. *The Mirage of Modernization*. New York: Monthly Review Press.

Kis, János. 1996. "The Transition is Over." *Beszelo III* 1 (6): 4–11.

Kowalik, Tadeusz. 2009. *www.PolskaTransformacja.pl*. Warsaw: Muza SA.

Oberschall, Anthony. 1996. "The Great Transition: China, Hungary and Sociology Exit Socialism Into the Market." *American Journal of Sociology* 101 (4): 1028–1041.

OECD. 1996. *Transition at the Local Level: The Czech Republic, Hungary, Poland and the Slovak Republic*. Paris: Organisation for Economic Co-operation and Development.

Ost, David. 2005. *The Defeat of Solidarity: Anger and Politics in Post-Communist Europe*. Ithaca: Cornell University Press.

Pickles, John, and Adrian Smith. 1998. *Theorizing Transition: The Political Economy of Post-Communist Transformations*. New York: Routledge.

Podemski, Krzysztof, ed. 2011. *Spoleczenstwa Europy Srodkowo-Wschodniej: Projekt Eurequal*. Poznan: Wydawnictwo Naukowe UAM.

Stark, David. 1996. "Recombinant Property in East European Capitalism." *American Journal of Sociology* 101 (4): 993–1027.

Szelenyi, Ivan, and Eric Kostello. 1996. "The Market Transition Debate: Toward a Synthesis?" *American Journal of Sociology* 101 (4): 1082–96.

Sztompka, Piotr. 2000. *Trauma wielkiej zmiany. Spoleczne koszta transformacji* [*Trauma of a Great Change. Social Costs of Transformation*]. Warsaw: ISP PAN.

Verdery, Katherine. 1999. "Fuzzy Property: Rights, Power, and Identity in Transylvania's Decollectivization." In *Uncertain Transition: Ethnographies of Everyday Life in the Postsocialist World*, edited by Michael Burawoy and Katherine Verdery, 53–81. Boulder: Rowman and Littlefield.

Walder, Andrew. 1995. "Career Mobility and the Communist Political Order." *American Sociological Review* 60 (3): 309–328.

Wozniak, Zbigniew. 2009. "Poklosie Okraglego Stolu. Przeszlosc dla przyszlosci." *Ruch Prawniczy, Ekonomiczny i Socjologiczny* 2 (71): 349–379.

Acknowledgments

All books are written in solitude, yet they are sustained by social support and ultimately are a social product. This one is particularly so. I struggled many years with this project first as a dissertation and, years later, when teaching at Haverford College, as a book manuscript, often doubting whether I could bring it to fruition. This doubt stemmed as much from facing tangible and formidable family and professional responsibilities that interrupted my writing, as well as from the recognition that the timing of the project has not been well paced with the mainstream of scholarly discourse.

Although Eastern Europe produced the 1989 revolutions that became the subject of intense debates in social sciences for the next decade or so, it was the Western academic world that produced hegemonic knowledge about these events, with a triumphalism of neoliberal perspective in interpreting them and in delineating the main domains of scholarly discourse. I was introduced to these debates when entering my cohort of Berkeley's doctoral program in sociology as the only foreign student. In contrast to my American counterparts all arriving at Berkeley with undergraduate trainings from prestigious U.S. universities, I entered the program with a degree from an Eastern European place no one knew or could pronounce—Poznan, Poland. This entry evoked in me deference to Western academia in general. Even as I intuitively formulated research questions for my dissertation that steered me away from the main themes of the transition discourse on Eastern Europe, I feared they were displaced or unwarranted and struggled with a nagging self-doubt in the validity of my project. By the time I gained trust in my perspective and turned to reworking the manuscript into a book, Eastern Europe and its reality after socialism had lost the attention of Western scholars, overshadowed by other developments and issues. Nonetheless, I continued to believe there was more to say.

From the large group of people who sustained me in this protracted project, I am most indebted to Michael Burawoy. As the chair of my dissertation committee, Michael was quintessential to my dissertation work. Beyond that, throughout the many years of my graduate studies in Berkeley, he embarked on a long, and often frustrating, mission to convince me that I can have my own meaningful voice in sociology. In that process, he had a dual effect on me. As a superb and renowned scholar and teacher, and foremost a person of unique integrity, he was always a towering figure who was a stark reminder of my own shortcomings. Yet he continuously inspired me to aim higher than I ever thought possible, and finally he instilled in me trust in my abilities. In that he gave me a far more priceless gift than the dissertation itself.

Throughout my stay at Berkeley, I was fortunate to learn sociology from the most accomplished scholars. I received generous support from Michael Watts. He mesmerized me with his passion and intellectual brilliance in the classroom and his scholarly work. Neil Fligstein engaged me in intellectual pursuit that revealed to me the broader theoretical ramifications of my work and stimulated me to look in new ways at my project. I found myself privileged to be a student of Neil Smelser. His writings, the courses I took with him, and his chairing my qualifying examination will remain with me as unforgettable experiences. Mark Gould, my mentor, colleague, and friend at Haverford College, with his analytical brilliance that tends to make everyone around him feel intellectually inadequate, provided tireless encouragement, intellectual guidance, constructive critique, and emotional sustenance during my reworking of the dissertation into this book. Laurie Hart, Linda Bell, Sid Waldman, Kathleen Wright, and Kay Edwards of Haverford College taught me how to be a wonderful colleague in ways I never imagined.

During different stages of working on this project as a dissertation, I developed many friendships that sustain me emotionally and intellectually. Terry Arendell, Judy Auerbach, Mary Waters, Gay Seidman, Steve Stoltenberg, John Torpey, Marc Garcelon, Veljko Vojacic, and Vedat Milor bring very fond memories of my stay within the department. I was fortunate to be a part of "The Smith Group." Bob Freeland, Patrick Heller, Mary Kelsey, Hyan OK Park, Chris Rhomberg, Brian Rich, Andres Schneiderman, Rob Wrenn, and Mona Younis provided me with a friendly, yet rigorous intellectual critique of my project in progress. I am grateful to Bob Freeland for our regular conversations about our respective projects that extended far beyond the Smith Group's life and over the years provided me with a great sense of comfort and one of the closest friendships. I am particularly indebted to Lynne Haney, whose support was indisputably most crucial to sustain me at the most critical stages of this project and who became a dear friend over the years.

I want to thank numerous people who assisted me in my fieldwork in Poland. I thank Czeslaw Janicki, the former deputy prime minister and minister of agriculture, for my discussions with him and for enabling me to contact other officials within the ministry of agriculture. I thank Congressman Waldy Dzikowski, the chairman of the local government during my fieldwork, who never hesitated to assist me with my needs and encouraged others within the local government to accommodate me in my work. I particularly thank personnel from the Agricultural, Planning, and Special Services departments. I cannot name all the peasants, agricultural cooperative members, state farm personnel, and many members of other local economic and political organizations to whom I extend my thanks. My visits with many of them became far more than just collecting sociological data. These meaningful encounters only reminded me why I was interested in doing sociology in the first place. I thank many sociologists from Poland—Henryk Domanski, Rafal Drozdowski, Krzysztof Gorlach, Elzbieta Tarkowska, Krzysztof Podemski, Zbigniew Wozniak, and Barbara Pawlowska—for the very insightful and engaging discussions during which they shared with me how they think about reality after socialism.

I thank the students from Haverford College for their assistance in the revisions of the manuscript. I am indebted to Amanda Amann for her tireless, very efficient, and professional editorial support. This book would not have materialized without the great support and understanding from Justin Race of Lexington Books and his very professional and diligent colleagues, particularly, Sabah Ghulamali and Lindsey Schauer. Last but not least, I am indebted to Ghassan for showing me the meaning of perseverance. I thank my children, Christina and Joseph—your love, moral support and tireless help allowed me to bring this project to completion.

Introduction: The Mystery of Property

The Events of 1989 in Eastern Europe: Imported Refolutions or Organically Grown Revolutions?

The 1989 revolutions that brought down socialism in Eastern Europe have been commonly marveled at as quite unusual, in their "velvet" and "by design" character. According to Samuel P. Huntington (1968: 264), "A revolution is a rapid, fundamental, and violent domestic change in the dominant values and myths of a society, in its political institutions, social structure, leadership and government activities and policies." By contrast, the events in Eastern Europe were not violent; rather, with the exception of the Romanian case, they appeared peaceful and were commonly referred to as "velvet revolutions" (Havel 1991; Glenn 1999; Shepherd 2000). The Eastern European revolutions seemed relatively short on explicit political or ideological agendas. This was because the 1989 revolutions proclaimed to be not a projection of a yet unrealized future, but a struggle for attaining societal forms and institutions already in existence in the capitalist West.[1] As one observer pointed out, the reality that Eastern Europe aspired to was a short train ride away to the West, in that the events of 1989 were about facilitating viable *means* rather than sorting out and articulating societal goals. Capitalism prevailed and thus the revolutions of 1989 aimed "back to the future": their point of departure, the political collapse of socialism, became synonymous with their destination—constructing capitalism.[2] Consequently, the Eastern European revolutions have been perceived as focusing pragmatically and narrowly on designing workable economic programs that would allow those countries to finally reach the prosperity levels enjoyed by their Western European neighbors (Przeworski 1991; Janos 2000). For politicians and analysts alike, the question of viable means seemed to start consistently with one answer—a creation of an incentive system for economic agents to be vested in efficient economic performance and producing economic growth. Creation of incentive systems to release the innate entrepreneurship of economic agents implied reintroducing an institution of private property as a way of overcoming chronically nonperforming socialist economies plagued by state property devoid of such an incentive system. Adam Smith's central thesis that unfettered private owners in pursuing their economic interests create societal prosperity was a guiding light in the design.[3] Hence, the 1989 revolutions have been equated with privatization drives and creation of private property.

The Eastern European revolutions of 1989 appeared also atypical when measured against another criterion commonly evoked to define revolutions. T. Skocpol (1976: 175), citing Lenin, posits that, in addition to rapid, basic transformations of socioeconomic and political institutions, the second distinctive feature delineating social revolution is massive class upheavals from below. In contrast, the destruction of socialism in Eastern Europe was generally conceived as a transformation permeating from the top—initiated by the political collapse of socialist ruling elites in 1989 (Burawoy and Lukacs 1992; Poznanski 1995) and *not* prompted by any mass unrest (with the exception of Romania). What looked like a void in the wake of the peaceful political collapse of socialism was quickly filled by the emergence of the post-socialist regimes, enthusiastically welcomed inside and abroad. These top-controlled political revolutions appeared to grant post-socialist regimes the opportunity to build by design radically new economic realities from the top down based on rational intentions, clear objectives, and methods and instruments for their realization that had been tested and proven earlier in the West. Thus the revolutions of 1989 were perceived as curious in part because the political revolutions preceded and spearheaded, from the top down, the economic revolutions or, more accurately stated, *refolutions*. This term, coined by Timothy Garton Ash (1990), alludes to the form in which the systemic change is realized—through induced reforms.

Implied in this dominant rendition of the distinctiveness of the Eastern European revolutions was their teleological and exogenous character: the objectives and means guiding the course of the social change were presumed to be defined and directed by the state in the form of an economic reform blueprint. This definition further implied that social change was imposed on the individuals from outside, with the individuals surrounded by society and unable to influence it. This version of the revolutions also asserts that those blueprints were not generated from within the host societies but instead were brought by Western experts from outside and adopted and incorporated by post-socialist leaders, who were inexperienced themselves in designing Western-type institutions. Such perception of the exogeneity of the Eastern European revolutions has been only reinforced by Western multilateral agencies and advisors to the Eastern Europe governments, thereby exporting vigorously the conventional, neoliberal view of transition as a relatively unproblematic implementation of a set of universalistic policies oriented for economic growth.

A dual challenge soon confronted this common account of the distinctiveness of the Eastern European revolutions and, in the early days, the triumphalism of neoliberalism associated with them. Whereas in 1989 to many observers it looked like the end of history, as manifested by capitalism and the reliance on the entrepreneurial instincts of private owners as the universal and only remaining option for societal organization, twenty years later, this end of history seems distant: not only the feasibility of successfully transplanting this option elsewhere revealed itself as problematic, but also the very viability of Western capitalism came powerfully into question with the financial crisis of 2008 erupting in the United States and spreading globally, followed by the European sovereign debt crisis. Thus, the ideal of Western capitalism has proven to be far more elusive to Eastern European societies rising from the ruins of socialism than initially foreseen. Attempts to replicate it have proven to be uneven, protracted, not fully consolidated, and potentially reversible. Privatization reforms have been difficult to implement, often unfinished, and frequently unfavorably received as a harmful course of actions economically and politically.

The stunning financial and sovereign debt crises in the West also prompted profound questions about the soundness of Western institutions and capitalism. Not long ago, laissez-faire Western advisors hailed private property as the fundamental instrument for transplanting capitalism to Eastern Europe and generating economic efficiency and prosperity. Recently capitalism, free markets, and private property became in desperate need of defense by smart states, when capitalism, laissez-faire, and private owners could no longer be assumed to benefit broader society, but could, instead, be seen as bent on destroying common good. Cornerstone institutions of capitalism presumed universally valid no longer appeared so, raising fundamental questions about their nature.

Grappling with the question of the feasibility of transplanting Western capitalism elsewhere, Hernando de Soto, in his book *The Mystery of Capital* (2000), admits that the privatization reforms pursued by the Eastern European post-socialist societies reflected a worldwide core strategy of accomplishing Western-level economic prosperity. Yet, as he also notes, the universal desire to emulate the Western capitalist model is persistently met by an inability to do so. To uncover the secret and fleeting formula of Western success, de Soto examines various unsuccessful privatization programs within the Latin American context. What he finds problematic about the non-Western institution of property is that it is unable to create capital. The burgeoning entrepreneurship of private owners is realized primarily within vast slums surrounding urban centers, institutionally isolated and deprived of the benefits of legal ownership. Therefore the creation of Western-style capital elsewhere, including post-socialist Eastern Europe, does not merely rest on the existence of private property. It further depends on the capacity of the state to create the *conditions of ownership*—to *judicially* integrate private property owners into unified national property systems. Such integration lowers the transaction costs of the private owners' extralegal economic activities, hence making their property rights efficient.

Despite the current global failures of privatization drives, de Soto reaffirms the universal feasibility of the Western capitalist trajectory with his time-lag thesis. As it took the Western states a few centuries to consolidate fragmented property arrangements into unified, national, and hence efficient property systems, the rest of the world still can construct capitalist prosperity, albeit at a delayed pace. De Soto thus contributes to the dominant debates on the question of how to get to capitalism successfully and expeditiously by pointing not to one but to two necessary types of actors—entrepreneurial private property owners *and* the state. As de Soto brings the state, even though only implicitly, back into the discourse on privatization and the capitalist trajectory, he directs our attention to the issue of how the state affects the deployment of property actions and the organization and aggregate performance of the broader economy.

Despite his original insights, de Soto's analysis yet again reaffirms the neoliberal assertion that an institution of private property, organically grown within Western capitalism over a span of centuries, can be *grafted by design* into other social contexts, including post-socialist Eastern Europe. This expectation implies a perception of property as a category that is timeless and fixed, involving an absolute individual or corporate right of a person *in things* to *dispose of* or *alienate* or *use*. Such property rights are further seen as unconditional; they do not depend on the owner's performance of any social functions or obligations in society. This conception of property is assumed sufficiently precise, consisting of articulated, detailed rules that can always be replicated in distinct contexts. It is further assumed to produce specific outcomes in practice—the efficient allocation of economic resources by rational, self-interested agents. Those outcomes are seen as the essence and justification of private property—ultimately not only protecting an individual's right to life, but also providing the entire society with "a good life," understood as a materially prosperous life. The mystery of capital for de Soto thus amounts to the consistent application of both key ingredients (private property and the state-generated "conditions of ownership") in the non-Western context to assure spreading economic prosperity beyond the Western boundaries.

In contrast to de Soto's thesis, the proposition underlying this book is that the promulgation of privatization drives does not attest to the universal feasibility of grafting Western capitalism into different contexts, and thus the puzzle of the *particular* privatization drives and their divergent outcomes cannot be solved by attending to an *abstract* mystery of Western capitalism. The spread of privatization drives in different parts of the world, including Eastern Europe, does not validate the assumption that neoliberalism was adopted in the reform packages because of its economic rationality and technical efficiency (Powell and DiMaggio 1991: 15; Meyer and Rowan 1991: 44; Zucker 1991: 85–88). The argument advanced in this book is that the adoption of the neoliberal reform package in post-socialist Poland stemmed from mostly political interests rather than from economic reasons[4] (Powell and DiMaggio 1991: 67–74; Babb 2001: 16–21; Centeno 2002).

Furthermore, contrary to neoliberal assertions, the general appeal of privatizations does not imply that its currency has rested on clarity or unity of meaning (Cole and Grossman 2002: 317). The point advanced in this book is that privatization has divergent and conflicting meanings for its different participants and hence cannot be transplanted to different contexts as the same "thing." Political leaders, scholars, and members of societies undergoing privatizations have had varying, sometimes divergent perceptions of what "private property" means. When we focus our attention on post-socialist transformations and privatization programs, property emerges as a complex concept with various meanings, rather than a fixed, economic entity with clearly delineated boundaries to be grafted within new host societies. Hence, in order to examine the question of the post-socialist privatization programs and their outcomes, we need to engage in tracing the *mystery of property* instead. And once we accept that a Western conception of property is not *the* conception of property, it would lead us to pose the questions of what the changes in property arrangements entailed in post-socialist Eastern Europe, when and how they originated, and what meaning these changes have for distinct actors involved in the privatization processes.

Examining such questions also prompts us to take a second look at the 1989 post-socialist revolutions, as measured against the criteria evoked by Skocpol, Lenin, and Huntington. I posit that the rendition of rapid privatization reforms as pursuing narrowly economic prosperity and devoid of political and ideological agendas obscures the particular nature of the post-socialist transitions. Even though commonly dated to 1989, the post-socialist revolutions were protracted. Their ultimate 1989 conclusion was rapid and unanticipated by observers and participants alike; nevertheless they were preceded by fundamental yet gradual transformations in the property arrangements decades earlier. These property transformations incubated and evolved within the socialist system. They initially stabilized that system, yet they simultaneously undermined its ideological legitimacy, which effectively led to the collapse of the socialist political elites.[5]

These gradual changes in socialist property arrangements before the political collapse of the socialist elites in 1989 framed the set of politically and economically viable alternative property arrangements available to post-socialist reformers. Thus, contrary to the common renditions of the post-socialist policies as imported from the West to emulate the West, the alternative perspective espoused in this book emphasizes the endogenous sources of post-socialist change from its top and bottom directions. The view proposed here, consistent with Bockman and Eyal's important thesis (2002), posits that, looking at the internal impetus of post-socialist change, the neoliberal post-socialist reform program was as much a home-grown product as a Western import. The post-socialist reforms were profoundly conditioned in the content of their policies by the antecedent property arrangements and became articulated in the long and complicated course of international and *internal* debates. The post-socialist reformers, far from being passive recipients of the Western neoliberal model brought to Eastern Europe after the collapse of socialism, had actively participated in those debates decades earlier (Bockman and Eyal 2002). The incorporation of the neoliberal ideas into their reform package was not predicated on their proven economic superiority, but derived out of economic exigencies in the aftermath of unsuccessful earlier reforms and the immediate political and ideological interests of the post-socialist elites to differentiate their reform program from that of the politically discredited late socialist regime. Thus, only on the surface did the property revolutions appear as narrowly economic in nature; hidden beneath the surface were salient, if not explicitly spelled out, political and ideological dimensions. An examination of these dimensions is necessary to understand the post-socialist transformations, the trajectories of which diverged in distinct ways from the projections made by post-socialist reformers and analysts.

Although the post-socialist revolutions of 1989 did not display upheaval of the masses, they were not the sole product of the great property redesigns from the top. The relative absence of mass mobilization is not equal to an absence of social conflict, resistance, or bargaining processes (Scott 1985, 1990). Hence, I will argue that the changing property arrangements resulted from the complex, mostly nonviolent, ongoing contestations between different social agents on the ground and the socialist and the post-socialist ruling elites. The formation of post-socialist property was thus articulated in the context of these political contestations before and after the 1989 revolutions. As such, the concept of property that informs the empirical analysis in this book of ownership changes in post-socialist Polish agriculture is not fixed and unambiguous in its content. Property is conceived as vague, evolving in its content, and essentially politically contested by interest groups. In my analysis, post-socialist property does not live in the present, articulated as a projection of the capitalist future. Rather, post-socialist property lives in the present, extending expectations into the future, which are solidly anchored in the meanings the ownership acquired within the socialist past. Thus my theoretical perspective acknowledges that the socialist past exerts a lasting impact on the post-socialist reality and replaces the initial notion that socialism as a social formation was unsustainable and, hence, could be simply deemed as irrelevant to ongoing social change in Eastern Europe.

Poland: The Vanguard of Transition to Capitalism?

If one adheres to a definition of state socialism as "the longest and most painful route from capitalism to capitalism" (Verdery 1996), Poland, holding the distinction of being the precursor to the 1989 "domino-like" collapse of Eastern European state socialism, would seem to represent the shortest socialist "loop" and the swiftest shift back to capitalism within Eastern Europe. The *Round Table* talks held in early 1989 paved the way for the imminent collapse of socialism in Poland. The initial astonishment over those unexpected historic events gave way in the early transition time to guarded optimism over whether the implementation of programmatic change from state socialism to capitalism would be successful. Poland appeared to be distinctive in the early stages of post-socialist transition in yet another way. Mixed economic results coming out of the Czech Republic, and to some extent Hungary, at the comparable time had undermined confidence in the soundness of their respective post-socialist reform programs and had induced doubt about their future trajectories.[6] By contrast, Poland seemed to generate confidence in many economic analysts about its economy's unprecedented expansion, which promised rapid prosperity for its citizens. Based on its impressive rates of economic growth relatively early on into the transition,[7] Poland was frequently depicted as the Eastern European equivalent to an "Asian tiger"—successfully proceeding along an irreversible transformation to a dynamic capitalist system. Only several years into the transition, the Polish experiment seemed to bear fruit and thus attest to the validity of its laissez-faire reform programs.

And, if Poland as a country was a precursor of fundamental changes in Eastern Europe, it was its western region, Wielkopolska (Greater Poland), that pioneered the post-socialist capitalist transformation within Poland. As the core of the Polish post-socialist program—price liberalization—was first implemented in agriculture and only later introduced in other sectors of the Polish economy, Wielkopolska as a prime agricultural region preceded other Polish provinces in post-socialist changes. Apart from its head start to the reforms, Wielkopolska's proximity to Poland's western border made it particularly prone to show quickly the effects of the post-socialist stabilization policies.[8] To a frequent visitor who could compare the "before" and "after" picture, Wielkopolska in the mid-1990s appeared to undergo an almost instantaneous transformation. This was the region most likely to generate the frequent enthusiastic reports depicting Poland as the emergent "East European tiger." The changes were palpable. Small retail businesses, food stands, restaurants, foreign car dealerships, and various product warehouses mushroomed almost overnight. Wielkopolska was also particularly attractive for scarce foreign capital. During my frequent visits in the first three years of transition, I ran into several foreign investors who were exploring this region for potential business because of its relatively developed communication infrastructure, transportation network, and proximity to Berlin. They considered the rest of Poland as "too deep in the East" and thus too risky.

Wielkopolska's history made it also best suited to revert to capitalism in comparison with other Polish regions. Before entering the "socialist detour," this region had a long capitalist legacy. During Wielkopolska's annexation to the Prussian Empire in the nineteenth and early twentieth centuries, the region was politically and economically integrated into the advanced Prussian capitalist system (Kochanowicz 1989; Topolski 1977). Thus it was exposed to the Prussian road to capitalism that left its lasting mark on the region. The 1918 unification of partitioned Poland and over forty years of state socialism never brought homogenization to its different provinces—often invoking customary references to the great divide between "Western Poland A" and "Southeastern Poland B." Wielkopolska of "Poland A" has been more economically advanced than Poland's eastern central and southern provinces formerly annexed by Russian and Austrio-Hungarian Empires. Wielkopolska under socialism had primarily been known as a flagship of Polish agriculture. It had fertile land interspersed with several dynamic urban and industrial centers that provided the countryside with the necessary resources for agricultural production. This region represented a quite advanced commodification of agricultural production—especially as compared with other major agricultural provinces in southern and eastern central Poland, which were dominated by highly fragmented and subsistence-oriented agricultural production.

Upon exiting the "socialist detour," Wielkopolska had an advanced rationalization of landholding and property structure particularly conducive to agrarian capitalism. The Prussian legacy left Wielkopolska with the long tradition of commodity relations and a unique heterogeneity of agricultural property forms. The formerly established Junker large agricultural latyfundia became suitable, ready-made bases for their subsequent conversion into socialist state farms. Thus, this region had a disproportional concentration of state farms under state socialism. Wielkopolska also contained a disproportionate share of medium and large private farms. Prussian law prohibited the subdivision of family farms among multiple family heirs in inheritance land transfers. As a result, Wielkopolska represented a relatively high rationalization of landholding (Kieniewicz 1969).[9] Equally, the disproportional concentration of agricultural production, trade, and service cooperative enterprises in Wielkopolska tied to Prussian legacy.[10] The rationalization of private agriculture in Wielkopolska was preserved under state socialism. The law sanctioned a unique landholding structure on these territories by allowing the upper limits of 100 hectares for farm size in Wielkopolska, compared to 50 hectares for the rest of rural Poland. Furthermore, the tradition of commodity relations in Wielkopolska was solidified. It stemmed from specific agrarian socialist policies of the 1970s and 1980s aimed to increase food production and yet to contain the spread of private agriculture (Kolankiewicz and Lewis 1988). As an outcome of these policies, the private agriculture sector became bifurcated and Wielkopolska became a central location for a small, yet dynamic, private subgroup of model agricultural enterprises with highly capitalized and specialized production. Created and reproduced by preferential investment and production state loans, these model agricultural enterprises operated based on family labor and seasonally hired labor.[11]

Methodological Note

Thus the Wielkopolska region, with its mixed industrial and agrarian economies and preexisting vast share of modernized individual farms, presented the best-case scenario for the post-socialist programmatic goal of a swift transition to capitalist agriculture. Given the heterogeneity of its agricultural property forms, Wielkopolska also represented a unique natural laboratory for a comparative study of the simultaneous changes in various judicial property forms (state, cooperative, private) in the aftermath of the post-socialist reforms. In the context of dominant debates about how to establish a capitalist system in the former socialist economies (i.e., through privatization of state property as advocated by neoclassical economists *or* the creation of a private sector as promoted by evolutionary economists), Wielkopolska provided an important empirical counterpoint to the envisioned transformations in post-socialist agrarian property relations.

As a result, I elected a rural community in the heart of Wielkopolska as a focus of my ethnographic research. The community that I named "Rolnicy" (Peasants/Farmers) consisted of a cluster of sixteen villages and constituted an administrative entity (*gmina*) under a local government. These villages were within an area of approximately fifty-six square miles, with a population of some thirteen thousand, out of which six thousand were registered as occupationally active. The geographical location of Rolnicy was vital to its economic standing and future prospects. The Rolnicy *gmina* was approximately ten miles from a major Polish urban center. Seven villages of the *gmina* were spread alongside an international highway that links Warsaw to Berlin.

Socioeconomically, the *gmina* was highly diversified. Only 45 percent of the occupationally active population engaged fully in agricultural production, while 45 percent were in services and transportation. The remaining 10 percent were employed in cottage industries, sales, and merchandise storage. The nonagricultural activities, such as trade, construction, small manufacturing, and service, were concentrated predominantly within the three central villages located alongside the international highway.[12] The *gmina's* eleven villages were mainly of agricultural production profiles. Uniquely, all three property forms of agricultural enterprises were present in this *gmina's* agricultural villages. The four agricultural production cooperatives were located in four of the "agricultural" villages. Each village's production activity was dominated by the collective grain and animal production. The cooperatives' members constituted a majority of these villages' population. They lived in apartment housing adjacent to their cooperatives. Within the borders of three other "agricultural" villages were spread agricultural enterprises that constituted the *gmina's* only state farm. The farm's employees worked and lived in these villages.

Private farms in the *gmina's* agricultural villages were quite diverse. In the southeastern villages, the soil was poorer than that of the remaining *gmina's* villages; their farms were quite small (five to seven hectares), their population was old, and their agricultural production was primarily for subsistence. On the other hand, the *gmina's* central and northwestern agricultural villages were characterized by medium-sized and large private farms (seven to twenty-five hectares). In particular, in six of them, there was a concentration of farms that led specialized production in the late socialism. If anyone anticipated a transition to capitalist agriculture, these villages appeared to be the cradle of the intended change.

As the legacy of specialization and production commodification by these medium and large farms appeared to lead to capitalistic agriculture, the overall *gmina's* economic development at the early stages of post-socialism seemed to further facilitate this process. In contrast to the national trend of deep shortages of investment capital stemming from the lack of internal reserves and meager foreign investments, the revenue base of the Rolnicy community consistently expanded. The local economy of the trade, services, and cottage industry generated a rich tax base for the local government. Furthermore, its location alongside the international highway and closeness to Poznan attracted foreign investors early on.[13] Thus, in the first four years of the transition, Rolnicy ranked second or third in the absolute amount of budget revenues among Wielkopolska's twenty-eight rural *gminas*. In 1995 Rolnicy moved up to first place among all the rural *gminas* in Wielkopolska. Furthermore, it was one of the leading communities nationwide in foreign investment per capita.[14] The structure of the *gmina's* expenditures was as sound as its revenue base. Roughly 30 percent of its funds were allocated to expand the *gmina's* infrastructure.[15] An additional 15 percent went to education, and 14 percent of revenues were spent on the *gmina's* administration.[16]

Thus, by all accounts, the community that I elected to study was clearly exceptional. It appeared to be particularly conducive to the construction of capitalist agriculture as advocated by two major camps of reform advocates. The community's long-established, commodity-oriented individual agricultural producers were expected to affirm the neoliberal economists' theory that market-regulated prices elicit positive economic responses. Also, the vast and dynamic individual agricultural subsector that existed alongside a relatively small agricultural state property sector quelled the evolutionist economists' general concerns about the state sector siphoning off the production resources from the ascending private enterprises. Through in-depth observation of the complex microeconomic transformations in all the agricultural subsectors, and the functioning of the local institutions, this unique community appeared to be well suited to shed light on the theoretical macroeconomic scenarios for building a capitalist system in the wake of the collapse of state socialism.

I was a participant observer in the Rolnicy *gmina* through four consecutive summers from 1991 to 1995. I maintained contact with many of the community members throughout and after the study during yearly recurrent visits over the subsequent several years to the *gmina* and broader region. I had special access to this community, as I was raised in the region, and my background knowledge of this general area facilitated my initial contacts. These personal connections were balanced by my long residence outside of Poland and lack of official affiliation with any Polish organization—affording me comfortable detachment from the community. As many of the residents stated more or less overtly, this mixture of familiarity and distance made me "safe" for revealing information that would otherwise be considered too sensitive to be shared with a sociologist working in Poland.

I began the research by contacting local government officials to inform them about my intention to conduct a study in their community, and to gain their consent. An energetic academic, who in the wave of the 1990 local government free elections became the *gmina's* popularly elected chairman (*wojt*) and who since 1997 became a member of the *Sejm* (Polish parliament), granted me several interviews and unrestricted access to personnel and local council meetings. In particular, I made contact with three members of his agricultural department.[17] Through numerous discussions and review of many documents in that department, I got a general overview of the production trends in the *gmina*, general characteristics of the *gmina's* individual agricultural villages, and lists of all its registered agricultural producers.

Given my research interest in the post-socialist transition in the agricultural system, when I constructed my sample, I eliminated vast segments of the *gmina* who belonged to the strata of peasants-workers.[18] Instead, I focused on agricultural producers, who derived their economic livelihood from full-time agricultural production under state socialism. This category included peasants, who sustained themselves through agricultural production, and who had farms that ranged in size from seven to twenty-five hectares, as well as four agricultural production cooperatives within the *gmina's* boundaries and one state farm conglomerate that consisted of five agricultural production enterprises. I observed these agricultural enterprises of distinct property forms as they mutually coexisted and functioned within their institutional local environment. Thus, my unit of analysis became the *gmina* Rolnicy, with its distinct agricultural enterprises from the private, cooperative, and state sectors as its critical components, which were undergoing concurrently changes in the wake of the post-socialist reform programs and were impacting each other in their distinct yet intertwined trajectories of change.

Of the registered agricultural producers on the *gmina's* list, I concentrated on peasants from the *gmina's* six agricultural villages. I randomly selected names within the categories of small (five to seven hectares), medium (seven to fifteen hectares), and large (fifteen to twenty-five hectares) farms. I contacted seventy-five individual respondents and conducted open-ended interviews with sixty-eight of them, often in multiple sessions. I also contacted the management teams in the four agricultural cooperatives. I conducted interviews with the general managers, bookkeepers, and agricultural workers in three cooperatives. The fourth declined to participate in the study, for never-specified reasons. I had five different interviews with the general manager of the state farms. There, I also interviewed the individual agricultural enterprises' managers and many state farm workers in the context of the state farms' local and regional strike preparations. Apart from conducting individual interviews, I also participated in many production meetings of the cooperatives, the state farms, and the *gmina's* council. In addition, I explored the local institutional environment. I conducted interviews with the local cooperative bank management, the management and personnel of the local agricultural procurement center, and the management and administrative staff of the service cooperative in agricultural circles. My study of the microeconomic responses in the context of the local institutional environment was coupled with my data collection on the central and regional institutional level. I contacted the ministry of agriculture and the regional offices of the state agency of agricultural property in charge of privatization of state farms.

Two Visions of Post-Socialist Development

Anthony Oberschall (1996) cautions researchers, in their pursuits to capture empirical reality, against an undue reliance on statistical data as a complete and sufficient basis for evaluating the relative merits of different substantive theories or for discerning the causes of given dependent variables. In his assessment, this "statisticism" derives from the weakness of theory. His cautionary note could well apply to the divergent accounts of early post-socialist transition, which employ quantitative statistics that project two contrasting visions of post-socialist development. Thus, selected macroeconomic indicators fed the enthusiastic projections about the early Polish post-socialist transition. However, other, frequently overlooked macroeconomic indices did not corroborate such optimistic prognoses. The post-socialist reforms that aimed to overhaul perennially inefficient socialist agriculture had generated instead a consistent production decline since their inauguration. In overall output across all production categories, and in the grain and animal husbandry yields, Polish agriculture showed a progressive drop to below the level of the mid-1980s and, in many instances, even below the crisis levels of the early 1980s. It also showed dramatic and consistent decline in the use of fertilizers throughout the transition years.[19] Thus, as one set of macroeconomic indicators evoked enthusiastic prognoses for Polish transition, other indices counterbalanced these conclusions. Moreover, the figures that generated these inconsistent projections artificially extracted the aspects of economic change from the multidimensional processes set in motion since 1989. By referring to the indices of economic growth alone, one could reduce the 1989 transition to a project of maximizing commodity production and of catching up with Western economic performance levels. Yet, the 1989 revolution signified more than an attempt to enhance production capacity of the former socialist societies. It represented a systemic *societal* change in its multidimensionality and simultaneity. This change was lived through social actors who, although being economic agents, were embedded in their local communities, institutions, and in society at large. Their economic decisions were inseparable from their political and social decisions.

Tracing the selected macroeconomic indicators gave a picture of post-socialist Poland as on a continuous and generally optimism-evoking trajectory, with the economy lifting up dramatically from a temporary traumatic recession of the early post-socialist years. Many scholars dismiss the early "growing pains" as inevitable, yet inconsequential, in the overall twenty-year transition. On the other hand, exploring less tangible and more complex microsocietal processes of the early transition, which were not registered by macroeconomic indices, allows us to contextualize these indicators. Furthermore, these processes might hold the key to understanding changes yet to come. From this perspective, the initial transition trajectory, rather than being dismissed as no longer relevant, warrants a close and careful examination in order to capture the overall nature of the post-socialist transition.

Peasantry as a Critical Social Actor

When setting up my analysis of individual agricultural producers, I faced some difficult analytical decisions with respect to farmers who I refer to here as "peasants." Scholarly efforts to delineate who constitute "peasants" have generated a vast literature (Wolf 1966; Potter 1967; Shanin 1971; Lenin 1971; Scott 1976, 1985; Chayanov 1986; Popkin 1980). The dominant conceptions of peasants, as perceptively depicted in one account (Leonard and Kaneff 2002), are constructions of a rural "other" formulated from an intellectual's frame of reference; for both socialist and capitalist thinkers, the term *peasant* derived from their respective macrolevel Enlightenment ideas about progress and modernity. For Western intellectuals, "ruralness" and the agricultural production of peasants signified the antithesis to progress based on rationalization and industrialization, whereas for the Marxist/Leninist thinkers, the peasants' small properties denoted the deepest constraint to a historic necessity of abolishing private ownership and creating socialism. These two models of development impute backwardness to the peasantry as an inherently insular force that operates outside, and in opposition to, the mainstream of history. An alternative perspective advanced by Western political economists,[20] which does not ascribe backwardness to peasants, declares them instead to be individualistic economic agents, not distinct from any other capitalist player.

In referring to post-socialist individual producers as "peasants" I reject either an inherent conservatism or utilitarian drive for economic gain as the peasantry's uniform and universal attributes. Instead, I adhere to a constructivist perspective where the peasant world is explored in its *totality* on the *micro*-level, rather than being assessed against the macrolevel blueprints of progress espoused by (urban) others. From such a perspective, the peasantry denotes diversified, historically specific, proactive, and reflexive agents who orient their actions to complex life circumstances. For many scholars, the relation to market presented an axis of comparison and internal division between agricultural producers who oriented their production for the market, and who therefore have been referred to as "farmers," and those who carried out subsistence production and were referred to as "peasants." My analysis of post-socialist changes centers not on the processes of marketization but on the evolution of socialist property relations with the private agricultural producers as property subjects distinct from cooperative and state owners, and on the relative collective political capacity of those owners to actively influence the direction of changes in the property arrangements. As their social homogeneity as cultural and economic forces operating within socialist society overshadows in significance their internal, market-related differentiation, I refer to them as "peasants."[21]

My attempt to understand the dramatic changes underway in Eastern Europe started with two diametrically different conversations that I had in Wielkopolska, in the summer of 1991. In an informal conversation over coffee at my parents' house, the former minister of agriculture in the Mazowiecki first post-socialist government recounted the main policy objectives of the shock therapy, projecting with confidence that the newly introduced price and trade liberalization measures would induce peasants to produce efficiently. I knew this deputy prime minister and the minister of agriculture to be an accomplished academic in agrarian science and a seasoned activist in Polish peasant parties, who understood agricultural production and championed peasant causes under socialism. I was amazed at the rapid transformation of this social activist under socialism into an advocate of neoliberal policy and its emphasis on individualism and material interests in its post-socialist aftermath. As he asserted, the cancellation of extensive agrarian subsidies and the introduction of "real" prices for agricultural resources would motivate peasants to allocate their production resources carefully and to produce efficiently and competitively. Those who would follow these inevitable requirements in economics would certainly flourish by developing modern, commodified farms. And those who could not learn the lesson would have to find a different line of work. This natural selection process would eventually bring results long awaited but unfulfilled under state socialism: fragmented land plots would be consolidated into efficiently sized farms.

His confidence in the value of agrarian economics was not echoed in my discussions with peasants. In one particular encounter, I got a glimpse of the complexity and intensity of peasants' assessment of the lessons spoken of by the former minister of agriculture. Visiting a large farm with modern-looking and well-maintained buildings in Rolnicy's village, I struck up a conversation with its owner, a proud-looking man in his sixties. Initially mistaking me for a government representative, he displayed apathy, mixed with distrust (engrained in him through the long years of living under socialism and its overt or covert attempts at collectivization of peasants' land), and resisted expressing any opinions. To put him at ease, I emphasized my long residence in the United States and my neutrality based on my lack of affiliation with any Polish governmental agency. I also remarked that the West wanted to learn about the changes in Eastern Europe from its "real" participants. This triggered a rapid change from apathy to visible anger. He charged that the post-socialist reform program was a conspiracy inflicted on Eastern Europe by the Western establishment in order to replace Soviet dominance over its societies and markets. He saw himself as a survivor of the failed state socialist collectivization drive. In the last twenty years, he had prevailed and ascended to become a successful farmer with a thriving specialized agricultural production and an elevated social status, due to a contract with the Agricultural Academy, a socialist state agency, to produce a special specimen of grass seeds. While he always approached the socialist agrarian policies with suspicion and uncertainty about their long-term intentions toward private owners, he expected the post-socialist Solidarity-based government to be unequivocally and principally supportive of private agriculture. Instead, as an agricultural producer, he saw the post-socialist policy ruining his specialized farm, forcing him to retreat from markets and run a subsistence-oriented production. As a citizen, he dreaded the impending collapse of domestic food production that would threaten Polish sovereignty. While this peasant's view was rather extreme, it essentially reflected individual agricultural producers' deep feeling of betrayal by the post-socialist reform program.

This set of two conversations reflected a deep split in the assessment of the reform package between policy architects and peasants, which was dramatically revealed in the September 19, 1993 parliamentary election. The 1993 election was as stunning in its result as the June 1989 parliamentary election that marked the unexpected end of the state socialism era. In both elections, peasants were the key constituency. In 1989, peasants were the critical voting block in Solidarity's unexpected electoral victory that led to the formation of the first post-socialist Mazowiecki government.[22] The 1993 electoral results effectively brought an end to the brief 1989–1993 post-Solidarity regime that dislodged the state socialist government from political power. The post-communist Union of the Democratic Left (SLD) and a post-1989 spin-off from the former United Peasant Party, the Polish Peasant Movement (PSL), dominated the elections. Together, they received close to 36 percent of the vote (Blazyca and Rapacki 1996). Based on the weighted electoral system, these votes translated into 66 percent of seats between these two parties in the 460-seat Polish parliament.[23] While the coalition government formed by these parties and headed by the PSL leader acknowledged the need to continue the reforms, it criticized the post-socialist government for taking excessively harsh economic measures and placing unfounded faith in the free market. In contrast, the new coalition emphasized a slow-down in privatization, pay hikes, measures toward curtailing unemployment, and pursuit of "capitalism with a human face."[24]

The second chapter in the peasants' pursuit of "capitalism with a human face," instead of laissez-faire capitalism, having further impact on the transition course, related to the collective, political responses ranging from different forms of protest[25] to the creation and dramatic rise of peasant "*Samoobrona*" (Self-Defense). Created in 1991 as a radical fringe organization in defense of indebted middle peasants, it transformed into a trade union and into a peasant party in 1992. By 2002, it became the third largest party in the lower house of the Polish parliament and its leader, A. Lepper, became the deputy parliament speaker. The party's populist demands had the support of over 20 percent of the Polish electorate. In 2006, Lepper won 15 percent of votes in the presidential election. These electoral results allowed his party to enter into the ruling coalition with the winning party of Law and Justice. Lepper became a Minister of Agriculture while other members of Samoobrona headed the Labor and Social Policy Ministry and Ministry of Infrastructure. Two years earlier, Samoobrona won over 11 percent of electoral votes, in the elections to the European Parliament, taking the fourth place among other political parties. As such, Samoobrona remained as a central political force in the first several years of post-socialist Poland.

Thus, only three years after the 1989 historic defeat of the socialist regime, this stunning reversal in the midst of the post-socialist transition seemed puzzling to the architects of the post-socialist reform program. Bronislaw Gieremek, a prominent figure in both Solidarity-based opposition and the post-socialist government, retrospectively pointed out that peasants were critically important to the fate of the post-socialist reform program and to electoral defeat of the post-Solidarity parties.[26] Their responses were unsuspected at the onset of reform. Although Gieremek identified peasants as the "awkward" class that resisted the project of the great transformation from state socialism to capitalism, his analysis left unanswered why a program that propagated private property elicited such a response from private property owners themselves.

Gieremek implicitly attributed to peasants reactionary tendencies that obstructed a progressive move forward. Such perceptions have been perpetuated since the inauguration of the post-socialist reforms[27] and were parallel to those articulated under state socialism. Under state socialism, peasants were an "awkward class" in a double sense. As both members of agrarian societies and private property owners, they represented remnants of the past, directly opposed to the state socialist central objectives of building an efficient socioeconomic system, industrial society, and socialized property. While completion of the collectivization drives of the 1940s and 1950s resolved the "peasantry" question in a majority of state socialist countries, unsuccessful collectivization programs in Poland preserved private agriculture alongside small, cooperative, and state subsectors.

Thus, by official ideology, peasants became "invisible" albeit indispensible under state socialism. Either they were eliminated as a social and economic entity through collectivization or they were presented as marginal and temporary, thus an irrelevant anomaly as in the Polish historical case. They had exhausted their role in history. They were similarly invisible in the scholarly debates. Analyses that aimed to theorize existing socialism pinpointed distinct social groups as pivotal to its dynamics, or as capable of changing the system (Szelenyi 1980; Bahro 1978; Rakowski 1976; Staniszkis

1984; Poznanski 1993). In their accounts, the agrarian question was omitted.[28]

Against these analyses stood the Polish empirical reality.[29] Under Polish state socialism, agriculture and peasants were more significant than socialist ideology, scholarly accounts, or economic statistics suggest.[30] Although state socialism promised a shift from agrarian to industrial societies, food expenditures persistently accounted for around 30 to 40 percent of family budgets, making agricultural goods the most vital consumer commodity on the domestic markets. All together, peasants were the main suppliers of domestic food needs. They held approximately 80 percent of Polish agricultural land and were comprised of divergent economic groups—ranging from small agricultural production units operating at close to subsistence level to a small (yet dynamic) segment of individual producers concentrated mainly in Wielkopolska with highly modernized, commodified, and specialized production. Furthermore, given the noncompetitiveness of socialist industrial goods on the foreign markets, peasants provided important export products, generating much-needed foreign currency. The political and economic stability of the whole system, and the fate of its leadership, seemed to be tied directly to the peasants. The major political crises of 1956, 1970, 1980, and 1989, which brought down state leaders and elevated new ones, were precipitated by inadequate food supply levels and placed food production at the forefront of political debates. As the agricultural sector held the key to the stability of state socialism, it equally became a precursor of post-socialist changes that were to follow in the rest of the economy once price liberalization was first introduced in the agricultural sector. Preexisting private agriculture seemed to spearhead the post-socialist reformers' daunting project of privatization in their quest for a growth economy.

In this book, I will make peasants and agrarian property relations "visible" in order to understand the initial phase of the 1989 post-socialist transition and its abrupt disruption in 1993. Many Polish observers and participants in the Polish post-socialist transition fixated on political elites in the initial transition period to account for its trajectory. According to many scholars, the rapid dissipation of Solidarity after its 1989 parliamentary victory into a myriad of infighting parties—"the war at the top"—weakened the post-socialist coalition government's ability to articulate the reform program in terms acceptable by society. It also undermined the post-socialist regime's resolve to implement the economic program consistently. Rather, this party polarization undermined the reform momentum by shifting focus from the critical economic issues to the symbolic, social, and religious issues (Osiatynski 1994; Smolar 1996; Michnik 1995). For others, the transition trajectory needed to be analyzed by focusing on workers' behavior in the context of both socialism and post-socialism. The trade union's opposition of Solidarity, with its doctrine of fighting for worker rights, was seen as indispensable to the abolition of state socialism. However, in the post-socialist transition, it undermined reform objectives by producing state enterprise resistance to the pressures of reforms for economic restructuring (Balcerowicz 1992). In the first view, the trajectory was explained by reference to the current political dynamics within the post-socialist period itself. In the second approach, the transition was connected to social processes before the initiation of the reform program. These processes account for the deviation of the actual transition's trajectory from its projected course as outlined by the reforms' planners. Yet, this book will show that the transition trajectory has been molded by the socioeconomic processes rooted in the deviations of the reforms in the implementation phase, as well as those encoded in the preexisting, specific, and distinct notions of property held by both reformers and social groups. These understandings guided the formulation of the economic program and provided the basis for the economic agents' reaction to it. Their dynamic interaction charted the post-socialist transition's course.

Dynamics of Agrarian Change

In this book, I will trace the evolution of property relations, particularly those that emerged in agriculture, from the early stages of state socialism to the early stages of the post-socialist period. Does the conventional notion of state property allow us to adequately conceptualize the property relations under state socialism? Was this system of a dynamic nature, and if so of what kind? Were changes in property relations of circular character, as some suggest (Kornai 1990; Brus and Laski 1989), or were they linear (Poznanski 1993)? Can significant shifts be demarcated in this process of property change? How did these changes originate? How do these shifts bear on the crystallization of property relations in post-socialism?

To trace the emergence of post-socialist property relations to those formed under state socialism, we need first to reexamine the notion used to describe property under state socialism. The conventionally applied category of state property does not provide an understanding of the complexity of existing property relations or their dynamic changes within state socialism. In its place, I develop the notion of conjoint property. This category refers to all judicial property forms under state socialism: private, cooperative, and state property. It suggests that, within each judicial property form, individual property rights—those over control of production, residual income, and asset exchange—were not vested in one class of ownership subjects. Rather, they were allocated to two categories of owners. The state extended ownership claims in each property form, alongside the claims of individual economic subjects.

The category of conjoint property lends itself to a dynamic analysis of state socialism. Mapping these changes in the allocation of specific ownership rights between these two ownership subjects allows us to distinguish between different periods of state socialism. These changes were associated with distinct economic policies that aimed to induce efficiency in economic agents. The policies that brought specific variations in the allocation of rights in joint ownership created clear demarcation points in the evolution of property relations. The 1956 policies brought the first change in conjoint ownership across all property forms. The 1970s policies set the second stage. The two different phases of the 1980s policies constituted the third stage in the reconfiguration of property relations. The 1989 post-socialist policies advanced the fourth stage.

These stages built upon one another. Policies that aimed to reform conjoint ownership build on preceding ones, leading to a progressive downward assignment of ownership claims from the state to the category of individual co-owners. The 1956 and 1970s reforms shifted the right of production control and the right to residual income downward, while centralizing control of asset exchange within the state. The 1980s reforms advanced this pattern further across all property forms. However, within private agricultural property, this downward allocation of rights led to the full consolidation of ownership rights in the hands of peasants and the state's withdrawal from ownership claims to this form of property. These former stages in reforming conjoint property led to substantive shifts by generating, within state socialist agriculture, exclusive private property. It implied an exclusive owner, unfettered by the state, vested with indivisible property rights.

While the changes in ownership coincided with major reforms in economic policy, they were also marked by historical contestations of power (Friedland and Alford 1991). In the 1956 and 1970s reforms, the impetus for change in joint ownership came from the reformist factions in the state socialist regime. In the 1980s, the locus of change had shifted. In conjunction with Solidarity attacks on the regime's economic efficacy and legitimacy, peasants, apart from their daily individual resistance to the state policies, launched their own political struggle. In the context of widespread food shortages, peasants successfully challenged the state to end the abrogation of their ownership rights, nearly a decade before the political collapse of socialism in 1989. The prolonged existence of peasants as exclusive owners within the state socialist regime imprinted on them historically specific connotations of private property. To preserve its political rule, the state socialist regime suppressed Solidarity by imposing martial law between 1981 and 1983. It also provided exclusive agricultural producers with many concessions in the form of protectionist measures to ensure uninterrupted, high-level commodified food production. These measures were designed to remove competition and risk from individual commodity production. They were also designed to remove earning differentials between urban and rural sectors according to the socialist principle of sectoral economic equality. Protected by such measures, and backed by state socialist ideology, peasants formed expectations for the individual outcomes and social consequences of the exercise of private property rights; they associated exclusive private ownership with the freedom to succeed in the market without the risk of failing, leading to the realization of economic equality between urban and agrarian sectors.

The series of joint ownership reforms not only generated historically specific private property within state socialism. It also impinged on the formulation of post-socialist reform measures. The previous reforms, which progressively reduced the state as an economic agent and property coclaimant, channeled the post-socialist reformers to form a liberal vision of private ownership and to accentuate anti-statism in their notion of property. Individual exclusive ownership outcomes encoded in the reformers' vision spelled a different kind of freedom that peasants learned to pursue under the late protectionist socialist state: freedom to fail as well as to succeed in the market. The critical evaluation of the efficacy outcomes that stem from the abrogation of ownership rights by the socialist state led the post-socialist reformers to focus on the free exercise of ownership against state barriers. It also prompted them to underestimate the effects of the absence of sufficient state-backed guarantees to, and regulation of the exercise of, ownership. Furthermore, the post-socialist program was formulated in the narrow language of creating a "normal" (replacing a "shortage") economy without explicitly embracing the model of capitalist *society* or explicitly rejecting the model of socialist *society*.[31] By default, the post-socialist regime implicitly upheld the social agenda of state socialism and reinforced peasants' previous expectations of social outcomes associated with the exercise of private exclusive ownership rights. The formulation of the post-socialist reform program in the context of the former reform attempts will be examined in chapter two of this book.

"Liberalizing" peasants as genuine exclusive private owners through the introduction of the post-socialist stabilization package adversely affected the peasants' capacity to exercise their property rights. These reforms restricted their access to production resources through price destabilization and the selective allocation of financial credits, they curtailed peasants' ability to accrue profits from production due to new institutional constraints and limitations, and they undermined peasants' capacity to transfer their ownership and to move into new agricultural markets. The comprehensive liberalization of prices reshaped the structure of agricultural prices and subsequently undermined the profitability of agricultural production. Price liberalization and wage controls dramatically curtailed domestic food demands. In their cumulative effect, peasants faced sharp increases in agricultural resource costs. They also experienced a dramatic decrease in the domestic demand for their output. They were subjected to a scarcity of financial resources, as stipulated by the post-socialist fiscal policies. In addition, both national-level and local-level credit allocation gave credit preferences to state and cooperative agricultural enterprises over individual peasants. The reforms also curtailed peasants' ability to accrue profits from their production by subjecting the peasants to a constricted demand for food, new institutional constraints, and enhanced opportunistic behavior of economic agents from other agricultural subsectors. In dealing with monopolistic procurement centers, peasants faced disproportionally high uncertainty in disposing of their output. They endured systemic and transparent siphoning off of their profits by procurement centers. In the context of these financial constraints and an insufficient institutional infrastructure, their repeated attempts to compete with monopolistic procurement centers were unsuccessful. Overall, peasants' high transaction costs in transition compared unfavorably with their position under late state socialism and relative to cooperative and agricultural subsectors.

These new sets of constraints contrasted with peasants' expectations of their individual outcomes and the social consequences of their exclusive private ownership status. This quickly triggered peasants' strategic responses. Economically, they responded through the involution of production, closed-cycle production, and a retreat from markets. To reduce their production costs and minimize their exposure to commercial transactions with procurement centers, peasants focused on reducing their costs rather than enhancing production efficiency. Increasingly, they relied on themselves to generate the production resources necessary for the renewal of their production cycles. Politically, they responded by waging collective action against the post-socialist regime and its program within a year of the reforms. Initially, their contestation was regional, centered on specific economic transactions and corporate concessions. In early 1992, their political resistance reached the national level. Peasants no longer focused on specific transactions. Rather, they challenged the overall market logic of the economic transactions imposed on them. Within a year, peasants successfully reformulated their class-based economic demands into national and societal grievances against the post-socialist state's program, articulating them as protection of citizens' rights. In effect, early on, the post-socialist state was pushed from its long-term goals toward damage control and the pursuit of short-term political and economic stability.[32] The liberalization of the private agricultural sector by the post-socialist reform program and the peasants' responses will be analyzed in chapter three of this book.

While the comprehensive removal of state-imposed constraints on private property owners did not lead to the effective exercise of exclusive ownership rights, the course of the transition trajectory of agricultural cooperative ownership also deviated from both the official objectives in the post-socialist program and the expectations of the "real" subjects of cooperative ownership. The regime aimed to reinstate voluntarism, self-aid, and self-governance as critical components of exclusive ownership in the cooperative sector. For post-socialist reformers, the spontaneous and firm reassertion of exclusive cooperative ownership rights rested on the rapid dismantling of the superimposed state socialist institutional superstructure. This structure, reflected in the socialist state's co-claims to the cooperative subsector, engulfed ground-level cooperative organizations. Contrary to the reformers' expectations, the mandatory dismantling of the cooperative superstructure created institutional and financial discontinuity that effectively undermined cooperative self-government. The rapid deinstitutionalization of local cooperatives lifted controls from above, giving the management of local cooperatives autonomy, but it also made it impossible for the creation of any effective control of managerial decisions from within. This led to the centralization of managerial control, rather than a revival of exclusive cooperative ownership. These policies, detrimental to the clarification of cooperative ownership, also seemed to preserve inertia and to narrow the organizations' capacity to adjust to the economic environment. The underdeveloped institutional infrastructure and heightened uncertainty in the economic environment narrowed the options for change—leading to economic behavior similar to forms under state socialism. Effectively, the process of change in the cooperative subsector was uneven. It was marked by a diversification in the responses on the individual cooperative level that depended on preexisting organizational and production profiles. The changes in cooperative ownership will be discussed in chapter four of this book.

The post-socialist agrarian program explicitly targeted state farms to be eliminated and reconstituted as exclusive private enterprises. In contrast, the trajectory of the agricultural state sector followed the specific microeconomic adjustments of individual state farms affected by the anticipation of privatization that later led to the state representative organs' reconsolidation of the state farms' ownership and the allocation of management control to the old managerial cadre. This effective reconstitution of joint ownership of state farms by the distinct state institutional representatives and the circulation of the economic nomenklatura stem from the process of formal privatization. The early pronouncements of state farm privatization had their effect already on the stage of the anticipated privatization by individual state farm enterprises, long before enactment of a new privatization bill and its actual implementation two years later. The explicit, yet ambiguous promise of privatization precipitated uncertainty concerning the future ownership status of state farms. It also inspired retroactive settling of the past (joint) ownership claims. By virtue of state farms' legal status as state enterprises with past economic obligations tied to the state's initial asset contributions for the creation of the state farms and to its subsidies, the state imposed on formally autonomous state farms quite extensive co-ownership claims in the allocation of productive resources during their initial period of economic adjustment. Restrictions placed on the general managers' ability to hire and fire, and the imposition of dividend and excessive income taxes, effectively eroded the state farms' resource base. This undermined their incentives and their ability to respond positively to market forces. Legal restraints placed on the state farms' general directors narrowed their room to maneuver, locked them into unchanged lines of production, and forced them into short-term time horizons. As a result, they were pushed into incurring debt more quickly than the other agricultural subsectors with little consideration for long-term economic viability or for production efficiency results.

Hence, on the supply side, state farms faced higher constraints to their adjustment strategies through state intervention than other agricultural subsectors. However, on the demand side, they appeared to gain advantageous position vis-à-vis other agricultural subsectors. Like other agricultural producers, state farms faced an increase in the price of inputs, higher credit costs, and persistently low product prices. While the irrational price structure derived largely from preexisting monopolistic agricultural procurement centers, state farms showed the ability to function within this monopolistic market quite effectively, squeezing individual and cooperative subsectors out of the agricultural output market. State farms were more effective than their cooperative and individual agricultural counterparts in reducing the uncertainty over the demand for their products and in exerting control over procurement prices.

The constraints on the immediate adjustment strategies pending the farms' privatization produced a short-term reinforcement of soft budget constraints and massive indebtedness of individual state farms. This impinged on the direction and pace of the *actual* process of privatization two years into the post-socialist reforms. To avoid transferring the assets of indebted state farms to their lenders (banks), rather than the policy-targeted recipients (peasants and state farm employees), privatization proceeded first among the few economically strong state farms, perpetuating the cycle of soft budget constraints and economic decline among the weak, indebted farms. While the actual privatization procedures left the weak and indebted state farms in a continual uncertainty about the exact privatization formula to be applied to them, they also induced uncertainty among potential recipients of state farms assets. Although the revised 1992 agricultural program proposed to create agriculture based exclusively on small private farms and family labor, economic efficiency considerations outlined in the governmental state farm privatization plans called for an asset transfer that would create economies of scale based on hired labor within the agricultural sector. The public articulation of these tensions between social outcomes and production performance objectives produced tangible microeconomic results. The small minority of peasants who sought to acquire state farms and who were not shattered by credit constraints withdrew their interest in light of these tensions in agrarian policy objectives. In effect, state farm general managers remained the effective contenders to steer the process of privatization. Various schemes of leasing or administering state farms allowed them to maintain control of state farm assets. These processes will be discussed in chapter five of this book.

Through both historical analysis of changes in agriculture and analysis of distinct yet interconnected trajectories of agricultural subsectors in the post-socialist period, I show the importance of property in the post-socialist transition. Yet, this property needs to be conceptualized more broadly than conventionally applied. The essence of post-socialist ownership changes does not consist of a shift from a homogeneous state ownership into private ownership, as the architects of post-socialist reforms assert. Neither does it rest on a legal transfer of ownership entitlements and assets. Rather, the post-socialist ownership changes should be conceptualized as *multifold*, mutually *interdependent* transformations of heterogeneous state socialist conjoint property into various (incomplete) exclusive ownership forms. These divergent ownership trajectories stem from combined outcomes of the policy makers' objectives, as well as the expectations and intentions of the respective properties' subjects. Such property has to be seen as historically specific. As such, its impact on macroeconomic performance has to be explored rather than assumed as universally leading to economic growth. Equally, my analysis shows that the conventional notion of transition, perceived as a shift from socialism to capitalism induced by post-socialist reform, obscures more than it reveals of the complexity and duration of processes of change on the ground. Hence, in the next chapter, I proceed with the closer examination of the notion of transition and of property as applied to capture the nature and sequence of post-socialist changes.

Notes

1. "When people made the transition from 'feudalism' to 'capitalism,' as well when they attempted to make the transition from 'capitalism' to 'socialism,' they were daringly sailing uncharted seas. They had a program, a 'vehicle' of principles and demands, but not any certainty as to where they would eventually land. As Albert Hirschman has shown in *The Passions and the Interests* (1997: 37), the early arguments for capitalism were very different from what were later seen as the actual accomplishments and essence of capitalism, namely, economic growth, efficiency, and prosperity. This is fundamentally different in the case of the transition from communism to capitalism. This transition is not a 'revolution,' but, as Habermas (1990) has argued, a project to 'catch-up' with 'the West.' In contrast to the earlier transitions, people know very well and from empirical evidence where they want to go (namely to 'Europe'), but just don't know how to get there" (Offe 2002: 250–251).

2. Leszek Balcerowicz, an economics professor, the Polish post-socialist finance minister, and the architect of the post-socialist shock therapy reform program, spoke of benefiting from the stock of innovations that were developed in the West which the Eastern European societies missed out on during the forty years that the command economy held sway in the East.

3. "The natural effort of every individual to better his own condition, when suffered to exert itself with freedom and security, is so powerful a principle, that it is alone, and without any assistance, not only capable of carrying on the society to wealth and prosperity, but of surmounting a hundred impertinent obstructions with which the folly of human laws too often encumbers its operations; though the effect of these obstructions is always more or less either to encroach upon its freedom, or to diminish its security." Adam Smith. *Wealth of Nations*. 1981 [1976] vol II: 49–50.

4. For an excellent account of the historical spread of neoliberalism in association with the interests of economists see Bockman and Eyal (2002).

5. The approach suggested here approximates Jadwiga Staniszkis' perspective of the evolutionary theory of discontinuous change in place of the notion of revolution. (Staniszkis 1992: 235).

6. In the Czech Republic, real growth rates were negative throughout the first years of transition. The decline in gross industrial production started in 1990, reached negative 24 percent in 1991, and remained within a high negative single digit for the subsequent two years. 1994 brought a positive 2 percent industrial production growth, only to decline below zero again two years later. Equally, the gross agricultural production stayed consistently negative for the first five years of the transition. In Hungary, the initial negative growth rate in gross industrial production turned into positive growth of 4 percent in 1993 and of 9 percent in 1994. The recovery was slower in the agricultural sector. Only in 1994 did the growth rate reach a positive 2 percent after preceding years of consistent decline in agricultural production output. See selected economic indicators for 1990–1994 for Czech and Hungary in WIIW (1995).

7. In gross industrial production (sales), Poland showed a positive growth rate already in 1992 with a 3 percent annual increase. The years 1993 and 1994 brought over 7 percent and 12 percent growth rates respectively. See WIIW 1995: 68.

8. Poznan, the region's capital, is closer to the capital of Germany, Berlin, than to the Polish capital, Warsaw, giving it advantage over other regions in Poland for the exposure to Western capitalism and its markets.

9. By contrast, in the Polish territories under Russian and Austrio-Hungarian domination, such land subdivision within individual families was permitted and, as a result, the excessive fragmentation of land ensued.

10. Commodity-oriented Polish peasants in the late nineteenth century created the first wave of a dynamic network of service and trade cooperatives in Wielkopolska (cooperatives of agricultural circles). Ostensibly, these cooperatives were to facilitate the peasants' agricultural production. But they were also formed to provide an institutional base for the peasants' political resistance to the Prussian occupation of these territories.

11. Many of them erected vast greenhouses to maintain highly profitable specialized production of vegetables and/or flowers. These producers gained visibility and evoked envy for their modernized form of production and high standard of living as compared to the vast majority of agrarian and urban dwellers. A select group of agricultural socialist barons in Wielkopolska, who utilized these preferential agrarian policies, became the talk of Wielkopolska's communities in the 1970s and 1980s. Allegedly, these entrepreneurial peasants could rival their most advanced capitalist counterparts. People were gossiping about the agricultural enterprises that produced exclusively for export and led to an equally exclusive consumption style for their owners.

12. Shortly after the 1989 reform program was initiated, merchandise warehouses, stores in residential homes, and foreign auto sale and repair shops opened up in record numbers in these communities. Another significant segment of these villages' population held steady employment in nearby Poznan's businesses. Their agricultural activities were conducted on small household plots, mainly as a second source of income. Two other villages, located by a picturesque lake in the eastern segment of the *gmina*, experienced rapid growth of the tourist industry. In these villages, vast areas of sandy soil, unsuitable for agricultural production, became converted to commercial lands, subdivided, and sold to urban clients for construction of recreational summer homes.

13. As early as 1991, the local government was reviewing investment offers from German, Italian, and American capital for the construction of chocolate, furniture, and soft drink factories.

14. See Wojewodzki Urzad Statystyczny. *Rocznik Statystyczny Wojewodztwa Poznanskiego* 1994: 82–83.

15. The *gmina*'s investments went into developing and expanding technical infrastructure—an installation of phones in commercial and private residences, natural gas heating system, central sewage system, improvements of the community's roads, and operation of the local bus service.

16. See Wojewodzki Urzad Statystyczny. *Rocznik Statystyczny Wojewodztwa Poznanskiego* 1994: 85.

17. The department was in charge of disseminating agrarian expertise about how to optimize production lines and resource use in individual farms and to transmit the central and local government policies and regulations as they applied to peasants.

18. They derived main income from nonagricultural jobs and supplemented their incomes by agricultural production on their small plots (0.5 to 2.0 hectares), primarily for their own consumption.

19. See Główny Urząd Statystyczny 1995: 420–421.

20. See Samuel Popkin 1980, "The Rational Peasant: The Political Economy of Peasant Society." *Theory and Society* 9 (3): 411–471.

21. Guided by the specific conceptual objectives of this study, my designation of individual agricultural producers as "peasants" contrasts on the surface with categorization applied in an excellent and rare ethnographic study of another Wielkopolska rural community in the early post-socialist period conducted by Polish anthropologist Michal Buchowski (2003). Buchowski asserted that these economic actors were "farmers," rather than Chayanovian (1986) "peasants," because of their integration into socialist macroeconomic system and their production oriented for markets. Yet, Buchowski acknowledged the existence of the common ethos of "real peasants" constituting these diversified economic agents into a more homogeneous social group (2003: 18). Equally, Polish sociologist Krzysztof Gorlach in his essay on the peasantry's agency (1998) considers ownership as a central element of the self-identity of peasants as a coherent group (despite their multifold inner differentiation) vis-à-vis the state agrarian policies toward them as owners of private property.

22. Heyns and Bielecki (1991) argued that the strongest support for Solidarity candidates in the June 1989 parliamentary elections came from rural areas rather than from the industrial and urban centers.

23. See Poland Update (1993, 1994).

24. The SLD, despite its vague election platform, was identified with the assertion that the first post-socialist economic adjustment was excessive. SLD-PSL incurred electoral debts to repay urban workers, peasants, seven million pensioners and three million unemployed. The need to deflect internal social anxieties, paired with the need to sustain the expectations and confidence of the international financial community, left very narrow room to maneuver for the SLD-PSL coalition when formulating future policy, leading to the public promise of a continuity in economic policy and fight against inflation (Blazyca and Rapacki 1996: 87–89).

25. Comparative research conducted by Kubik and Ekiert (1999: 175) indicated that in the period from 1989 to 1993 "Poland had the highest incident of protest among the East Central European countries." The study included East Germany, Hungary, Poland, and Slovakia. For more on the evolution of the peasant protests, see Gorlach (1999, 2000).

26. In a conference on November 1–2, 1996, held at Stanford University, Bronislaw Geremek (the principal author of the 1981 Solidarity program, the chief Solidarity negotiator at the 1989 Round Table discussions with the late state socialism government, and the chairman of the foreign policy committee of the Polish parliament), Jerzy Osiatynski (minister of planning in Mazowiecki's government and the minister of finance in Suchocka's government), and other high officials in the post-Solidarity governments shared their reflections on the lost 1993 elections.

27. While some scholars attributed inequalities seen soon after the onset of the transition to the market (see Szelenyi and Kostello 1996), other Eastern European scholars attributed the

exacerbation of inequality for, particularly, agricultural producers not to neoliberal reforms but to agricultural producers' social attributes, reactionary attitudes, and resistance to the continuation of the reforms. See Michal Buchowski (2009) for a more general discussion on the intellectual tradition among Western and socialist thinkers, which imputes backwardness to the peasantry as an inherently insular force that operates outside, and in opposition to, the mainstream of history. See also the introduction to *Post-Socialist Peasant? Rural and Urban Constructions of Identity in Eastern Europe, East Asia and the Former Soviet Union* (Leonard and Kaneff 2002).

28. The notable exceptions to this tendency are presented in the analyses of Szelenyi (1988) and Nagengast (1991).

29. With the advancement of socialism, the chronic inability of the socialized agricultural sector to produce adequate food supplies became a sufficiently significant threat to the regime's political stability to prompt an internally contradictory agrarian policy: maintenance of an ideological commitment to collectivize private owners, combined in time with a growing reliance on the private producer's food production based on the provisional policy measures to stimulate segments of private agriculture.

30. For a discussion of the importance of agriculture under state socialism, see Bell (1984); Creed (1999); Lampland (1995); Hann (1985); and Buchowski (2009).

31. The dual objectives of the post-socialist reform package were articulated in terms of building democracy to replace party-state under socialism and of a construction of a market economy to replace the command economy of socialism. Together, they were to lead to an outcome of "joining the West." Reference to "capitalism" was avoided as it carried a negative connotation of a social formation, which generates social and economic inequality and evokes socialistic critique.

32. In early summer of 1990, the Mazowiecki government showed visible signs of deviating from its original program and of inner government fractions. In May, the Economic Council within the Council of Ministers proposed loosening fiscal discipline and some state intervention. Particularly, it proposed preferential loans and minimum prices in agriculture. Those changes provoked the resignation of Marek Dabrowski, the first vice-minister in the Balcerowicz team. For more details on the economic program debates see Balcerowicz (1990), Przeworski (1993), and Mack (1994).

References

Ash, Timothy Garton. 1990. *We the People: The Revolution of '89 as Witnessed in Warsaw, Budapest, Berlin, and Prague*. Cambridge: Granta Books.

Babb, Sarah. 2001. *Managing Mexico: Economists from Nationalism to Neoliberalism*. Princeton, NJ: Princeton University Press.

Bahro, Rudolf. 1978. *The Alternative in Eastern Europe*. London: Verso.

Balcerowicz, Leszek. 1992. *800 dni. Szok kontrolowany*. Warsaw: Polska Oficyna Wydawnicza "BGW."

———. 1990. "The Price of Polish Economic Reform." In *Without Force or Lies: Voices from the Revolution of Central Europe in 1989–1990*, edited by W. Brinton and A. Rinzler. San Francisco: Mercury House Books. U.K. Ltd.

Bell, Peter. 1984. *Peasants in Socialist Transition*. Berkeley: University of California Press.

Blazyca, George, and Ryszard Rapacki. 1996. "Continuity and Change in Polish Economic Policy: The Impact of the 1993 Election." *Europe-Asia Studies* 48 (1): 85–100.

Bockman, Johanna, and Gil Eyal. 2002. "Eastern Europe as a Laboratory for Economic Knowledge: The Transnational Roots of Neoliberalism." *American Journal of Sociology* 108 (2): 310–352.

Brus, Wlodzimierz, and Kazimierz Laski. 1989. *From Marx to the Market*. Oxford: Oxford University Press.

Buchowski, Michal. 2009. "Property Relations, Class, and Labour in Rural Poland." In *Postsocialist Europe: Anthropological Perspectives from Home*, edited by L. Kurti and P. Skalnik, 51–75. EASA Series 10. New York: Berghahn Books.
———. 2003. "Redefining Social Relations Through Work in a Rural Community in Poland. *Max Planck Institute for Social Anthropology Working Papers*. Working Paper no. 58.
Burawoy, Michael, and Janos Lukacs. 1992. *The Radiant Past: Ideology and Reality in Hungary's Road to Capitalism*. Chicago: The University of Chicago Press.
Centeno, Miguel A. 2001. "Isomorphic Neoliberalism and the Creation of Inevitability." Paper presented at SASE Conference, Amsterdam.
Chayanov, A. V. 1986. *The Theory of Peasant Economy*. Madison: The University of Wisconsin Press.
Cole, Daniel, H. and Peter, Z. Grossman. 2002. "The Meaning of Property Rights: law vs. economics." *Land Econ.* 78:3 8:317–330.
Creed, Gerald. 1999. "Deconstructing Socialism in Bulgaria." In *Uncertain Transitions: Ethnographies of Change in the Postsocialist World*, edited by Michael Burawoy and Kathrine Verdery, 223–244. Lanham: Rowman & Littlefield Publishers, Inc.
de Soto, Hernando. 2000. *The Mystery of Capital: Why Capitalism Triumphs in the West and Fails Everywhere Else*. New York: Basic Books.
Friedland, Rodger, and Robert Alford. 1991. "Bringing Society Back In: Symbols, Practices, and Institutional Contradictions." In *The New Institutionalism in Organizational Analysis*, edited by Walter W. Powell, and Paul Di Maggio, 232–266. Chicago: University of Chicago Press.
Glenn, John K. 1999. "Competing Challengers and Contested Outcomes to State Breakdown: The Velvet Revolution in Czechoslovakia." *Social Forces* 78 (1): 187–211.
Główny Urząd Statystyczny (GUS). 1995. *Maly Rocznik Statystyczny*. Warsaw: Główny Urząd Statystyczny.
Gorlach, Krzysztof. 2000. "Post-Traditional Family Farm in the Post-Communist Modernity: The Case of Poland." Paper delivered at the Working Group 22 on Family Farming. *International Rural Sociological Association X World Congress*, July 30–August 2, Rio De Janeiro, Brazil.
———. 1999. "Presenting 'New Face': Polish Peasants' Protests in the Era of Post-Communism." Paper delivered at the Working Group 1: Social Movements in Rural Areas: Sources, Rationalities and Identities in the Process of Change. XVIII *Congress of the European Society for Rural Sociology*, August 24–28, Lund, Sweden.
———. 1998. "Chlopi jako podmiot procesow spolecznych." In *Sociologia Wsi*, edited by Roman Zych. Rzeszow: Wydawnictwo Wyzszej Szkoly Pedagogicznej.
Hann, Chris. 1985. *A Village without Solidarity: Polish Peasants in Years of Crisis*. New Haven: Yale University Press.
Havel, Václav. 1991. *Open Letters: Selected Writings 1965–1990*. Edited by Paul Wilson. New York: Knopf.
Heyns, Barbara, and Ireneusz Bialecki. 1991. "Solidarnosc: Reluctant Vanguard or Makeshift Coalition?" *American Political Science Review* 85 (2): 351–370.
Hirschman, Albert, O. 1997. *The Passions and the Interests. Political Arguments for Capitalism before its Triumph*. Princeton. Princeton University Press.
Huntington, Samuel P. 1968. *Political Order in Changing Societies*. New Haven: Yale University Press.
Janos, Andrew C. 2000. *East Central Europe in the Modern World: The Politics of the Borderlands from Pre- to Post-Communism*. Stanford: Stanford University Press.
Kieniewicz, Stefan. 1969. *The Emancipation of the Polish Peasantry*. Chicago: University of Chicago Press.
Kochanowicz, Jacek. 1989. "The Polish Economy and the Evolution of Dependency." In *Origins in Backwardness of Eastern Europe. Economics and Politics from the Middle Ages until the Early Twentieth Century*, edited by Daniel Chirot, 92–130. Berkeley: University of California Press.
Kolankiewicz, George, and Paul Lewis. 1988. *Poland: Politics, Economics and Society*. London: Pinter Publishers.

Kornai, Janos. 1990. *The Road to a Free Market Economy*. New York: W. W. Norton Publishing.

Kubik, Jan, and Grzegorz Ekiert. 1999. *Rebellious Civil Society and the Consolidation of Democracy in Poland, 1989–1993*. Ann Arbor: University of Michigan Press.

Lampland, Martha. 1995. *The Object of Labor: Commodification in Socialist Hungary*. Chicago: University of Chicago Press.

Lenin, V. I. 1971. *Selected works [of] V.I. Lenin: One-volume edition*. New York: International Publishers.

Leonard, P., and D. Kaneff. 2002. *Post-Socialist Peasant? Rural and Urban Constructions of Identity in Eastern Europe, East Asia and the Former Soviet Union*. New York: Palgrave.

Mack, Wales. 1994. *Rethinking the Market, Reconfiguring Institutions: The Case of Polish Agriculture*. Berkeley: University of California Press.

Meyer, J. W., and Brian Rowan. 1991. "Institutionalized Organizations: Formal Structure as Myth and Ceremony." In *The New Institutionalism in Organizational Analysis*, edited by Walter W. Powell and Paul Di Maggio, 41–62. Chicago: University of Chicago Press.

Michnik, Adam. 1995. *Diabel naszego czasu*. Warsaw: Niezalezna Oficyna Wydawnicza.

Nagengast, Carole. 1991. *Reluctant Socialists, Rural Entrepreneurs: Class, Culture, and the Polish State*. Boulder: Westview Press.

Oberschall, Anthony. 1996. "The Great Transition: China, Hungary and Sociology Exit Socialism into the Market." *American Journal of Sociology* 101 (4): 1028–1041.

Offe, Claus. 2002. "An Excursion to the Transitology Zoo." In *Postcommunist Transformation and the Social Sciences: Cross Disciplinary Approaches*, edited by Frank Bonker, Klaus Muller, and Andreas Pickel, 247–253. Lanham: Rowman & Littlefield.

Osiatynski, Wiktor. 1994. "Decommunization and Recommunization in Poland." *East European Constitutional Review* 3 (3–4): 36–41.

Poland Update. 1994. *East European Constitutional Review* 4 (1).

———. 1993. *East European Constitutional Review* 3 (4).

Popkin, Samuel. 1980. "The Rational Peasant: The Political Economy of Peasant Society." *Theory and Society* 9 (3): 411–471.

Potter, Jack M. 1967. Introduction. In *Peasant Society: A Reader*, edited by Jack M. Potter, May N. Diaz, and George M. Foster. Boston: Little Brown.

Powell, W. W., and P. J. DiMaggio, eds. 1991. *The New Institutionalism in Organizational Analysis*. Chicago: University of Chicago Press.

Poznanski, Kazimierz. 1995. *The Evolutionary Transition to Capitalism*. Boulder: Westview Press.

———. 1993. "Restructuring of Property Rights in Poland: A Study in Evolutionary Politics." *East European Politics and Societies* 7 (3): 395–421.

Przeworski, Adam. 1993. "Economic Reforms, Public Opinion and Political Institutions: Poland in the Eastern European Perspective." In *Economic Reforms in New Democracies: A Social-Democratic Approach*, edited by L. C. B. Pereira, J. M. Maravall, and A. Przeworski, 132–198. Cambridge: Cambridge University Press.

———. 1991. *Democracy and the Market: Political and Economic Reforms in Eastern Europe and Latin America*. Cambridge: Cambridge University Press.

Rakowski, Marc. 1976. *Toward an East European Marxism*. London: Allison & Busby Ltd.

Scott, James C. 1990. *Domination and the Arts of Resistance: Hidden Transcripts: 1990, xiii*. New Haven: Yale University Press.

———. 1985. *Weapons of the Weak: Everyday Forms of Peasant Resistance*. New Haven: Yale University Press.

———. 1976. *The Moral Economy of the Peasant: Subsistence and Rebellion in Southeast Asia*. New Haven: Yale University Press.

Shanin, Teodor. 1971. "Introduction." In *Peasants and Peasant Societies*. Harmondsworth: Penguin.

Shepherd, Robin H. E. 2000. *Czechoslovakia: The Velvet Revolution and Beyond*. New York: Palgrave.

Skocpol, Theda. 1976. "France, Russia, China: A Structural Analysis of Social Revolutions." *Comparative Studies in Society and History* 18 (2): 175–210.

Smolar, Aleksander. 1996. "Civil Society after Communism from Opposition to Atomization." *Journal of Democracy* 7 (1): 24–38.
Staniszkis, Jadwiga. 1992. *Ontology of Socialism*. Translated and edited by Peggy Watson. Oxford: Oxford University Press.
———. 1984. *Poland's Self-Limiting Revolution*. Princeton, NJ: Princeton University Press.
Szelényi, Ivan. 1988. *Socialist Entrepreneurs: Embourgeoisement in Rural Hungary*. Madison: University of Wisconsin Press.
———. 1980. "Whose Alternative?" *New German Critique* (20, Special Issue 2: Germans and Jews) (Spring–Summer): 117–134.
Szelenyi, Ivan, and Eric Kostello. 1996. "The Market Transition Debate: Toward a Synthesis?" *American Journal of Sociology* 101 (4) (01): 1082–1096.
Topolski, Jerzy. 1977. *Gospodarka polska a europejska w XVI–XVIII wieku*. Poznań: Wydawn. Naukowe.
Verdery, Katherine. 1996. *What Was Socialism, and What Comes Next?* Princeton: Princeton University Press.
WIIW (Wiener Institut für Internationale Wirtschaftsvergleiche). 1995. *Countries in Transition* Vienna: The Vienna Institue for Comparative Economic Studies..
Wojewodzki Urzad Statystyczny. 1994. *Rocznik statystyczny wojewodztwa poznanskiego*. Poznan: WUS.
Wolf, E. R. 1966. *Peasants*. Englewood Cliffs, NJ: Prentice-Hall.
Zucker, Lynne G. 1991. "The Role of Institutionalism in Cultural Persistence." In *The New Institutionalism in Organizational Analysis*, edited by Walter W. Powell and Paul Di Maggio, 83–107. Chicago: University of Chicago Press.

Chapter One

The Post-Socialist Transition and Formation of Post-Socialist Property Relations

The year 1989 has been generally perceived as a demarcation point, a revolution that delivered East European societies from their state socialist past and onto a path of fundamental historical change. For reformers and scholars alike, the apparent end of state socialism left capitalism as the only conceivable alternative destination point for Eastern Europe. Whether they enthusiastically or begrudgingly endorsed the ostensible inevitability of the capitalist destiny, the divergent accounts of the changes in Eastern Europe tended to address these societies as *post*-socialist or *post*-communist rather than pre-capitalist. Hence, they accentuated the historically specific departure point of the transition, leaving its destination implicit. These societies' departure from state socialism caught both analysts and participants off guard. It thus stimulated debates and struggles to account for the unfolding events of *post*-state socialism as well as to influence their course. These debates generated vastly different assessments of the up-to-date status of the changes. More importantly, they reflected distinct conceptualizations of the overall characteristics and the nature of the transition.

Overall, the prolific transition literature can be divided into two broad camps. One group contained neoliberal, evolutionist, and neomarxist analyses that were united by the shared perception of post-socialist transition as a *project of designing* the capitalist system. Within this orientation, "the *post*-socialist transition" connoted a discontinuity with the former system. In the words of Tadeusz Mazowiecki, the first prime minister of the Polish post-socialist regime, it referred to drawing "the thick line" separating state socialism and the nascent system. Post-socialism implied abandoning a discredited experimentation with the socialist project and resuming the construction of a capitalist system so as to ensure sustainable economic development. These were *convergence* accounts that invoked comparisons across socialist and capitalist systems. They saw inevitability for Eastern Europe to switch to, and follow the tracks marked earlier by, the advanced capitalist systems. From this perspective, the 1989 collapse of state socialism unmistakably attested to the superiority of the capitalist system. The transition's trajectory was delineated by mapping specific reform strategies and measures that were imperative for realization of this project (Balcerowicz 1992; Kornai 1990; Przeworski 1991; Lipton and Sachs 1990). What separated the approaches within this perspective was a debate that centered on the appropriate strategies to successfully accomplish this system-switch. Neoliberals saw the rapid, large-scale reprivatization of state enterprises as securing the transition to a capitalist system. For evolutionists, the switch could only be accomplished gradually through a slow growth of private sector. This strategy implied progressing for some time along two tracks—those marked by socialist and capitalist systems. For some sociologists, the strategy of rapid implementation of reforms was the only possibility given the double system-switch: the move to market economy *and* to parliamentary democracy.

The second broad category of the transition literature encompassed different analyses that view the post-socialist transition as anchored in, yet departing from, socialism. These accounts emphasized lasting legacies of state socialism that mediated the course of the post-socialist transition. They pronounced across-time comparisons within Eastern European societies and downplayed the validity of intersystem parallels between the East and West. These were *divergence* theories that posited distinct historical trajectories for East and West Europe. The past legacies set the path of future development. The switch cannot be engineered by any prepackaged reform strategy, but was triggered as a product of social processes within state socialism. These accounts posited the ascendancy of a specific East European capitalism from within state socialism that is distinct from West or East Asian contemporary counterparts. These accounts differed in identifying specific processes and pinpointing historical moments that generate this particular capitalism. They also differently evaluated this ascendant capitalism's economic capacity. In one approach, a high adaptive efficiency of economic units during the initial phase promised this capitalism to advance along the trajectory of economic growth. In another analysis, the emerging East European capitalism systematically undermined production and allocation efficiency, sending Eastern Europe on a track of economic involution.

Accepting the notion that the past cannot be discarded, but must be dealt with as generating unique and uncharted developments in Eastern Europe, incites us to pursue a specific theoretical project. It prompts scholars to scrutinize the heuristic value of the dichotomous categories applied by the proponents of the first theoretical camp. The concepts that evoke a contrast between socialism and capitalism are grossly inadequate to theorize the concrete historical processes distinct to Eastern Europe. In an attempt to theorize the unfolding, key socioeconomic processes in the post-socialist period, there is important scholarship that strives to provide the conceptual retooling for an analysis of nascent property relations in the post-socialist period. Based on a reexamination of state socialism, these accounts propose that the emerging post-socialist property forms cannot fit the reformers' projections of private property replacing state ownership. One analysis posits that a new hybrid form of recombinant property that blends public and private ownership spontaneously evolved out of state property in the stage of late socialism. In another account, unambiguously defined state, cooperative, and/or private ownerships can arise in the post-socialist period out of the ambiguous communal property that dominated state socialism. While providing distinct conceptual frameworks that reflect dynamic ownership changes in post-socialism, both approaches impute inertia to state socialism and homogeneity to its ownership structure. Yet state socialism underwent distinct stages in its duration and contained evolving multiform property structures. These analyses' inability to account for change within state socialism ultimately impairs their capacity to accurately delineate the dynamics of post-socialist property relations.

To capture the dynamics of the post-socialist period, strands of theoretical debates about the transition's trajectory and the nature of property relations need to be integrated. To fully understand the transition, we need to focus on property relations as its key social processes. To adequately map out the dynamic changes in property relations in state socialism and their reconfiguration in the post-socialist period, we need to conceive of the transition as a process and to demarcate its specific phases. Thus, in my approach, I will build on the conceptualizations of transition advanced by the "divergence" camp *and* on the debates on post-socialist ownership forms. Proposing a notion of conjoint ownership as a dominant property in state socialism, I will present the distinct phases of its evolution under state socialism. I will tie the departure point of the post-socialist transition to a specific stage in that evolution that is associated with the unintended systemic transformation of conjoint property into historically specific exclusive private property in the early 1980s. Given the prolonged existence of private property owners within state socialism, they formed historically specific expectations regarding exclusive private ownership. Those expectations bear on their responses to the post-socialist reform measures. I will also propose that the stages in reconfiguration of conjoint property affected post-socialist reformers in their conceptualization of how to establish genuine owners. In my rendition, we will be able to map the transition's trajectory by tracing the interplay between economic actors' reactions mediated by historically formed expectations regarding ownership, and the effects of reform measures introduced by post-socialist reformers.

The Post-Socialist Transition: Designing a Capitalist System or Departing from State Socialism?

The initial conceptualization of the post-socialist transition was translated from the concrete experience of designing a post-socialist reform program to lift the economy from deepening crisis. For Polish post-socialist reformers and their advisors, the paramount and imminent realities of economic failures, in the wake of socialist reform measures that combined state property and limited market mechanisms, were sufficient to discredit completely those measures as not viable and the former system as unreformable. This also prompted them to adopt a neoliberal perspective that declared the superiority of capitalist economic systems and thus to begin their search for appropriate reform strategies drawn from Western economies. In their rendition, the post-socialist transition was synonymous with designing a comprehensive reform blueprint and its consistent implementation to replace a failed economic system with a new, capitalist one.

The scholarly debates prompted by the neoliberal reform program initially preserved this conceptualization of the post-socialist transition. The debates revolved around what axis of comparison should guide the formulation of reform measures and which strategies would lead to economic outcomes characteristic of the West. For neoliberal economists, the axis of comparison was drawn around private property and markets as the defining features of capitalist systems. For evolutionary economists, the emphasis was on the institutional superstructure as the critical dimension of the Western economic performances to form the centerpiece of appropriate post-socialist reform strategies. For sociologists, the neoclassical model was faulty due to its singular axis of comparison. They argued that the reform strategies should be guided by the realization that the transition not only involves the construction of an economy based on Western models, but also the simultaneous building of Western parliamentary democracy. Despite the disparities in these approaches, they shared a common ground—viewing the post-socialist transition as a project from above to be guided by the reformers' objectives.

In other debates, the point of contention becomes the impetus of post-socialist change. For sociologists like Poznanski (1992, 1993), Szelenyi (1988), Nagengast (1990), Stark (1996), and Burawoy (1992, 1995), complex socioeconomic processes that occurred in state socialism generated systemic change that originates in transition. The transition's trajectory does not derive from appropriate post-socialist reform programs. Rather, processes integrally connected to the past sent these societies on a uniquely Eastern

European path. The accounts of these respective sociologists diverge in terms of whether this path is comparable to Western capitalism in generating economic growth.

The Post-Socialist Transition: Destined for Capitalism?

The 1989 political revolution in Poland, initiated by the Round Table resolutions and leading subsequently to the stunning electoral victory of the opposition groups and the formation of a Solidarity-based post-socialist government, was a revelation both to active political participants and analysts alike. In the words of a leading Solidarity figure, A. Michnik (1990: 36), "What we have learned during the past year is that there is no determinism in history, that our history depends far more on ourselves, on our will and our decisions than any of us thought." However, in the context of the severe economic problems gripping Poland, the initial revelation of political development quickly turned into pressure on the newly formed government and the Solidarity prime minister, Tadeusz Mazowiecki, to delineate a reform program that was distinct from the series of failed economic reform attempts of the socialist regimes. Furthermore, the program required quick and tangible economic results. At the inauguration of the post-socialist reform program in 1990, its main architect, Leszek Balcerowicz, proclaimed: "The system we have inherited from our predecessors can no longer exist. It has become the source of disintegration of the economy and disorganization" (Balcerowicz 1990: 224). He posited that the newly attained political liberty of 1989 allowed the economists to abandon their earlier reform initiatives in search of a "Third Road" of economic development and enabled them to follow a path that had proven itself in Western societies. "Our proposal is an economy based on market mechanisms with an ownership structure that occurs in highly developed countries and is open to the world" (Balcerowicz 1992: 39–43).

In Balcerowicz's own words, the reform design was driven by the realities of the economic performances of the East and West. Deep economic crisis, precipitated by the former reform attempts, led the team of post-socialist economists to the unshakable conclusion that a system based on state property and state coordination was untenable. Thus, the reform package's conceptualization reflected what Rawski (1992) refers to as a "nirvana approach," in which the results of nonoptimal arrangements observed in the actual socialist economies were used as a sufficient reason to invoke the *superiority* of an unexamined alternative of the capitalist market economy. In short, the conviction of the nonviability of socialism reaffirmed capitalism's viability. Furthermore, the critique of the integration of state property with limited market coordination provided a clear axis for the favorable comparison of economic experiences in capitalist economies and socialist ones—private property and unrestrained market coordination. This critique pushed for the adoption of a perspective that uniquely declared the superiority of capitalism: the neoclassical model.[1]

From the Balcerowicz program's neoclassical perspective, the post-socialist transition's departure point was a straightforward, unequivocal break from socialism. This carried a twin and transparent vision of its destination. This vision was confined to the sphere of economy, realized through explicitly formulated instrumental objectives—macroeconomic stabilization and privatization. Without explicitly labeling the projected system as *capitalist*, Balcerowicz announced that the desired system was to be based on different types of private property, organized according to the principle of open domestic and foreign competition.[2] The adoption of a theoretical perspective that enabled Polish reformers to declare the superiority of one set of economic arrangements also allowed them to see the issues of allocation and production as separate from redistribution. Thus, they abstracted from the political processes in their conceptualization of the destination point of their program and of the transition itself. With privatization as its cornerstone, broader social and political priorities of the projected new society were left unarticulated in the Balcerowicz program. The vision of the destination was conspicuously narrow.

For neoclassical reformers, these changes were not only *viable*, but they were *feasible*. Jeffrey Sachs, one of the leading consultants to the Balcerowicz reform program and an advisor to other Eastern European and Latin American governments, expressed confidence in the successful transition of socialist societies to capitalist economies. He projected that economic prosperity, similar to that in the West, would come to Eastern Europe early on, if it adopted a comprehensive and radical reform strategy (Lipton and Sachs 1990). Sachs argued for the necessity of a "shock therapy" approach, a strategy of rapid and comprehensive stabilization and restructuralization measures in order to construct a capitalist economy.[3] He acknowledged the unavoidably high aggregate social and economic transitional costs, such as a decline in the standard of living, an increase in labor displacement and unemployment, and a decrease in productive output. Although unavoidable and profound, a *swift* implementation of the reform program would shorten the duration of these transitional costs and ensure a speedier recovery to a healthy economy. For Sachs, the potential impediments to this transformation were limited to recalcitrance on the part of policy makers and state officials in the face of popular resistance to the transition costs.[4]

From the "invisible hand" perspective adhered to by Polish reformers, the post-socialist transition delineated a thick line. The disintegration of the particular political configuration of late state socialism and the failure of the socialist reform efforts created a clean slate, a beginning upon which to launch the transition. In this perspective, the distinction between the extrication from socialism and the reforms' origin was collapsed, and the departure and destination points were confounded. From the prism of neoclassical reformers, the only thing that stood between the transition's points of departure and destination was a reform blueprint that could be imposed comprehensively on different societies. Since the model did not refer to any political, cultural, or social influences from below that could systemically restrain its implementation, it obfuscated any distinction between the reforms' conceptualization and the reforms' realization. For neoclassical reformers, the post-socialist transition was conceived of as a revolution from above.

As neoclassical analysts propagated a shock therapy strategy to ensure the successful "grafting" of the program on a host society and to reduce transition costs, prominent economists spoke against rapid change. Instead they prescribed a strategy of gradual change to the post-socialist economies. Evolutionary economists such as Kornai (1990), Murrell (1991), North (1990), and Poznanski (1993) warned that extreme reform measures would bring institutional discontinuity. They argued that the insufficient organizational, legal, and financial infrastructure associated with abruptly imposed change would cause grave dislocations in economic activity and manifest themselves in production decline (Kiss 1993).

Their distinct approach to reform stemmed from a different axis of comparison of state socialism and capitalism. For instance, Murrell (1991) argued that the neoclassical model rests its explanation for the different performances of capitalist and socialist economic systems on false premises. He disputed the neoclassical thesis that capitalism outperforms state socialism in allocative or static efficiency. Therefore, he objected to placing the emphasis of the transition program on creating competitive markets and private property. For him, the superiority of capitalism lies in its dynamic or adjustment efficiency—in promoting technical and organizational innovation in economic behavior. The source of this innovation is an institutional environment that provides regulation, uniformity, and stability in economic activities. In doing so, it minimizes uncertainty, promotes learning, and preserves accumulated knowledge through organizational routines. Thus, Murrell's distinct axis of analysis generated specific recommendations for the policy formulation. As both North (1990) and Murrell (1991) argued, building an institutional framework that promoted stability and learning would advance economic performance more than privatization.

In his influential critique of the shock therapy approach, one of the leading analysts of East European socialism, Janos Kornai (1990), emphatically cautioned against underestimating the considerable gap between wishes for rapid change and the realistic pace of the transition to a market economy. Adhering to the theoretical assumptions of evolutionary economics, Kornai viewed institutionally promoted incentives as indispensable to the advancement of economic performance. In the wake of the economic experience of state-owned enterprises, he questioned whether state property could ever meet the efficiency test or present a viable alternative to a capitalist economic system.[5]

Kornai concluded that, ultimately, the inferiority of state socialism stemmed from its systematic undermining of dynamic efficiency. He argued that decades of soft budgetary constraints and impersonal property in the state sector eroded incentives for economic performance and a sense of ownership. His affirmation of the vision of a capitalist economy is predicated on his perception of the source of disintegration of state socialism. Thus, in order to arrive at a capitalist economy, behavioral patterns that proved detrimental to economic performance under state socialism must be altered through a reconstruction of complex incentives to stimulate competitive and financially responsible behavior.

Thus, the fundamental project of the post-socialist transition is not to create private property per se. Rather, it is to reconstitute economic behavior positively oriented to market forces. Such reconstitution could not result from a government policy enactment, such as the massive reprivatization proposed by neoclassical reformers. Rather, it must be associated with the emergence of a new entrepreneurial class and the creation of historically specific "personalized" private property. For Kornai, embourgeoisment implies socializing economic agents into specific expectations, behavioral patterns, and routines to cultivate calculation, accumulation, and competitiveness. Thus, it is a lengthy historical process that will consist of step-by-step changes over decades. Furthermore, Kornai envisioned the process of embourgeoisment in the post-socialist transition to progress *unevenly* across different branches of the economy.

Contrary to the neoclassical, antistatist agenda, evolutionary economists view the involvement of a strong state as indispensable because the embourgeoisment process cannot be spontaneous. Rather, it must be promoted through state-regulated credit. Therefore, given the unavoidable, prolonged coexistence of an ascending embourgeoisment sector with a state sector replete with soft budget constraints, the most important act of the reform program is the state's protection of the new entrepreneurial class. For him, the state must protect this sector against state enterprises' inherent abilities to siphon off limited credit resources intended for private investment.

Kornai's embourgeoisment theory reconceptualizes the transition as the outcome of a constellation of specific social forces that underlie and shape the market structure. In his perspective, the transition's trajectory is no longer the intended result of reforms implemented from above, but more of an *unintended* consequence of the actions of individuals responding to market forces. Kornai very explicitly points out the socioeconomic conditions inherited from state socialism that can limit the relevance of applying Western economic models to Eastern Europe.

In his early debates with neoclassical analysts, Kornai disaggregated the demarcation points in his notion of the post-socialist transition. In the neoclassical model, the transition connoted a clean line that divided two contrasting and static economic systems. In the evolutionary economists' perspective, the transition acquired a temporal character that connoted a prolonged process of hybrid economic forms that drew from both systems—the state sector remained alongside the emerging private sector.[6] In this perspective, the departure point of these processes begins to be articulated in the *disintegration* of state socialism and the *initiation* of the post-socialist transition trajectory. Evolutionary economists see the absence of effective incentive mechanisms to promote dynamic efficiency as the source of state socialism's disintegration. This disintegration produced lasting results by encroaching on the transition's initiation. It did not leave reformers with free reign to decide what form of private property to develop in the post-socialist economy. The socioeconomic conditions inherited from state socialism locked reformers' efforts into the creation and protection of "personalized" property. Consequently, while it sends Eastern Europe on a path toward capitalism, it is a different path than its Western counterparts. Thus, for Kornai, the post-socialist transition is a passage by intent toward a capitalist economy, but a passage affected in its route by socialism. Hence, he agrees with neoliberal economists about the nonviability of state socialism and the inevitability of its collapse. He also upholds the capitalist economy as the only viable system left to map the destination point of the post-socialist transition.[7] However, given the socialist past, he sees its feasibility as problematic. Within the evolutionary perspective, the departure and destination are no longer collapsed and the destination point becomes dimmer.

Kornai formulated his analysis shortly after the initiation of reforms and thus had little distance from them. Therefore, he left unexamined the constellation of social forces that shaped the transition's trajectory. Although he acknowledged the state sector's tendency to siphon off limited credit resources, he did not scrutinize the sector's ability to continue this tendency and effectively reproduce itself to the detriment of the private sector's expansion and overall economic growth. Furthermore, although Kornai acknowledged that the state needed to protect the private sector, he left unexamined the state's capacity and interest to provide the nascent private sector with a conducive environment. Hence, Kornai's delineation of the post-socialist transition's trajectory was not done in descriptive terms of what *was* but rather in prescriptive terms of what *should have been.*

The contribution to the progressive unveiling of the demarcation points in the conceptualization of the post-socialist transition came from other theoretical orientations as well. Many scholars applied a broader axis of comparison between state socialist and capitalist systems than implied in the debates between neoliberal and evolutionist economists. The post-socialist transition was not a process merely oriented to reconstruct the market economy, but also a process to build concurrently a democratic political system. Such a conceptualization was evident in Przeworski's work (1991). Contrary to the neoclassical model depicting the transition as a replacement of one economic system by another, in Przeworski's account the post-socialist transition gained a broader connotation and becomes a genuine passage. The feasibility of arriving at capitalism in the post-socialist transition was far more problematic for Przeworski than for Kornai. However, contrary to Kornai's analysis, it was not rooted in the detrimental behavioral patterns that precipitated state socialism's disintegration. For Przeworski, it stemmed from the problematic viability of the destination point itself. This is because the goal of constructing capitalism was less viable in the context of *contemporary* societies. The features that coexisted in "mature" capitalist systems, developed separately over time, were mutually undermining if pursued simultaneously in the process of post-socialist transition.

Przeworski posited that market reform programs pursued in Eastern Europe and Latin America were basically in conflict with the simultaneous pursuit of building a democratic system. The implementation of an economic reform program with its inherently painful transition costs unavoidably engendered opposition from the popular electorate, which had a low tolerance for austerity measures and the means to derail the reform measures. According to Przeworski, the context of a democratic electoral system imposed the necessity of adopting a "bitter pill" strategy in the program of an economic transition to capitalism that imposed deep, but short-term, transitional social costs. "The success of the bitter pill strategy depended on its initial brutality, on proceeding as quickly as possible with the most radical measures, on ignoring all the special interests and all immediate demands" (1991: 183).

In this way, Przeworski concurred with Sachs, arguing that adopting an alternative strategy would produce a repetition of the Latin American experience of protracted, stumbling, and retreating reform programs, with each successive reform plan encountering an increasingly skeptical and resistant population. Yet, unlike neoliberals and evolutionists, Przeworski's analysis was marked by a deep (although not fully articulated) pessimism regarding the chances for a successful transition to capitalism in Poland. For him, prosperous capitalism was unlikely in Poland on logical, as well as on empirical, grounds. Tensions inherent in the concurrent pursuit of democracy and market-economy reform were unavoidable. In addition, Przeworski saw that some political, ideological, and cultural barriers specific to Poland would prevent the consistent application of the "bitter pill" approach.

Przeworski's analysis of the transition implicitly addressed the significance of the *historical sequencing and timing* of the attempted construction of capitalism. It is a post-socialist transition in that the building of capitalism in the aftermath of socialism is far distinct from the starting point of the capitalist transition from feudalism. Then, the transition into an electoral system occurred *after* the construction of a market economy, contrary to the reality of East European societies facing these two projects *simultaneously*. Przeworski's emphasis on the post-socialist transition as an ongoing process is a vivid reminder not to confuse the dynamics of an established, mature system with the dynamics of an emerging system. From this perspective, the post-socialist reformers' idea of borrowing a model of the transition from advanced capitalist societies rests on the confusion of both.

Like Kornai, Przeworski's intent was to conceive of the transition as a combined outcome of multiple forces from above and below. Ultimately, both of their transition models are prescriptive/strategic in nature, as they map the strategy that *should* be pursued from above. However, Przeworski's approach is devoid of Kornai's confidence that the actual trajectory will in fact lead to the intended outcomes. Pressures from below, although acknowledged in Przeworski's model, remain uncharted in the assessment of their results. Thus, his analysis comes short of the *actual* trajectory of transition. Hence, Przeworski's approach attempted to integrate economic and political domains in the conceptualization of the post-socialist transition. However, he captured the relation of these two spheres and their mutual incompatibility at the origination point of the transition, leaving unexamined the dynamics of these two spheres in the *process* of transition.

The Post-Socialist Transition: Legacies of State Socialism

By proclaiming the nonviability of state socialism on empirical and theoretical grounds, the above approaches viewed the transition's trajectory as a function of reform prescriptions that post-socialist regimes ought to implement in order to construct capitalist systems. The contrasting, "socialist legacy" perspective replaced the strategic approach's preoccupation with what the transition's course should be and theorized what the actual post-socialist trajectory *was*. In the "socialist legacy" perspective, the past was not dismissed but, rather, was accounted for as an active force that could not be easily demarcated from the transition's origin. Accordingly, state socialism has to be perceived as a dynamic system evolving to capitalism. By interweaving the origins of post-socialism with the past, the "socialist legacy" approach replaced the notion of an unqualified break with that of continuity. In this approach, the fundamental changes of the post-socialist period stem from the evolutionary changes of late state socialism. However, the individual models of the "socialist legacy" approach vacillated between macro-policy programs and the microlevel actions of economic units as the loci of these momentous changes.

Challenging both the notion of the revolutionary nature of the post-socialist reform policies and their discontinuity from the past, the policy-oriented studies of the reform programs (Poznanski 1993; Wolf 1991) reacted to the overly static, restrictive assessments of state socialism and posited the progression of the reform-induced redesigning of state socialism in the direction of capitalism. In an attempt to account for the dynamics of the post-socialist transition, Poznanski (1993) focused on the changes initiated by socialist reformers and linked them to the changes by their post-socialist followers. Akin to the approach that Walder (1996) adopts in his study of the trajectory of economic changes in China, Poznanski deems socialist reforms in Eastern Europe significant in the context of the overall direction of subsequent post-socialist changes. For Poznanski, the socialist reforms were relevant regardless of their incomplete applications, unintended outcomes, and incessant failures in stimulating economic growth. They were significant because they set off a chain of consequences that constituted the initial conditions for subsequent reforms. These posed limits to future alternative policy objectives and strategies.

For Poznanski, the alleged 1989 revolution that abolished state socialism was in fact an evolution of state-sponsored reforms. The post-socialist reform program was a direct product of the long-standing efforts from above to reform the property structure of the socialist system. Based on his careful reexamination of state socialist and post-socialist policies, Poznanski posited a thesis of the linear reform evolution in the direction of the state-induced, progressive undermining of public ownership. In Poznanski's view, the 1989 post-socialist reform built directly on its antecedents. Rather than creating private property, it produced the "weakest" version of public property to date. Thus it led to the deepest Polish economic recession since the beginning of state socialism, rather than to the intended economic growth.

Other theoretical models also proposed a dynamic evolution of state socialism and its potential for transformation into capitalism. While Poznanski posited the pattern of policy initiatives from above as the locus of critical evolutionary changes within state socialism that prefigured the post-socialist trajectory, others within the "socialist legacy" approach identified factors from below as most critical in the continuous system changes. Thus, in contrast to Poznanski's thesis on the emergence of an underperforming capitalism out of the gradual weakening of public property, Nagengast (1990, 1991) asserted that the sequence of state socialist agricultural policies, which aimed to resolve recurrent food shortages in late state socialism, generated capitalist private property and gave rise to genuine agricultural capitalist entrepreneurs. Nagengast argued that these policies led to the gradual capitalization of farming and marketing and thus the economic polarization of peasantry. Although the agrarian reforms generated the economic polarization of the peasantry, Nagengast (1991) emphasized the evolution of ideological and cultural traits in the countryside, that is, changes in the ideology of populism, which provided the legitimation base to sustain and advance this agrarian polarization.

Similarly to Nagengast, Szelenyi (1988) posited a thesis of the nascent bourgeoisie in the context of late Hungarian state socialism. Szelenyi pointed out that the late socialism reform programs promoted expansion of second economies parallel to formal economies. For Szelenyi, the officially prescribed parallel structures of late socialism emerged as the foundation for a new era. However, through his notion of "interrupted embourgeoisment," Szelenyi accorded greater importance to cultural traits in the evolution of state socialism to capitalism. He argued that, given the market-oriented policies of late socialism, only heirs of pre-socialist entrepreneurs, via their cultural capital, took advantage of these policies' incentives. Both the theoretical frameworks of Nagengast and Szelenyi were formulated before the 1989 changes took hold. The implications of these analyses were that these nascent capitalist processes should carry over into the post-socialist transition and lead to a dynamic macroeconomic performance. As they anchored the origin point of the post-socialist transition solidly in the past, the dynamics of the post-socialist transition in these analyses was collapsible into the dynamics of state socialism.

Stark's (1996) theoretical model presented a particularly significant contribution to the "socialist legacy" approach. For Stark the disintegration of the past could not be easily demarcated from the transition's origin. Although 1989 brought a collapse of the formal structures of state socialism, Stark argued that the parallel, quasi-legal economies *endured* the foundation for post-socialist transition. The changes in Eastern Europe have occurred "not *on* the ruins, but *with* the ruins of communism" (1996: 995). Stark emphasized the utility value of the fragmented remnants of socialism for the construction of a new period.[8] Conceptually blending the complex processes of extrication from socialism with the inception of post-socialism, Stark dispensed with the concept of the transition as a passage from one order to the next. In its place, he proposed the notion of "transformation." "Change, even fundamental change, of the social world is not the passage from one order to another but rearrangements in the patterns of how multiple orders are interwoven" (1996: 995).

For Stark, the fundamental changes of the post-socialist period stem from the spontaneous and evolutionary changes of late state socialism. The locus of these momentous changes in his framework is the microlevel actions of economic units. These changes are the sum total of the evolving adjustment strategies of economic enterprises, guided by their immediate, pragmatic goal of survival in the context of the changing economic environment of late state socialism. These adjustments amounted to a complex redressing of organizational boundaries into the intricate crisscrossing of enterprise networks. These organizational innovations produced a blending of distinct ownership forms: state ownership and the second economy's private ownership. This resulted in a hybrid post-socialist ownership form of recombinant property.

With his notion of organizational innovation and the progressive reconstitution of state ownership into recombinant property, Stark breaks the pattern of the prescriptive/strategic models of transition. The recombinant property that emerges from the spontaneous adjustments of economic agents leads to uncharted territories. It thus challenges the earlier strategic approaches that affirm a predeclared destination point in the transition. Instead, Stark posited that the organizational innovations and transformations of late state socialism delineated the actual post-socialist transition's trajectory and generated a uniquely East European capitalism.[9] Contrary to the divergent approaches that insisted that the road to capitalism would inevitably lead through "privatization" and some form of *asset transfer*, Stark pointed to *asset recombination* as a uniquely East European road to capitalism.

Can this East European post-socialist capitalism be expected to amount to a superior model as compared to its state socialist's predecessor? Stark posits that post-socialism tentatively passes the superiority test. Subscribing to an institutional analysis, Stark cites adaptive or dynamic efficiency as the critical dimension to differentiate and evaluate socialism and capitalism. Following Hannan (1986) and Boyer (1991), Stark views organizations as bundles of routines and practices that are based on shared organizational knowledge. The multiplicity of organizational forms implies an increasing flow of organizational information. Thus, economies that maximize a diversity of organizational forms are superior because they generate a broad repertoire of organized solutions to a changing economic environment. Thus, they enhance adaptive efficiency. Because state socialism was based on a homogenized property form that implied low organizational diversity, its economy was characterized by low adaptive efficiency.

For Stark, post-socialism is synonymous with organizational diversity and networks of cross-ownership that allow for flexible adaptation and therefore promote dynamic efficiency. Yet he closes his analysis by expressing ambivalence over whether the post-socialist organizational reconfiguration will translate to *sustainable* economic development. Although recombinant property tends to promote adaptive efficiency, recent results suggest central shortcomings for the post-socialist enterprises. Accountability and production efficiency are problematized by recombinant property.[10] The results contrast to the capitalist counterparts of West Europe and East Asia where organizational diversification produces both adaptive and production efficiency.

Stark broke new ground in the study of the East European transition. He rejected those strategic approaches, which he called "transitology," because they assumed that social changes could be designed and directed based on a reformer's expert knowledge. Stark challenged the notion that the post-socialist transition represented an exogenous change modeled on Western patterns and imposed from above that ultimately would convert the East into the West. Thus, he firmly established the endogenous bases of the transition, integrally linking past and present. The organizational recombinations that drove the post-socialist period did not derive from the economic programs of post-socialist reformers. Rather, they were rooted in the dynamics of late socialism.

The strength of Stark's analysis is also a source of its shortcomings. By rejecting strategic approaches because they reduce the transition's trajectory to reformers' programs and objectives, Stark negates the reform program's impact on the transition course. By doing so, his model deprives the transition of its element of linearity and intentionality. Furthermore, his model is itself somewhat reductionist. Based on an impressive data set from Hungary, Stark showed the burgeoning rate of the reconstitution of state enterprises into recombinant, cross-ownership property.[11] However, the post-socialist organizational recombination lacks any demarcation point that differentiates it from the processes produced under late state socialism. It thus becomes collapsible into the earlier processes. Also, he fell short of tying the emergence of organizational reconfigurations to their original conditions, as he set out to do. Furthermore, despite Stark's explicit notion of the multiplicity of structures and domains involved in the post-socialist transformation, his concept of recombinant property limits the analysis to the realm of economy and explains the principal players through a purely economic view of action without reference to the cultural and political constructedness of their action.

Burawoy (1995) also anchored the post-socialist transition in late state socialism. Yet Burawoy established the transition as a sui generis process that could not be reduced to the preceding system.[12] To distinguish the dynamics of the post-socialist transition as separate in their logic from those of late state socialism, he drew an analytical distinction between the extrication from state socialism and the onset of reforms in his notion of the transition's point of origin. Although he emphasized the importance of the antecedent political and economic structures in releasing specific responses at the micro-level, he also accounted for the effects of post-socialist reform policies. Thus, he preserved an element of intentionality in the course of the post-socialist transition. Hence, for Burawoy, the transition's trajectory was charted through the combined effects of post-socialist policy intentions and reactions to them from below.

Furthermore, in Burawoy's model, the reactions of economic agents are no longer reduced to pure economic responses. Instead, he offers a tripartite analysis of fluctuating relations between enterprises and the state administrative bodies, individual enterprises and managers, and workers. These three levels shape Burawoy's conception of the formation of agents' responses: He sees them as a function of the complex constellation of forces and interests. In Burawoy's approach, politics becomes an inherent aspect of microlevel economic relations and it is inseparable from the economic transition on the macrolevel.[13]

For Burawoy, the distinctive stage of disintegration of state socialism associated with the collapse of the party system generated "merchant capitalism" by altering the tripartite relations of economic agents. The collapse of the party-state strengthened preexisting monopolies, replaced dissipating hierarchical relations with increased lateral exchanges between and within enterprises, and increased workers' control over production vis-à-vis managers. These sets of changes made the maximization of profit through *trade* the driving force behind enterprises' strategies, thus signifying the rise of merchant capital. A primitive form of capitalism that does not have its own system of production, merchant capital grafted itself onto preexisting systems without altering them (Burawoy 1995: 27–28). Burawoy argues that this particular form of capitalism emerged out of the proliferation of trade and markets and combined with existing institutions and forms of production. It then undermined production efficiency and was unambiguously translated into the involution of production rather than economic development.

In effect, merchant capitalism immediately preceded, and thus conditioned, the subsequent stage and overall trajectory of the transition. At the next point of the transition, the onset of the post-socialist reform programs, it generated constraints that radically undermined the implementation of reforms. The reform's central measures—the monetarization and the privatization of the economy—were intended to impose financial accountability on enterprises by hardening soft budget constraints and to induce enterprises to production efficiency. Yet these measures were doomed from the onset because of the party-state's disintegration and the resulting institutional void. This left reformers without the necessary political instruments to adequately regulate or enact the measures. Consequently, the outcomes of the reforms deviated from the intended results.

Hence, the monetarization of the economy led to a dual process. It resulted in the systematic transfer of capital to trade enterprises. In a parallel outcome, it depleted individual industrial firms of investment resources and strengthened soft-budget constraints on their attempt to reproduce the production circle. The privatization led to the depletion of enterprise assets by both managers and workers. It also prompted them to combine their efforts to extract government credits based on their political influence rather than economic merit. The unintended outcomes further solidified the trajectory of the transition initiated by the disintegration of the party-state and nascent merchant capitalism.

Thus, both Stark and Burawoy saw the transition's trajectory as anchored in the spontaneous actions of economic agents. For both of them, late socialism generated and "incubated" a uniquely East European capitalism. For Stark, it was enterprise or ownership network capitalism. For Burawoy, it was merchant capitalism. Stark was reluctantly optimistic that nascent capitalism, synonymous with organization innovation and adaptive efficiency, would lead eventually to sustainable economic growth. Burawoy pointed to the unambiguous trends in industrial relations that systematically undermined adaptive and production efficiency and led to economic decline and social disintegration.[14]

In Burawoy's approach, the post-socialist transition acquires a dynamic of its own. Although its origins can be traced to the disintegration of state socialism, they cannot be reduced to it. The transition consists of clearly delineated stages. The implementation of the post-socialist reforms is constrained by merchant capitalism, yet the reforms produce their own dynamics and outcomes. Thus, in Burawoy's approach, the transition is linear. Each stage is constrained by the preceding phase, but develops according to its own dynamics. Thus, in his model, unlike that of Stark, the notion of continuity between state socialism and post-socialism entails demarcation points separating one phase of the transition from the next. Furthermore, for Burawoy, the transition is uneven across sectors and industries. The complex political and economic processes at the local and national levels result from the systemic favoring of the trade sector in the distribution of financial capital.

Like Burawoy, I also subscribe to the conceptualization of post-socialist transition as a dynamic process of linear progression that is rooted in the crisis of state socialism. In order to capture the dynamics of transition, I also concur with him that the transition's departure point needs to be disaggregated from the extrication from socialism and the onset of the reforms. Thus, like him, I conceive of the transition as charted by the disintegration of socialism and the effects of reformers' efforts from above. These processes are path-dependent in that they build on one another, yet acquire independent dynamics at each stage.

Yet, I perceive the crisis of socialism differently. Burawoy views it somewhat narrowly, as synonymous with the collapse of the party-state's function as economic coordinator that subsequently gave rise to a merchant capital form of market coordination. He also sees the disintegration of party-state coordination as a rather *instantaneous* collapse. From the vantage point of Polish state socialism, where the party-state faced powerful opposition to its rule in regard to both its political legitimacy *and* economic efficacy, the conceptualization of the extrication from state socialism requires broader terms that reflect the complex disintegration of economic and political structures. I posit that the disintegration of the economic and political domains did not coincide; the economic crisis preceded the political collapse of state socialism. Burawoy clearly traces the origins of East European capitalism by the collapse of the central economic coordination mechanism and its replacement with historically constructed markets that together undermined production growth. In my approach, the extrication from socialism and the genesis of Eastern European capitalism was a *prolonged* process that stretched from the beginning of the 1980s.[15] In this decade, the asynchronic socialist crises were associated with the emergence and consolidation of a historically specific private property that preceded and precipitated the political collapse of the socialist regime several years later. These property relations were further solidified under the post-socialist reform program and led to the involution of production and the development of specific state paternalism.

Furthermore, in Burawoy's model, the constraining effect of the disintegration of socialism on the transition's trajectory plays out at the stage of the reforms' implementation. After the party-state's collapse, it was the initial institutional void that altered microlevel economic behavior. Subsequently, the insufficient institutional infrastructure at the post-socialist state's disposal undermined its capacity to steer the economic agents to actions consistent with the expected outcomes. Problematizing only the implementation of reforms in an attempt to account for unintended outcomes left unexamined the issue whether the post-socialist program had the internal coherence required to elicit the results it projected. Was the constraining effect of the past limited to weakening post-socialist capacity to enforce its program on economic actors, or did it impinge on how reformers defined the change? I will argue that the program was inherently affected by the extrication from socialism at the stage of its conceptualization as well as its implementation. The path dependency of post-socialist transition needs to be analyzed at the level of how the reformers sought to stimulate appropriate economic actions as reflected in their policies. The post-socialist reformers viewed property as the key determinant of economic actions. Thus, they made property transformation the core of their program. Hence, my discussion will turn to the issue of how to account for changes in property relations associated with post-socialist transition.

Property Relations in the Post-Socialist Transition: From Universal to Historically Specific Property

In juxtaposing state socialism with capitalism, the prescriptive approaches frame the debate about post-socialist ownership changes around the issue of *how* to move from an economy dominated by state property to one based on private ownership. Neoclassical approaches advocate the massive transfer of state assets into private hands. The passage from state to private property is synonymous with assuring economic growth. Within this approach, the only problem lies in implementation—how to valuate the assets to be distributed or where to find the financial capital needed for this asset transfer.

Within the evolutionist perspective (North 1990; Murell 1991; Kornai 1990), the debate on how to move toward private property inherently contains the question of what *type* of private property could be correlated with economic growth given the socialist past. For Kornai, state socialism imposed a historically specific narrow passage to an economy of sustained growth by eroding any sense of ownership. The post-socialist reconstitution of economic behavior positively oriented to market forces can only be accomplished with personal property ownership. Only by fusing control and ownership functions in property can the effects of the past be neutralized through the introduction of incentives to stimulate competitive and financially responsible behavior. For Kornai, neoliberal proposals supporting massive asset transfers imply the creation of diffuse private property that would perpetuate socialist behavior patterns and thus undermine production efficiency and economic growth.

The actual state asset transfer and the creation of the private sector reveal a stark deviation from both projections. Both perspectives would explain this gap as merely a delay in an otherwise predictable outcome. Each approach reasserts the validity of its theoretical stand and calls for a strengthened commitment to their privatization strategies as a way of closing the gap between projected and real outcomes (Balcerowicz 1992; Blanchard 1993). The renewed commitments are underpinned by the assumption that the distinctive categories of ownership possess universally valid characteristics. Private property is desired because it has an affinity with markets and consequently results in economic growth, while state property is its direct antithesis.

The centrality of ownership change in the post-socialist transition is addressed differently in the "socialist legacy" models. Divergent empirical results and theoretical expectations prompted many analysts to reexamine the adequacy of imposing dichotomous concepts—categories that were developed to contrast socialism with capitalism—on the empirical reality of post-socialism. Stark's prominent standing within, and his undisputed contribution to, the debate on the descriptive approaches to the post-socialist transition are rooted precisely in this kind of careful reexamination of the heuristic value of dichotomy-based notions to inform analysis of post-socialist property relations.

Stark (1996) argues that opposing the notion of private property to state property is a grossly inadequate way to theorize post-socialist ownership transformations. Instead, he proposes the concept of recombinant property. Drawing from his empirical analysis of post-socialist Hungary, Stark posits that the actual changes in property relations do not follow the transition from public to private as outlined in the privatization programs of the post-socialist reforms. For Stark, post-socialist property blends the boundaries of private and public ownership and results in a new, hybrid recombinant property. It is a product of individual enterprises' strategies to adjust to the acute uncertainties of the new economic and organizational environment.[16] Their attempts rest on employing two strategies simultaneously. They *spread* risk through a downward diversification of assets involving the creation of the parent enterprises' organizational spin-offs. Also, they *shed* risk by accumulating liabilities on the individual enterprise level, which, in their global effects, periodically prompt state-sponsored, massive bail-out programs.

As Stark points out, these two adjustment strategies shape post-socialist property relations. The downward diversification of assets and the creation of semiautonomous satellite companies produce crisscrossing lines of interenterprise ownership networks. State-sponsored bail-out programs transform private debt into a public liability. These acquired public liabilities are subsequently converted into public shares within the insolvent enterprises that qualified for debt restructuralization funds. Thus, an interenterprise ownership network is characterized by the complicated blending of the boundaries between public and private ownership.

For Stark, risk shedding by the economic firms results in the centralized management of liabilities and a combination of market and redistributive coordination in the post-socialist period. Large liabilities can be converted into assets once they are translated into qualifications for more resources from massive debt restructuring and bail-out programs. Thus, the post-socialist period is marked by a distinct state paternalism. "Whereas in the state socialist economy, paternalism was based on the state's attempts to centrally manage assets, . . . in the first years of the post-socialist economy paternalism is based on the state's attempts to centrally manage liabilities" (Stark 1996: 15). The emergence of a recombinant property structure, as it produces the combined forms of market and redistributive coordination, also results in ambiguous organizing principles legitimizing economic activity. In their strategies of survival, economic enterprises aim to be profitable in market transactions and to be eligible for state allocation of resources.

Stark distanced himself from the dichotomous concepts of property that derive from comparisons between socialism and capitalism. His conceptual retooling assumes an endogenous comparison of systems across time—state socialism transforms into post-socialism. Yet this comparison is not consistently carried through. In his effort to grasp the nature of ownership changes, Stark proposes an innovative reconceptualization of the ever-reconfigured post-socialist *present*. However, he retains the depiction of state socialism developed through comparisons with capitalism. Therefore, Stark's endogenous comparison is pursued only halfway. In his analysis, he preserves the notion of state property as descriptive of property relations under state socialism. Stark replaces the "state ownership versus private ownership" divide presented in the prescriptive models with a duality of "state property and recombinant property." The latter implies economic dynamism, organizational reconfiguration, and heterogeneity. It is contrasted to the static character and organizational homogeneity of the former. However, to chart the trajectory of the post-socialist transition and to assess fully the legacy of state socialism, the depiction of state socialism needs to be equally carefully reexamined.

Comisso's (1991) work provides this kind of framework for understanding the nature of ownership under state socialism and the subsequent changes in property relations. Comisso posits that state socialism was based not on state property as is conventionally assumed. Instead, the dominant form of ownership was *communal*. Comisso emphasizes the social and legal nature of property rights because they delineate persons into two categories—those possessing rights that are socially recognizable, specific, and sanctioned, and those excluded from exercising rights. The delineation of rights involves the operation of the exclusion principle separating two classes of persons: owners and nonowners. It involves the parallel separation of two domains: private and public. The specification of property rights, as Comisso argues, is a "collective/political act par excellence," since property rights involve the recognition by others of what individuals holding them may do. Because of the "two-sided" aspect of any given property right system, those who exercise rights cannot unilaterally specify what the rights are. "Rather, an authority 'above' economic transactions must specify the conditions under which they can take place and be bound by their own rules should it engage in them" (1991: 173). Hence, this property right specification implies the existence of independent institutions to elaborate the rules of conduct and to enforce these rules. As the constitution of property rights involves establishing genuine economic actors, its corollary is establishing genuine political authority. Hence, Comisso's notion of property rights integrates the political and economic domains. Furthermore, her "two-sided" notion of property rights (implicitly) points out that, at the same time as an exercise of specific rights results in specific production performances by those entitled, it also produces broader consequences for those excluded from the ownership. Therefore, their continuous acceptance of the given property relations must be predicated on some broader agreement on the *social outcomes* that stem from specific property rights. The study of property relations must thus encompass economic and social realms.

Given this conceptual framework, Comisso asserts that state socialism was dominated by communal property. Under state socialism, the exclusion principle did not operate to delineate property's subjects or to apply uniform laws enforcing property rights. She argues that, in state socialism, institutions lacked the necessary independence to elaborate rules of conduct and to enforce them. "The party's 'leading role' continually eroded the boundaries between the subjects of the property and those excluded from it. Because laws in general were subordinated to political priorities, property rights defined in laws necessarily suffered the same fate, regardless of who held them" (1991: 168–169). Inevitably, the ad hoc, case-by-case assignment of property rights, combined with a lack of appropriate state-enforced norms, lead to the overexploitation of production assets and a decline in production efficiency.

Distancing herself from transition models predicated on the state property–private property dichotomy, Comisso asserts that socialism based on communal property presents a *third* alternative to both private and public (cooperative or state) property rights. The latter are constituted on the bases of unambiguously specified and uniformly enforced rights. The post-socialist transition then is about establishing genuine owners. By definition, this process involves the creation of political institutions to specify and enforce ownership rights. Like Burawoy, Comisso argues that the institutional collapse of socialism has to be distinguished from the initiation of the post-socialist transition, for the latter requires the existence of an independent and efficient institutional framework to begin ownership restructuring. Therefore, she proposed that the post-socialist reformers' goal to rationalize resource use, and ultimately to bring about economic growth, could be met by the reconstitution of communal property into any of these alternative property systems. As she asserted, none of these alternative ownerships could be rejected as a priori "inefficient" based on previous experience.

The approach advanced in this book builds on Comisso's work. She provides the conceptual retooling for the study of the formation of post-socialist property relations by breaking further away from approaches that rely on a binary conception of state property and private property to describe the passage from state socialism to post-socialism. Yet her notion of communal ownership and its underlying ambiguity in the specification of property norms and subjects is too broad a category to describe the property relations under socialism. Moreover, it is too static to account for the changes in ownership within state socialism.

Kathryn Verdery's important anthropological work on the decollectivization of the agricultural sector in Romania (2003) greatly advances the rethinking of property transformations in the former socialist societies. In her book, she challenges the Western-specific conceptual content of the notion of property, applied as a universal category within the post-socialist context, and emphasizes the intense promotion of the notion of property in the 1990s as a political and ideological project: "Property was the idiom used by international organizations, which made economic assistance conditional on changes in property rights, as well as by . . . politicians wanting either aid from abroad or symbolic capital against the former party apparatchiks . . . ; villagers, too, had a property discourse, speaking of 'my land' and 'my rights'" (2003: 15).

Distancing herself from the dichotomous approaches that oppose state and private properties, Verdery (2003) examines socialist property on its own terms rather than as a failed form of Western property. Thus, she emphasizes the relative advancement in economic efficiency accomplished by the socialist collectivization when, based on administrative mechanisms of control, it transformed peasants' farms into institutional forms and production units far better adapted to monitoring, managing, and appropriating from above (1998: 203).

Targeting economists, political scientists, and policy makers, who are actively involved in promoting private property for the Eastern bloc, she aims to attune her divergent audience to the great complexity of property arrangements within post-socialist societies, and to their origins from within socialism itself rather than from the 1990s post-socialist privatization reforms (2003). Verdery argues that the socialist system included multifold property regimes, thus challenging the prevalent simplistic tendency to homogenize socialism as dominated by state property. She asserts the existence of four property types: state, cooperative, private, and personal properties, owned by three property subjects—the state, cooperatives, and individuals. Furthermore, similarly to other anthropologists (for example, Hann 1993; Buchowski 2009), Verdery ascribes a broader social nature to socialist property than merely economic, as is assumed in the Western connotation of property, arguing that property rights were accorded as attributes of status, not merely for economic benefit. The distinct property forms had a hierarchical ranking of differential status: "state socialist property was *more* inalienable, *more* exclusive, *more* property than any other form, and judicial practice was to shore it up, buttressing its status over that of other kinds" (2003: 52). Descending status ranking was associated respectively with the cooperative, private, and personal property forms.

Verdery conceives of socialism based on heterogeneity of property arrangements and proceeds to integrate the delineation of distinct property forms, with the theory of the state as a central component of her conception of socialist property. Challenging the Western notion of property as *pre*-political, in that the state legitimizes and guarantees the already existing private owners with the bundle of their economic rights, Verdery assumes socialist property is *post*-political. That is, property arrangements and the allocation of related property rights are a function of who has political power at the time of their determination. Under socialism, ownership rights originated within the political domain and their implementation was subsumed under the *right of direct administration*. Verdery argues that the right of direct administration imposes a dual nature on socialist enterprises by combining their simultaneous subordination to the state and autonomous legal functioning distinct from it. Directors of state-owned enterprises and cooperative units exercised administrative rights in their own name rather than as state agents. Although the administrative rights were extensive, the power to exercise them was premised on the prior existence of the state's power as owner, from which the administrator's power was derived. Those hierarchies of administrative and productive entities, held together by delegating administrative rights to state and cooperative enterprises in agricultural and industrial sectors, were established by socialist party-states to coordinate processes of production within a system of centralized appropriation. The administrative rights were to link the different property types, establishing specific relations to values and goods.

To articulate further the distinctive, post-political nature of ownership under socialism, Verdery evokes an analogy to Gluckman's anthropological analysis (1943) of the organization of property in the Lozi kingdom of Central Africa. In both instances, the ownership rights to all types of property were vested within the superior political power, whereby the socialist state and the Lozi king, respectively, exercised ownership by passing downward the rights to lower-level entities in the bureaucratic hierarchy. The administrative grants allowed the endowed subjects to act as conventional owners, short of the right to alienate property assets permanently, in return obliging them to allegiance and to generating products that the state appropriated and redistributed. Crucial to the argument advanced in this book is Verdery's assertion, echoing Gluckman's thesis, that the party-state's downward allocation of ownership rights, similarly to the Lozi's case, has not compromised its claim to supreme ownership.

In her efforts to integrate the theory of the state into her conception of socialist property, Verdery perceives the state as the institutional structure. Hence, she analyzes the socialist institutional vertical relations of farm directors and the bureaucratic hierarchy exercising the administrative right superimposed on the institutionally and informally structured system of horizontal relations among distinct socialist (state and cooperative) property managers. Finally, she traces villagers' position in, and attitudes toward, socialist property arrangements. In Verdery's view, socialist property arrangements are the institutionally defined network of relations and obligations that bind the distinct property forms together on the microlevel. These, conditioned by systemic economic shortages, produce an aggregate macrolevel result of a complex *gift* economy– a barter system of gifts and favors.[17]

The network of favors and gifts as a crucial dimension of socialist property had both the effect of affirming and undermining the socialist system. Unauthorized appropriations by many officials lubricated the planned economy, reinforcing the officials' positions of authority and reinstating them as effective socialist cadres, while common theft from the collectives, done by its members in the spirit of self-respecting persons resisting the system, drained the collective property by diverting its assets downward to the personal property.

Verdery shows that, with the advancement of socialism, the process of downward assignment of ownership rights has allowed the administrators of the respective property arrangements to gain growing autonomy from the state. "Once central control began to disintegrate, the managers abrogated the state powers, even selling off state assets—often to themselves. By the time privatization officially commenced by the initiatives of post-socialist reformers, many of socialism's erstwhile directors were well on their way to being private owners, a process that socialism's hierarchy of administrative estates had facilitated" (2003: 59). Thus the transformation of property arrangements in post-socialism stems from bottom-up, evolutionary processes within socialism rather than from the top-down reforms of the new post-socialist regimes.

Verdery's seminal work has opened new discourse on the socialist property regimes, inspiring further scholarly efforts at the conceptualization of the nature and direction of property arrangements in the aftermath of socialism. Her challenge to the approach that inscribes dichotomies of state and private property on the Eastern European post-socialist dynamics enabled her to advance new, fruitful lines of analysis. Her references to the African kingdom allowed her to show how property arrangements have emerged in both systems outside of the political domain, engendered by a network of informal obligations and coordinated not by market but by administrative methods. By drawing an analogy between post-political property arrangements in socialist administrative regimes with those in the Lozi kingdom, Verdery, echoed by C. Hann (1993) and other anthropologists, points to the fusion of micro- and macrolevels and between economic and political domains, thus necessitating an incorporation of the theory of the state as an integral part of the conception of property.

This innovating analogy creates at the same time limitations in her analysis. Emphasis on the exercise of the administrative right in both cases leads her to conceive narrowly of the state as an administrative structure. As she addresses the institutional embodiment of administrative right in the regulation of property arrangements, she does not examine the state as *an actor*, and, consequently, she leaves unanswered how these two respective political authorities in the Lozi kingdom and in the socialist regime legitimate their supreme ownership rights, which in turn have a bearing on the specific content, terms, and mode of granting downward ownership rights.

She ascribes the absolute property rights to the socialist state akin to those vested in the African king. Yet, the distinct principle legitimating the supreme ownership of the socialist state considerably attenuated its administrative right: socialist right could not be inherited, and its maintenance was contingent on performance—delivering specific economic and social results. Hence Verdery's analogy of African and socialist administrative rights is not sensitive to the temporal contextuality of these two types of societies. Competing with modern advanced capitalism as an alternative way to bring modernity to backward Eastern European societies, the socialist administrative right carried a serious constraint for its central authority—an obligation to establish such property arrangements as would produce an economic efficiency and growth sufficient to provide a vast range of social benefits to a broad spectrum of society. Such obligation was not built into the administrative right of the African king of traditional society.

In practice, the socialist state's obligation as an actor with administrative right to provide tangible results led to the mounting and effective pressures from low levels of the property hierarchy for the change in the granted property arrangements. Thus, in my book, I focus on deepening the analysis of the socialist state as an actor and on the factors shaping the downward assignment of property rights by more precisely pinpointing the distinct phases of that process and locating each one's impetus. I show that, in early socialism, the state initiated the reconfiguration of property entitlements, while the later phase of the process was precipitated by the subjects from below. Hence, rather than assuming one downward direction in the assignment of property rights, I argue that property arrangements emerge out of political contestation between distinct claimants to property rights with the outcome of a diverging balance of power between them.

In short, Verdery's main shortcoming is an incomplete theory of the state that is embedded in her notion of property; she perceives the state mainly as an institutional structure without articulating also its dimension as an *agent*. As a result, she refers to state administrative *right*. When she discusses obligations in socialist property arrangements, essentially she locates them only within the realm of formally and informally induced favors within a horizontal network of divergent property subjects, without sufficiently scrutinizing the relations between rights and obligations associated with the downward assignment of property by the socialist state. This book will advance her work by integrating the theory of the state into the conception of socialist property.

Property appears to elude sociology, given, as Swedberg (2003) and Kowalik (2009) acknowledge, the relative absence of a comprehensive analysis of property in Western and Eastern European scholarships, respectively. However, a recent discourse among organizational sociologists and law and society scholars on the nature of property within Western advanced capitalist societies provides a fruitful springboard to the conception of property necessarily involving both rights and obligations, and, with that, it allows us to understand the distinctiveness of socialist property. The sociologists (Fligstein 2001; Emigh 1999; Carruthers and Ariovich 2004) and legal scholars

(Radin 1993; Edelman 1992; Dobbin and Sutton 1998; Edelman and Suchman 1997; Singer 2000; and others) quarrel with the traditional view of property, which, in its absolute approach, assumes that property is objectively definable or identifiable apart from social and political context and that it represents and protects the sphere of legitimate absolute individual autonomy.[18] Legal theorist Joseph Singer (2000) is particularly relevant to the considerations in this book. He argues that this traditional view rests on the understanding that property denotes an individual ownership, whereas property should instead be viewed as a social institution involving *many* owners. This implies that, even if we do assume a strong position for the protection of individual autonomy from the intervention of government, such requirement implies protection for individual owners against theft, trespass by others—property holders or nonowners—and any wrongful abrogation of individual property rights. Thus, since, in practice, the bundle of rights of some owners may impinge upon the exercise of property rights of other owners, property exhibits inherent *internal tensions*. These tensions may stem from the clash of the same right exercised by many owners, or a specific right within the property might come into conflict with other rights. These tensions and disputes between different claimants over property call for their constant adjudication by judicial systems.

Singer's conception of property as a social institution pertaining to *many* owners has three implications that are of interest here: First, an effective protection of the exercise of property rights and autonomy for *any* individual owner is predicated on his recognition and respect of the property of others and hence carries an *obligation* not to make claims to, or harm the property of, others. Thus, when we conceive of property, we need to speak of both rights *and* obligations accorded to property rather than to refer merely to property rights. Second, although, in the traditional approach, regulation seems to be perceived as threatening property, property cannot exist without regulation. Hence, even within the traditional notion of property, we can point out the embedded direct reference to the state. The affirmation of property claims and the adjudication of disputes over property, when they emerge, require state and judicial regulations. Further, as it emerges from the legal discourse on property, the judicial regulation is not of a nature that the traditional approach suggests—that is, it does not follow the rule of law (Radin 1993: 160). The liberal ideal of the rule of law requires that individuals, including property owners, be governed by general rules. These rules are presumed to predate the action to be judged by them. It is further presumed that these rules are known, understood, and agreed upon by those to whom these rules apply. Hence, the ideal of the rule of law impels the courts to seek preexisting formal uniform solutions. However, legal scholars have uniformly attested to the problem of trying to achieve formal rules in the face of the persistent relevance of circumstances that make only feasible practice-based contextual judicial solutions. The only general principle followed in the judicial adjudications of situated cases "is that judgments rendered expressed the requirement that property owners be *reasonable*" (Radin 1993: 149, emphasis added). Invoking "reasonable" behavior, the legal scholars point out, reveals the operation of a narrow definition of governmental/judicial intervention, which expects of individual owners a level of self-restraint in light of concerns for others, preventing the property claimant from inflicting harm on the community. A stronger definition of "reasonable" behavior would aim at forcing the claimant to confer a benefit on a community.[19] Applying this connotation of "reasonable" behavior by the judicial system within capitalist societies means that, if the state requires the claimant to yield up a benefit, then courts would need to decree compensation to the owner.

Thus, as evidenced in legal scholars' discussions of the distinct meanings of the "reasonable" behavior of owners, the institution of property in advanced capitalist societies is organized around the principle of *individualization of owners*, whose entitlements are *not* contingent on fulfilling any social duties to the community or society at large. As my analysis will show, along these very lines, the intent and design of the institution of property under socialism differs from its counterpart in capitalism. The principle of *communitarianism of owners* whose entitlements are not individualized, but are contingent on providing service to the immediate community and broader society, undergirds socialist regimes, affecting, in turn, expectations associated with post-socialist property arrangements. The third implication of the conception of property as a social institution containing many owners is that property rights and obligations cannot be defined by reference to ownership alone. In adjudicating property disputes, courts are compelled to give consideration to the effects the claims and exercise of property entitlements have on others. They do so by considering the ultimate normative bases for ownership, through reference to such values as freedom, security, distributive fairness, economic efficiency, promotion of the general welfare, and social justice. In the words of Joseph Weintraub: "Property rights serve human values. They are recognized to that end and are limited by it" (cited in Singer 2000: 37).

However, such reference to values when making choices regarding ownership is a complex and ambiguous process. The complexity stems from several sources: it arises from the pluralism of values that drives the partial and temporary judicial solutions to particular cases. A commitment to values that can be in tension with each other (such as freedom and distributive fairness) might inform a judicial decision on property. The difficulties equally stem from ambiguities as to the precise meaning of, and requirements for realizing, a value—be it distributive fairness, economic efficiency, or social justice. The complexity of invoking normative bases is also associated with changes over time in commitment to specific values and in the meanings attributed to them. Furthermore, reference to the complicated and changing normative framework, when making judgments on property, implies also attaching unequal moral weight to distinct property arrangements, hence producing a hierarchy of property claims and entitlements. Commonly associating private property with the development of personhood in the ideology of Western capitalist society elevates tacitly or more overtly private property to a greater legal protection than any communal property. I will show in a later discussion that both socialist and post-socialist property arrangements were also morally ordered on respective continua, with differing strengths of distinct property holders' claims. Lastly, rulings pertaining to property holders' claims often cannot be adjudicated in isolation, but instead must be considered simultaneously and might compete with the protection of other nonproperty interests of individuals.

In his important work "Citizenship and Social Class," T. H. Marshall (1998) delineated in the course of Western capitalism from the eighteenth through the twentieth century a gradual and sequential rise of civil, political, and social rights. These nonproperty rights of individuals, as they have gained articulation and become increasingly affirmed within Western capitalist societies as measures of tempering social injustices and overall social progression of societies, have often come to supersede and attenuate individual property rights. Hence, in advanced Western capitalism, the affirmation of property, understood as a social institution containing many owners, is based on a process of searching for "reasonable" individual behavior and a specific content of entitlements that oblige individual owners to avoid harm to others. Avoiding harm implies not merely consideration of protecting ownership entitlements of others but more broadly safeguarding civil, social, and political entitlements of property and nonproperty owners as citizens of society. The rights of an owner to control his own production and to produce most efficiently need to be reconciled with multitudes of other rights: for example, the rights of his neighbors/owners to exercise their property entitlements, the rights of his workers to safe and healthy working conditions and legally expected hours, the rights of citizens to a clean environment, and so on.

The legal scholars' discourse on property in Western capitalist society, posing a challenge to the traditional, neoliberal narrow economic notion of property as a dyadic relation between a person and a thing, reveals that property is of a triadic nature, involving, as well, socially recognized and politically sanctioned rights to assets. Thus, it is a broad, perennially contested concept, as are the normative concepts on which it rests. The values implicit in choices among property rules are various, incommensurable, and often in conflict, making justifying and affirming specific property arrangements a complex and ambiguous process.[20] From this legal debate in the context of Western advanced capitalist societies, we can imply that, in order for any property regime to have reasonable stability and respect from members of society, it must be rooted in a preexisting consensus on what is the guiding hierarchy of societal values and what are the broad social objectives. These conclusions can help shed light on the nature of emerging property arrangements out of the fallen socialism.

The Post-Socialist Transition: From Conjoint Property to Incomplete Exclusive Property

Similar to Comisso (1991), who emphasized the rule of exclusion, separating owners from nonowners and revealing property's triadic nature, Nobel laureate Douglass North (North and Weingast 1989) points to the right to exclude as essential in defining and enforcing property rights. As North posits, the state has a relative advantage in violence; it has therefore a key role in the formation of property arrangements. Thus, he formulates a theory of the state as an integral part of the theory of property. In doing so, he extends the Coasian (1960) theorem of transaction cost economics, based on an exchange view of the relationship between ruler and constituents, where the state exchanges protection and justice for tax revenues from the constituents.

Elaborating on his theory of the state as part of a theory of property, North (1981) traces the historical links between economic development and property, in which the state operates as a revenue maximizer. "The ruler as a revenue maximizer acts like a discriminating monopolist, separating each group of constituents and devising property rights for each so as to maximize state revenues. He is constrained, however, by the existence of potential rivals who provide the same services" (North 1981, cited in Nee 2001: 3). Thus, he examines the conditions that provide incentives for *political* actors to establish formal institutional arrangements supporting efficient property rights. These entail the dilution of state control over resources and the emergence of some form of political pluralism. As North points out, this does not imply a weak state, but a state and society context in which the tension between ruler and constituent allows for the evolution of institutions that limit the capacity of the state to expropriate resources from producers (North and Weingast 1989).

The installation of socialism in Eastern Europe after World War II was a top-down, alternative modernization project, pursuant to which the state aspired to surpass Western societies in their production and allocation efficiency and to build an egalitarian society. In exchange for this promise, constituents did not deliver revenues to the state, but rather "permitted" the state to impose its preemptive proprietary claim to control productive assets as a property subject. I will argue that, by imposing these ownership claims to assets, the state created its own constraints as a political actor, making an obligation to deliver on its promise of economic and property efficiency and equality, and thus subjecting the state to recurrent tensions with its coclaimants and constituents when it failed to do so. Thus, instead of functioning as a homogeneous and static social system with the state as exclusive owner, as commonly assumed, socialism was marked by a succession of crises and corresponding attempts by the state to reallocate property rights among constituents as property co-holders in a manner that would calm the crises and bring economic efficiency to property relations. Thus, I argue, based on an examination of the agricultural sector of Polish state socialism, that the principle of exclusion was partially operational, rather than indiscriminately preempted, as argued by Comisso.

My analysis affirmed the delineation of horizontal boundaries between ownership forms, thus concurring with Verdery that state socialism, throughout its duration, contained a *plurality* of legal ownership forms. State, cooperative, and private properties constituted a horizontal delineation of distinct property arrangements coexisting side by side within Polish state socialism. Rather than being ambiguously shared by *all*, as characteristic of the communal type of state socialist property implied by Comisso, these forms differed according to the distinct, *specified* property holders who exercised the ownership rights.

State, cooperative, and private property forms were subjected to the vertical delineation of ownership, which was subsumed to the state socialist principle of "the party/state's leading role" and its changing articulation over time. The principle reflected the central aspiration of the socialist party/state to achieve social modernization marked by a commitment to the value of economic efficiency combined with distributive and social equality. T. H. Marshall has shown in reference to Western capitalist societies the *sequential* emergence of civil, social, and political rights in the time span of centuries, long after property rights were instituted and consolidated. By contrast, the inception of the socialist societies was predicated on a commitment to provide simultaneously those rights to "deserving" citizens. Rather than having an individualistic focus, an anticipated economic prosperity for those backward societies had a collectivist objective—it was to advance the social and economic standing of all. This aspiration to construct a new society led by the political authority emerged from the critique of the alternative modernization processes developed earlier in capitalist societies. The socialist state as *an actor* aimed to transcend social and economic consequences stemming from the exercise of capitalist private property affirmed by the capitalist state and coordinated by market mechanisms. As Verdery writes, citing Marx: "The distinguishing feature of communism is not the abolition of property generally, but the abolition of bourgeois property" (2000: 48, from Marx and Engels 1968: 34–35).

Commitment to this core set of normative values constituted the legitimation basis of the socialist state and hence obliged it to their realization (di Palma 1991). Further, this commitment led the state to undertake direct participation in the exercise of property rights and the use, appropriation, and distribution of assets. This normative basis of the socialist state therefore implied from the onset a very distinct positioning of the state as an actor to ownership. Rather than performing a function of guarantor and protector of distinct subjects in their exclusive exercise of ownership, as was the case in capitalist societies,[21] the socialist state became itself a claimant of property. The state/party supreme ownership of assets was premised on the state's commitment to realizing societal nonproperty rights. In contrast to the Western states pursuing civil and societal rights as a way of mitigating inequality caused by individual private property, the socialist state aimed to constitute those higher, nonproperty rights by shaping appropriately socialist property arrangements. Thus its granting of the property entitlements was conditional on the provision of civil and social rights to its citizens.

Thus, the socialist state became an ownership contestant and shared ownership with individual physical subjects within each judicial ownership form—state, cooperative, and private property. The ownership entitlements were not associated with the specific property form as an indivisible entity exercised by one specific property owner. Rather, the entitlements were specified in relation to individual *divisible* rights shared by two kinds of property holders within each ownership form. As such, the bundle of rights within each property form was disaggregated into distinct property rights, and thus assigned not to one ownership subject but distributed among *two categories* of ownership claimants—the state as a fictive person and the natural persons. Based on this key feature of property under Polish state socialism, I develop the concept *conjoint ownership*. It characterizes a distinct state socialist property *type* that is represented in private, cooperative, and state *forms*. As such, the conjoint property of state socialism finds its post-socialist alternative in *exclusive ownership*. The latter type of ownership vests ownership entitlements in a singular rather than a dual category of ownership subjects.

Furthermore, the nature of conjoint ownership cannot be fully captured by mere reference to a shared bundle of property *rights* between dual categories of claimants. Instead, conjoint ownership reflects a mutual bundle of entitlements *and* obligations faced by both coclaimants and vis-à-vis each other. I invoke here again Joseph Singer's analysis carried out in the context of capitalist societies, that the notion of property, understood as a social institution of many owners, contains both rights and obligations: just as it grants entitlements, it too imposes on each category of owners an obligation. The self-restraint obligation, enforced by the state, prevents each claimant of individual property from inflicting harm on other owners, hence allowing them to exercise fully their property rights. Thus the self-restraint obligation is central to the perpetuation and efficient functioning of the institution of private property under capitalism.[22] I claim that, similarly, socialist property in its many forms, in addition to being shared by distinct subjects, with the state as a coclaimant in each, was not unconditionally granted but, too, was predicated on an obligation. However, conjoint claimants were presented with a stronger, and different in nature, obligation than the exercise of self-restraint required of capitalist property holders.

The physical subjects were obliged to confer a benefit on a broader community, to serve collective, economic, and noneconomic interests of society. Hence, under the system of state coordination of the national economy, the state would lay claims to the right to control production in terms of its levels and content within each property form; the state farms, cooperatives, and individual agricultural producers were to achieve a given level of the production output and engage in the production of goods specified by the state in order to contribute toward the centrally defined aggregate needs of society. The state then would make a claim to a significant share of the production output within each property form and reapportion it on behalf of society.

For example, the socialist state legitimized its co-claims to the private owners' rights over residual income by heralding economic equality in society and thus the need to control the private owners' profits. At one stage of conjoint property relations, the state exercised this co-claim by erecting an institutional network of compulsory deliveries. Agricultural owners had to surrender a specified share of their production output under the threat of severe sanctions (Gorlach 1999). Thus, the state laid claims to the right of appropriation of a share of output produced by agricultural producers. Given that often the share to be surrendered was in kind (i.e., milk, wheat, etc.), the state was impinging on the individual owners in their decision making regarding production profile, thus directly laying claims to the right of controlling production. Equally, the agricultural private owners were not given the right to alienate their property. At another time, the same ownership co-claim advanced by the state was realized by tying individual owners to a network of procurement centers that paid the private subsector administratively set, lower prices than it paid cooperative or state agricultural subsectors.

As the socialist state imposed rights and obligations on the physical subjects within each distinct property form, the state, too, faced obligations attached to its co-claim of ownership rights vis-à-vis its physical property coclaimants. The overt commitment of the socialist state to an advancement of distributive and social equality obliged the state to herald such specific constellation of property arrangements that would generate sufficient material base to safeguard and advance realization of these central societal values in practice. An inability or ineffectiveness in meeting these obligations, on the part of the state, potentially undermined its legitimacy as an ownership coclaimant, thereby providing an opening for physical co-owners to contest the state's standing as an ownership co-subject.

In turn, the state's ownership entitlements and obligations affected the differential standing of distinct property forms in the hierarchy of socialist ownership, which was revealed by a distinct content and configuration of entitlements assigned by the state to them. Large state farms were considered economies of scale and were favored for their alleged link to the value of economic efficiency. They were considered higher economic contributors to the national economy than their cooperative or private counterparts, respectively. Furthermore, they were understood as rightly connected to the advancement of a society that emphasized collectivity and social and economic equality. As a result they were considered not only more efficient producers but also more "deserving" citizens in terms of not only property entitlements but also nonproperty rights.

By contrast, individual agricultural producers, as small in size, were perceived as far less economically viable to contribute to societal economic needs, and socially less fitting, if not outright incompatible, with advancing the objectives of social and economic equality. As a result, based on those combined economic and social considerations, the socialist state in its allocation of entitlements tended to severely attenuate their property rights with an ongoing intent that this particular ownership form could be altogether eliminated and replaced by more economically viable property forms (cooperative or state form). It further considered them as the least "deserving" citizens for nonproperty and property entitlements. They consequently were granted far more limited property entitlements, as compared with state or cooperative farms, and received far steeper sanctions for noncompliance. While potential noncompliance by state farms and cooperatives, which were obliged to contribute to the national economy as stipulated by state production targets, would evoke fines and administrative measures, the sanctions for the private sector in similar circumstances were far more imposing. Private owners at different stages in state socialism faced sanctions that ranged from heavy fines to land confiscation to imprisonment.

Furthermore, the hierarchy of nonproperty entitlements for "deserving" citizens was superimposed on the hierarchy of socialist ownership in its distinct property forms in accordance with their respective ownership entitlements and obligations. For a long time under socialism, while the state farm and cooperative members were granted free education, health care, retirement pensions, and family vacations, private property owners were excluded from such nonproperty social entitlements.

The distinct position of the state as an actor directly involved in the exercise of ownership was also reflected in the other dimension of the socialist state—its institutional structure. The state implemented the reform stipulations and executed its ownership co-claims by embedding each property form within a distinctive and complex institutional network that also molded each property's organizational representation. State farms, cooperatives, and individual agricultural producers, rather than being coordinated in their activities by market mechanisms, were integrated into hierarchical structures of command, allowing the state to exercise its ownership claims to each property form (Piotrowski 1980; Domanski 1990). The extensive administrative mode of vertical coordination of activities within the various property forms was further combined with horizontal links between them allowing the sharing of, among other things, equipment and implements.

The term conjoint property aims to reflect this dynamic character of property relations in socialism. It refers to a changing configuration in which specific rights were distributed among these two classes of property subjects. The reconfiguration of the allocation of property rights and resulting changes in property relations marked distinct phases in state socialism. However, the changes did not come about as a product of spontaneous economic adjustment, as postulated by Stark. Rather, they were associated with an interplay between economic and political actions that produced recurrent economic crises. The subsequent initiatives of reformers aimed to alter existing property relations to overcome these crises. In Poland, the three major stages in the reconfiguration of ownership rights were associated with the reforms of 1956, the 1970s, and the 1980s. Each reform called for a specific reconfiguration of entitlements within each property form between its respective subjects and the state. Each stage of these three distinctive reform efforts was manifested in different institutional and organizational representations of reconfigured property relations. In each stage economic agents formed different expectations regarding their economic dealings with others.

From my perspective, the origins of a specific stage in the development of conjoint property cannot be seen in the economic realm alone. Rather it must be seen as a combined outcome of economic responses *and* political contestations of two categories of subjects over the production implications and economic and social consequences of the specific distribution of property rights. My approach raises the issue addressed by Verdery (1996) in her work on post-socialist property relations—the importance of *how* the specific configuration of property rights came about. The way in which individual rights were allocated among its coclaimants within property forms (whether inspired by internal socialist reformers and/or prompted by political pressures from below) bears on such coclaimants' subsequent social recognition, expectations, and economic performance. While the specific stages of state socialism coincided with the major attempts to reform property relations, they also proceeded in a *linear pattern* historically and across property forms. They followed a pattern in which the state decreased its share in the bundle of ownership rights and progressively assigned individual property rights to the physical owners.

In the efforts to reform socialism, the trend toward the downward assignment of rights culminated in the consolidation of ownership rights in the hands of *one* category of subjects within the agricultural private property form. Hence, in the early 1980s, the conjoint ownership of state socialism was transformed into an *exclusive ownership*. The combined effects of the peasants' political struggle to end the state's abrogation of their ownership rights and their overall societal standing, and the pressures on the socialist government to overcome food shortages, prompted the state to abandon its ownership claims to agricultural private property. Agricultural private ownership transformed within socialism from being a property considered initially as inefficient and wrongfully held (thus constantly a subject of elimination by the state) to one being heralded as highly productive and safeguarding national sovereignty. This implied that property rights were legally recognized as *indivisible* and allocated to one category of subjects. It effectively signified an ascendancy of an alternative type of *exclusive* ownership. Such legal recognition of exclusive private property transcended the logic of the state socialist redistributive economy, engendering a fundamental crisis in the system.[23] Thus, I would argue that the origins of the Polish post-socialist trajectory should be shifted back to the early 1980s rather than 1989.

Yet, despite the emergence of exclusive subjects of private property in the early 1980s, the political collapse of the system was deferred for almost a decade. This produced an *asynchronic extrication from socialism*—the nonparallel reconfiguration of the economic domain and political regime. The protracted extrication from state socialism implied that, although exclusive property rights were won within state socialism, the social and legal expectations of the *individual outcomes* as well as the *social consequences* stemming from exclusive property rights were formed and solidified within the bounds of state socialism and its ideology. Exclusive owners expected not to be abrogated in their economic decision making by the socialist state's interventions, yet to remain protected by the state from the adverse outcomes of their individual economic pursuits. Furthermore, in accordance with the socialist equality principle, exclusive owners also held the state responsible to elevate them as a collective to a comparable economic standing of other socioeconomic groups. Thus, the historically specific connotation of exclusive ownership incubated in state socialism merged two elements that were in tension—an antistatist notion of freedom in, and state protectionism of, individual economic action.

This specific form of the disintegration of state socialism profoundly shaped the post-socialist transition at its inception and its subsequent trajectory. The protracted extrication from state socialism initially revealed itself not on the level of reform implementation, as Burawoy posits, but already on the level of conceptualization of post-socialist property relations. From the onset, it created a *disjunction* in the respective connotations of exclusive ownership held by the post-socialist reformers vis-à-vis those held by preexisting exclusive owners. Against the broad socioeconomic expectations that emerging exclusive owners formed, the 1989 negotiated exit from state socialism and the worsening economy channeled the post-socialist reformers' visions of the future into a narrow scope. They concentrated on outlining instrumental strategies for stimulating economic growth based on creating genuine owners and enhancing their production levels, thus making privatization the core basis for the political legitimacy of the post-socialist regime and its transition program. The historical emergence of private property based on a single category of owners affected post-socialist reformers' conceptions of how to protect ownership rights. The historical context of the consolidation of property rights, free from state constraint in late socialism, led the post-socialist reformers to overemphasize the barriers to genuine ownership that come from the state's abrogation of property rights and to ignore those that stem from the absence of state protection and the underdevelopment of legal and institutional infrastructure.

Furthermore, the narrow scope of the post-socialist reform agenda obstructed the formulation of the general social ends of the transition (Wagener 2001). The absence of clearly articulated social and political objectives meant that the true realization of general socialist principles was not explicitly rejected and hence lingered (by default) over the agenda of the post-socialist regimes.[24] Despite the fact that the post-socialist reformers heralded an antistatist notion of individual economic freedom to experience both the benefits and risks of market exposure, their narrowly formulated reform program promoted a distinct connotation of exclusive ownership: although not explicitly or comprehensively articulated, the ideology of the post-socialist regime perpetuated expectations of the exclusive owners formed under state socialism—to be unfettered from the state's abrogation of their ownership rights, but to remain protected by the state from the adverse outcomes of market pursuit. In short, the post-socialist program *implicitly* sustained expectations to pursue *freedom to succeed* in the market economy without equally accepting the *freedom to fail*.

Hence, the universalism of the post-socialist project to build capitalism was not based on the *prospect* of becoming a successful entrepreneur, as was the case with the emergence of classical capitalism. Rather, it was based on utopian universalism promising *real* participation in the economic success of all. To paraphrase Comisso, from its initiation, the post-socialist system lacked the principle of exclusion that specified who could legitimately *not* benefit from the reformers' projected quick success of the capitalist experiment. Post-socialism attempted to emulate capitalism in its economic efficiency and its level of individual consumption.[25] But it did not seek to emulate its system of redistribution. Thus, the asynchronic crisis of socialism generated *incomplete* exclusive property that engendered antistatist connotations, yet entailed specific expectations of state paternalism. In contrast to Stark's view, it was not a paternalism of centrally managed liabilities, but a paternalism of centrally sponsored opportunities for all.

From my perspective, long before the initiation of post-socialist programs aimed to construct capitalist systems, state socialism generated a capitalism specific to Eastern Europe. Parallel to Burawoy's perspective, this East European capitalism was based on the incubation of historically specific private property that proved to have no affinity with the market. The historical emergence of private property of a single category of owners not only molded economic agents' expectations, but also affected post-socialist reformers' conceptions of how to protect ownership rights. Their antistatism-laden conceptions underpinned the dismantling of socialist institutional frameworks as a post-socialist strategy to establish the genuine exercise of ownership rights. While the economic agents' expectations and the reformers' strategies for redesigning ownership were independently molded by state socialism, the interaction between them set the dynamics of the subsequent period of post-socialist reforms.

My argument as to the multiplicity of property forms and their reconfiguration within state socialism implies an unevenness in the post-socialist transition. In Burawoy's model, this unevenness runs along industrial and economic sectors. In my approach, the unevenness is implied within sectors, among different property forms. Given the distinct institutional and organizational arrangements associated with the distinct property forms under state socialism, they should undergo different, yet interconnected, transition trajectories with the onset of post-socialist reform programs.

These early transition trajectories did not correspond to the outcomes envisioned by the post-socialist reformers. Although the reformers were correct in seeing the centrality of property in the post-socialist transition, they defined property inaccurately and thereby effected changes in property relations that they did not intend. Their reform program was predicated on what Comisso would refer to as a one-sided notion of property that delineated only "owners." Their notion of property was underpinned by the assumption that the capacity to exercise property rights resided within entitled economic agents. Once formally designated and free from state intervention, these agents were presumed to possess universally valid behavioral characteristics—a propensity to enhance, and an economic interest in enhancing, their production performance through increased production efficiency. Hence, unfettered property owners were expected to bring about economic growth consistently. Such a notion of property resonated with reformers' perceptions that the spontaneous release of enhanced economic performance among entitled owners coincided with the collapse of state socialism and the dismantling of its institutional structure. For them, the extrication from state socialism was equated to the initiation of the post-socialist transition and the liberation of owners' capacities to exercise their rights in production activities.

From my perspective, the capacity to exercise property rights does not derive from the inner characteristics of the formally entitled agents, nor are the agents driven in their production activities by expectations that are narrowly economic in nature and exclusively focused on individual economic outcomes (Scott 2008; Sewell 1992; Clemens 1997; Friedland and Alford 1991; Giddens 1979). State socialism was not an aberration that caused economic agents to deviate from their otherwise constant behavioral predispositions. State socialism could not be corrected by lifting up the institutional framework to liberate economic agents in their economic pursuits. Institutional structures were erected under state socialism to bring about a specific configuration of shared ownership rights. It follows that, in order to facilitate the exercise of ownership rights by exclusive subjects, an appropriate institutional structure needs to be created, as opposed to just dismantling the old one that supported the previous ownership. Thus the capacity to exercise ownership rights does not hinge on agents' behavioral predispositions, but is mediated by legislative and institutional context, in which entitled owners are embedded. Furthermore, from my perspective, rather than being an aberration, state socialism was a formation that produced a historically specific conjoint ownership. The significance of conjoint ownership did not merely rest on combining two categories of subjects in one ownership form. Instead, it is tied to the dynamics between these two co-owners that reverberates with historically specific expectations regarding individual dealings with others (economic agents within other property forms), and with broader sociopolitical outcomes for the coexisting ownership forms. Such a notion of property is what Comisso considers as two-sided; it articulates the outcomes of property rights for those entitled vis-à-vis those outside any given property form.

In the following four chapters, I will develop an *interactive* approach to the post-socialist transition, marked by an interaction between policy intentions and the mutually interdependent behavioral responses of economic agents within ownership forms. First, I will show the path-dependency of the post-socialist reform program. I will assess how the reformulations in the allocation of ownership rights under socialism shaped the formulation of the post-socialist reformers' program in general, and in agriculture in particular. I will show the continuity in terms of the content, the scope, and the method of implementation of the post-socialist Balcerowicz reform program, and of earlier efforts to reform conjoint ownership. Then, focusing on the private subsector within agriculture, I will examine the interaction between policy stipulations and the responses they elicited among "liberated," exclusive private agricultural owners. I will show how introduction of the post-socialist stabilization package that was intended to consolidate exclusive private ownership adversely affected peasants' capacity to exercise their property rights and undermined the profitability of their production. I will show that the new sets of constraints for private owners compared unfavorably with peasants' real individual and collective gains in late state socialism. These new constraints also presented higher transaction costs in transition for private owners relative to those endured by cooperative and state property subjects. These constraints contrasted with peasants' earlier formed expectations of the individual and social outcomes of their exclusive ownership status. This contrast provoked peasants' economic and political responses. In their individual production activities, they retreated from market exposure and focused on reducing costs, often at the expense of undermining production efficiency. In their collective action they contested the post-socialist state and its policies, not only to avert adverse individual consequences of market transactions for peasants but also to reverse broader social consequences brought about by the post-socialist program. Their collective actions induced revisions to the agricultural policy that partially restored the earlier state paternalism of private exclusive ownership. Subsequently, I will analyze whether post-socialist policies evoked changes that solidify exclusive cooperative ownership as they intended to do. I will show that the rapid, mandatory dismantling of regional and central institutional cooperative superstructure led to institutional and financial discontinuity. The rapid deinstitutionalization of local cooperatives, while it lifted controls from above, granting autonomy for the local cooperative management, also made impossible any effective control of managerial decisions from within. I will show that the change brought about by the implementation of the reforms was consistent with the centralization of managerial power. It led to the weakening of exclusive cooperative ownership and the undermining of adaptive efficiency of these economic enterprises. I will then reveal how the transformations in cooperative agricultural organizations negatively affected the exercise of ownership rights within the private subsector. Finally, I will examine how the stabilization measures channeled the initial economic adjustment of state agricultural enterprises and subsequently led to their regression into conjoint ownership, rather than the transfer of their assets to exclusive private agricultural owners as outlined in the privatization plans.

In short, in contrast to the neoliberally oriented reformers' presentation of post-socialist transition as a massive transfer of assets from the state to the private sector, or the evolutionary economists' depiction of the transition as an expansion of private property, my analysis of the distinct yet interconnected trajectories of the three agricultural subsectors presents the transition as an incomplete reconfiguration of conjoint property into exclusive ownership. The incomplete shift to exclusive ownership was evident in all property forms, yet manifested in each form differently. In the private sector, it revealed itself in a partial reinstating of state paternalism over individual exclusive owners. In the cooperative sector, the incomplete shift manifested itself in the regained autonomy of individual cooperatives, mixed with cooperative members' inability to counteract managerial centralization. In the state sector, the incomplete shift revealed itself through joint-stock arrangements, with the state reclaiming part of the state farms' assets while transferring the rest of them for administration or lease to physical subjects. These early post-socialist changes in property relations were not consistent with enhancing either production or adaptive efficiency.

Notes

1. Murrell (1991) points out that, unlike all other economic models that point to the trade-offs between competing visions in economic reform, only neoclassical perspective declares the superiority of one set of arrangements over any other—that of free markets.

2. Balcerowicz 1992: 39–43.

3. Thus, the rapid transfer of state assets to private hands and the elimination of nonviable enterprises were declared priorities. Divestment of at least as much as half of the book value of existing state-owned enterprises within three years was adopted as a policy guideline in Hungary and Poland (Bolton and Roland 1992). Accordingly, preference was given to the least complicated forms of such transfer, that is, giveaway schemes that bypassed both the barrier of costly asset valuations and that of limited personal savings (Gomulka 1991; Blanchard and Layard 1992).

4. His confidence in the success of the reform in Poland, in particular, and Eastern Europe, in general, stemmed from his assumption that the reformers in Eastern Europe would strengthen their will to consistently implement the program by learning from the negative experiences of some modernizing Latin American societies. Compromising the integrity of the reform program by caving in to pressure from political opposition could lead to a renewal of inflationary policies or to governmental protectionism. Both were perceived by Sachs as being incompatible with the rationalization of production resources allocation and orienting the economy for growth.

5. See Kornai (1990), and also Brus and Laski (1989).

6. In his assessment of the evolutionist model of transition, Brada (1995) critiques the evolutionist perspective precisely for leaving very vague the element of time and the question of when the state can transition assets from the state to the nascent private sector. Ericson (1991) questions the feasibility of the long-term coexistence of elements of socialistic and capitalistic systems in a single economy.

7. The assumption of nonviability of socialism leads Kornai to sustain the Smithian image of the superiority of capitalism. This allows him to sustain the end point despite problematizing the transition trajectory itself. Thus, according to Kornai, the units of the private sector need no stimulation, agitation, or directives in order to act along the lines of the market, as this is their natural mode of existence (1990: 36).

8. Those parallel structures are "routines and practices, organizational forms and social ties, that can become assets, resources, and the basis for credible commitments and coordinated actions in the post-socialistic period" (Stark 1996: 995).

9. As a product of its socialist legacy, it is a specific capitalism, distinct both from Western European capitalism and East Asian versions of capitalism. All those capitalist economies are no longer based on choices between market or plan but combine both types of economic coordination into a specific mix. As Stark argues, these economies are market oriented but not market coordinated. These economies also merge property forms into a specific mix. (1996: 995).

10. "By dampening the performance of the stronger and facilitating the survival of the weaker firms in the enterprise recombinant, they might even impede creative destruction in the conventional sense" (Stark 1996: 1019).

11. For an equally important contribution to the debate on hybrid property forms based on an analysis of China, see Nee (1992).

12. Based on his ethnographic studies of timber, banking, and coal industries in the former Soviet Union and post-socialist Russia, Michael Burawoy (1994, 1995) traced and clearly delineated changes in these distinct industries in their specific phases.

13. In his *The Politics of Production*, Burawoy (1985) lays out the integration of political and economic elements at both the microlevel and macrolevel of analysis.

14. On the reopened general debate about the efficiency of socialism as compared to capitalism, see Joseph Persky (1991), "Lange and von Mises, Large-scale Enterprises, and the Economic Case for Socialism." *Journal of Economic Perspectives* 5 (4): 229–236.

15. My point on the timing of extrication from socialism in Poland is paralleled by analyses of Hann (1993), Elek (1991), and Rona-Tas (1997), which associate the systemic collapse of socialism in Hungary with property reforms introduced in the early 1980s.

16. Analyzing changes in Polish property relations, J. Staniszkis (1991) conceptualizes the original point of transition in a way parallel to Stark. She places the origins of transition within state socialism. She ties it to the emergence of a "political capitalism" based on a hybrid property form that blends public with private ownership.

17. Verdery surmises, "If we stop with the allocation of *administrative rights*, we miss this crucial aspect of socialist property, so dependent on a corresponding system of *obligations*. . . . The central actors of socialism's property regime were not just the state, cooperatives and individuals but networks" (2003: 63).

18. The primary liberal theories of property, as advanced in Radin (1993: 153), find property to be necessary for the proper flourishing of individuals. They find and forge a link between private property and the differentiation, maintenance, and development of the self. Different strands of liberal thought emphasize different aspects of such a connection. Some theories emphasize a positive aspect—proper self-development and flourishing are linked to property connection with the external world. Others (Reich 1964 and Nozick 1974) emphasize the negative aspect—property self-maintenance and flourishing are linked to proper protection from the external world. For Marx, bourgeois property abolished the connection between property and individual personhood in the context of the full-blown market society.

19. History shows that in different societies, as was the case within socialist societies, reasonable behavior implied obligations of owners to confer a benefit to the community, such as under feudalism, or in ancient Greece.

20. As Joseph Singer asks rhetorically (2000: 38): How do we compare the value of freedom and the value of security and choose one over the other? Disputes over property use can be solved only by reference to human values, to a normative framework that helps us choose between freedom and security. As J. Radin emphasizes (1993), the legal process of adjudicating ownership disputes redefines property as containing within it the normative values and tensions that characterize such disputes.

21. See historical sociology scholars, particularly Barrington Moore (1966), whose class analysis of comparative modernization points to a specific historical power struggle underlying the emergence of private property in England. Moore attributes the state's role as a guarantor of private property to its relative political weakness vis-à-vis the ruling social classes, which preempted the state from becoming the ownership claimant and relegated it instead to the role of guarantor of the exclusive ownership rights of individuals.

22. In his *Toward a Theory of Property Rights*, Demsetz states: "Property rights are an instrument of society and derive their significance from the fact that they help a man form those expectations which he can reasonably hold in his dealings with others. These expectations *find expression in the laws, customs, and mores of a society*. An owner of property rights possesses the consent of fellow men to allow him to act in particular ways. An owner expects the community to prevent others from interfering with his actions, provided that these actions are not prohibited in the specifications of his rights (1974: 31, emphasis added).

23. In a confidential communication to the first secretary of the Polish Socialist Party (PZPR), an official spokesman for the Polish regime recognized already in 1981 impending systemic change: "We are facing disaster, since, in my opinion, the time has already passed when PZPR could effect a renewal, remodel the system of government, advance a program and

obtain the acceptance and support of society." (J. Urban, Letter to the First Secretary, *Uncaptive Mind* 1, 4 [1988: 3]).

24. In his *Radiant Past*, Burawoy and Lukacs (1992) showed that the critique of state socialism was predicated not on the rejection of the socialist principles but rather on an unrealized implementation of them. Over a decade into post-socialism, and after Burawoy's comments, Pascall and Kwak (2005) point to an established pattern of expectations by reference to Polish surveys of the mid-2000s, which showed that the rejection of socialism had by no means equaled the rejection of collectivist and statist solutions as well. Rather, the surveys clearly show the demand for the latter has even increased. Similar patterns are reported most recently in a massive comparative study of transformation processes in distinct former socialist societies, headed in Poland by Podemski (2011).

25. See Janos (2000) for a discussion of the demonstration effect.

References

Balcerowicz, Leszek. 1992. *800 Dni. Szok Kontrolowany*. Warsaw: Polska Oficyna Wydawnicza "BGW."

———. 1990. "The Price of Polish Economic Reform." In *Without Force or Lies: Voices from the Revolution of Central Europe in 1989–1990*, edited by W. Brinton and A. Rinzler, 223–238. San Francisco: Mercury House Books, U.K. Ltd.

Blanchard, Olivier. 1993. "Consumption and the Recession of 1990–1991." *The American Economic Review* 83 (2, Papers and Proceedings of the Hundred and Fifth Annual Meeting of the American Economic Association): 270–274.

Blanchard, Olivier, and Richard Layard. 1992. "Post-Stabilization in Poland." In *Wage Policy during the Transition to a Market Economy, Poland 1990–1991*, edited by F. Coricelli and A. Revenga. Washington, DC: World Bank.

Bolton, Patrick, and Gérard Roland. 1992. "Privatization in Central and Eastern Europe." *Economic Policy* 15: 276–309.

Boyer, Robert. 1991. "Markets within Alternative Coordinating Mechanisms: History, Theory and Policy in the Light of the Nineties." Conference on the Comparative Governance of Sectors. Bigorio, Switzerland, April 1991.

Brada, Josef C. 1995. "Editor's Introduction." *Eastern European Economics* 33 (6): 3–4.

Brus, Wlodzimierz, and Kazimierz Laski. 1989. *From Marx to the Market*. Oxford: Oxford University Press.

Buchowski, Michał. 2009. "Property Relations, Class, and Labour in Rural Poland." In *Postsocialist Europe. Anthropological Perspectives from Home*, vol. 10, edited by L. Kurti and P. Skalnik, 51–75. New York: Berghahn Books.

Burawoy, Michael. 1995. "Industrial Involution: The Russian Road to Capitalism." In *A La Recherche des Certitudes Perdues*, edited by Burgit Müller, 11–57. Berlin: Centre Marc Bloch.

———. 1994. "Why Coupon Socialism Never Stood a Chance in Russia: The Political Conditions of Economic Transition." *Politics and Society* 22 (4): 585–594.

———. 1985. *The Politics of Production: Factory Regimes Under Capitalism and Socialism*. London: Verso

Burawoy, Michael, and Janos Lukacs. 1992. *The Radiant Past: Ideology and Reality in Hungary's Road to Capitalism*. Chicago: University of Chicago Press.

Carruthers, Bruce G., and Laura Ariovich. 2004. "The Sociology of Property Rights." *Annual Review of Sociology* 30: 23–46.

Clemens, Walter C. 1997. "An Alternative to NATO Expansion." *International Journal* 52 (2, Leaders and Leadership 3): 342–365.

Coase, R. H. 1960. "The Problem of Social Cost." *Journal of Law and Economics* 3: 1–44.

Comisso, Ellen. 1991. "Property Rights, Liberalism, and the Transition from 'Actually Existing' Socialism." *East European Politics and Societies* 5 (1). 162–188.

Demsetz, Harold. 1974. "Toward a Theory of Property Rights." In *The Economics of Property Rights*, edited by E. G. Furubotn and S. Pejovich, 31–42. Cambridge, MA: Ballinger.

di Palma, Giuseppe. 1991. "Legitimation from the Top to Civil Society: Politico-Cultural Change in Eastern Europe." *World Politics* 44 (1): 49–80.

Dobbin, Frank, and John R. Sutton. 1998. "The Strength of a Weak State: The Rights Revolution and the Rise of Human Resources Management Divisions." *American Journal of Sociology* 104 (2): 441–476.

Domanski, Henryk. 1990. "Dynamics of Labor Market Segmentation in Poland, 1982–1987." *Social Forces* 69 (2): 423–438.

Edelman, Lauren B. 1992. "Legal Ambiguity and Symbolic Structures: Organizational Mediation of Civil Rights Law." *American Journal of Sociology* 97 (6): 1531–1576.

Edelman, Lauren B., and Mark C. Suchman. 1997. "The Legal Environments of Organizations." *Annual Review of Sociology* 23: 479–515.

Elek, S. 1991. "Part-Time Farming in Hungary: An Instrument of Tacit Decollectivization." *Sociol. Ruralis* 31: 82–88.

Emigh, R. J. 1999. "Means and Measures: Property Rights, Political Economy, and Productivity in Fifteenth Century Toscany." *Social Forces* (78): 461–490.

Ericson, Richard E. 1991. "The Classical Soviet-Type Economy: Nature of the System and Implications for Reform." *Journal of Economic Perspectives* 5 (4): 11–27.

Fligstein, N. 2001. *The Structure of Markets. An Economic Sociology of Twenty-First-Century Capitalist Societies*. Princeton, NJ: Princeton University Press.

Friedland, Rodger, and Robert Alford. 1991. "Bringing Society Back In: Symbols, Practices, and Institutional Contradictions." In *The New Institutionalism in Organizational Analysis*, edited by W. W. Powell and P. Di Maggio, 232–266. Chicago: University of Chicago Press.

Giddens, Anthony. 1979. *Central Problems in Social Theory: Action, Structure, and Contradiction in Social Analysis*. Berkeley: University of California Press.

Gluckman, Max. 1943. *Essays on Lozi Land and Royal Property*. Livingstone, Rhodesia. Rhodes-Livingston Papers, no. 10.

Gomulka, Stanislaw. 1991. "The Causes of Recession Following Stabilization." *Comparative Economic Studies* 32 (2): 71–89.

Gorlach Krzysztof. 1999. "Presenting 'New Face': Polish Peasants' Protests in the Era of Post-Communism." Paper delivered at the Working Group 1: Social Movements in Rural Areas: Sources, Rationalities and Identities in the Process of Change. XVIII Congress of the European Society for Rural Sociology, August 24–28, Lund, Sweden.

Gorlach, Krzysztof, and Zygmunt Serega. 1993."From 'Repressive Tolerance'to 'Oppressive Freedom': Polish Family Farms in Transition." In *Post-Communist Poland: From Totalitarianism to Democracy*?, 109–118, edited by Jaques Coenen Huther and Brunon Synak. Commack, NY: Nova Science.

Hann, Chris. 1993. "Property Relations in the New Eastern Europe: The Case of Specialist Cooperatives in Hungary." In *The Curtain Rises: Rethinking Culture, Ideology, and the State in Eastern Europe*. edited by H. G. De Soto and D. G. Anderson, 99–121. Atlantic Highlands, NJ: Humanity.

Hannan, Michael T. 1986. "Uncertainty, Diversity, and Organizational Change." In *Behavioral and Social Science: Fifty Years of Discovery*, National Research Council, 73–94. Washington, DC: National Academies Press.

Janos, Andrew C. 2000. *East Central Europe in the Modern World: The Politics of the Borderlands from Pre- to Post-Communism*. Stanford, CA: Stanford University Press.

Kiss, Yudit. 1993. "Lost Illusions? Defense Industry Conversion in Czechoslovakia, 1989–92." *Europe-Asia Studies* 45 (6): 1045–1069.

Kornai, Janos. 1991. "Privatization: The Great Problem of Transition in Eastern Europe." *Bulletin of the American Academy of Arts and Sciences* 44 (8): 32–40.

———. 1990. *The Road to a Free Market Economy*. New York: Norton.

Kowalik, Tadeusz. 2009. *www.PolskaTransformacja.Pl*. Warsaw: Muza SA.

Lipton, David, and Jeffrey Sachs. 1990. "Creating a Market Economy in Eastern Europe." In *Brookings Papers on Economic Activity 1990: 1*, edited by W. C. Brainard and G. L. Perry, 75–147. Washington, DC: Brookings Institution Press.

Marshall, T. H. 1998. "Citizenship and Social Class." In *The Citizenship Debates*, edited by G. Shafir, 93–111. Minneapolis: University of Minnesota Press.
Marx, Karl, and Frederick Engels. 1968 [1848]. "Manifesto of the Communist Party." In *Selected Works*, 35–71. Moscow: Progress Publishers.
Michnik, Adam. 1990. "The Moral and Spiritual Origins of Solidarity." In *Without Force or Lies: Voices from the Revolution of Central Europe in 1989–1990*, edited by W. Brinton and A. Rinzler, 239–250. San Francisco: Mercury House Books, U.K., Ltd.
Moore, Barrington. 1966. *Social Origins of Dictatorship and Democracy; Lord and Peasant in the Making of the Modern World*. Boston: Beacon.
Murrell, Peter. 1991. "Can Neoclassical Economics Underpin the Reform of Centrally Planned Economies?" *Journal of Economic Perspectives* 5 (4): 59–76.
Nagengast, Carole. 1991. *Reluctant Socialists, Rural Entrepreneurs: Class, Culture, and the Polish State*. Boulder, CO: Westview.
———. 1990. "Populism and the Polish State." *Socialist Review* 90 (2): 80–101.
Nee, Victor. 2001. "Sources of the New Institutionalism." In *The New Institutionalism in Sociology*, edited by Mary C. Brinton and Victor Nee. Stanford, CA: Stanford University Press.
———.1992. "Organizational Dynamics of Market Transition: Hybrid Forms, Property Rights, and Mixed Economy in China." *Administrative Science Quarterly* 37: 1–27.
North, Douglass. 1990. *Institutions, Institutional Change and Economic Performance*. Cambridge: Cambridge University Press.
———. 1981. *Structure and Change in Economic History*. New York: Norton.
North, Douglass, and Barry W. Weingast. 1989. "The Evolution of Institutions Governing Public Choice in Seventeenth-Century England." *Journal of Economic History* 49: 803–832.
Nozick, Robert. 1974. *Anarchy, State, Utopia*. New York: Basic.
Pascall, G., and A. Kwak. 2005. *Gender Regimes in Transition in Central and Eastern Europe*. Bristol: Polity Press.
Persky, Joseph. 1991. "Lange and von Mises, Large-scale Enterprises, and the Economic Case for Socialism." *Journal of Economic Perspectives* 5 (4): 229–236.
Piotrowski, Klemens. 1980. "Direct and Indirect Instruments of System of Management of the Polish Economy in the 1970s." *Soviet Studies* 32 (4): 500–514.
Podemski, Krzysztof, ed. 2011. *Spoleczenstwa Europy Srodkowo-Wschodniej: Projekt Eurequal*. Poznan: Wydawnictwo Naukowe UAM.
Poznanski, Kazimierz. 1993. "Restructuring of Property Rights in Poland: A Study in Evolutionary Politics." *East European Politics and Societies* 7 (3): 395–421.
———. 1992. "Privatization of the Polish Economy: Problems of Transition." *Soviet Studies* 44 (4): 641–664.
Przeworski, Adam. 1991. *Democracy and the Market: Political and Economic Reforms in Eastern Europe and Latin America*. Cambridge: Cambridge University Press.
Radin, Margaret J. 1993. *Reinterpreting Property*. Chicago: University of Chicago Press.
Rawski, Thomas. 1994. "Progress Without Privatization: The Reform of China's State Industries." In *Changing Political Economies*, edited by V. Milor. Boulder, CO: Lynne Rienner.
———. 1992. "Ideas About Studying China's Rural Economy: A Comment on the Commentaries." *Republican China* 17 (1): 146–159.
Reich, Charles A. 1964. "The New Property." *Yale Law Journal* 73 (5): 733–787.
Rona-Tas, Akos. 1997. *The Great Surprise of the Small Transformation: The Demise of Communism and the Rise of the Private Sector in Hungary*. Ann Arbor: University of Michigan Press.
Scott, James C. 2009. *The Art of Not Being Governed: An Anarchist History of Upland Southeast Asia*. New Haven, CT: Yale University Press.
Scott, W. R. 2008. *Institutions and Organizations: Ideas and Interests*, 3rd ed. Thousand Oaks, CA: Sage.
Sewell Jr., W. H. 1992. "A Theory of Structure: Duality, Agency and Transformation." *American Journal of Sociology* 98: 1–29.
Singer, Joseph W. 2000. *Entitlement: The Paradoxes of Property*. New Haven, CT: Yale University Press.

Sorensen, A. B. 2000. "Toward a Sounder Basis for Class Analysis." *American Journal of Sociology* 105: 1523–1558.

Staniszkis, J. 1991. "Political Capitalism in Poland." *East European Politics and Societies* 5: 127–141.

Stark, David. 1996. "Recombinant Property in East European Capitalism." *American Journal of Sociology* 101 (4): 993–1027.

Swedberg, Richard. 2003. *Principles of Economic Sociology*. Princeton, NJ: Princeton University Press.

Szelenyi, Ivan. 1988. *Socialist Entrepreneurs: Embourgeoisement in Rural Hungary*. Madison: University of Wisconsin Press.

Urban, J. 1988. "Letter to the First Secretary." *Uncaptive Mind*. 1 (4): 1–7.

Verdery, Katherine. 2003. *The Vanishing Hectare: Property and Value in Postsocialist Transylvania*. Ithaca, NY: Cornell University Press.

———. 2000. "Nationalism, Internationalism, and Property in Post-Cold War Romania." In *Nationalism and Internationalism in the Post-Cold War Era*, edited by K. Goldmann, U. Hannerz, and C. Westin, 87–102. London: Routledge.

———. 1998. "Property and Power in Transylvania's Decollectivization." In *Property Relations: Renewing the Anthropological Tradition*, edited by C. M. Hann, 16–80. Cambridge: Cambridge University Press.

———. 1996. *What was Socialism, and What Comes Next?* Princeton, NJ: Princeton University Press.

Wagener, Hans-Jürgen. 2001. *The Welfare State in Transition Economies and Accession to the EU*. San Domenico di Fiesole, Italy: European University Institute, Robert Schuman Centre.

Walder, Andrew G. 1996. "Markets and Inequality in Transitional Economies: Toward Testable Theories." *American Journal of Sociology* 101 (4): 1060–1073.

Wolf, Thomas A. 1991. "The Lessons of Limited Market-Oriented Reform." *Journal of Economic Perspectives* 5 (4): 46–57.

Chapter Two

Continuity of Reform Policies: From Conjoint Ownership to Exclusive Ownership Reform

The concept of *refolution*, coined by T. Garton Ash (1990), succinctly captures the nature of predominant debates on the 1989 post-socialist transition. Unlike previous revolutions from below, the revolutions of 1989 are seen as velvet revolutions emanating from above by reform designs. Overwhelmingly, economists, sociologists, and reform architects credited these "reform revolutions" with the epochal role of radically breaking with the socialist past and redirecting the post-socialist future so that it converges with a capitalist path. Subsequent debates revolved around which proven capitalist patterns should be the guiding posts in designing programs that would mold the post-socialist future.

Within this frame of reference, the historical dynamics of state socialism are deemed irrelevant. If the influence of the state socialist past is acknowledged, it is seen as delaying the reform objectives, not shaping them. Thus, with growing distance from the onset of reform initiatives, Leszek Balcerowicz no longer emphasized the radical break of his reform program from its recent economic past. Moreover, he denied the impact of the past on the overall direction of the reform initiatives. In his more recent reassessments, he claimed that 1989 was not a tabula rasa upon which reforms were written. Rather, he argued that the pace of the reform process was affected by "the poisonous inheritance of the past."[1] For Balcerowicz, a deleterious influence of the past on the arrival of the capitalist future could be corrected for through two key reform strategies: less generous social spending and a speedier, more consistent implementation of privatization before strong opposition to it could develop.[2]

Many evolutionary economists challenged Balcerowicz's radical therapy by advocating reform strategies that differed in terms of speed, locus, and sequence of reforms (Kornai 1990). However, these debates on viable reform strategies only underscore the shared assumption that the reformers' goal is an active force that drives the careful selection and balancing of reform strategies in the post-socialist transition. From both perspectives, the introduction of private property and market-based models signifies a radical discontinuity and sets a qualitatively new course: it marks a complete break from socialism by planting the seeds of capitalism "imported" from Western experiences. Continuity is drawn between the post-socialist present and capitalist future. Any connections to the past are openly dismissed. State socialism is portrayed as a centrally planned system, dominated by state property, that proved to be untenable and hence is historically irrelevant.

Another approach emerged to challenge both the notion of the revolutionary nature of the post-socialist reform policies and their discontinuity from the past. This perspective reacted to the overly restrictive assessment of state socialism inherent in the teleologically oriented debates on transition. In an attempt to account for the dynamics of the post-socialist transition, it re-opened an analysis of state socialism and linked post-socialist reforms to those initiated by the reformers' socialist predecessors (Poznanski 1993; Wolf 1991; Kowalik 2009; Bockman and Eyal 2002). Poznanski (1993) focuses on the systemic changes effected by post-socialist reformers in the context of reform attempts by the previous regime. For Poznanski, the 1989 reforms did not constitute a revolution. Rather, they represented yet another step in a continuous process of restoring capitalism. Contrary to those who dismiss the previous regime's efforts as following a circular pattern of incomplete reforms and a regression to pre-reform status (Brus 1988; Kornai 1989), Poznanski posits a linear pattern of reforms—the continuity of the policies, each building on the others. Poznanski views this continuity of reforms through a prism of ownership changes progressively weakening public ownership. Other more recent and thought-provoking scholarly accounts reveal the gradual emergence and increasing importance of economic liberalism in public policy formulation both under socialism and in the post-socialist period (Bockman and Eyal 2002; Katznelson [1996], 2005; Kowalik 2009; Walicki 1988). These accounts challenge the commonly held perception that the neoliberalism that informed the shock therapy reforms of the post-socialist regime was external to the intellectual tradition of the Eastern European societies at the time of socialism's fall and was imported wholly from the West. These perspectives instead find an endogenous evolutionary growth of economic liberalism within socialism, reaching a dominant influence on policy in the 1980s and leading radical and systemic reforms of property relations and economic coordination. These accounts, therefore, refocus how we view periodization of the systemic changes in Eastern Europe, implying that the post-socialist reforms did not mark a radical discontinuation from the previous regime, but, to the contrary, the shock therapy was their extension, profoundly impacted in its conception and execution by its predecessor.

Building his conceptual framework on Migdal's concept of weak and strong states (1988) and Kornai's work (1992), Poznanski's analysis centers on the change in property structure triggered by the reform sequence in socialist and post-socialist Poland. He argues that the reform sequence represents a systemic evolution of the undermining of public property, resulting in what he calls "weak" public property. In Poznanski's view, the 1989 post-socialist reforms produced the "weakest" version of public property, as reflected by the deepest Polish economic recession since World War II. In order to argue that the systemic evolution of the economic system progressively undermined public property, he develops a reform typology based on the links that different reforms produced between public ownership and economic coordination mechanisms. Thus, he claims that the 1970–1980 Polish reforms, which granted industrial lobbies control over economic coordination, led to a "weak" state and "strong" public ownership. He then argues that the 1981–1988 reforms replaced state with market coordination. However, the market was "weak," marred by overregulation and monopolistic structures. The weak market was combined with uncertainty over ownership status in the public sector ("weak" public ownership as measured by the collapse of enterprise-level party supervision). The 1988–1989 reforms once again produced a "weak" market as reflected in gross macroeconomic imbalances. The "weak" market was coupled with "weak" public ownership, manifested by the massive, uncontrolled ownership claims. Finally, the post-socialist reforms of 1989–1991 perpetuated "weak" monopolistic market structures and "weak" public property, severely undermined by fluid privatization laws (Poznanski 1993: 410).

Poznanski's work brought a new perspective to the study of post-socialist transition. Contrary to the view that finds unintended policy outcomes or incomplete policy applications as sufficient conditions to render the policy irrelevant, Poznanski argues that reforms initiated under state socialism *do* matter. Poznanski's assertion that socialist reforms matter and, thus, "history matters" reflects what Paul David describes as a genealogical explanation—one that "links the present state of arrangements with some originating context or set of circumstances and interpolates some sequence of connecting events that allow the hand of the past to exert a continuing influence upon the shape of the present" (David 1994: 206). The most famous proponent of the "history matters" approach, Nobel Prize winner Douglass C. North, points to institutions as "carriers of history," and states that institutions "evolve incrementally, connecting the past with the present and the future; history in consequence is largely a story of institutional evolution in which the historical performance of economies can only be understood as a part of a sequential study" (1991: 98). Furthermore, North's emphasis on "history matters" or, in other words, path dependency leads him to the recognition that institutional or reform change does not inevitably result in growth or improvement but can also lead to stagnation or decline, given that "institutions are the humanly devised constraints that structure political, economic and social interaction. They consist of both informal constraints (sanctions, taboos, customs, traditions and codes of conduct), and formal rules (constitutions, laws, property rights)" (1990: vii).

Poznanski posits that socialist reforms may not have been fully implemented, and may have produced unintended outcomes, but they were not irrelevant. This is because the policies and their objectives formed specific social expectations. The realization or the frustration of those expectations affects future alternative policy strategies and objectives.[3] Thus, state socialist reforms shaped the subsequent trajectory of the transition and therefore require close reexamination instead of an instant dismissal. It can be further inferred from Poznanski's perspective that the initial reform policies have significant long-lasting effects on the overall course of changes and therefore they are not easily reversible. Because the preceding policy's outcomes constitute the initial conditions for reforms, they pose limits to subsequent policy choices.

In this chapter, I will provide this kind of reexamination of state socialist policies and the initial post-socialist reform package. I concur with Poznanski that the proclaimed revolution against state socialism was in fact an *evolution of state-sponsored reforms*. The 1990 program was a product of a long process to reform the socialist system. I also agree with Poznanski that the reform sequence follows a linear path. Yet, although he alludes to the continuous *process* of reform, his analysis is based on a *typology* of reform initiatives. His analysis then acquires static connotations and limits our understanding of how the particular reforms built on one another.

I will argue that earlier reform strategies both constrained and facilitated the options that the first post-socialist Mazowiecki government had at its disposal to respond to socioeconomic conditions at hand. Hence, like Poznanski's analysis, my account of the reform *pattern* will focus on the progression of reform-induced changes in *ownership structure*. Yet I will depart from Poznanski's thesis of the linear reform evolution by arguing that this pattern contained a *systemic transformation* that did not coincide with the 1990 post-socialist reform initiatives. Rather, supported by recently emerging scholarly accounts, I posit that the "rupture" was produced by the ownership reforms of the socialist regime of the 1980s. Those reforms qualitatively demarcated the stage of conjoint ownership reforms from that of exclusive ownership reforms. This shift was reflected most starkly in the area of agricultural policy, although subsequently it was applied to the whole economy.

The reform-induced shift from conjoint to exclusive property inadvertently was associated with the erosion of the legitimacy of the central government, leading in the decade that followed to an unanticipated consequence of political crisis and negotiated political extrication from socialism. Hence, contrary to the common perception of the *rapid* 1989 political revolutions bringing about the radical economic change of the shock therapy, this account argues the opposite: that the *gradual* economic changes amounted to a systemic rupture that decades later was completed by a political collapse of the system. The way this systemic radical change unfolded as a protracted asynchronic process fundamentally conditioned the conceptualization and implementation of the 1990s shock therapy with its laissez-faire privatization package and further impacted the longer-term dynamics of transition.

I. History Matters

The Balcerowicz reform program adopted by the first post-socialist Mazowiecki regime can be traced to the three major reform attempts within state socialism (Szurek 1987; Hare 1981; Magyar 1984; Kolankiewicz 1981; Hare and Wanless 1981; Korbonski 1989).[4] The three reforms aimed to alter the dynamics of real existing socialism conditioned by the contradictory basis of its legitimation. The core of the legitimacy of real existing socialism was a promise of a permanent, purposeful efficiency with a creation of socialized property arrangements, feeding an ambition for a social and political alternative to domestic backwardness and to global market democracy. Such self-authenticating claim to the right to rule on behalf of the whole society carried an implication of cognitive infallibility of the socialist, virtuous regime, preempting the need to derive it from the popular support of its citizens (Szelenyi and Konrad 1979; di Palma 1991). Yet, given that the goal of building the alternative superior society was prospective, this normative self-legitimation principle, or legitimation from the top, was inherently self-contradictory. Thus, although in principle its legitimacy did not flow from popular support, inadvertently, the long-existing socialist regime subjected itself with such claim of legitimacy to the ongoing popular verification of its results vis-à-vis its ambition, with the progress of market democratic systems as a tangible yardstick to measure its own advancement toward the self-proclaimed goals of catching up to, and surpassing, the West.

The cognitive infallibility claim to the right to rule implied in turn a singular unity of purpose and cohesive, top-down coordination of the economy, prompting many scholarly accounts to depict the real existing socialism as a command economy. Yet, early on the cognitive infallibility claims became subject to test by the reality of persistent and growing problems with allocative efficiency, manifested by shortages and bottlenecks in production.

These economic problems stemmed from the planners' inherent imperfect information gathering, indispensible for a formulation of a sound economic plan, and from the distorted information fed to the planners by the "investment hungry" subjects to the economic plans' commands. The production delimited by the supplies of production inputs, rather than by output demand, as is the case in a capitalism economic system, was identified by Kornai (1979) as a key systemic feature of socialist economic system. He famously denoted it as a (production) resource-constraint or shortage economy, comprised of microeconomic units operating on soft budget constraints.[5] The disappointing economic outcomes challenged the "infallible cognition" claim and imposed, from the late 1950s forward, a recurrent pressure for reforms to alter the system. Initially, these pressures were internally generated from within the ruling elite, revealing growing fractions within the regime rather than the claimed internal cohesion; later, the pressures were mounted from the outside, by social resistance, increasingly subjecting the regime to the politically damaging and nagging question of who should be granted a right to decision making regarding economic resources and production. These questions revealed an advancing claim for participation in these decisions by others, as pointed out by Korbonski (1989).[6]

The underlying principle that linked the Balcerowicz plan to the main reform attempts within socialism was an overriding objective to *increase the efficiency* of the economic system at both the micro- and the macrolevels. The pursuit of this objective manifested itself in a more or less continuous movement toward the *decentralization* of economic decision making and the *downward* assignment of economic rights to various economic agents and institutions. Decentralization also implied initiatives for the *lateral democratization* of economic decision making on the macrolevel, through institutional reorganization and the enlargement of the pool of participants entitled to partake in devising and monitoring economic plans. Since the processes relating to the delineation of economic rights over production resources on micro- and macrolevels are at the heart of the definition of ownership, the continuity among all of these reform efforts lies in the fact that all of them constituted *property rights reforms*. The Mazowiecki administration's post-socialist privatization reform represents a more specific form of the ownership reforms undertaken under state socialism.

In the scholarly debates, property has been long associated with a "bundle of rights." In the early twentieth century, the legal scholar Wesley Newcomb Hohfeld drew an association between ownership and a bundle of rights: "Ownership, in its most comprehensive signification, denotes the relation between a person and any right that is vested in him. That which a man owns is in all cases a right. When, as is often the case, we speak of the ownership of a material object, this is merely a convenient figure of speech. To own a piece of land means in truth to own a particular kind of right in the land"

(Cook 1919: 727). The economist Armen Alchian tied property to economic rights when he asserted: "In essence, economics is the study of property rights over scarce resources. . . . The allocation of scarce resources in a society is the assignment of rights to uses of resources" (1967: 2–3, cited in Furubotn and Pejovich 1972: 1139). Sir William Blackstone defined property as "that sole and despotic dominion which one man claims and exercises over the external things of the world, in total exclusion of the right of any other individual in the universe" (Blackstone 1979 [1766]: 2). Carruthers and Ariovich (2004: 23) echo this conception of property by stating: "Ownership involves socially recognized economic rights. Property is that over which such rights obtain, and owners are those who possess the rights. In a sense, property concerns the dyadic relationship between people and things." According to an economist, Demsetz (1974), property rights entail three broad categories of rights—control, income, and transfer. First, they entail the right to control economic production. This implies the right to acquire and dispose of production inputs such as machines and equipment, production services, and financial capital and the right to determine the goal of production. Second, property rights include the right to appropriate the return or income from the assets. And, third, they include the right to transfer (through inheritance or sale) and liquidate property assets.[7] Horwitz (1977) points out that property rights confer power through rules that constrain and enable and by vesting decision-making rights over assets in a property subject: a physical or fictive party or in multiple parties. Given that those rules can change over time, property rights change over time. Reeves asserts that "Owner A owns property P if and only if: 1) A has the right to use P; 2) A may exclude others from using P; and 3) A may transfer rights defined by rules 1 and 2 to others by consent" (1986: 11).

In this chapter, I will show that all ownership under socialism was in fact of a conjoint nature. The decision-making power over assets was not exclusively located within, respectively, industrial enterprises, private agricultural owners, cooperatives, or state farms. The state was a constant coclaimant in the decision-making process, and particularly the right of transfer by consent was almost completely removed from the owners on the ground and reserved for the state. As the state throughout socialism claimed its ownership rights to all of those property forms in smaller or larger extent, the chapter will show the pattern of evolution in the power relation between the respective property subjects and the allocation of rights among them, progressing toward divesting the state from the ownership claims and assigning downward the rights to the subjects on the ground. I will show that underlying this process was a growing contestation of power between the state and society, culminating in the early 1980s, with recognition by the state of Polish peasants as exclusive private property subjects with unalienable rights to their assets. Although this changed rule guiding property arrangements was motivated by the attempt to preserve the socialist regime in the midst of a growing Solidarity challenge, it was tantamount to a systemic change.

Thus, I will discuss in this chapter three major economic reforms in state socialist Poland that preceded and impacted the Balcerowicz post-socialist reform and that shaped the distribution of these categories of rights among economic agents on micro- and macrolevels. Agricultural policies will be of special interest here, although their discussion cannot be separated from some broader description of reform initiatives. As the reforms were advancing, more bundles of rights were assigned downward, increasingly exhibiting features of a *bargaining* economy[8] instead of a *command* economy, as a political contestation between the state and many social groups was driving the process of downward property right rearrangements.

More specifically, in the first section of this chapter, I will discuss the conjoint ownership reforms of 1956 and those of the 1970s. These were revisionist reforms that asserted the state as the central economic agent and primary de facto claimant in the distribution of ownership rights across all legal property forms (state, cooperative, and private). The next section will examine the reforms of the 1980s. These reforms established the constitutional equality of economic agents of different legal property forms in place of the earlier proclaimed superiority of state and cooperative ownership over private property, and promoted the ability of local economic agents to advance their ownership rights at the expense of state ownership claims. These reforms were revolutionary in nature. They represented a shift from conjoint ownership reform to exclusive ownership reform. In this way, they constituted what Staniszkis (1991) calls an "ontological opening" or what Gramsci (2011 [1992]) characterizes as an "organic system crisis."[9] Finally, the third section of this chapter will analyze the completion of the shift and consolidation of exclusive ownership reform as pursued in the 1990 Balcerowicz plan. These reforms emphasized the comprehensive removal of the state as an economic agent and as an ownership claimant. They also liberated local ownership claimants from state-imposed restrictions, thus completing the process initiated in the state socialist period.

II. Early State Socialist Reforms: Redefining Conjoint Ownership Rights

The 1956 and 1970s reforms constituted two distinct steps in conjoint ownership reform of state socialism. They enacted divergent arrangements in the distribution of individual ownership rights between the state and economic agents within respected legal property forms. In broad terms, the reform of 1956 was primarily focused on a partial downward transfer of rights from the center to the economic agents on the microlevel mainly in the *area of pro-*

duction control, more specifically, in the determination of enterprise production goals. At the microlevel, the self-management principle advanced the rights of workers to share with management in the decision making over production goals. The reform of 1976 rested on a pronounced downward shift in the right to appropriate return on income from assets. Economic enterprises gained the right to retain some portion of the income, while the right to control production was effectively reclaimed by the center, and recentralized within the enterprises by management.

Both reform initiatives reserved the ownership right of transfer and exchange intact within the state. Also, the right to allocate production inputs remained centralized under both waves of reforms. Severe restrictions on the transfer of asset rights not only pertained to state property, but also applied to the cooperative and private properties in agriculture.

The Conjoint Ownership Reform of 1956: The Downward Delegation of the Right to Control Production

The disappointing economic results of the first three economic plans triggered wide-ranging public debates about excessive centralization and management planning. A reform program emerged out of proceedings of the 2nd Polish Economist Meetings in June 1956 and out of the government-appointed Economic Commission, chaired by Oscar Lange. The commission's conclusions were contained in the 1957 Thesis of Economic Commission on the Directions of Changes of Economic Model (*Tezy Rady Economicznej w sprawie kierunkow zmian modelu gospodarczego*), referred to herein as the 1957 Thesis on Reforms. The reform program reflected a compromise between the more radical government faction who supported market-oriented reforms and conservatives who preferred the status quo. The thesis contained the conceptual seeds for the subsequent reform initiatives in Poland (and some other Soviet bloc countries), especially the reforms of the 1980s. The reforms were predicated on two fundamental assumptions. First, they were premised on the idea that the centralization of decision making at the macrolevel removes incentive, responsibility, and authority from economic agents at the microlevel by inhibiting them from utilizing production resources efficiently. Second, these reformers were guided by the notion that the center can never have the information necessary to plan economic activities efficiently at the microlevel. In accordance with these assumptions, the 1957 Thesis on Reforms called for less intervention and the issuance of special orders in an attempt to ensure plan fulfillment. Thus, the thesis proposed to reduce the number of annual plan targets and to move toward more strategic planning through indirect economic instruments such as prices, interest rates, taxes, and tariffs. Although the reform commission was headed by Oscar Lange, a famous proponent of "a competitive model of market socialism," it proposed only a marginal introduction of the market.[10] Under the thesis program, the values of the proposed indirect economic instruments (especially those regarding basic inputs in short supply) were to be determined by central authorities. With the reduction in the number of annual plan targets, the November 1956 legislature reduced the power of the center in relation to state enterprises.[11] These changes in the system of macroeconomic decision-making granted more autonomy to state enterprises within the scope of broadly defined plan objectives. Enterprises gained more rights in the area of production goals, such as orienting enterprise production for profit making, and in management, such as the right to establish work norms.

Mapped out in the 1957 Thesis on Reforms, the effective reduction of the center's power vis-à-vis more autonomous state enterprises was matched by the proposed dispersion of economic decision making at the microeconomic level, through legislation that provided for the establishment of workers' councils. The authority within the firm was to reside in the workers' council and the enterprise director. However, the legislation on workers' councils left a very imprecise division of authority between them.[12]

The 1957 Thesis on Reforms remained predominantly in the zone of legislated reform policy—replete with ambiguities and an unspecified outline for implementation. Although the thesis was left mostly unimplemented or was abruptly reversed, it signified a partial conjoint ownership reform of state property. It represented a clear downward shift in the control of production from the center to economic agents at the microlevel of state enterprises.[13]

Agricultural policies, with decollectivization as their cornerstone, were placed squarely within the economic reforms of 1956. In order to analyze the 1956 policies of decollectivization, one must understand the specific initial conditions of Polish agriculture that shaped the content of subsequent policy makers' efforts at reforming the agricultural sector. Within the bounds of the Stalinist ideology, socialist Poland's agrarian policies exhibited a significant deviation from several of its Eastern European counterparts. The very specific historical conditions present at the installation of the socialist regime in Poland led to the promulgation of private property in agriculture and to the temporary programmatic exclusion of private agriculture from the initial period of state socialism until 1948. The specific constellation of political parties struggling to take power in Poland in the aftermath of World War II impacted the shape of the first agrarian program. The newly installed provisional communistic government supported by the Soviet Union proclaimed radical land reform on July 22, 1944, to compete with the Peasant Party for support in the countryside. The reform program codified on September 1944 called for the distribution of land (without indemnity) to agricultural laborers and peasants with less than five hectares. The land was to be confiscated from estates of fifty or more hectares of arable land and from property seized from Germans or German collaborators. In the western provinces of Poznan, Pomerania, and Silesia, with the history of annexation to Prussia and a tradition of large commodified agricultural estates, the limit for estates was raised to one hundred hectares. Although in principle the new socialistic regime intended to include middle peasants as beneficiaries of the reform, the small amount of land available for redistribution was insufficient to even satisfy the needs of farm laborers and small holders. Despite the policy prescription regarding the minimum size for a self-sufficient farm to be five hectares, the average land grant was only 1.93 hectares per family (Polonsky and Druker 1980: 75). Yet, by comparison with the previous time, the reform brought an increase in the average amount of land per household (Dziewianowski 1977: 156). Politically, this specific land reform was indispensable to the new regime in earning it a gradual acceptance by the rural population. In Korbonski's words: "There is no doubt that they [the communist party] scored a significant political success managing with one stroke to gain if not support, then at least the neutralization of well over half the population, destroying at the same time one of the most important centers of opposition, the land owning class" (Korbonski 1965: 89). However, the political considerations that guided the formulation of the land reform resulted in severe fragmentation and regionalization of the agricultural structure at the beginning of state socialism.

The first secretary of the United Workers Party, Gomulka, explicitly pointed out the specificity of Polish historical conditions reflected in the agrarian policy, making it unwise to follow in the footsteps of Soviet agrarian policy. He thus rejected collectivization because in the Polish condition it would be harmful economically and politically. Further, Gomulka explained his opposition to the Soviet model: "In order to introduce collective farming it is necessary to obtain the agreement of the peasants besides a technological and industrial base which Poland does not possess. No changes in the agrarian system can even be contemplated against the will of the peasants since no government in Poland could maintain itself without peasant support" (see Korbonski 1965: 62–63).[14]

Drastic changes in Polish agrarian policy were initiated in 1948 when the party formally proclaimed responsibility to mobilize the poor and middle peasants for a rural class war with rich peasants (*kulaks*).[15] However, contrary to the official proclamations of a class war, the collectivization was not advanced in rural regions with the most pronounced inequalities and with the highest concentration of poor peasantry. Rather, collectivization advanced primarily among middle and wealthy peasants, in the relatively egalitarian agrarian western territories, as opposed to the more economically heterogeneous other regions (Sokolovsky 1990). Instead, the pattern of collectivization and the strategies used support the thesis that the regime's priority in the collectivization movement was production efficiency.[16]

The collectivization drive in Poland was conducted under two specific historical constraints. First, there was the constraint of primitive socialist accumulation, the transfer of agrarian capital for the early socialist industrialization of 1956, which implied the state's unwillingness to allocate significant resources to the task of collectivization. Second, it was constrained by the Polish regime's choice to conduct collectivization on a voluntary basis, stemming from the lessons of the Soviet Union's earlier forced collectivization.[17] This precluded the application of coercion as a legitimate tactic against private owners in the collectivization drive. Instead, the officials implementing collectivization were pressured to create economically viable socialized agricultural enterprises. It was believed that this was the best means to convince the peasantry of the superiority of socialist agriculture. Also, carrying out the collectivization campaign in the context of a six-year plan that emphasized heavy industrialization added pressure to create efficient cooperatives that did not need subsidies that drained limited state resources. Therefore, the state targeted areas of traditionally high productivity in the collectivization campaign.[18]

Inhibited from applying coercion, the abrogation of individual property rights was used to induce peasants to leave their private property and join cooperatives. Thus the twin element of the campaign of voluntary collectivization was the *statization* of private property—the state asserted claimant rents (positive and negative) and rights that superseded the rights of the individual agricultural owners. The state laid claims to certain parts of farm produce through a system of gradually implemented *compulsory deliveries*. In this system, peasants had to supply the state with a range of food items at official prices that were substantially lower than market prices (Korbonski 1965; Sokolovsky 1990; Mosley 1958).[19] The compulsory delivery system and the state's requests for specific kinds of produce contingents not only implied the state's direct appropriation of the share of output, but also its co-claims to peasants' control over production goals (Jarosz 1998; Bolkowiak 1978). Further, the state severely restricted the rights of individual owners to acquire implements for agricultural production. Favored access to improved seeds, fertilizers, and building materials was reserved for cooperative members (Korbonski 1965).[20] Restrictions were also made on land transactions and on hiring agrarian labor (Magyar 1984). Above all, the state assumed the right to revoke the property titles from peasants who elected to refrain from land cultivation and agricultural production.[21] This last threat was progressively perceived by peasants as overly encompassing and not just tied to a specific infraction of the law. The 1952 Constitution only enhanced this perception—it established the favored status of socialized ownership without guaranteeing the inviolability of peasant ownership (Daniel 1994). This precipitated a sense of the uncertain and transitory status of private ownership.

In 1953, disappointing economic results in agriculture prompted a reconsideration of these agricultural policies.[22] Under measures that restrained their private property rights, individual producers reduced their production, and the cooperatives did not produce at nearly the levels delineated by the six-year plan targets. By 1956, earlier proposals to correct the implementation of the agrarian program were replaced by a full-blown critique of the central tenets of the collectivization movement and a change in the course of the agricultural program. Gomulka pointed to an incompatibility in the agricultural program's objectives—between the voluntary collectivization and the imposition of production targets for the socialized agricultural sector. "A quantitative development of producer cooperatives cannot be planned because, on the basis of voluntary entry into a cooperative, this would amount to planning the growth in human consciousness, and that cannot be planned" (Zinner 1956: 222). He also denounced the squandering of resources associated with the tactics of the statization of the agricultural private property used in the attempted socialization of agriculture.[23]

In line with the conceptual philosophy of the 1957 Thesis on Reforms, the 1956 Gomulka decollectivization plan called for the abandonment of any specific production targets for the collective agricultural sector, while it did not reject the socialization of agriculture in principle. The plan sought to reinstate the truly voluntary nature of the transition to socialized agricultural production. Gomulka's new wave of the 1956 reforms called for abandoning the strategy of negative inducement of peasants to the collectivization movement. Gomulka denounced subsidizing unprofitable collectives and recommended their dissolution. The policy recommendations were met by massive exodus away from the cooperatives. Half a year after an introduction of the policies of decollectivization, 83 percent of collectives had disbanded, with 86 percent of collective membership and 87 percent of total collective land. Those that remained within the collective sector were predominantly composed of former estate workers.[24] Thus, Gomulka initiated a partial de-statization of peasants' ownership rights. First, the state substantially retreated in its claims to residual income from individual agricultural production. The price structure for the state procurement of the agricultural products was then revised and the compulsory quotas were adjusted downward. Peasants were allowed to pay their taxes in installments and to market their surpluses after their state obligations were fulfilled. Second, the former state-imposed abrogation of the peasant's right to control their production through restrictions on their access to production resources was lifted. Gomulka created a network of *agricultural circles* at the local level to function as traditional peasant service cooperatives for joint purchase of agricultural machinery and implements. This was his strategy for the decentralization of control of access to agricultural production resources.[25] However, while peasants' cooperative membership in agricultural circles gave them easier access to machines, individual peasant owners were unable to purchase new farm equipment until 1971.[26]

As Gomulka's agrarian policy removed the negative incentives to join cooperatives and limited state residual property claims to agricultural private ownership, it failed to provide a positive inducement to transform agricultural landholdings into a socialized form. With most capital investment allocated in heavy industry, the new wave of reforms left the agricultural sector *undercapitalized* and *undermechanized*. By reasserting the primacy of heavy industry, the Gomulka reform program essentially continued the earlier policy of collectivization "on the cheap." This approach failed to induce the small peasantry to join cooperatives. Consequently, the fragmentation of landholdings, originating with the land reform and deepening with the collectivization campaign, continued during Gomulka's decollectivization program. Between 1950 and 1960 an increase of four hundred thousand in the number of new farms coincided with the reduction in average farm size. As the state exercised the ownership right to transfer assets by implementing the law that banned the division of private farms, there was a proliferation of illegal, informal land sales. According to data received by the ministry of agriculture in December 1980, the unregulated ownership that resulted from these informal land sales accounted for approximately 60 percent of all farms (Daniel 1994: 147). This led to new difficulties in distinguishing ownership from the mere possession of land.[27]

This failure to rationalize agricultural landholdings and to create efficient-sized farms erected long-term barriers to the increase in agricultural productivity. Thus, agricultural production showed slowing growth—3 percent annually in the period from 1956 to 1970 but only 2 percent annually in the 1960s. This declining growth rate for agricultural production coincided with the increasing gap between the growth of the urban population and the stagnation of the rural population. It created an impetus for the next agricultural reform program under the Gierek regime in the 1970s.

The 1956 reforms sought to build systemic incentives to enhance the performance of economic agents and thus to increase production efficiency through accentuating a specific element in ownership reform. The 1956 reforms delegated the right to control production to the microlevel of economic enterprises, allowing them to co-exercise that right with the state's central economic planning institutions. The delegation of this ownership right in the agricultural sector was expressed by the creation of agricultural circle cooperatives that liberalized peasants' access to the production resources. The limited downward liberalization of this specific ownership right, while preserving the centralization of others, led to economic performance (particularly in agriculture) that was far below the central plan's projection. The result was an impending economic crisis.

Conjoint Ownership Reforms of the 1970s: The Downward Delegation of the Right to Income

In an attempt to correct the growing imbalances between the supply and demand of food in the late 1960s, Gomulka's government attempted to increase consumer food prices to minimize government food subsidies. The official announcement of impending food price hikes in December 1970 produced worker riots in several major cities across Poland, leading to bloody confrontations between protesters, militia, and army units. The resulting political crisis led to Gomulka's removal and his replacement by the Gierek regime. The economic and political crises in the 1970s precipitated a new wave of reform. Predicated on the assumption that the center could not efficiently allocate production resources to enterprises or plan their production, the 1973 Gierek reforms further departed from direct central planning toward decentralized management (Wanless 1980; Piotrowski 1980). Believing in the advantages of organizational concentration, the 1973 reforms pursued the improved efficiency objective through a more economical use of inputs by stipulating the horizontal integration of state enterprises into the associations of multiplant state enterprises, or WOGs (Large Economic Organizations).[28] Such reorganization entailed an increase in the concentration of WOGs' management authority vis-à-vis workers, as well as an increase in the authority of directors within individual enterprises.

According to many observers, the reforms of 1973 to 1975 represented a reversal of the 1957 policy. Yet the conceptual continuity in the policy formulation between these two reform attempts cannot be overlooked. Although Gierek's reform abandoned workers' councils at the enterprise level and promoted the concentration of authority at the microlevel, it partially dispersed economic decision making at the macrolevel. It did this by enhancing the power of branch ministries (to whom the WOGs were subordinated) and by delegating downward some ownership rights to a newly created intermediary set of institutions located between the center and the WOGs. Through the increased use of indirect economic parameters, the center attempted to inform the WOGs of the general state of economic activity and to induce the WOGs to draw up "parallel" investment plans based on their own self-interest that would coincide with the center's projected output and value targets (Wanless 1980; Piotrowski 1980; Kalinowski 1978).[29]

Instead of promoting the control of production goals at the microlevel through self-management, as was advanced by 1957 reform policy, the Gierek reform package attempted to induce economic motivation at the microeconomic level by assigning rights to state enterprises to *retain a share of production surpluses* (realized both in internal exchanges and in limited foreign exchanges).[30] This was to be realized in accordance with two remuneration principles: to tie wage fund increases proportionally to the WOGs' rate of growth and to relate managerial bonuses to the WOGs' rate of profit growth. The decision regarding how to divide up the increases in the wage bill among the constituent enterprises within WOGs were left to the WOGs themselves. As a result, the connection between wage increases for individual workers and individual enterprise and their performance were very weak and therefore very ineffective as a mechanism to induce workers to increase their productivity.

The second element of the Gierek economic reform was a new "development strategy" designed to modernize industry through massive imports of production equipment and machinery from the nonsocialist bloc. From 1971 to 1975 import volumes from non-socialist countries grew annually on an average of 25 percent and capital investments increased in excess of 15 percent annually.

Under immediate pressure to meet increasing food demands of the urban population and to raise productivity through an efficient use of production inputs, Gierek's new agricultural program heralded the motto "any farm that makes profits is socialistic, whatever its form." It appeared that Gomulka's earlier policy that simply removed negative incentives for the socialization of private agricultural production transformed into a positive reaffirmation of individual agricultural ownership under Gierek's agricultural plan. The Act of September 26, 1971 recognized peasants' ownership right to asset exchange by granting and recording the deeds of those who had obtained their land through informal trade. It became one of the first measures to address the concerns of private farms.[31] As it turned out, the act was met by deep-rooted suspicion of the peasants about the true intention of the act. They feared that the legalization of the land transactions would be a pretext for the government to take the land of the "enfranchised farmers" and bypass their heirs (Daniel 1994: 141).

In an attempt to stimulate economic growth and overcome the dismal results of the Gomulka reforms, Gierek's agrarian program aimed to stimulate private agrarian producers to increase their production. His program toward individual agricultural producers was based on increasing their share of agricultural income and abating the state residual claims to profits from private agricultural production. Thus, in January 1972, the government abolished compulsory deliveries of meat, grain, and potatoes. It also increased procurement prices for agricultural produce. Long-denied social insurance plans were extended to individual peasants. At the same time, state procurement prices for agricultural products were raised several times from 1971 to 1976 (Magyar 1984; Szurek 1987).

However, the objective to stimulate agricultural production within individual agricultural enterprises coincided with the objective to *constrain the agricultural private sector*. This implied tighter state restrictions on peasants' ownership rights in the acquisition, transfer, and exchange of land. In

1973, the state allocated ninety thousand hectares for sale to individual peasants from the state land fund. This share decreased to only twenty thousand hectares in 1975.[32] Equally important, the state imposed lower and upper limits for the landholdings of individual peasants. Throughout the 1970s, land transactions below eight hectares were prohibited and transactions resulting in holdings exceeding fifteen hectares required approval by the commune heads.

Gierek's reforms assigned the right to appropriate a higher share of income from agricultural production by individual agricultural producers themselves. At the same time, the state strengthened the abrogation of the individual agricultural owners' right to access production resources.[33] The main mechanism of curtailing the latter was the centralization of local agricultural circles to form cooperatives of agricultural circles. Thirty-five thousand local agricultural circles were consolidated into approximately three thousand cooperatives of agricultural circles, and reduced further to less than nine hundred. In the process of centralization, a cooperative of agricultural circles was set up for a group of fifteen to twenty villages. The machine stock of agricultural circles was removed from villages and transferred to the newly formed communal centers. This reorganization and relocation of the machinery park resulted in very difficult access to mechanized land cultivating services for peasants.

The centralization of agricultural circles not only partially curtailed peasants' ownership rights. It also served to contain the spread of the private farm sector and to expand the socialized sector. Beginning in 1973, the cooperatives of agricultural circles were given land from the state land fund for direct cultivation. In 1970, the land under the disposal of agricultural circles was 56,000 hectares; by 1979 it soared to 260,000 hectares. The gain in land shares of the cooperatives of agricultural circles implied direct losses of land from the state land fund available for purchase by individual peasants.

In addition, land expansion of the centralized cooperatives and their involvement in agricultural production resulted in a reduction in the availability of mechanized land services to individual peasants. By 1980, 25 percent of all mechanized land services provided by agricultural circles were carried out on their own land instead of the land of individual peasants. The centralization of agricultural circles was connected further to the constriction of investment funds designated for the private sector. Thus, the private sector's share of investment expenditures in agriculture fell from 37 percent in 1970 to 25 percent in 1976. In the same time frame, the share of the cooperatives of the agricultural circles reached 18 percent of investment expenditures, as compared with an earlier 4 percent.

The Gierek policy to increase the productivity of the private farms and to restrict the growth of this subsector as a whole led to a *bifurcated* private sector (Swain 2000). Thus, the government pursued a French model and created a distinct group of specialty-model farms. The bifurcated mode of development of the private sector was closely connected with the regionalization of the private sector. Most of the model farms were concentrated within the western part of Poland. The owners were engaged in one type of production. Their "specialty" status granted them advantageous government contracts consisting of long-term, low-interest loans, and tax exemptions, as well as priority for the purchase of machines and production resources, and guaranteed demand for their agricultural output. Often, the loans were drastically reduced or forgiven altogether if their recipients met production targets set forth in their production contracts with the government. Small peasants were to be phased out through the granting of retirement pensions in exchange for transferring their land to the state land fund for its further incorporation into the socialized sector.[34] Thus, consistent with the Gierek agricultural policy objective to concentrate land in the state sector ("collectivization without peasants"), state agriculture's share of arable land increased from 24.9 percent in 1970 to 31.6 percent in 1978. That was the highest share of socialized agricultural land during the whole socialistic period, higher than during the overt collectivization drive. Parallel to the rise of the socialized sector, the private sector's share dropped from 75.1 percent to 68.4 percent.

Thus, despite official proclamations of the equality of all forms of agricultural ownership, Gierek's agrarian policy represented a new, covert approach to advance the cause of the collectivization of agricultural land at the expense of the private subsector. Gierek could no longer pursue overt collectivization, where the statization of private property was the main means to force peasants to transfer their private land to cooperative ownership. In the face of his own reform-induced growth in WOGs, workers' wages, and the resulting pressures for increased foodstuffs, Gierek could no longer afford a policy of "the worse off the private peasant the better," which was the guiding motto of earlier overt collectivization policy. To prompt a rise of agricultural production in the private sector, Gierek's partial conjoint ownership reform allowed for the limited accumulation of capital in the private subsector through a downward assignment of rights to individual owners to retain the income from their agricultural production. Yet this differential policy of land allocation and capital investment was constricted by increased limitations on ownership rights in the area of exchange and acquisition of land. The differentiated agrarian policy toward the private and socialized sectors led to the creation of mutually isolated agricultural subsectors.[35]

The initial results of Gierek's reform program were quite impressive. From 1971 to 1975, national income grew by nearly 10 percent, as compared with 6 percent for the preceding four-year period. Despite the increase in the proportion of the national income allocated to investments, this heightened economic growth allowed for the total volume of consumption to increase by approximately 50 percent between 1970 and 1975. Wage rates during this period grew by 7 percent annually, tripling the rate of the prior five-year period.[36] The state-induced wage increases led to heightened consumption pressures. Given the strong emphasis on the development of heavy industry, increased consumer power was directed into the consumption of agricultural goods. Thus, per capita meat consumption rose from fifty-three kilograms in 1970 to seventy kilograms in 1975.[37]

Following the Gierek ownership reform that granted peasants higher income based on heightened procurement prices and no compulsory deliveries, peasant production rose to unprecedented levels. From 1971 to 1973, private farm production for commercial purposes rose by 33 percent. Between 1971 and 1975, cattle production increased from 10.8 million to 13.2 million, and swine production from 13.4 million to 21.5 million in the same period.[38] However, the rise in domestic demand, which stemmed from the wage reform, quickly outpaced the production capabilities of the agrarian sector.[39] Thus, to sustain consumption levels, the Gierek regime relied increasingly on the import of food and agricultural supplies for domestic production.

However, the widening gap among domestic food production, consumption needs, and the state's reliance on imports forced the government to make two failed attempts to address the growing macroeconomic imbalances. First, in order to offset the increasing financial burden of agricultural subsidies, it aimed to curtail consumption by bringing retail prices for foodstuffs closer to the level of the procurement prices. In 1976, this initiative was met by food riots, similar to those in 1970 that toppled the Gomulka regime. The government then withdrew the proposed price hikes. Second, the government attempted to lower the consumption level by reducing the expensive fodder imports for domestic livestock production. This solution led to a breakdown in livestock production and prompted further food shortages.[40]

The state's subsequent attempt to bring livestock production to pre-1975 levels was linked to its goal of restructuring livestock production. The regime essentially shifted livestock production from the previous main livestock producers—small and middle-size family farms—to agricultural circles and specialty private farms by granting the latter special subsidies and exclusive access to animal feed. However, the 1978 upswing in livestock production was connected to an enormous waste in production resources and the duplication of capital investments.[41] Furthermore, the attempted restructuring of livestock production encouraged a wasteful approach to production resources among small peasants.[42] By 1980, as a consequence of Gierek's economic reform, Poland faced growing food shortages, an enormous foreign debt, and a pressing need for further reforms (Korbonski 1989; Wanless 1980).

The Gierek agrarian policy partially relaxed state claims to income from private agricultural production. Yet it virtually expropriated private producers' rights in the areas of property asset transfer. It also narrowed their access to the means of production. This further enhanced the perception among the peasants of the *overall temporary status* of private property. The uncertain and disadvantageous status of private property removed incentives from the private subsector to rationalize the use of production resources and to increase agricultural production. Effectively, Gierek's partial ownership reform in the private agricultural subsector pushed over 30 percent of full private producers and another 30 percent of partial agricultural producers into the new category of "peasant-workers." No longer concerned with the rationalization of production or the improvement of allocative efficiency, small peasants viewed their agricultural enterprise as a place for preserving independence and securing their livelihood while seeking supplementary income elsewhere in the socialized economy.

Gierek's agricultural program reflected the ad hoc nature of political decision making in the aftermath of popular opposition to the food price hikes. Agriculture became the most volatile terrain upon which all the internal tensions of Gierek's economic reforms revealed themselves. Eventually, this led to a deep internal breakdown of the reform movement and the rise of Solidarity.

III. The Systemic Change of the 1980s: From Conjoint Ownership to Exclusive Ownership Reform

The reform initiatives of the 1950s and 1970s were precipitated by preexisting economic crises, social unrest and riots, and the reshuffling of political leaders. Yet the 1980s reform efforts were formulated and conducted under the unprecedented pressures of severe economic and social crises and the Solidarity movement.

Although shaped by writings of Oscar Lange, Wlodzimierz Brus, and other advocates of competitive socialism, the reformers' debates on the strategies for the improvement of state socialist central planning were reinvigorated by severe economic and political crises precipitated by the Gierek reform initiatives. The patron-client bargaining relationships between WOGs and the planning and management centers over price setting and subsidies renewed concerns about the policy makers' accountability. Furthermore, Gierek's partial, administratively controlled price reform produced a price structure that only aggravated economic shortages by producing a gap between retail and procurement prices and creating severe foreign trade imbalances.[43] The 1980s reform initiatives attempted to address these concerns. They followed the principles of the 1957 Thesis on Reforms, yet they were more ambitious and comprised of explicit proposals with more specific and comprehensive measures.

Thus, the far-reaching socialization that included the lateral and downward enlargement of institutional participants in the planning process was to assure the accountability of policy makers. As stipulated in the program, the monopolistic position of the Polish United Workers Party (PUWP) in economic policy formulation was curtailed by enhancing the effective policy-making role of the Polish parliament and the council of ministers, and by including various consultation groups in the economic policy and reform process. At the same time, a reduction in the size of the central economic administration was proposed.

In September 1981, the legislation ruled that enterprises were no longer required to belong to industrial associations at the intermediate level. As a result, in 1982, some four hundred obligatory associations of enterprises were abolished. However, the legislation provided that, "when it is socially and economically indispensable," enterprises could be obliged by the government to join such organizations for a period of up to five years (Plowiec 1988). The institutional reorganization of the planning process went hand-in-hand with a change in its nature. The program stipulated that the center significantly relinquish its ability to bind enterprises to specific production targets and tasks. Equally important, the scope of the central allocation of material inputs and foreign exchanges was reduced. The center's planning commission responsibilities shifted from operational planning to a more analytical and advisory role.

With the decline in the role of directives in central planning, the further expansion and strengthening of indirect economic instruments (and thus markets) became viewed as an indispensable mechanism to remedy macroeconomic imbalances, and thus guide enterprise activities in the efficient use of resources and in the direction of the planners' priorities. Thus, the reform program emphasized enterprise self-financing as the dimension of the autonomous economic activities of enterprises most critical to the overall success of the program. Financial discipline was to be accomplished through more comprehensive price reform than had been introduced in the Gierek program.

The January 1982 law on prices established three price categories: administrative, regulated, and contract prices.[44] The price system reform was highly complex and thus implemented slowly. Furthermore, it was applied with sectorial differentiation in the proportion of administrative versus contract prices.[45] Lessons drawn from the experiences of the inflexible pricing system of the Gierek reforms prompted Jaruzelski to emphasize the continued revision of the proportion between price categories and price level controls within each category. This was to reduce state subsidies and to ameliorate market imbalances. However, the negative aspect of the frequent adjustments in the system of price categories, and in continually changing combinations of price controls, was the creation of a very unstable regulatory environment for operation of the enterprises.

To strengthen price reform, the Jaruzelski regime also included reforms in the banking system. It proposed a two-tier banking system, autonomous from the state. The program also attempted to bring about the progressive demonopolization of the economy—to introduce competition as a measure to prevent price setting based on monopolistic positions and to increase production output in the conditions of the shortage economy. Although the principle of the demonopolization of state economy was strongly emphasized in the 1981 reform program, it lacked any tangible strategies for its implementation.

The redefinition of the nature of centralized control over economic enterprises signified a further progression in the ownership reforms initiated in the 1956 and 1970s programs. It entailed the downward assignment of a broad range of rights to individual enterprises. State enterprises gained the right to set their own production targets, to make their own investment decisions, to choose their sources of supply, and to decide on their level of employment. The 1981 legislature permitted state enterprises to seek production opportunities in fields not stipulated in their founding statutes.[46]

In 1980, workers' protests and the demands of Solidarity created a powerful impetus for reformers to reconceptualize the specific form of decentralization articulated in the 1981 reform initiatives. Diverging from Gierek's WOGs decentralization reform that shifted authority from the center to particular managers, and thus became synonymous with technocratism, the 1981 reform program reaffirmed the principle of self-management. It therefore returned to the tenets of the 1957 Thesis on Reforms. The program granted an important role for workers' councils in appointing managers, distributing profits, evaluating directors, allocating investments, and determining firm production profiles.[47]

The most comprehensive ownership reform thus far within state socialism did not merely constitute a linear progression and deepening of the earlier ownership reforms. As a natural outgrowth of conjoint ownership reform, specific forms of exclusive ownership emerged in the 1980s. New measures sponsored by Jaruzelski aimed to utilize both capital and labor more efficiently and to facilitate state enterprise self-financing. This allowed for changes in the organizational structures of enterprises, effectively transferring the share of state enterprise capital to emerging new forms of property.

State property was spun off to group and individual ownership enterprises that were functionally closely associated with state enterprises. This effectively led to the transformation of state property into a *hybrid* form of property (Staniszkis 1991; Stark 1996; Rona-Tas 1997).[48] Furthermore, there were also initiatives that assigned the state a more passive position within state enterprises and converted these enterprises into joint stock companies with the participation of private investors. As a result of these new regulations, the mid-1980s showed rapid growth of the private initiatives taken within the framework of state enterprises. At the eve of postsocialist privatization reform there were approximately three thousand joint ventures, out of which 75 percent were created within the framework of the state enterprises and close to half of them were headed by the directors of the state enterprises.

These transformations in conjoint ownership were not exclusive to the Polish experience of reforming state socialism (Stark 1996; Rona-Tas 1997; Staniszkis 1991). Nor did they directly undermine the priority *of state ownership*. However, the ownership changes within Polish agriculture did undermine this priority. Antagonized by the Gierek agrarian policy that was predicated on the temporality of private property, as reflected in the selective granting of specific ownership rights, the majority of the Polish peasantry had pushed the issue of the status of private property to the forefront of the national discourse. Polish agricultural producers in the 1980s questioned the fundamental principles of socialism about the superiority of social (state or cooperative) ownership over private property and opened the debate on the proposed ownership changes conceivable within state socialism.

As workers' Solidarity challenged the Jaruzelski regime and pressed its demands in the 1980 to 1981 period, peasants moved to set up their own separate farm union. Pressured by the increasing food shortages, the Polish regime was forced to recognize Rural Solidarity (NSZZ RI "*Solidarnosc*") by signing the *Ustrzyki Dolne -Rzeszow* Accord on February 20, 1981. Subsequently, the regime was forced to incorporate Rural Solidarity's demands in its reform program.

Peasants understood that only by securing the *permanence* of private property as a specific ownership form within state socialism could they attain a solid basis for exercising their specific private ownership rights. Thus, one of Rural Solidarity's central demands was to guarantee the unconditional existence of family farms and to put them on an equal footing with other agricultural property forms. Built on the central demand of the permanency of private property within Polish socialism, the main clauses of the Accord of the Ustrzyki Dolne-Rzeszow called for the abolition of the state's continued attenuation of specific private property rights, particularly with respect to access to production resources and property exchange rights.[49] This request implied the de facto demand for a formal and complete withdrawal of all state claims to private property rights based on the socialist principles of production and redistribution. Thus, it called for a *destatization* of private property—the removal of the dual category of claimants to private ownership rights and the reinstatement of individual peasants as *exclusive* proprietors.

On the one hand, the permanency demand coexisted with Rural Solidarity's assessment that no feasible alternative to the socialist system existed and that a challenge to the regime had to be done within the confines of state socialism. On the other hand, by accommodating Rural Solidarity's demands, the Jaruzelski regime recognized private property as an *economic asset* within state socialism rather than an inconvenient and persistent foreign element. Pressured by growing food needs, Polish economists increasingly recognized the private sector as an economic asset for socialist Poland, given the relative productivity of the socialized sector and private one. "What state would our country be in now if we had to furnish the same level of agricultural production with a socialized farm economy that used twice as much capital equipment as the private sector? Where would we find enough fertilizer to satisfy a state farm system that uses twice as much to produce 30 percent less?" (Szurek 1987: 252). The shortages generated by the socialist economies had come to be perceived as more destructive to the system than any potential threat from renascent capitalism. Thus, he proclaimed that the reforms provided for more *effective economic tools* without altering the fundamental principles of socialism.

Together, Rural Solidarity's demands for unfettered private property rights, free from any state intervention, and the regime's reluctant (yet comprehensive) recognition of this represented *a half-limited revolution*. It was qualitatively distinct from earlier attempts to reform state socialism. Propelled by demands from below for economic autonomy and freedom from governmental control, these reforms represented a highly pronounced, antistatist, liberal approach that was discontinuous from earlier attempts to refine state coordination of the economy. It effectively transcended the logic of command economies and channeled the future post-socialist reforms into an antistatist, laissez-faire privatization drive. In the process of "using up and exhausting" the strategy of ownership reform, the system had moved to a new stage of specific privatization processes by the early 1980s. The recurrent economic and food crises in Poland since 1956 always threatened the political stability of the system; by the early 1980s, they had revealed incurable problems connected to refining state ownership and coordination, and thus made the shift to privatization imperative. Thus, the 1980 to 1981 period constituted a Gramscian "organic crisis" of state socialism. The genesis of the economic shift in the mechanisms for achieving greater economic efficiency should therefore be traced to the early 1980s, and the state's strategy of "growth without development"[50] in the attempted revival of socialism (Gorlach 1999), rather than the 1990s.[51]

Yet, the 1980 reforms were a half-limited revolution in that the fight for private property rights remained ideologically and politically welded to the campaign for the realization of socialist ideals. Rural Solidarity's demand for the destatization of private property was absorbed within the populist platform of the worker Solidarity's self-limiting challenge to the system. It was an integral part of Solidarity's moral crusade to reform state socialism from within and to empower society vis-à-vis the regime. Rural Solidarity's fight for economic self-rule and private property rights free from governmental obstruction resonated with Solidarity's repudiation of the authoritarian and arbitrary socialist state and its call for the democratization and the prevalence of legal rule in macro- and microlevel economic processes. Furthermore, one of peasant Solidarity's main demands for a fair and equitable distribution of goods and production resources across agricultural subsectors included a demand for the equal treatment by the state of private agriculture's segments—a *correction* of increasing economic differentiation between the specialized model farms and the rest of the peasantry.[52] The campaign for the destatization of private property was intrinsically connected to the campaign for the fulfillment of socialist egalitarian ideals.

Although the 1981–1982 ownership reform was introduced by a parliamentary legislature and represented a systemic discontinuity that opened the gates for exclusive ownership reform, it remained predominantly "on paper" (Gorlach 1999; Korbonski 1989: 14–17). Any comprehensive implementation of it proved to be impossible in the context of increased social tensions, widespread strikes, and intensified confrontations between Solidarity and the regime. The lawless and chaotic environment of the 1980–1981 period was not conducive to the decentralization and democratization called for by the 1981 reform program. Neither was the imposition of martial law in December 1981, which suspended civil rights, curtailed economic self-management on the enterprise level, and cut off Poland from external markets. Reform strategies to preserve the economic system that generated shortages clashed with the strategy of averting immediate political threat to the regime by the Solidarity-led opposition. Economically, Polish state socialism underwent systemic discontinuity in the early 1980s. Yet the regime was able to preserve its political rule for another decade, through a deployment of coercive and consent-building means. This *asynchronic* crisis of socialism had a profound impact on the post-socialist transition and the actual post-socialist privatization reform.

The clash between economic and political imperatives revealed itself in a reform "paralysis," a progression of external and internal disequilibria that further pushed Poland into deep economic crisis. On the agricultural front, the insulation from external markets and the government's attempt to reduce the staggering foreign debt amassed by the Gierek regime meant that imports of agricultural production resources were radically reduced. Jaruzelski's agricultural policy stipulated that production had to be based on domestic resources. Discouraged by the past economic performance of state and cooperative agricultural subsectors, the government expressed its confidence in the private agricultural subsector. It granted this sector permanent status within state socialism and equality with the socialized agricultural sector.[53] Its intended equal treatment of all sectors was reflected in the fiscal reform package. In 1983, land tax reform was introduced that equalized the tax burden for all agricultural sectors. Also, all forms of property were supposed to be taxed equally on their profits. Furthermore, the government liberalized the land market for private agricultural owners. From 1981 to 1984, the share of arable land in the private sector increased from 74.9 percent to 76.4 percent, with the trend toward land concentration among farms of more than ten hectares. From 1981 to 1984 their number increased by 7 percent, rising from 15.1 percent of the total number of farms to 16.3 percent.[54]

However, given the past policies of systematic underinvestment in agriculture, the domestic industrial production of agricultural inputs was not adequate for the needs of the agricultural sector. The supply of fertilizers, pesticides, and construction materials for use in private agriculture decreased. Insufficient supplies were reflected in the decline in livestock production and in sudden drops in the supply of many consumer food products. Food shortages from 1982 to 1985 ensued. Sugar, meat, butter, flour, and other commodities were rationed; the black market flourished and inflation ballooned (Nagengast 1991: 119; Kolankiewicz and Lewis 1988: 131). Constrained by the shortage of agricultural production inputs, from 1982 to 1986 the Jaruzelski regime repeated the dual treatment of the private agricultural sector practiced earlier by Gierek. Subsidies and low interest rates for the development of specialized private agriculture were granted in order to raise productivity within this segment, at the expense of the remaining small agricultural producers.

The ineffectiveness of the early 1980s reform initiatives manifested by the disappointing economic results in agriculture also marred other segments of the economy where the regime was not able to resolve various dislocations and growing inequalities associated with the persistent dominance of heavy manufacturing over other economic and social priorities (Domanski 1990). The worsening economic situation, combined with increasing political pressures on the regime stemming from the more or less clandestine spread of Solidarity chapters within state enterprises, resulted in yet another wave of reform initiatives between 1986 and 1989, the so-called "second stage" of reform, guided by a strategy to continue and advance the regime's exclusive ownership reform as a way of reversing the economic slide. Increasingly, neoliberal theory became an influential conceptual guide for the socialist reform architects in the formulation of their policies.

The influence of intellectuals on the formation of the governmental economic policy is a highly complex and protracted process, as revealed by the famous British economist John Maynard Keynes, considered as one among few scholars having profound effect on the economic policy of governments. Drawing from his years of failing to influence public policy with his ideas, until he published in 1936 *The General Theory of Employment, Interest and Money*, Keynes describes as "roundabout" the process by which an intellectual theory gains influence over public policy by first gaining recognition within the academic community, after overcoming its deep divergences of opinion "which have for the time being almost destroyed the practical influence of economic theory. Only then would the new, academically accepted theory powerfully guide the initiatives of politicians and civil servants."

Keynes points out that the time lag can in normal times extend to a quarter of a century, although in the midst of a crisis the process might work very quickly (Keynes, *General Theory*, 383–384, quoted in Evans 1985: 116).

The process described by Keynes reflects the emergence and growing prominence of neoliberalism in Poland. Walicki (1988), Bockman and Eyal (2002), Katznelson (2005), and Kowalik (2009) all traced an active participation by the members of Polish and Eastern European opposition intellectuals in an international discourse close to three decades prior to the introduction of the post-socialist reforms. This challenges the prevailing view that neoliberalism was introduced to Eastern European societies after the fall of socialism by the Western advisors guiding the unexposed and inexperienced Eastern European reform architects in the formulation of post-socialist policy. Instead, Bockman and Eyal (2002), in their important article, point to a confluence of interests between the Western and Eastern European economists. The authors show that, in the ascendance of their theory to a dominant stand within the economics discipline, Western neoliberal economists sought cooperation within an international intellectual community, while their Eastern European counterparts actively engaged in the international discourse and espoused the economic liberalism to lend them a conceptual base for articulation of the critique of the socialist regime and its approach to macroeconomic problems. Thus the members of the opposition intellectuals, who later participated in the Round Table negotiation with the socialist regime, and from whom later emerged architects of the post-socialist reforms, have had a long and active exposure to, and participation in, the neoliberal discourse.

With the neoliberalist perspective infiltrating the Polish opposition intellectual community for decades, by the mid-1980s it had become a conceptual platform used by a majority of the intellectual elite representing the Solidarity movement to reorient the hitherto critique of real existing socialism into a rearticulation of the *socialist ideals*.[55] Seeking for its members the right to full participation in policy decision making, Bronislaw Gieremek, a prominent intellectual within Solidarity and one of the key members of the Round Table negotiators, saw in the market economy and in the neoliberal antistatist postulate a conceptual ground for the renewal of socialism. For Gieremek, (socialist) state paternalism attenuates an individual's exercise of free ownership of oneself; hence Gieremek proposed self-governance of citizens within a market economy (Wesolowski 1991). Miroslaw Dzielski embraced neoliberalism by conceptualizing private property as a basis for the future construction of procedural democracy—thus he saw granting all citizens economic ownership and creating a society of private property owners as a way to renew societal trust in, and thereby the legitimacy of, the socialist regime. Lech Walesa, the leader of the trade union "Solidarity" and the Solidarity movement, in late 1988 in the context of dire economic crisis, concluded:

"We will not catch up with Europe if we build the strong labor union, which will certainly oppose the reforms. Solidarity started these reforms and we must help to rebuild the economy" (Michnik 1989).

The influence of economic liberalism on the socialist regime and its policy began with intellectual expertise sought by and delivered to government officials, and it went on to become a dominant intellectual current of the reforms in the later part of the 1980s when Prime Minister Mieczyslaw Rakowski handpicked his cabinet members primarily from the liberally oriented intellectual elite. The reform package prepared under Prime Minister Rakowski, in its major contours, was a precursor of the subsequent post-socialist shock therapy.

Against the background of a rapidly deteriorating economic situation, a surge of violent strikes in 1988, and a spreading wave of local Solidarity chapters formed illegally within the state enterprises, thereby challenging the state's ownership right to control them, Prime Minister Rakowski in the Jaruzelski government proclaimed at the Central Congress of the Polish Socialist Party in the winter of 1988 the necessity to legalize Solidarity and to include its representatives in the formulation of future economic policy.[56] As he proposed this unprecedented societal participation in the formation of policy, the content of the proposal prepared for the government was equally far reaching. The government's decentralization reform package, the so-called Sekula Package,[57] contained many specific policies furthering three postulates consistent with economic liberalism: *freedom* of economic activity of economic units; *equality* of all property forms, thus economy-wide recognition of private property; and *competition* free from state redistributive intervention. The reform package (*Ustawa o dzialalnosci gospodarczej*) was accepted by the Polish parliament (*Sejm*) on December 23, 1988. The regime issued several proposals that also liberalized foreign market access to Polish economic enterprises and allowed for limited foreign exchange auctions. The parliament approved the law on economic activity with the participation of foreign capital on December 23, 1988. In addition, consistent with its efforts to expand the private sector, the regime proposed to streamline the central government by eliminating some ministries.

However, the most far-reaching reforms were those regarding agriculture. To deal with growing food shortages and to bring further incentives to agricultural producers, in early 1989 the regime advanced its price reform by liberalizing agricultural procurement prices. The resulting differences between the low, still mostly administered prices for industrial goods as compared with high, contract prices for agricultural goods made 1989 a very profitable year for the peasantry. Furthermore, the government established minimal agricultural prices based on a parity in the standard of living between the rural and urban populations.

Thus, Polish agriculture became the flagship of the shift from conjoint ownership to exclusive ownership reform under state socialism. To overcome deepening shortages, the regime moved to promote private property actively and unequivocally. Yet its incentives to stimulate *production* within the private sector inherently contained redistributive implications that were unmistakably consistent with the socialist principle of economic egalitarianism (that is, urban-rural parity).

The Rakowski reform package became the basis of the Round Table negotiations, staging a negotiated exit from socialism in Poland (and subsequently in the rest of the Soviet bloc).[58] As documented by one participant, the economist Tadeusz Kowalik (2009), neoliberalism became a conceptual frame within which the Round Table negotiations were carried out by the socialist government and its opposition represented by Solidarity, revealing a broad convergence on fundamental points of the proposed economic policy. Both sides endorsed the socialist regime's reform initiative called the Sekula reform package in its pursuit of political democratic pluralism and territorial decentralization, and both sides agreed on the gradual advancing of privatization and marketization of the economy to be completed in 1991. Both sides also agreed that the main recipients of assets transferred from the state enterprises should be their employees, leading to employee-owned enterprises run according to the principle of self-governance.[59]

Thus, the asynchronic character of these socioeconomic crises was manifested in the non-concurrence of economic discontinuity (marked by a shift from ownership to privatization reform occurring early in the 1980s and deepened throughout the 1980s) and political discontinuity (marked by the 1989 Round Table negotiations and parliamentary elections). This asynchronism paradoxically resulted in an expressed compatibility between private property and socialistic principle of economic equality. It spelled profound implications for the course of development of the post-socialist era both in terms of policy formulation and societal reactions to them.

Although they marked a political departure from state socialism, the outcomes of the 1989 elections, although stipulated by the Round Table agreement, were unexpected to both the opposition and to the Jaruzelski government. Parliamentary elections with the participation of the opposition were pursued by the embattled Jaruzelski regime as a stabilizing mechanism. They aimed to draw the opposition to join in responsibility for new attempts to reform the economy. Although the opposition did not seek the elections, it did accept a compromise formula for the electoral process at the Round Table negotiations. Furthermore, it did participate in the elections as a concession in exchange for the relegalization of Solidarity. Against the regime's most careful calculations and the opposition's disbelief in the feasibility of any real shift of power, the opposition was peacefully swept into power by the June 1989 election results (Staniszkis 1991; Banac 1992).

IV. Post-Socialist Program: Reform of the Reforms

The political transition of 1989 installed the post-socialist, Tadeusz Mazowiecki regime. Mazowiecki, an intellectual journalist and philanthropist, long-connected with the Solidarity movement, which led directly to the Round Table negotiations, saw a connection between socialism and Christian ideology that could constitute a common base for rebuilding society around a social agenda of combating poverty and social exclusion. At the time of his unexpected ascent to the office of prime minister, Mazowiecki sought out "his Erhard" in the person of economist Leszek Balcerowicz.[60] It has been reported that Mazowiecki, turning to Leszek Balcerowicz, stated: "I am looking for my Ludwig Erhard. We will be fighting inflation and redirecting the economy toward a normal free market direction. Will you be willing to assist me in this work?" (Kuczynski's report cited in Kowalik 2009: 81; my translation). On January 1, 1990, the new economic reform program, named after the finance secretary and the deputy prime minister, Leszek Balcerowicz, was unveiled.[61] The Balcerowicz plan represented itself as a clear demarcation from past reform efforts and as a direct negation of former socialist regime initiatives.[62] It expressed a negation of the infallibility claim of the socialist regime revealed by the *economic* deficit of an inefficient state with its failed strategy of modernization as an alternative to Western capitalism. While the continuous search for sustained economic growth was the driving force for all reform attempts, the Balcerowicz plan explicitly staked out its distinctiveness from its socialist counterparts by emphasizing the discontinuity in the *mechanisms* needed to reach this shared objective. By insisting that a necessary precondition to increased productivity of economic units, and consequently to economic growth, was a change to private property as the only ownership form capable of responding to market logic, the post-socialistic reformers negated all earlier formulas for reforming state property on both conceptual and practical grounds.

In his inaugural speech to the Polish parliament (*Sejm*), the first post-socialist prime minister, Tadeusz Mazowiecki, stated that "the government will undertake steps initiating the transition to a modern market economy, tested by the experience of developed countries" (Przeworski 1993: 141). The minister of economic cooperation, Marcin Swiecicki, reiterated this point: "In reforming our economy, we do not seek experiments. We do not want our economists to invent new systems but to adopt solutions that work elsewhere. We simply want to construct a market economy like the West's" (Przeworski 1993: 141). Addressing the International Monetary Fund (IMF) and the World Bank in September 1989, Balcerowicz declared his main objective as a transformation of the "Polish economy into a market economy with the ownership structure changing in the direction of that found in the advanced industrial economies." He further stated that "the long-term goal of reforms is to turn an economy of shortages into a normal economy."[63]

The projected economic system was to be based on different types of private property, organized on the principle of open domestic and foreign competition, and backed by a strong convertible currency. In order to achieve this outcome, the following measures were perceived as necessary: the massive privatization of state enterprises; the breaking up of monopolies; the liberalization of foreign trade; the liberalization of Polish currency; the straightening up of the financial system; and the limiting of extensive state intervention in the economy (Balcerowicz 1992: 39–43).

In its broad guidelines, the agricultural policy of the first post-socialist regime was well integrated into the overall reform package. The policy clearly delineated the intended outcome: to create an agricultural system that consisted of highly specialized, capitalized, and commodified private production units. Despite the shrinking of arable land supplies and continuing population growth, such an agricultural system was expected to provide for national self-sufficiency in food production through growth of agricultural productivity and the expansion of production. The government projected an annual increase of 2.0 to 2.2 percent in agricultural production to attain such self-sufficiency. The forty years of agricultural policies under state socialism never met that long-sought-after goal.

In the Balcerowicz program, the intended borrowings from the West and the corresponding rejection of state socialism were one-dimensional. By rejecting the shortage economy, the program sought from Western advanced societies mechanisms to achieve economic affluence. The convergence tendencies of the new economic program were centered on the search for increased production output and consumption. They were expressed in the language of efficiency and rationality but without embracing or even addressing the capitalistic logic of distribution. As J. Gross eloquently expressed it:

> The 1989 East European revolution is still encapsulated in a set of technical prescriptions; it stands or falls, apparently, on the accuracy of experts' advice. . . . Revolutions used to be export commodities, presumably because the exporters had a blueprint for a better society to offer or, in any case, because they represented something new. This one, judging by the number of outside experts crisscrossing Eastern Europe (from business-school graduates to constitutional lawyers), apparently can be imported. Evidently there is a know-how somewhere—experience, ability, resources, knowledge, certainly money—that simply needs to be transplanted to carry the revolutionary task to successful completion. It is so because, unlike those of its predecessors (that is, other great revolutions), the future, the destination and the end point of this revolution is well-known. It actually exists. It can be reached by an overnight

> train. A lot of people from East Central Europe have seen that future. And it works. (1994: 69)

Thus post-socialist reformers collapsed the Polish revolution of 1989 into a blueprint for economic reform as identified by the Balcerowicz plan. They asserted their legitimacy primarily within the economic sphere by claiming to provide a successful and long-term resolution to the successive series of economic crises that plagued state socialism and that proved insurmountable to the previous socialist regime. *Privatization* and *shock therapy* rose to the level of the most identifiable ideological elements of the post-socialistic reform plan—connoting a rejection of the state's role in the economy and the previous protracted modes of reform implementations. The opening statement of the post-socialistic government's economic program reads: "The causes of the striking economic indolence of the economy rest deeply embedded in the previous economic system. Without their fundamental change we will continue to be stuck in an atmosphere of general indolence and a situation of permanent crisis. No partial measures can change this situation" (cited in Przeworski 1991: 147). Balcerowicz, in his presentation of the reform program to the weekly *Polityka*, put forward the principle of "quickly or not at all" as necessary in order to account for the disastrous results produced by the earlier reforms.[64]

As much as members of the post-socialist regime, who were caught by surprise by their electoral victory, sought to distance their program from the former attempts at reform and invoke imported Western economic models in the debates on the optimality of economic strategies, I will argue that the specific design of the Balcerowicz program and its neoliberal overtones came about from endogenous processes of policy conceptualizations, their subsequent reformulations, and the respective social responses to them. An analysis of the former reform attempts makes it apparent that the Balcerowicz program was path-dependent—it was a reform of the socialist reforms with respect to its mode of implementation, its content, and its scope.

Hence, one of the central elements of the post-socialist economic program, the stabilization measures that affected the overall character of the reform package, derived from the necessity to account for hyperinflation produced by the immediate predecessor's price and wage reforms.[65] The Balcerowicz program was formulated in the context of a critical assessment of state socialist failed reform attempts. It reflected the negation of the mode of implementation of the earlier reform initiatives, rather than their content. The protracted and limited implementation of price reform was criticized as the main culprit in the creation of a confusing and uncertain economic environment for the enterprises, macroeconomic imbalances, and the rampant price speculations by state enterprises (Kolankiewicz and Lewis 1988). In line with a critical assessment of the previous reform attempts, Balcerowicz proposed a "shock therapy" approach—a radical, comprehensive, uniform, and speedy implementation of reform measures as the main element to ensure the success of the reform efforts.[66]

Pointing to the adverse economic outcomes brought about by the gradual commercialization of specific economic sectors under earlier reform programs, Balcerowicz emphasized the necessity of a comprehensive and uniform implementation of the post-socialist reform program. Despite his acceptance of the uniqueness of agricultural production, he emphatically rejected suggestions to single out the agricultural sector in the reform program. "Agriculture is part of the whole economic system and we need to look at the economy as a whole" (Balcerowicz 1992: 92). In his opinion, the nonuniform, sectorial marketization of agricultural prices in early 1989 had led to an excessive increase in food prices and contributed to hyperinflation. Further, following the principle of a uniform approach across sectors, he also rejected proposals of minimum procurement prices for agricultural goods, a measure that was introduced in the second phase of Jaruzelski's reforms before the Balcerowicz program.

In terms of the *content* of his reform, the Balcerowicz program reflected *a conceptual deepening* of the measures that constituted integral elements of the previous state socialist reform package. The central element of his stabilization program was an immediate and comprehensive price liberalization to replace the previous transitional marketization of the price system. The other critical elements of his plan included wage reforms, banking system reforms, and the liberalization of foreign trade. All of them had been conceptualized, although not consistently implemented, in the previous reform package.

The second fundamental element of the Balcerowicz reform package, restructuration and privatization, was presented by its architects as affirming the vision of a new emerging society that negates the existence of state socialism and its property relations. This vision of a nascent post-socialist society, fundamentally distinct from its socialist counterpart due to its private ownership structure, rested on the assumption of the universal affinity between private property and the market. The privatization of the economy was elevated to the ideological trademark of the Balcerowicz plan, separating it from the earlier, politically bankrupt initiatives. Yet this failed to acknowledge that the post-socialist reform could not be divorced from the state socialist measures introduced earlier. It also failed to recognize that property relations under state socialism underwent a dynamic evolution that included changes in private ownership. Furthermore it did not acknowledge the historically specific connotation of private property that had emerged under state socialism through a long process of contestation between the regime and its opposition over private property rights. All of these factors influenced the construction of private property in the transition period.

Thus, the Balcerowicz privatization reform signified a subsequent step in the gradual progression from various stages of conjoint ownership reforms into an exclusive ownership reform already originated within state socialism. The post-socialist privatization reform caught in progress two modes of exclusive ownership that evolved within state socialism. First, it built on the *spontaneous privatization of the state sector* that led to hybrid property formations in the process of enterprise adjustments to the progressive marketization of the economy. Second, in the realm of the preexisting private subsector in Polish agriculture, the Balcerowicz privatization plan followed the gradual decoupling of the dual categories of claimants to private ownership—a process that culminated in late state socialism with the consolidation of private ownership rights exclusively in the hands of individual private owners. This evolution from conjoint private property based on two classes of property rights' claimants (individuals and the state) toward exclusive private property (with peasants as the only ownership claimants) manifested itself in late socialism through the reaffirmation of the permanency of agricultural private property unfettered by the state. In the post-socialist transition, it expressed itself through the clear neoliberal conceptualization of private property rights in the Balcerowicz plan and its programmatic rejection of any role for the state in the regulation of economic activity.

The post-socialist reform program was also path-dependent in terms of its *scope*. In an attempt to emulate Western advanced economic systems in their efficiency and strategies of its attainment, the plan never explicitly referenced capitalist society as a template for the Balcerowicz program. The economic program began with the declaration: "The Polish economy requires basic systemic changes. The goal is to construct a market system similar to the one existing in developed countries" (Rychard 1993: 34). In fact, responding to long-held and strong anticapitalist traditions in Poland, Balcerowicz emphasized that "privatization does not mean the entering by Poland into the savage capitalism in its 19th century version" (Rychard 1993: 21). These anti-capitalist overtones reflected immediate state socialist legacy, strengthened by traditional Catholicism and the beliefs of the noncommunist Left (Przeworski 1993: 142; Staniszkis 1991: 132–133). Yet as much as he explicitly distanced his model from capitalist redistributive patterns and antagonistic social relations, Balcerowicz did not pronounce affirmatively what the social objectives of his plan were or how it attempted to establish social harmony. This omission at the inauguration of the post-socialist reforms characterized subsequent government policies. Twenty years into the post-socialist change, a report on Poland as a part of a multinational comparative study of social inequality and its impact on the economic and democratic development of Central and Eastern Europe stated: "The analysis of the 'quality' of Polish economic policy indicates the fact that there is lack of . . . relation between economic policy and social policy. The realization of the social policy has been so far concentrated mainly around problems concerning reduction in the negative social occurrences (unemployment, poverty, health service) resulting from privatizing of economy and reduction in the social service sector" (Podemski 2011: 32–33).

Thus the post-socialist reform package was left without any explicitly formulated social policy. In so doing, the proclaimed break with the past contained a huge element of ambiguity in terms of the reformers' intended *telos* of the transition and subsequently in terms of their own basis of legitimacy.

In effect, the Balcerowicz plan subjected itself *by default* to the inheritance of state socialist social objectives. These crystallized during the *asynchronic crisis* of late socialism when the progressive repudiation of the socialist state's economic function integrally evolved with Solidarity's decade-long campaign for "moral socialism"—it condemned an oppressive state for failing to deliver the socialist ideal while upholding at least some of these ideals as still important and binding.[67] Hence, the post-socialist reformers' negation of the socialist past carried an element of a tacit obligation to deliver what the previous socialist regime failed to deliver. In reality, the proclaimed break with state socialism signified its transcendence—a projection of past unfulfilled goals and compensations for past wrongdoing as salient dimensions of the social objectives of the post-socialist regime.

The economic program, formulated in technical language of formal rationality and economic efficiency designed to stimulate accumulation, inevitably inherited the historically specific prescriptions for providing social harmony that became the legitimation basis for the post-socialist regime. From the onset, this combination of the explicit program for the stimulation of economic output and implicit requirement for social harmony resulted in an inner tension and ambiguity. The stabilization and privatization programs were designed to remove the state's responsibility for managing and planning capital accumulation. They were also designed to provide a solution to a profound fiscal crisis that engulfed the late socialist state through the removal of permanent state subsidies to economic enterprises. Yet the inherited pledge of social harmony was modeled on socialist distributive patterns and implied a state willing to maintain a prominent role in the regulation of the economy and able to increase its expenditures in the face of social dislocations generated by the comprehensive economic restructuration.

In its agrarian policy, the first post-socialist government explicitly addressed the shortcomings of real socialism by pointing to its double exploitation of Polish agriculture and by proposing broad measures to overcome them. The first post-socialist regime acknowledged the intersector profit transfer from agriculture to industry and the inequities in capital investments that they fostered. This left all of the industries supporting agricultural production chronically and grossly underinvested.[68] It also recognized the socialist state's wrongdoing as it pertained to intrasector transfer of profit from private agricultural owners to socialized forms of agricultural production. Explicitly alleging the previous regime's wrongdoing toward agriculture, the Mazowiecki post-socialist regime incorporated into its reform platform a broad objective to bring the living standards of the rural population on par with the industrial sector through active state involvement in economic development and the restoration of balance between economic sectors.[69] Thus, in broad terms, the agricultural program called for governmental intervention to provide for the development of industries supporting agriculture; to stimulate the growth of agricultural processing sectors; and to develop infrastructure in rural communities. At the same time, an attempt to compensate private agricultural owners for their past persecutions and economic exploitation added to the strictly economic arguments on production efficiency the political and ideological imperatives to stress an *antistatist agenda* of the post-socialist reform program—a comprehensive withdrawal of any state regulation in an already existing, predominantly private agriculture.

Thus, the Balcerowicz program explicitly represented itself as a radical departure from state socialist policies made possible *only* by the 1989 political revolution. Yet adhering to Poznanski's thesis on policy continuity, I suggest that it was a reform of the former reforms. The formulation and implementation of the post-socialist reform program was path-dependent, as reflected in its elected implementation strategy, content, and scope. As a reform of reforms, the post-socialist reform package spelled out enormous pressures for itself already at the level of its conceptualization, setting the dynamics of post-socialist transition. In its articulated objectives it aimed to "liberalize" private owners and thus to induce them to create economic growth. Yet in its salient implied redistributive patterns, it projected the state's commitment to alleviate social expenses, dislocations, and economic inequalities associated with the liberalization of economic activities. Thus, in its explicit objectives, the program sought to generate accumulation and to overcome fiscal crisis by cutting the state's expenditures, while in its redistributive patterns it assumed an existing economy of sustainable growth that provided sufficient revenue base for increased state expenditures. In addition, by emphasizing the comprehensive and rapid mode of its implementation, the post-socialist program projected a short-term horizon for the realization of these conflicting objectives.

In the next chapter, I will examine the effects of the policy of "liberalizing" exclusive owners and what expectations and responses it met within the private agricultural subsector.

Notes

1. Balcerowicz pointed to two factors. First, the trade unionist opposition of Solidarity, with its doctrine of fighting for worker rights, was indispensable in abolishing state socialism, but, in post-socialist transition, it resulted in state enterprise resistance to reforms aimed at economic restructuralization. Second, populist sentiments pushed for preserving a pension plan that escaped control of the post-socialist government and plunged the state into a fiscal crisis and undermined macroeconomic stability (1992: 166–187).

2. Balcerowicz 1992: 12.

3. North further points out that institutional changes (which include property changes as is argued in this book) come about not for social efficiency, but instead they are established to serve the interests of those who are powerful enough to establish them (1991).

4. The first reform was the Gomulka program of 1957. Although not mentioned in Poznanski's analysis, it was significant to the subsequent reform initiatives. The Gierek reform of 1973 to 1975 was the second reform initiative. These two reforms were followed by the Jaruzelski reform program of 1981 to 1982 and its second phase from 1986 to 1989.

5. See Janos Kornai's (1979) "Resource-Constrained versus Demand-Constrained Systems," *Econometrica* 47 (4). See his further elaboration of this theoretical model in *The Socialist System: The Political Economy of Communism* (Princeton, NJ: Princeton University Press, 1992).

6. Korbonski (1989: 4) stated: "The . . . 1960s, which witnessed the emergence of the crisis . . . in several countries, reflected in the slowdown in the rate of economic growth, . . . and general stagnation and non-fulfillment of popular expectations, coincided to a large extent with increasing demands for greater access to, and participation in, governmental decision making, especially on the part of certain groups in society." Instead of claimed cognitive infallibility, as Korbonski pointed out (5), "the . . . East European regimes, faced with an impending economic crisis, found themselves, rather suddenly, in need of expert advice."

7. For a discussion of the distinction between ownership and privatization reform and the content of both, see Walder (1992), Rawski (1992), and Putterman (1995).

8. See Charles Sabel and David Stark (1982), "Planning Politics, and Shop-Floor Power: Hidden Forms of Bargaining in Soviet-Imposed State-Socialist Societies," *Politics and Society* 11: 439–475, and their analysis of the shifting power of conflict and alliance, with an emphasis on the growing mutual dependence and complex ties among planners and various social groups pursuing their separate ends, instead of relations of command and subordination.

9. For Staniszkis, the ontological opening characterizes a change in property rights, signifying a systemic change. For her, the breakdown of the system in Eastern Europe, the ontological opening, happened in 1989–1990 and implies the convergence of socialism to capitalism. She finds privatization the major mechanism of this convergence. According to Staniszkis, the convergence took the form of political capitalism whereby the former ruling elite (nomenklatura) converted its political authority into economic power by becoming private property owners. See Staniszkis (1991).

10. See Oscar Lange (1936–1937). Equally influential for the course of the attempted reforms was a theoretical analysis of economist Wlodzimierz Brus (1961). In his *Ogólne problemy funcjonowania gospodarki socjalistycznej* (*General Problems of the Functioning of the Socialist Economy*), Brus outlined a model of a centralized socialist economy as an inflexible, inefficient, and overly bureaucratic system and juxtaposed it with a model of a decentralized socialist economy based on semiautonomous production units, coordinated by a multilayered decision-making system, replacing the centralized one.

11. The State Commission for Economic Planning had been reconstituted as the Planning Commission of the Council of Ministers with the staff cut by half and its function changed from an economic decision-making body to an advisory organ.

12. For comprehensive analysis of the early stages in the socialistic economic programs, see Montias (1962).

13. For example, by the decree of the Council of Ministers in 1958, spontaneously growing workers' councils were seriously circumscribed by the creation of industrial associations, which mostly re-created the functions of the old central boards. The 1958 law on workers'

councils was modified to create "conferences of workers' self-management," which effectively subordinated the workers' councils to the trade union committees of enterprises and to political directives. See more on this in Brus (1988), Montias (1962), and Zielinski (1973).

14. For delineation of the seven different agricultural regions, as far as the size of holdings, technological development, and level of inequality are concerned, see Sokolovsky 1990: 38, table 2.1. The inequalities in landholdings were more reflective of interregional differences than intraregional disparities. This fragmentation could not be offset by the addition of frontier regions to western Polish territories out of German occupied land following a postwar settlement that provided considerably more land for distribution—6,497,000 hectares of agricultural land as compared to 2,751,000 hectares in old provinces—and resulted in a disproportionally bigger average size of farms than in the other regions. In the western territories the average size of holdings was 7.9 hectares while elsewhere the figure was just 4 hectares (Magyar 1984).

15. The minister of industry, Hilary Minc, recounted on the pages of *For a Lasting Peace* that socialism in Poland unavoidably involves collectivization of agriculture and "elimination of the kulaks as a class" (October 1, 1948: 5). That statement initiated the collectivization phase in the Polish agrarian policies of 1948 to 1956.

16. See Sokolovsky (1990) for delineation of different models of collectivization.

17. For examples of the party's frequently issued directives against violation of the voluntary principle in the establishment of collective farms, see *For a Lasting Peace*, September 14, 1951: 3; February 27, 1953: 2; and November 20, 1953: 2.

18. Thus, state farms were set up as model farms in overwhelming concentration in the frontier region out of confiscated German estates. By January 1950, seventy-five of the 533 existing collective farms were located in one of the most productive regions of Poland, in the province of Poznan. Another sixty were set in the next most collectivized area, the frontier province of Wroclaw (East Europe, March 16, 1950: 8). By the end of 1954, over 55 percent of all advanced collective farms were located on the former German territories (GUS, *Rocznik Statystyczny* 1955: 108). They received favored access to improved seeds, fertilizer, credit, modern equipment, and breeding stock. The six-year plan allocated 41 percent of all state investment in the rural sector to state farms and projected approximately 20 percent of the nation's grain supply and approximately 10 percent of meat supply from the state farms (Barnett 1958: 235; Korbonski 1965: 174).

19. As the collectivization movement was progressing, so was the gap between market and compulsory prices of agricultural output. The quotas for compulsory deliveries varied by product, specific year, and type and size of holdings. The classification of holdings derived from a complex procedure of assessing the type of arable land, specific region, fifteen types of private peasants, and eleven brackets for progressive taxation. In 1952 and 1953 peasants officially classified as kulaks had 50 percent of their output affected by compulsory deliveries. The numbers for middle peasants and poor peasants were 30 percent and 14 percent, respectively. Only landholdings smaller than one hectare were exempt from compulsory delivery of meat. See Magyar 1984: 33, GUS, *Rolniczy Rocznik Statystyczny* 1945–1965: 331–333; GUS, *Rocznik Statystyczny* 1971; GUS, *Statystyka Rolnictwa* 1946–1957: 258–259.

20. The state abrogation of access to production resources was more pivotal for commodity-oriented production. It therefore proved to be far more effective to drive middle-size peasants and those afraid to be labeled kulaks into the collective farms than the small-holding peasants oriented for subsistence production.

21. In February 1953 a decree was passed "On the Reclamation of Unsatisfactorily Cared for Lands." The National Council of Cooperatives was given the right to confiscate agricultural land determined to be "not properly husbanded." Owners were to be given some compensation and the land distributed among poor and middle peasants as well as among the cooperatives and state farms. Farmers who failed to report their inability to cultivate their lands or to surrender their property faced jail sentences of up to three years, fines, and two to five years of exile from their native villages (*News from Behind the Iron Curtain*, May 1953: 28, cited in Daniel 1994: 141).

22. As measured from 1949, agricultural production rose only by 9 percent, while industrial production increased 150 percent (*News from Behind the Iron Curtain*, January 1954: 6).

23. "Thoughtless is the idea still heard today that the positive effect of the agricultural policy pursued in the past is the surrender of the ruined kulak to the people's power. This kind of surrender could have been achieved at any time and there was no need for the years of the policy of so-called restricting the kulak, which in reality was not a policy of restricting exploitation, but a policy of ruining the kulak's farm. After all, even today, it would be possible to achieve the wholesale surrender of all remaining prosperous peasant farms not yet ruined. There is nothing easier than to achieve such a surrender, such a cheap, or rather costly victory, bearing in mind how much we are paying for the import of grain" (Zinner 1956: 223).

24. For more details, see Korbonski 1965: 258. For more on the evolution of collectives, see chapter 4.

25. For more detailed discussion of agricultural circles, see chapter 4.

26. See table 12 in Magyar (1984) for changes in the private sector of agriculture after 1956. The new agricultural program resulted in a steady increase in agricultural productivity as the official statistics indicated. The agricultural productivity index increased from 113 in 1955 to 121.4 in 1956 and to 135.9 in 1960. See Korbonski (1965: 214). However, despite increases in domestic agricultural productivity, Poland's dependence on food imports was increasing. The rate of import of agricultural products more than doubled between 1955 and 1960, and tripled in the period between 1960 and 1974. See Daniel (1994: 141).

27. The Act of June 29, 1963 in Polish Civil Code limited the division of farms. *Dziennik Ustaw* no. 16, pos. 93, April 23, 1964.

28. Introduction of Gierek's reform was marked by cautious incrementalism. The new management system did not entirely displace the old one. It was introduced very gradually in the associations of enterprises called WOGs (Wielkie Organizacje Gospodarcze or Large Economic Organizations), which were largely self-selected. In 1973, some twenty-four WOGs began to operate the new system in industry and accounted for approximately 20 percent of the industrial output. By 1975, the reform covered WOGs producing about two-thirds of the sector's output, almost all domestic retail trade and parts of construction and foreign trade, but Gierek's reform never became universal.

29. In Gierek's model of indirect economic management, administratively set prices played a central role, as well as interest rates, internal exchange rates, and a system of subsidies. The system of subsidies consisted of direct subsidies to specific WOGs (subjective subsidies), price subsidies, and taxes, aimed to reflect the economic plan's sectorial priorities. In light of the branch ministries retaining their powers over the microlevel, the management freedom of decision making was not guaranteed nor was it respected in practice. As economic difficulties mounted between 1973 and 1975, bureaucratic interference in the running of WOGs became more common (Kalinowski 1978; Hare and Wanless 1981: 511).

30. WOGs were permitted to retain a certain amount of their foreign exchange proceeds earned through exports, according to a norm set on an individual basis.

31. See "Uregulowanie wlasnosci gospodarstw rolnych i zmiany w kodeksie cywilnym" (Regulating Ownership of Farms and Changes in the Civil Law), *Panstwo i Prawo* (1971: 8–9).

32. These figures should be compared with the land allotment policy in the subsequent period, with the transfer of 165,000 hectares of land from the state land fund in 1981, and 240,000 hectares (thus close to 90 percent of the land allocation) in 1982 into private hands despite the imposition of martial law (see Magyar 1984, fig. 6).

33. The state restricted the main access to production resources through the centralization of agricultural circles, even though it liberalized its policy on machine purchases. In 1971 private agricultural owners were allowed to buy new tractors. That policy was preceded by the 1967 ruling that allowed peasants to buy tractors discarded from units of the "socialized" sector. Before 1967, even during Gomulka's decollectivization drive, the peasants were barred from buying tractors. During the 1970s, in the wake of the new liberalized policy on tractors for the private sector, peasants purchased over 325,000 tractors, starting from the initial level of 54,000 in 1971. As a result, the private sector's tractor stock surpassed that of the socialized sector by 130,000. Yet, in 1981, over 200,000 peasants were on a waiting list for the purchase (Magyar 1984: 90–92). In the climate of permanent uncertainty about the status of their property in general, and about their narrowing access to the machines from agricultural circles in particular, the liberalization of the access to tractors was met by peasants with an excessive

demand. This was a function of a desire to gain independence from the state, rather than deriving from economic rationality. In fact, in many instances the size of landholdings did not justify the purchases of the tractors.

34. Initially, the retirement plan was positively received by small peasants. However, in 1977 and 1978, when the rate of pension benefits was linked to productivity, it discouraged small peasants from contributing to the retirement system. Thus, the aspect of "agricultural reconstruction" connected with the attempted phasing out of the small holdings did not produce the desired outcomes. The share of small holdings (within the range of two to five hectares) decreased marginally during the 1970s, constituting over 30 percent of all the landholdings in 1978. In addition, the holdings of one-half to two hectares slightly increased from 26.9 percent in 1970 to 30.5 percent in 1978 (GUS, *Rocznik Statystyczny* 1979).

35. Procurement prices for agricultural goods were administratively determined and differentiated by subsector. The subsectors had separate organizational networks for, among other things, trade.

36. GUS, *Rocznik Statystyczny*, various issues; Domanski 1990: 424–445; Hare and Wanless 1981: 492–493.

37. GUS, *Rocznik Statystyczny* 1985: 128.

38. Szurek 1987: 240.

39. This was primarily due to the fact that there was a continuation of disproportional investments in heavy industry (45 percent), while only 15 percent of investments were allocated to the development of all agricultural sectors (Szurek 1987: 240).

40. The drastic cuts in wheat imports (from 1.7 million tons in 1974 to 1.4 million tons in 1975) following the rise of wheat prices on the world market coincided with poor domestic harvests of wheat and potatoes in 1974 and 1975. As a result, the supply of livestock feed to family agricultural producers was cut almost by half in 1976, to a level of 3.7 million tons as compared with 6.9 million tons two years earlier. Furthermore, the government introduced unequal access to animal feed, with preferential treatment for the state farming sector (GUS, *Rocznik statystyczny rolnictwa i gospodarki zywnosciowej* 1978: 387; Szurek 1987: 241).

41. A kilogram of meat produced within the agricultural circles required 8.5 kilograms of feed compared with 3 kilograms for the state farms and the private farms, respectively. State farms consumed 300 kilograms of fertilizer per hectare, as compared with 150 kilograms on private farms (Szurek 1987: 244). The restructuring of livestock production required extensive capital investments for the construction of buildings for animal raising within the socialized sector and specialized farms, while small and middle-size peasants already possessed such accommodations.

42. As Szurek (1987: 244) reported: "Deprived of (access to) imported animal feed, private farmers took advantage of blocked retail prices and the rise in production prices to speculate. For example, producers were paid 6.2 zloty for a liter of milk which was sold to consumers for 2.9 zloty. Similar discrepancies existed for meat, bread, etc. Farmers bought up consumer stocks of these products in towns and proceeded to use them, mostly to feed livestock. The main aim of ration coupons, first issued in 1981, was to put a stop to this speculation."

43. Although the socialist regime was influenced by Lange's writings, it did not implement his recommendation consistently or comprehensively. As Wanless (1980) pointed out, in his writings, Lange restricted the directive role of central planners to prescribing trends in investment and exercising control over prices as the main indirect regulator of production. Poland however failed to carry out consistent price reform and also failed to modify the process of drawing up the central plan that was necessary for the price regulation to be effective.

44. Administrative prices, set by the center at prices lower than the production costs, but offset by heavy subsidies, covered basic consumer goods and services indispensable for daily consumption, basic agricultural produce purchased by the socialized sector, and other basic goods and services (such as postal and telecommunication services). Regulated prices, set by producers, based on costs and monitored by authority, were considered to be a transitional stage to contract or market prices. The latter, in principle, were set freely in the marketplace, yet the governmental agencies followed a complex set of regulations to monitor rises in contract prices (Gomulka and Rostowski 1984).

45. Still, in 1988, six years after the inception of the reform program, only 18 percent of all retail prices were market-determined. Within the agricultural sector, approximately 30 percent of all retail prices were set by the market.

46. In specific cases, though, drastic deviation in the production profile required prior approval from the founding body.

47. Through the extension of the self-management principle to the individual factory level, the program provided for development of work teams. The organizational form of involvement of workers varied according to the size of the enterprise and the type of industry the enterprise was in—some enterprises were exempted from the workers' selected management.

48. See Staniszkis (1991) on political capitalism in Poland, as well as Stark (1996) and Rona-Tas (1997) on the evolution of state property forms in Hungary.

49. The main clauses of the Ustrzyki Dolne-Rzeszow demanded the following in respect of property rights: (1) a free land market of up to one hundred hectares for a single owner, as stipulated in Polish law; (2) equal rights to subsidies and loans for all agricultural sectors, including specialty farms; and (3) aid programs for private farms. In addition to economic demands regarding property rights, RI "Solidarnosc" made vast political and cultural demands. See Protokol porozumienia w sprawie zwiazkow zawodowych rolnikow indywidualnych (Rzeszow-Ustrzyki Dolne: NSZZ, February 18–20, 1981: 12).

50. Krzysztof Gorlach (1999, 1989), one of the leading Polish rural sociologists, termed the bifurcated strategy of modernizing small segments of the private agricultural producers while stifling overall development of the private agricultural sector, subject to overt or covert attempts at collectivization, as the strategy of "growth without development" in the 1970s and 1980s period when the socialist regime applied "oppressive tolerance" to peasants.

51. See Rona-Tas (1997) for a similar conclusion in the context of the Hungarian reform of socialism. He, too, looks at unintended consequences of the reforms of the 1980s and associates the "rupture" moment leading to the collapse of socialism in Hungary with the 1982 reforms, which for the first time allowed private owners to conduct business transactions with the state enterprises. This reform effectively made the regime's claims to ownership baseless, showing society a tangible and feasible alternative of "private entrepreneurship" to the dependence on the state.

52. See Staniszkis 1984: 98.

53. The state "protects the individual family agricultural land holdings of working peasants, guaranteeing their permanence; proffers assistance in increasing production and raising their technical-agricultural standard; supports the development of agricultural self-management, in particular agricultural circles and collectives; supports the development of cooperation and specialization of production; and broadens the ties of individual agricultural land holdings within the socialist national economy" (*Dziennik Ustaw*, no. 39, section 175, July 22, 1983). See also Lonc 1992: 220; Gomulka and Rostowski 1984.

54. The overall agricultural structure of the private sector has changed very insignificantly within the forty-year period under state socialism and with substantial land fragmentation—leaving over 58 percent of peasant holdings sized between one-half and five hectares. (GUS, *Rocznik Statystyczny*, various years; Szemberg 1993).

55. See Adam Michnik (1989), "Zwiazek zawodowy juz nie wystarcza," Gazeta Wyborcza, 108: 1. T. Mazowiecki, the future first post-socialist prime minister, best reflected this shift of orientation when he stated that "the struggle against has to be reoriented into a struggle for." See Kowalik 2009: 112.

56. Baka (2007: 200) cites Rakowski's rationale presented at the Central Congress of the Central Committee of the Polish Socialist Party: "Currently, in the large state enterprises over 200 local chapters of "Solidarity" operate openly or semi-openly. If, in the next several months, another several hundred are created, what are we to do? Ignore them? Try to dismantle them?" And further: "The time has come for the Party to answer whether we can meet the enormous challenge facing Poland, or whether we should do it together with the constructive opposition, which after its legalization would share part of the responsibility for it" (my translation).

57. See Kowalik 2009: 48–49.

58. The Round Table talks between Solidarity leaders and Jaruzelski's regime were held in February and March 1989 (Dubinski 1990). In the aftermath of strike waves, the talks were

initiated by the government side—they were proposed by Prime Minister Mieczyslaw Rakowski. The talks produced four major compromise items between the government and the opposition—the legalization of Solidarity, outlawed since imposition of martial law in December 1981; freer elections to the lower chamber in Parliament (the Sejm) and free elections to the upper chamber (Senat) in exchange for the opposition's sharing responsibility for the difficult economic decisions; the creation of the new, powerful institution of the president at the expense of the diminished Sejm's power, in exchange for a further reduction of the "leading role of the party'" and the gradual move toward a "government of law." Staniszkis 1991: 77–78. For a reflexive synthesis of the events of the Round Table negotiation and their lasting impact on the transition, see the accounts of a participating economist, Tadeusz Kowalik (2009); and a sociologist, Zbigniew Wozniak (2009). For a more detailed account chronicling the experiences of 232 participants in the negotiations, see Adamecki, Mogielnicka, and Wujec (1989).

59. For a detailed account of the agreement on economic matters, see Kowalik 2009: 49–51.

60. Mazowiecki was looking for the equivalent of Ludwik Erhard, the postwar German economic minister and chancellor who, on the basis of his social market economy reform package, rebuilt the German economy after World War II.

61. The Balcerowicz Plan "Economic Program: Main Assumptions and Directions" was adopted by the Council of Ministers in October 1989.

62. Economist Marek Belka stated: "The Mazowiecki government in some sense was a "Dictatorship." It offered society a program, which was endorsed—as there was no way to go back—behind us were only queues and vinegar on the empty shelves. We did not have an alternative, so we were given a new system, or, if someone prefers to say, a new system was imposed on us. This was the dictatorship of experts." (Panel, "Premierzy o 15 latach transformacji ustrojowej, wypowiedz Marka Belki," *Gazeta Prawna*, 21 lutego 2005, cited in Kowalik (2009: 81; my translation).

63. See "Balcerowicz's Address to IMF." *Financial Times*, July 16, 1990.

64. Pawel Bożyk (1989), "Cudu nie będzie." *Polityka*, December 16, 5; also Paweł Bożyk (1990), "Niech ruszy z bezruchu: bronie Balcerowicza." *Polityka*, August 11, 4.

65. In the prolonged process of the implementation of the hybrid system of administered and market prices, the provisions enacted between 1982 and 1986 to control the levels of price setting proved to be ineffective. They were insufficient to prevent drastic manipulations by the enterprises to continuously increase their products' prices only in loose relation to increases in their production costs. Equally, the wage regulation system in its implementation produced disappointing results. It led to excessive wage growth, unrelated to productivity increases and running counter to the main objective of the reforms to instill self-financing discipline within enterprises. Combined, the price and wage reforms had led to spectacular hyperinflation.

66. Contrary to the approach presented here that the past reform influenced the formulation of the post-socialistic reforms, Przeworski (1991) refers to the incompatibility of the complex goals of the prior reforms—whereas the simultaneous projects of building a market economy and a political democracy dictate the shock therapy approach as more likely to succeed.

67. The post-socialist regime was expected to continue to, for example, provide universal social capital and services in areas of education, medical care, and housing, and maintain economic equality. For an analysis of the nature of the crisis of state socialism, see Burawoy and Lukacs (1992).

68. The actual outcomes deviated radically from the reformer expectations and persisted at the disappointing levels. Buchowski (2003) cited the following data: In the fall of 1996, 1.126 million rural inhabitants were unemployed (43 percent of all unemployed). The Polish Employment Office estimates that hidden unemployment in rural areas amounts to 0.6 to 0.9 million. After years of improvement, the situation started to worsen at the beginning of 2000, and in mid-2003 unemployment had reached more than 18 percent.

69. See World Bank 1990, *An Agricultural Strategy for Poland. Report of the Polish European Community*. World Bank Task Force, Washington, DC: World Bank.

References

Adamecki, W., M. Mogielnicka, and L. Wujec. 1989. "Okrągły Stół. Kto jest kim. 'Solidarność'—opozycja." In *Okrągły Stół. Kto jest kim, 'Solidarnosc'—opozycja. Biogramy, wypowiedzi*, edited by W. Adamecki, M. Wnuk, and E. Kisielinska, 3–328. Warsaw: Wydawnictwo Mysl.

Ash, Timothy G. 1990. *The Uses of Adversity: Essays on the Fate of Central Europe*. New York: Random House.

Baka, Wladyslaw. 2007. *Zmagania o Reformę: Z Dziennika Politycznego 1980–1990*. Warsaw: Wydawnictwo Iskry.

Balcerowicz, Leszek. 1992. *800 Dni. Szok Kontrolowany*. Warsaw: Polska Oficyna Wydawnicza "BGW."

Banac, Ivo. 1992. *Eastern Europe in Revolution*. Ithaca, NY: Cornell University Press.

Barnett, Clifford R. 1958. *Poland, its People, its Society, its Culture*. New Haven, CT: HRAF Press.

Blackstone, W. 1979 [1766]. *Commentaries on the Laws of England*. Vol. 2. Chicago: University of Chicago Press.

Bockman, Johanna, and Gil Eyal. 2002. "Eastern Europe as a Laboratory for Economic Knowledge: The Transnational Roots of Neoliberalism." *American Journal of Sociology* 108 (2): 310–352.

Bolkowiak, I. 1978. *Polityka finansowa w stosunku do gospodarki nieuspolecznionej I ludnosci w okresie wstepnego uprzemyslowienia w Polsce*. Warsaw: Panstwowe Wydawnictwo.

Bożyk, Paweł. 1990. "Niech ruszy z bezruchu: bronie Balcerowicza." *Polityka* 32 (1736): 4.

———. 1989. "Cudu nie będzie." *Polityka* 50 (1702): 5.

Brus, Wlodzimierz. 1988. "Utopianism and Realism in the Evolution of the Soviet Economic System." *Soviet Studies* 40 (3): 434–443.

———. 1961. *Ogólne problemy funcjonowania gospodarki socjalistycznej*. Warsaw: Panstwowe Wydawnictwo Naukowe.

Buchowski, Michal. 2003. "Redefining Social Relations through Work in a Rural Community in Poland." *Max Planck Institute for Social Anthropology Working Papers*. Working Paper no. 58.

Burawoy, Michael, and Janos Lukacs. 1992. *The Radiant Past: Ideology and Reality in Hungary's Road to Capitalism*. Chicago: University of Chicago Press.

Carruthers, Bruce, and Laura Ariovich. 2004. "Sociology of Property Rights." *Annual Review of Sociology* 30: 23–46.

Cook, Walter W. 1919. "Hohfeld's Contributions to the Science of Law." *The Yale Law Journal* 28 (8): 721–738.

Daniel, Krystyna. 1994. "Private Farm Ownership in a Changing Poland: Myth and Reality." In *A Fourth Way?: Privatization, Property and Emergence of New Market Economies,* edited by Gregory Alexander and Grazyna Skąpska, 138–150. New York: Routledge.

David, Paul, A. 1994. "Why Are Institutions the 'Carriers of History': Path Dependence and the Evolution of Conventions, Organizations and Institutions." *Structural Change and Economic Dynamics* 5 (2): 205–220.

Demsetz, Harold. 1974. "Toward a Theory of Property Rights," in *The Economics of Property Rights*, edited by E. G. Furubotn and S. Pejovich. Cambridge, MA: Ballinger Publishing.

di Palma, Giuseppe. 1991. "Legitimation from the Top to Civil Society: Politico-Cultural Change in Eastern Europe." *World Politics* 44 (1): 49–80.

Domanski, Henryk. 1990. "Dynamics of Labor Market Segmentation in Poland, 1982–1987." *Social Forces* 69 (2): 423–438.

Dubiński, Krzysztof. 1990. *Magdalenka: Transakcja epoki*. Warsaw: Sylwa.

Dziewanowski, M. K. 1977. *Poland in the Twentieth Century*. New York: Columbia University Press.

Evans, Peter, Dietrich Reuschemeyer, and Theda Skocpol, eds. 1985. *Bringing the State Back In*. Cambridge, UK: Cambridge University Press.

Furubotn, Eirik G., and Svetozar Pejovich. 1972. "Property Rights and Economic Theory: A Survey of Recent Literature." *Journal of Economic Literature* 10 (4): 1137–1162.

Gomulka, Stanislaw, and Jacek Rostowski. 1984. "The Reformed Polish Economic System, 1982–1983." *Soviet Studies* 36 (3): 386–405.

Gorlach, Krzysztof. 1999. "Presenting 'New Face': Polish Peasants' Protests in the Era of Post-Communism." Paper delivered at the Working Group 1: Social Movements in Rural Areas: Sources, Rationalities and Identities in the Process of Change. XVIII Congress of the European Society for Rural Sociology, August 24–28, Lund, Sweden.

———. 1989. "On Repressive Tolerance: State and Peasant Farm in Poland." *Sociologia Ruralis* 29 (1): 23–33.

Gramsci, Antonio. 2011 [1992]. *Prison Notebooks*. New York: Columbia University Press.

Gross, Jan T. 1994. "Poland After the Revolution: The Obfuscated Autonomy of Politics." In *Transition to Capitalism? The Communist Legacy in Eastern Europe*, edited by J. M. Kovács, 173–185. New Brunswick, NJ: Transaction Publishers.

GUS (Główny Urząd Statystyczny). 1979a. *Rocznik Statystyczny*. Warsaw: Główny Urząd Statystyczny.

———. 1979b. *Rocznik statystyczny rolnictwa i gospodarki zywnosciowej*. Warsaw: Główny Urząd Statystyczny.

———. 1978. *Rocznik statystyczny rolnictwa i gospodarki zywnosciowej*. Warsaw: Główny Urząd Statystyczny.

———. 1955. *Rocznik Statystyczny*. Warsaw: Główny Urząd Statystyczny.

Hare, P. G. 1981. *Allocation Rules for Publicly Provided Goods: Aggregation of Planning Information*. London: Economic and Social Research Council (ESRC).

Hare, P. G., and P. T. Wanless. 1981. "Polish and Hungarian Economic Reforms: A Comparison." *Soviet Studies* 23 (4): 491–517.

Horwitz, M. J. 1977. *The Transformation of American Law 1780–1860*. Cambridge, MA: Harvard University Press.

Jarosz, Dariusz. 1998. *Polityka wladz komunistycznych w Polsce w latach 1948–1956 a chlopi*. Warsaw: Wydawnictwo Dyg.

Kalinowski, H. 1978. "Wpływ systemu zarządzania na kontrolę gospodarczą." *Problemy Organizacji* (3): 102–114.

Katznelson, I. 2005 [1996]. *Krzywe Kolo Liberalizmu. Listy do Adama Michnika*. Wroclaw: Wydawnictwo Naukowe Dolnoslaskiej Szkoly Wyzszej Edukacji.

Kolankiewicz, George, and Paul Lewis. 1988. *Poland: Politics, Economics and Society*. London: Pinter Publishers.

Kolankiewicz, George. 1981. "Renewal, Reform or Retreat: The Polish Communist Party after the Extraordinary Ninth Congress." *The World Today* 37 (10) (October): 369–75.

Korbonski, Andrzej. 1989. "The Politics of Economic Reforms in Eastern Europe: The Last Thirty Years." *Soviet Studies* 41 (1): 1–19.

———. 1965. *Politics of Socialist Agriculture in Poland*. New York: Columbia University Press.

Kornai, Janos. 1992. "The Post-socialist Transition and the State: Reflections in the Light of Hungarian Fiscal Problems." *American Economic Review* 82 (2): 1–22.

———. 1990. *The Road to a Free Market Economy*. New York: Norton.

———. 1989. "Some Lessons of the Hungarian Experience for the Chinese Reformers." In *Market Reforms in Socialist Societies. Comparing China and Hungary*, edited by P. Van Ness, 75–106. Boulder, CO: Lynne Rienner Publishers.

———. 1979. "Resource-Constrained versus Demand-Constrained Systems." *Econometrica* 47: 801–819.

Kowalik, Tadeusz. 2009. *www.PolskaTransformacja.pl*. Warsaw: Muza SA.

Lange, Oscar. 1936–1937. "On the Economic Theory of Socialism." *Review of Economic Studies* 4 (1–2): 53–71, 123–124.

Lonc, T. 1992. "Social and Economic Adjustment and Policies in a Period of Crisis and Emergence from It: The Experience of Poland in the 1980s." In *Just a Sack of Potatoes? Crisis Experience in European Societies. Past and Present*, edited by A. Hakkinen, 220–235. Helsinki: SHS.

Magyar, Balint. 1984. "Peasantry and Agrarian Policy in Poland, 1944–1982." Manuscript.

Michnik, Adam. 1989. "Zwiazek zawodowy juz nie wystarcza," *Gazeta Wyborcza*, 108: 1.

Migdal, Joel. 1988. *Strong Societies and Weak States*. Princeton, NJ: Princeton University Press.
Montias, John M. 1962. *Central Planning in Poland*. New Haven, CT: Yale University Press.
Mosley, Phillip E. 1958. "The Collectivization of Agriculture in Soviet Strategy." In *The Collectivization of Agriculture in Eastern Europe*, edited by I. T. Sanders and E. E. Kraehe, 49–66. Lexington: University Press of Kentucky.
Nagengast, Carole. 1991. *Reluctant Socialists, Rural Entrepreneurs: Class, Culture, and the Polish State*. Boulder, CO: Westview.
North, Douglass. Winter 1991. "Institutions." *Journal of Economic Perspectives* 5: 97–112.
———. 1990. *Institutions, Institutional Change and Economic Performance*. Cambridge: Cambridge University Press.
Piotrowski, Klemens. 1980. "Direct and Indirect Instruments of System of Management of the Polish Economy in the 1970s." *Soviet Studies* 32 (4): 500–514.
Plowiec, Urszula. 1988. *Polityka Gospodarcza USA Wobec Krajow Socjalistycznych*. Warsaw: Ksiazka i Wiedza.
Podemski, Krzysztof, ed. 2011. *Spoleczenstwa Europy Srodkowo-Wschodniej: Projekt Eurequal*. Poznan: Wydawnictwo Naukowe UAM.
Polonsky, Antony, and Boleslaw Druker. 1980. *The Beginnings of Communist Rule in Poland*. London: Routledge & Kegan Paul.
Poznanski, Kazimierz. 1993. "Restructuring of Property Rights in Poland: A Study in Evolutionary Politics." *East European Politics and Societies* 7 (3): 395–421.
Przeworski, Adam. 1993. "Economic Reforms, Public Opinion and Political Institutions: Poland in the Eastern European Perspective." In *Economic Reforms in New Democracies: A Social-Democratic Approach*, edited by L. C. B. Pereira, J. M. Maravall, and A. Przeworski, 132–192. Cambridge, UK: Cambridge University Press.
———. 1991. *Democracy and the Market: Political and Economic Reforms in Eastern Europe and Latin America*. Cambridge, UK: Cambridge University Press.
Putterman, Luis. 1995. "The Role of Ownership and Property Rights in China's Economic Transition." *China Quarterly* 144: 1047–1064.
Rawski, Thomas. 1992. "Ideas About Studying China's Rural Economy: A Comment on the Commentaries." *Republican China* 17 (1): 146–159.
Reeves, A. 1986. *Property*. Atlantic Highlands, NJ: Humanities.
Rona-Tas, Akos. 1997. *The Great Surprise of the Small Transformation: The Demise of Communism and the Rise of the Private Sector in Hungary*. Ann Arbor: University of Michigan Press.
Rychard, Andrzej. 1993. "Limits to the Economic Changes in the Post-Communist Poland: Sociological Analysis." In *Reforms, Adaptation, and Breakthrough. The Sources of and Limits to Institutional Changes in Poland*, edited by Andrzej Rychard, 54–76. Warsaw: IFiS Publishers.
———. 1991. "Politics and Society after the Breakthrough: The Source and Threats to Political Legitimacy in Post-Communist Poland." In *Democratization in Poland*, edited by G. Sanford, 246–263. London: Macmillan.
Rzadowe Centrum Legislacji. 1983. *Dziennik Ustaw*, no. 39, section 175, July 22.
———. 1964. *Dziennik Ustaw*, no. 16, section 93, April 23.
Sabel, Charles F., and David Stark. 1982. "Planning, Politics, and Shop-Floor Power: Hidden Forms of Bargaining in Soviet-Imposed State-Socialist Societies." *Politics and Society* 11: 439–475.
Sokolovsky, Joan. 1990. *Peasants and Power: State Autonomy and the Collectivization of Agriculture in Eastern Europe*. Boulder, CO: Westview.
Staniszkis, Jadwiga. 1991. *The Dynamics of the Breakthrough in Eastern Europe*. Berkeley: University of California Press.
———. 1991. "Political Capitalism in Poland." *East European Politics and Societies* 5: 127–141.
———. 1984. *Poland's Self-Limiting Revolution*. Princeton, NJ: Princeton University Press.
Stark, David. 1996. "Recombinant Property in East European Capitalism." *American Journal of Sociology* 101 (4): 993–1027.

Swain, Nigel. 2000. "The Rural Transition in Post-Socialist Central Europe and the Balkans." *Max Planck Institute for Social Anthropology Working Papers* 9.

Szelenyi, Ivan, and George Konrad. 1979. *The Intellectuals on the Road to Class Power*. New York: Harcourt Brace Jovanovich.

Szemberg, Anna. 1993. "Rural Population: Changing Pattern." *Polish News Bulletin*, August 27, 2–6.

Szurek, Jean-Charles. 1987. "Family Farms in Polish Agricultural Policy: 1945–1985." *East European Politics and Societies* 1: 225–254.

Walder, Andrew. 1992. "Corporate Organization and Local State Property Rights: The Chinese Alternative to Privatization." Paper presented at the conference "The Political Economy of Privatization and Public Enterprise in Eastern Europe, Asia and Latin America." Brown University, April.

Walicki, Andrzej. 1988. "Liberalism in Poland." *Critical Review* 2 (1): 8–36.

Wanless, P. T. 1980. "Economic Reform in Poland 1973–1979." *Soviet Studies* 32 (1): 28–57.

Wesolowski, Wlodzimierz. 1991. "Transition to Democracy: The Role of Social and Political Pluralism." *Sisyphus Sociological Studies* 7: 79–94.

Wolf, Thomas A. 1991. "The Lessons of Limited Market-Oriented Reform." *Journal of Economic Perspectives* 5 (4): 46–57.

Wozniak, Zbigniew. 2009. "Poklosie Okraglego Stolu. Przeszlosc dla Przyszlosci." *Ruch Prawniczy, Ekonomiczny i Socjologiczny* 2: 349–379.

Zielinski, Janusz. 1973. *Economic Reforms in Polish Industry*. London: Oxford University Press.

Zinner, Paul E. 1956. *National Communism and Popular Revolt in Eastern Europe: A Selection of Documents on Events in Poland and Hungary, February–November, 1956*. New York: Columbia University Press.

Chapter Three

Private Agricultural Property Owners in the "Valley" of Post-Socialist Transition

The previous chapter dealt with the post-socialist reform program's relationship to past reform efforts and the impact of this past on the transition trajectory. Challenging the notion of a "revolution," I proposed that the post-socialist reformers' design was not of a revolutionary character, but was more of a "refolution"—a linear, progressive pattern of policy adjustments with the 1980 systemic rupture. Furthermore, I argued that, even unsuccessful, these policies had an influence on the nature of post-socialist changes. However, an analysis of the post-socialist transition trajectory cannot be reduced to the reformers' programs from above. This chapter focuses on the other component in the dynamics of the post-socialist transition—the changes "on the ground." It examines the behavior of the most critical social agent, the Polish peasants, as it interplays with the reformers' intentions to chart the direction of the post-socialist transition.

Theorists and reform strategists of the post-socialist transition have underlined the problem of introducing capitalist institutions without a bourgeoisie (Staniszkis 1991; Ekiert 1990; Lewandowski and Szomburg 1990). In the absence of such historical subjects invested in these changes, the East European transition was to be guided by theoretical rather than real interests. In this view, which takes the patterns of the capitalist transition in the West as a point of reference for the East European transition, Polish agriculture appeared to be in a particularly advantageous position. The unique historical development of Polish agriculture under state socialism left approximately 80 percent of agricultural land in private hands at the time of the inauguration of the post-socialist reforms.[1] The neoliberal post-socialist reform program seemed to be in harmony with the peasants' continuous struggle against administrative control and the systematic abrogation of their property rights under state socialism. The agricultural sector was therefore characterized by the existence of historical subjects with potentially real interests in the objectives of the transition at the *onset* of the stabilization phase of the reform. Hence, the Polish transition was to be fueled from below, through the process of the *embourgeoisment of the peasantry.*

While the rest of the economy faced the daunting project of fundamental restructuring, these historical subjects were expected to move into a capitalist type of production once prompted to do so by reform-induced incentives. Neoliberal reform strategists viewed the removal of state regulation as synonymous with the protection of private ownership rights and the operation of market regulation. With the full liberalization of prices and trade, individual agricultural producers were expected to find it in their rational self-interest to increase efficiency and volume and to commodify production. By liberalizing foreign trade, reform strategists attempted to restore the peasants' ownership right to unrestricted access to production resources. Furthermore, by liberalizing foreign trade, they expected to introduce competition to the state-owned and pseudo-cooperative monopolistic agricultural outlets surrounding individual agricultural production, both at the input and output levels. Reformers also foresaw an increase in economic rationality on the microlevel to be concomitant with a *rationalization of private landholdings* and the progressive *transformation of the ownership structure*. By shifting to capital-intensive farming methods, they projected that successful peasants would consolidate and expand their landholdings, thus reversing the long trend of the fragmentation of private land under state socialism.[2] In addition, approximately 20 percent of all agricultural land owned by state farms was envisioned to be absorbed by these prosperous peasants. Consistent with their programmatic proclamations of the economic and ideological superiority of private property, reformers favored the physical breakup and auctioning of the state farm productive units, and the distribution of land to private local peasants.

The post-socialist reformers' reliance on peasants as a social base was not only limited to their economic behavior. It also applied to their social ethos, thought to permeate throughout society. The reformers posited the distinct peasant ethos as a legitimizing force in the transition, arguing that peasants would help chart the social agenda for the transition and accept its unavoidable hardships. They referred to the peasant "ethos of labor" as derivative of their direct contact with nature. As Staniszkis (1991: 133) put it, reformers drew on peasants' "tenacity, patience, and resistance to setbacks" and saw their "pragmatism" as essential to the success of the reforms.

While the post-socialist strategists counted on reforms to spearhead the embourgeoisment of peasantry, some scholars posited that a rural bourgeoisie had already emerged under late state socialism. In her work, C. Nagengast (1990, 1991) argued that state socialist agricultural policies precipitated the gradual capitalization of farming and marketing and thus had led to the economic polarization of peasantry. While the agrarian policies, which aimed to combat inherent food shortages in late state socialism, gave rise to internal economic fragmentation of the previously homogenous Polish peasantry, the evolution of ideological and cultural traits in the countryside provided the legitimation bases for economic polarization.[3] Szelenyi advanced a similar thesis regarding the nascent rural bourgeoisie in the context of late Hungarian state socialism (Szelenyi 1988). However, through his notion of "interrupted embourgeoisment," Szelenyi accorded greater importance in the rise of agricultural capitalism to cultural traits. He argued that, given the market-oriented agricultural policies of the late socialism, only heirs of pre-socialist entrepreneurs, via their cultural capital, took advantage of those policies' incentives. Hence, both Nagengast and Szelenyi presupposed the existence of *actual* and *real* interests as opposed to potential ones. Although the interests of the rural bourgeois were formed under socialism, they were expected to carry over into the post-socialist transition and to be congruent with the objectives of the post-socialist reforms.

Yet the Polish post-socialist reality had been far from the expectations of reformers and from the scholarly accounts. Instead of driving production efficiency and economic growth, peasants "involuted" their production and retreated from markets. Rather than simply accepting the hardships of the transition or promoting economic individualism and independence of economic enterprises, peasants were among the first social groups to stage massive political opposition to the reform program. Within a few months of the inauguration of the Balcerowicz program, peasants in unison, stretching across their differential landholdings, called for its significant reformulation and elicited great support from the general Polish population. Once perceived to be allies of the post-socialist transition, peasants turned out to be its greatest foes.[4]

In this chapter, I will explain this unanticipated turnaround. I will do so by starting from a different conceptual and comparative base. Instead of superimposing ahistoric images of capitalism in the West, I will contextualize peasants' behavior by drawing comparisons to their immediate past. However, rather than directly extrapolating from their context-specific past behaviors to project their responses to the post-socialist reforms, I will demonstrate how the past was mediated in the context of the transition's realities.

To do so, I will draw on the work of Przeworski (1985). In his theory of transition, Przeworski problematizes Marx's thesis that workers' economic interest under capitalism inevitably leads them to embrace socialism. In his reformulation of Marx's theory, Przeworski upholds the Marxist premise that (a) workers' behavior is rational, (b) workers are interested in a continual improvement of their material conditions, and (c) socialism is superior to capitalism in its potential economic capacity. Przeworski challenges Marx's thesis because of its failure to acknowledge the historical alternatives available to workers, in particular the possibility of reforming capitalism to improve workers' welfare. He also rejects the thesis on the grounds that it leaves unexamined the economic deprivations connected to the transition to the socialist alternative, what he calls the "valley of transition." By advancing their economic interests along the capitalist path through a compromise with capitalists, workers could avoid "the transitional valley" to socialism and safeguard their material welfare. According to Przeworski, if suitable historical conditions exist to allow for such compromise, they could deter workers from pursuing the socialist path, despite their sustained perception of the economic superiority of socialism. Hence Przeworski's "valley of transition" focuses on the relative cost of transition as compared with historical alternatives, and points to the necessity of examining the *absolute* and *relative* deprivations experienced by economic agents as the essential components shaping their responses to reform measures.

Przeworski's work deals with the worker's valley of transition *from capitalism to socialism*. Yet I would claim that Polish peasants' transition *from socialism to capitalism* can be understood in similar terms. The peasants' responses to the post-socialist reform measures have to be filtered through the historical possibilities opened up to them under state socialism; the economic deprivation experienced under the post-socialist reform program must be compared to the costs and benefits of *previous* reforms. Since the 1980s, the compatibility between private property and economic egalitarianism had become a historical possibility *within* state socialism. Although General Wojciech Jaruzelski's socialist government crushed the Solidarity movement with the imposition of martial law in 1981 and reasserted its *political* rule, it also introduced fundamental economic changes in an effort to preserve the system. Food shortages in 1980 and 1981 forced the regime to recognize the demands of Rural Solidarity and to grant constitutional guarantees to agricultural *private ownership*. Unprecedented in the history of state socialism, the constitutional guarantee affirmed the *permanent* and *equal* standing of private property with other forms of ownership. The further deepening of the food crisis in the late 1980s pushed the socialist government to move beyond the legal recognition of private property rights and toward the realization of the socialist promise of economic equality for private property owners. In 1988, it institutionalized protectionist measures of minimal prices for agricultural outputs based on a parity of incomes between rural and urban sectors rather than on production costs. Through the combined effect of the partial liberalization of agricultural prices and guaranteed minimum agricultural prices based on income, Polish peasants received windfall profits; they were encouraged to succeed commercially while protected by the state from the risks of market failure.[5]

The responses of Polish peasants to the market transition must be seen through the prism of these historical possibilities opened up under state socialism. In addition to this historical comparison, peasants' experiences of the transition must also be related to the deprivations endured by economic agents from other agricultural subsectors in the post-socialist transition. Thus, given the post-socialist government pronouncements about the superiority of private property, peasants might have expected *differential bottoms* of the "transitional valley" for different ownership subsectors within agriculture; they might have assumed that the transition costs for private owners would be less than those experienced by the state and cooperative agricultural subsectors. But, in practice, peasants faced higher transition costs (Dzun 1993; Podemski 2011). Hence, the peasants' response to reforms must also be viewed in relation to the deprivations of these other economic agents. Once seen in these terms, the peasants' threshold of tolerance was much lower than the reformers had counted on.

From Neoliberal Myth to the Polish Reality: The Outcomes of Post-Socialist Agricultural Policy

The post-socialist stabilization package introduced in Poland had profound effects on the peasants' capacity to exercise private ownership. First, these reforms restricted their access to production resources through price destabilization and the selective allocation of financial credits. Second, they curtailed the peasants' ability to accrue profits from production by subjecting peasants to new institutional constraints and limitations. Finally, these reforms undermined the peasants' capacity to transfer their ownership and to move into new agricultural markets. In short, far from neoliberal expectations, the post-socialist agrarian policy ended up undercutting key components of the peasant economy.

Price Liberalization or Destabilization?

The rapid and comprehensive liberalization of prices under the Balcerowicz stabilization plan fundamentally reshaped the structure of agricultural prices and, subsequently, the profitability of agricultural production. Since retail food prices were commercialized under Jaruzelski's partial price reform, the post-socialist price liberalization had its main impact on the prices of agricultural inputs (previously administratively controlled and state subsidized). This liberalization raised them to astronomical heights. The hyperinflation that occurred immediately prior to the inauguration of the Balcerowicz plan raised the prices of agricultural inputs by an average of 800 percent. Yet in the immediate aftermath of the Balcerowicz stabilization plan, their prices soared by 1800 percent, quickly approaching the level of world prices.[6] On the other hand, retail food prices rose at the disproportionally lower pace of approximately 250 percent, hence lagging below world prices.[7] Although quite modest in comparison to the jump in input prices, this increase in food prices was at the high end of what was economically and politically tolerable for Polish society. In order to target the galloping hyperinflation engulfing the Polish economy, the Balcerowicz stabilization plan coupled price liberalization with the control of the population's spendable incomes. However much wages increased, they were drastically outpaced by the cost of food products. Far exceeding the predictions of Jeffrey Sachs, Balcerowicz's foreign advisor, some estimates indicated that in 1990 the purchasing capacity of the Polish population fell by 40 to 60 percent for both agricultural and nonagricultural goods.[8] In their combined effect, price liberalization and wage controls significantly constrained domestic food demand. Hence, agricultural producers faced sharp increases in agricultural resource costs *and* a reduction in the domestic demand for their outputs.

Given the past socialist experiences of chronic excess food demands and shortages on the supply side, this insufficient food demand triggered by the stabilization program was unprecedented and unanticipated. Its implications for agricultural production were not fully recognized by policy makers. The rise of agricultural input price levels, disproportionate with increases in the prices for agricultural products, resulted in a reversal of the price scissors formed under the partial price reform of Jaruzelski in the early 1980s.[9] By 1988, as an outcome of Jaruzelski's reform, a peasant's average income exceeded that of an urban worker by 17 percent. However, by the first quarter of 1990, Polish peasants' income dropped to 86 percent of workers' income.[10] With the inauguration of the Balcerowicz stabilization program, the dramatic reversal of the price structure was further amplified, with no clear correlation between the procurement price levels paid to the agricultural producers for their outputs and the retail food price increases.[11]

Peasants' Access to Production Resources

From the onset, the previous agrarian policies created a tension for the fiscal policies of the post-socialist agricultural program. To ensure the balanced development of the agricultural sector—a sector that had been chronically and grossly underinvested under state socialism—the plan pointed to the need for a substantial infusion of capital into agriculture as a whole and into its specific branches (most notably in the production of agricultural inputs and food processing).[12] Simultaneously, the stabilization plan's essential objective was a drastic reduction in budgetary expenditures as a way of lifting the post-socialist state from a deep fiscal crisis. As an outcome of these two contradictory objectives, the actual funds advanced for agriculture did not come close to the estimated needs.[13]

The allocation of credits for individual peasants increased by nearly 50 percent from 1989 to 1992. This appeared to be in line with the programmatic commitment to the development of individual agricultural production. However, it represented a negligible amount of the credits allocated to all economic units within this period.[14] In fact, the proportion of credits issued for the private agricultural sector showed substantial decline. Immediately prior to the inauguration of the post-socialist reform program, peasants received roughly 40 percent of all credits designated for private initiative. From 1990 to 1992, the average per year dropped to nearly 20 percent.[15]

In addition to the sheer scarcity of available financial resources, local-level implementation of credit allocation guidelines also constrained individual peasant access to financial capital. From 1991 to 1992, the majority of peasants in the studied community reported having no information about available funds for agriculture. Many complained about discrepancies in the information provided on national and local levels. Following media announcements about new financial assistance for the private agricultural sector, local financial institutions frequently denied the existence of such funds to inquiring and frustrated peasants. Overall, very few peasants reported obtaining any preferential credit for the purchase of agricultural inputs, such as fertilizers and pesticides. The small group that did get it received negligible amounts in comparison to their production needs. These peasants also alleged that timely notification and acceptance of the preferential credit petitions by the local cooperative bank were extended only to a select few who had preexisting personal connections within local and regional financial institutions, dating back to state socialism.

When the local cooperative bank received a limited amount of preferential credits designated for the community's individual agricultural production, the bank extended a total of 18 billion zloty of credits for the construction of two new food processing sites located within the borders of Rolnicy.[16] A meat processing and a dairy processing plant were started by former directors of regional state processing enterprises. Initially, peasants viewed these sites as potentially absorbing their output. Yet this perception was short lived. Both projects far exceeded the original projections of necessary capital investment. Short of funds, neither facility ever reached the completion stage. The servicing of the advanced investment loans on these sites led the local cooperative bank to declare bankruptcy in early 1994. Uncertain about the fate of their own deposits, peasants (as cooperative members of the bank) voiced a deep resentment of the bank's loan allocation policies—particularly its support for two outsiders with undeniable ties to the former ruling elites and its lack of funds for its own cooperative membership.

In addition, the requirements attached to these preferential credits artificially reduced the demand for them, despite the fact that production needs far exceeded the level of available financial assistance. In 1991, the bank received one billion zloty from the European Foundation for the Development of Polish Agriculture for the preferential credits for fertilizers and pesticides. Because the European Fund made those funds available in April, too late in the agricultural production cycle for the application of fertilizers and pesticides, and would not consider petitions retrospectively, only half of the funds available were utilized. The same thing occurred in 1992. Funds made available by the local cooperative bank were advanced by the European Commission (EC) for the purpose of modernizing Polish agriculture. A sophisticated business plan had to be submitted with the credit application. With no such skills of its own, and no services available to assist peasants to meet this requirement, the fund generated no demand within Rolnicy.

Hence, the tightening of the money supply consistent with the stabilization program produced a shift in credit preferences. Despite the government's programmatic commitment to the modernization and restructuring of agriculture, and specifically its preferred private subsector, few financial resources were extended to peasants for the renewal of their production cycle. And none were given for the expansion and modernization of their farms.[17] For the latter, peasants were expected to generate their own funds through increased productivity.

The absolute deprivation that peasants experienced in their access to financial resources in the post-socialistic period was compounded by their sense of relative deprivation vis-à-vis economic agents within agricultural sectors that the post-socialist agricultural plan claimed to eliminate.[18] Fearing temporary imbalances in the grain market, the government provided monopolistic procurement centers with preferential credits for the storing and drying of grain. The government justified such allocation as indirect support for individual producers by reducing uncertainty in demand for their crops. For these peasants, there was a rapidly growing and inescapable realization that, contrary to the government promises, they carried the disproportionally high costs of the transition.

In addition to limited access to credit, peasants also experienced restricted access to agricultural machinery. Defying conventional economic measures, the agricultural private subsector emerged from state socialism as curiously both under- and overcapitalized (Brooks 1991). Unable to successfully implement a collectivization drive, the successive Polish socialist regimes adopted divergent measures aimed at denying peasants the right to own agricultural implements. A vast network of agricultural circles was designed to provide machinery services for the private agricultural sector. The initial prohibition of private ownership of agricultural machinery was partially liberalized in the mid-1970s, allowing peasants to acquire used machines from state and cooperative agricultural enterprises. The peasants' strong drive to remove themselves from a dependence on the ever-capricious agricultural circles generated increasing mechanization. Hence, secondhand machines designed and produced for agricultural economies of scale steadily found their way to the individual subsector with its highly fragmented landowning structure.[19] This progressive mechanization of the private subsector was not only grossly unsuitable for relatively small plots, but it was also of progressively outdated stock.

The liberalization of trade in the Balcerowicz stabilization program was designed to rationalize and renew the mechanization of agriculture. This was to be achieved by opening up access to foreign markets with their assortment of agricultural implements suitable for small-scale agricultural production and by introducing price competition to a highly concentrated, monopolistic domestic agricultural industry. In Rolnicy, the agricultural machinery dealer expanded in a way that seemed to attest to the dynamic mechanization of Polish agriculture sparked by the reforms. Opened in the late 1980s, this one-man agricultural machinery parts exchange shop grew in the first two years of the post-socialist reforms. It became a modern company of an impressive size in terms of employment and sale revenues. Its market stretched to several *voivodships* in western-central Poland. The owner's continually expanding lot displayed countless new tractors and other domestic and imported machinery that gave the impression of a thriving machinery dealership.

Yet only on rare occasions was the new machinery sought after. His clients were primarily from state farms and agricultural cooperatives and were mainly interested in the replacement or repair of *parts* for their exiting equipment. Few of the peasants I interviewed had purchased any new machines during the three years of the post-socialist transition. Nor did they foresee an ability to do so in the near future. The new structure of agricultural prices created by the reforms did not allow them to put aside any funds for the amortization of their existing agricultural equipment. A few young peasants in the *gmina* who had the misfortune of pressing mechanization needs at the onset of the post-socialist reforms and who had tried to increase their production efficiency by investing in higher-quality imported machinery were rapidly threatened with the very survival of their farms due to the mounting interest on their loans.

Just as access to new agricultural machinery failed to materialize, peasants' ability to hire machinery services narrowed in the wake of the reform. The liberalization of prices for energy and fuel radically raised the fees for machinery services charged by agricultural circles. Although fees for machinery services became a significant portion of the overall cost of private agricultural production in the 1980s, the new fees became prohibitive for many peasants. Unable to meet the new machinery service fees of the agricultural circles, several of these peasants reverted to outdated and barely operative equipment.[20] Two such families proudly reported assembling an operational grain combine out of three dilapidated combines purchased from a liquidated state farm for a sum equivalent to the fee charged by an agricultural circle for grain harvesting. After assembling it, the peasants-turned-mechanics jointly harvested their individual crops and serviced a few of their neighbors.[21]

Hence, in this new market-oriented economic environment, the acquisition of agricultural machinery was highly constrained due to the high cost of these resources relative to the peasants' income. This resulted in the steady decapitalization and aging of the machinery park. The alternative way of gaining access to agricultural machinery through the machinery services of agricultural circles became limited too, due to increased fees for those services as well as a decline in their quality.

Peasants Face Monopsonistic Buyers

The constant shortage in the domestic food supply and the socialist legacy of the drastic underdevelopment of industry for agricultural purposes led post-socialist reformers to identify the *supply* of agricultural inputs as potentially the most uncertain point in the transition period's food production and distribution system. Yet, as it turned out, the *disposal* of agricultural outputs became the most critical and uncertain point in the transition of the agricultural system. While uncertainty in the disposal of agricultural output was caused *indirectly* by the decline in consumer purchasing capacity and shifting preferences (for foreign food products), it stemmed *directly* from the procurement centers' strategy of adjustment to the reform programs.

At the outset of the post-socialist reforms, the procurement of crop and animal commodity production was handled almost exclusively by the state-controlled agricultural trade cooperatives.[22] Policy makers' commitment to a comprehensive reduction and removal of subsidies subjected procurement cooperatives and state-owned agricultural processing enterprises to hard budget constraints almost overnight.[23] To adjust, procurement centers cut their operations to the level of sales and reduced their operation.[24] Both strategies directly affected their economic relations with individual agricultural producers.

Shortly after the introduction of the post-socialist reforms, peasants reported experiencing frequent difficulties in selling their output.[25] Procurement centers handled agricultural output purchases on a first-come-first-serve basis—without any prior notice to their agricultural suppliers regarding the size or type of procurement for a specific day. By the first post-socialist harvest, peasants were standing in line for several hours or even days with containers full of grain, only to be told that the procurement was finished for an undetermined period. Their ability to gather accurate and updated information about open sites of agricultural procurements was constrained by several factors: the lack of advance information from procurement centers; the shortage of phones in the countryside, especially in peasants' households; the insufficient network of roads; and the increased cost of gasoline and thus transportation. In several instances, peasants reported that, by the time they located an open procurement center and reached it, they were turned away again. Furthermore, because working with the larger agricultural supplier was more cost effective, agricultural cooperatives and state farms had easier access to the agricultural output market.[26]

The procurement centers reverted to various measures to lower the cost of their own operations and to transfer some of these costs to agricultural producers. Thus, the peasants I interviewed often pointed out that, facing the prohibitive cost of commercial credits, procurement centers dealt with their cash flow problems by delaying payments to their suppliers for undetermined periods of time—often by three months or more. Uncertainty in the payment level and schedule even extended to crops (for example, rapeseed) that had been under delivery contracts. These contracts, which specified various elements of the transaction including the size, price, and quality of the procurement, were unilaterally modified in the post-socialist period. Hence, the centers were obliged to absorb only specified amounts of output, thus leaving the issue of price and quality open to current market fluctuations. In addition to postponing payments for grain and animal deliveries, the centers began to charge individual agricultural producers for the storage of the grains procured from them.

The procurement centers' adjustment strategy was also manifest in how they determined the quality of agricultural output. The peasants I interviewed claimed that the procurement centers artificially raised quality standards in order to pay lower prices for their output. Moreover, they questioned the validity and accuracy of the center-administered tests that determined output prices. Unlike the agricultural cooperatives or state farms, peasants did not possess the equipment to verify the test results independently.[27] A good example of this can be seen in milk classification practices. Given that milk production provided the only steady source of yearly income for over 1 million agricultural households, the milk classification practiced by the procuring and processing centers was one of the most contested issues. Although the Balcerowicz plan's removal of milk subsidies implied low procurement prices in relation to agricultural input prices and retail prices for milk, peasants and the procurement centers battled over the validity of milk testing and classification practices.

From the date of their creation in state socialism, the peasantry viewed the milk procurement centers with a deep suspicion—as local organizations integrated into the complex system of redistributive economy and designed to exercise state control over private agricultural owners. Peasants in their "game for survival" with the procurement centers oscillated between the strategies of passive resistance and what Gorlach (1999) and Wilkin (1988: 32) called "domestication of the communist system" involving a complex set of informal clientele relations.

The story of an older widow, who, for over twenty years, farmed with her son on ten hectares of land, illustrates the typical transaction relations between the individual milk suppliers and the procurement centers. As she emphasized to me, milk procurement centers exercised an unusual level of arbitrariness in their transactions with peasants. In contrast to swine or cattle procurement, there were no safeguards for her milk transactions. The former transactions were guided by weight scales and price-per-weight tables; their trade terms were therefore subject to easy verification. She dated her problems with the local milk procurement centers back to the early 1980s. In the 1980s procurement centers used fat content and milk cleanness criteria in milk classifications. If daily delivered milk was contaminated or not properly chilled, the peasant was to receive a warning. An uncorrected problem would lead to the temporary withdrawal of milk procurement from an individual peasant.

In one incident, the widow was notified by the procurement center at the end of the delivery period that her whole half-month milk supply was declassified to level C due to detected contaminants. As stated by the center's veterinarian, these were symptoms of an infection present in her milk cows. The widow contested the diagnosis itself and the subsequent milk declassification. She argued that, since she did her milking manually, the alleged infection symptoms would not escape her attention. She further objected to the center's failure to notify her immediately about the milk's impurities. In response, the procurement center offered to send a staff veterinarian to reevaluate the widow's milk cattle. When the center did not follow through and the veterinarian did not appear for a month, the widow requested in writing that her milk be reinstated at class A and that she be financially compensated for the disputed period. Her request prompted a veterinarian's visit the following day. The widow claimed that he threatened to declassify her milk supply for the whole month because the fumigation of the facilities housing the milk cattle was not updated. The widow charged back that she could not meet this requirement since the milk procurement centers and the agricultural circles no longer provided peasants with spraying equipment. Given her health condition, manual application was not an option either. Then, with calm defiance, the widow asserted that she would never again provide him or anyone else from the procurement center with the opportunity to inspect her farm. She withdrew her milk deliveries to the center all together and diverted the existing milk supply for her family's consumption, for neighborhood sale, and for a fodder supplement for her piglets. Within two years, she reduced her milk cattle herd by half, stopping at the subsistence level. Her retreat from market transactions and separation from the procurement institutions were representative of broader peasant responses, which, as Halamska (1991: 47) pointed out, indicated the "incomplete" character of modernization of Polish peasant farms, and, as Gorlach (1999, 2000) described, constituted peasant "strategies of separation and preservation" developed during the long contestation with the socialist regime.

Echoing the widow's assertions, local peasants complained about the system of bi-monthly *retroactive* notification about the quality of milk, claiming it was costly and unfair to the milk suppliers. Notification of milk contamination on the *last* day of the bi-monthly pay period led to a significant loss of income. The bi-monthly system of milk classification, long practiced within state socialism, had effectively led the peasants I studied to withdraw from milk cattle production. Local peasants' production responses to this unequal bargaining position were represented in a steady decline in the number of milk cattle in the Wielkopolska region and nationwide.[28]

Ironically, with the reforms, these contested classification practices were perpetuated. In the face of milk shortages, monopolistic procurement centers were unable to lower their own operation costs based on arbitrarily restricting procurement, as was the case with grain. Instead, the centers attempted to maintain their own profits by manipulating the milk classification system. All of the peasants I interviewed contested subjecting their milk supply to an increasingly complicated system of classification that was tied to different payment levels, while the procurement centers passed this supply to the retail distribution in a unified bottling system, under one price tag. Peasants also objected to the implementation of the classification procedures itself. Suspecting notoriously unfair practices with milk testing, many peasants used amateur verification methods. They reported submitting identical milk samples in two batches under two separate names, or resubmitting the same milk sample on separate days, only to have them classified by the centers into two distinct categories and levels of payment.[29]

All of these measures heightened the antagonistic transaction relations with the milk suppliers that dated back to the socialist period. Although one of the first legislative initiatives of the post-socialist government was to restructure the local cooperatives in the spirit of genuine cooperative ownership, peasants as formal collective co-owners of the milk procurement centers felt increasingly alienated by these local organizations. Peasants did not perceive the increased membership fees in exchange for guaranteed milk procurement as a way to enhance their cooperative ownership within the centers. Rather, they saw it as an abrogation of their individual ownership right to income—as a way to expropriate further their milk profits. Peasants, as private property owners and agricultural suppliers of the procurement centers, simply saw the replacement of large national monopsonies by local-level ones.

This resulted in the development of spontaneous private competition in specific agricultural markets. In the case of pork distribution, peasants began to bypass the monopsonistic centers altogether, slaughtering swine themselves and selling the meat directly to consumers on the open market. Although these practices began prior to the 1990 market reforms, they were impeded by a number of barriers that prevented this alternative distribution system from effectively challenging the monopsonistic control of the state procurement centers. More specifically, the previous system of selling meat on the street was supplanted by a more organized meat market. After obtaining special permits, peasants who were able to provide a substantial down payment received permanent stands in the open market in a nearby major urban center. Very often, these sales exceeded that of their domestic production, prompting them to purchase meat directly from other local individual peasants. However, due to tax disincentives and an awareness of the risks involved in a complete specialization in retail, these independent distributors maintained their primary agricultural production and treated this distribution as a sideline activity. This set limits on the potential scope of their sales operations. Their lack of investment capital and an underdeveloped transportation system also impeded this nascent distribution network from expanding into areas where market demand was relatively high, such as in the industrial mining region of Silesia in southwest Poland. In the end, these systemic restraints limited the development of individual distributors, leaving local procurement centers in monopsonistic control. The weak competition of the private sector was insufficient to instill market regulation of meat prices. The higher prices private meat distributors paid to producers in 1990 and 1991 eventually fell to match the lower price level dictated by procurement centers.

Just as the systemic constraints worked against the successful *expansion* of the spontaneously started network of private meat distribution, the *creation* of private food processing enterprises also faced multiple constraints. The experiences of one young peasant, Robert S., embody the difficulties of venturing into private agricultural processing. For several years, Robert ran a specialized poultry farm in Rolnicy. He seemed to symbolize the kind of entrepreneur that the post-socialist agricultural policy sought to build. He had high qualifications and true passion for his work. On his inherited two hectare farm, he produced annually sixty to seventy thousand poultry in the late 1980s. In the wake of post-socialist reforms, Robert S. was almost immediately squeezed to the breaking point by increasingly unfavorable prices and an uncertain demand for his poultry. As Robert S. recounted the reasons for closing his poultry production, he told me of his last negotiations with a director of the state poultry procurement and processing plant. The state poultry plant, built in the 1970s, had a production capacity of fifty thousand poultry a day, and served the whole Wielkopolska region. It had an extensive administrative network of two thousand employees. Its machinery, equipment, and freezers designed for handling large amounts of poultry input were not suitable for subdividing and reorganizing efforts in the context of the new economic environment. As the enterprise lowered its production by 60 to 70 percent, reflecting the decline in consumer demand and the collapse of specialized poultry farms, its costs of production increased dramatically per unit of output. Having no existing private competition in procuring poultry, the enterprise began reducing its costs by lowering the procurement poultry prices offered to suppliers. A week before the scheduled delivery of twenty thousand contracted poultry, Robert S. visited the plant's director to negotiate the procurement price. The director offered him 4,000 zloty, when the average nationwide price was 6,000 to 7,000 zloty per chicken. For three days Robert S. hesitated. Each day, these deliberations cost him an additional one million zloty in feed. On the fourth day, feeling outraged and defeated, he delivered a batch of twenty thousand chickens at the price the director originally offered. He closed his poultry production and threw himself feverishly into staging a challenge to the state poultry processing plant.

The small size of his farm and its specialized equipment did not enable Robert to exit into subsistence production. In his consideration of adjustment strategies available to him within the new economic environment, Robert realized that just reducing the size of chicken production was not feasible. Given the character of his specialized equipment, the profile of production was limited to either ducks or geese, for which the demand was even more limited than for chicken. Thus he decided to establish a midsized poultry slaughtering and processing plant.

At the time of my first contact with him in 1991, he had already invested over a year of his time and 500 million zloty in processing fees.[30] Robert's strongest and most unique asset was his extensive knowledge of the field he was about to enter. He also had partial access to input and output markets. He understood that the drastic decline in the aggregate demand for food was a forced one. Thus, he saw the potential for a vast market for cheaper products, given the rapidly impoverished population. He also understood the limited flexibility of the state processing plants to restructure themselves in the face of new economic requirements. Therefore, he aimed to bring competition to state poultry processing enterprises by developing new lines of production. He estimated that the production of chicken hamburgers and nuggets, out of chicken parts that were wasted under the processing system of state enterprises, would find high demand among the population with significantly reduced purchasing power. Those who could afford it would also have the option of higher-priced chicken filets. All products were to be handled in modern, vacuumed, and easily managed packaging, which was not offered by state processing enterprises.

As he developed his business plan, Robert opened a small fodder outlet for local poultry production. The outlet allowed him to stay afloat financially. Yet it also provided him with an opportunity to locate poultry producers and to identify the local potential for his upcoming plant. Through his contacts with the poultry producers, he determined that the output of local poultry production would be sufficient to meet his processing plant's capacity of two million chickens annually. Along with his vision of switching to more genetically improved chicken, he also planned to organize the existing fragmented poultry food chain into a horizontally integrated network of contract-bound fodder suppliers, chicken producers, medical and veterinary services, and a poultry processing plant. Producers of genetically improved chickens would be contractually obligated to rely on the more expensive, high-protein fodder supplied by designated outlets. Producers, in turn, would be guaranteed demand for their output by his processing plant. The elimination of the uncertainty inherent in transactions with state procurement plants would lead to an overall reduction of costs.

Robert's business plan called for the installation of Dutch machines. The imported equipment would be 50 percent more expensive than the domestic equivalent. But he estimated that its higher energy efficiency and reduced labor costs would amortize quickly the original higher expense. Robert focused on the need to bring costs per unit of production down in order to compete with the state enterprises.[31] In researching his alternatives, Robert established contacts with Dutch poultry production and processing enterprises. Together they identified a genetically improved chicken that required 20 percent less feed and a shorter production cycle. Along with the sophistication of his business plan were his contacts with foreign investors and creditors. Robert had secured funds for all the poultry processing and packaging machinery based on credit issued by the Dutch company. He had also secured access to the Dutch market for the first three years of his production output, contingent on obtaining governmental permits for the start-up and domestic credits to build housing for the processing equipment.

The Ministry of Agriculture in Warsaw repeatedly gave him words of encouragement, but no actual support. He was told that they could not furnish him with the necessary authorizations or refer him to the officials who could. Robert's case of being referred from one level of government to another without any tangible result reflected system-wide problems pointed out by Waclaw Wilczynski (1996). As Wilczynski asserted, proper infrastructure of regional government was essential for successful development of a market economy and exercise of ownership rights in Poland. Self-governing bodies at the regional and local level must be able to have administrative and fiscal power, so as not to be dependent on central distribution and allocation of finances. Yet, as Wilczynski indicated, citing M. Kulesz (1994), Poland was the only large European country to have virtually no regional government beyond the local level of *gmina*. Moreover, this layer had negligible financing capabilities and was effectively subordinated to central authorities.[32]

Hesitantly, Robert was sent to the central cooperative bank (BGZ) to obtain the financial backing for his foreign credit.[33] There he was told he could apply for funds under the World Bank program with a processing time of five months. The application required a very detailed business plan, but the bank provided applicants with no assistance.[34] Eventually, his application was denied without any detailed justification. In addition, due to an insufficient number of independent sanitary inspectors, the *voivodship* authority required that Robert obtain authorization for the location of his future processing plant from a qualified staff member at the state poultry processing plant—Robert's direct competitor. After three years of continual attempts at obtaining authorizations and permits to take foreign loans for specialized equipment and to get domestic loans for erecting buildings, Robert's construction site remained incomplete, halted in the early stages of laying the foundations. Two years later, as I visited the community, a "for sale" sign was displayed in front of the lot with unfinished construction.

The Involution of Production and the Evolution of Peasants' Political Resistance

In an attempt to free private property owners from the state, the post-socialist price and trade liberalization reforms subjected peasants to a new set of constraints—higher costs of production resources, uncertain demand for agricultural outputs, and heightened arbitrariness in their business transactions. Furthermore, in contrast to reformers' expectations that peasants would remain patient and tolerant of these hardships, peasants reacted quite strongly against these new constraints. Economically, they responded through an involution of production and a retreat from markets. Politically, they responded by waging protests that challenged the post-socialist reforms at their foundation.

Economic Adjustment: Involution of Production and the Closed-Cycle Production System

In the new post-socialist economic environment, peasants were not motivated to increase productivity, as the reformers would have it. Rather, they sought to reduce their production costs and to minimize their exposure to commercial transactions with procurement centers. These considerations led peasants to an overall involution of production and to a *closed-cycle production system*. That is, peasants increasingly relied on themselves to generate the production resources necessary for the renewal of their production cycles. All production lines became interdependent. Peasants selected field crops in order to use them as production input for animal husbandry, while the by-products of animal production (mainly manure) became the input for renewing crop production. With the exception of wheat, rapeseed, and sugar beets, for which they actively sought markets, peasants diverted almost all of their other field crops away from the market into animal husbandry.

In switching to closed-cycle production, peasants drastically limited their demand for chemical fertilizers, pesticides, and improved seed strains. Regardless of their land size holdings or past practices of input utilization, all my respondents reduced the use of fertilizers by 50 to 70 percent in 1990. They maintained this level through 1991 and 1992.[35] Some of them reported abandoning chemical fertilizers altogether on selected grains. Peasants reported an approximately 30 percent reduction in the application of pesticides and herbicides. Staying away from the markets of genetically improved grain seeds, peasants began to rely on neighborhood seed-exchanges to renew their crop production. Similarly, they seriously curtailed or eliminated purchases of mineral and high-protein feed supplements that had previously been considered indispensable to animal husbandry.

Despite the new emphasis on animal production, however, not all lines of animal husbandry were expanded. The rapid withdrawal of milk subsidies stipulated by the Balcerowicz reform package only accelerated a clear trend of decreasing milk cattle herds in the private agricultural subsector. Even those few peasants in the studied *gmina* who had successfully engaged in specialized milk cattle production for over twenty years had reduced their production to a self-sufficiency level.

Instead, all peasants in Rolnicy concentrated their efforts on starting or expanding their swine production. Its production cycle was five or six times shorter than that for cattle husbandry, and hence provided relatively frequent and steady incomes for peasants with limited financial reserves. The scale of the swine production expansion was dictated by production cost considerations. All the peasants I interviewed increased their production only within the capacity of existing facilities, steadfastly refraining from starting any new investments toward swine husbandry expansion. Sporadically, they spent a substantial amount of their own labor to adapt existing cattle production facilities to accommodate an enlarged swine stock.[36]

These cost-cutting measures and the shift to closed-cycle production had a ripple effect in the agricultural sector. The piglet market virtually collapsed as peasants started to rely on their own stock for reproduction rather than piglets purchased from specialized breeders. Also, the high cost of feed almost completely eradicated the market for partially grown swine that had flourished in the socialist period. In the post-socialist transition, peasants returned to the markets only when their swine were fully fattened. However, the market they returned to was persistently dominated by monopolistic procurement centers.

The logic of closed-cycle production not only implied a purposeful retreat from specific markets; it also affected areas where peasants actively sought markets. In 1990, the construction of a modern vegetable oil plant in the vicinity of the studied community prompted peasants to see real prospects for a significant and stable demand for rapeseed. Yet all the peasants I interviewed who had previously cultivated rapeseed planned to increase their rapeseed production only marginally, if at all. Adopting a closed-cycle production as an overall strategy of adjustment to the post-socialist reforms meant keeping the relative balance among lines of production, which had the effect of significantly restricting their abilities to positively respond to favorable market opportunities.

For the majority of peasants I interviewed who had a diversified agricultural production, adopting a strategy of closed-cycle production involved a shift in emphasis among existing lines of production. However, for those peasants who engaged in specialized agricultural production, an adaptation to the rapidly changed economic environment in 1990 proved to be far more difficult. One young peasant, who inherited his eighteen-hectare farm from his father six years prior to the introduction of the Balcerowicz economic program, had continued to specialize in sheep husbandry as originated by his father. Prior to 1990, whatever amount of wool and baby sheep (export commodities) he produced, he was able to sell at a satisfactory profit to any wool processing cooperative. Once the state subsidies to the local processing cooperatives ceased in 1990, they found the New Zealand wool cheaper and of better quality than domestically produced wool. Instantly, the young peasant shared the same fate of five other small sheep producers in the Rolnicy *gmina*. There was no demand for their product. He found himself lucky to sell his breeding sheep early in 1991. The rest of the herd was progressively slaughtered for meat.

After the liquidation of his sheep production, the peasant attempted to adapt a newly vacated building in order to expand his previously marginal swine production. However, the falling swine procurement prices of 1991 reoriented his efforts into a different direction. He subcontracted with a private, limited liability company to intensively fatten ducks. The company, which was established in the late socialist period, was a joint venture with French capital and produced the ducks for the American market. As stipulated by the agreement between the peasants and the duck company, the company provided the feeding machines free of charge. The costs of duck transport, special corn feed, vitamins, and electrical energy were to be covered by the subcontracting peasants.

The task was both labor and energy intensive. Force-feeding with the machinery required five hours daily. The facility required a steady temperature and thus called for human supervision around the clock. At its completion, the one-month process of fattening the first batch of ducks (from approximately 3.5 kilograms to approximately 5 to 6 kilograms of live weight) brought the peasant considerable profit.[37] However, with his subsequent two batches of ducks, he experienced rapidly decreasing profits. By the fourth batch, he incurred a loss of over two million zloty (the equivalent of a worker's one-month salary). Rapid increases in the cost of corn feed and the high rate of losses in ducks triggered by an overly intensive scheduling of weight gain imposed by the duck company outran his net income.

He attributed this fiasco to an unfavorable price structure in agriculture—with costs of production fast outpacing the output prices. However, he also blamed what he perceived as the clearly dishonest practices of the company toward the producers. He was not paid on the basis of the birds' net live weight gain. Rather, his payments were calculated in reference to the weight of the slaughtered, defeathered, and internally cleaned ducks with the provision of a constant 12 percent for the differential between slaughter and live weight. The peasant found this calculation formula to be very conservative and unfair to the producers; its application was arbitrary and lacked verification by the contracting producers. He acknowledged that his financial losses resulting from the four-month contract with the firm were very humiliating. He was somewhat consoled by the realization that several other peasants in the village had similar experiences with the firm and came out with even more significant losses. Initially, all of them were ashamed and attempted to conceal their failed endeavors and high-cost transactions associated with pursuing new lines of production. However, their initial embarrassment quickly gave way to a collective view of the emerging private firms, representing formally the new post-socialist era, yet started in the previous regime, as unscrupulous, dishonest organizations. They saw these firms as oriented toward quick profits and as using the regulatory and legal infrastructure to escape accountability for their actions. The peasants had no procedural guidelines as to whether and how to pursue their grievances of unfair contractual arrangements and compensations. The unfavorable experiences with the limited liability joint venture company led them to refocus on the closed-circle production with minimum market involvement.

For those peasants who specialized in swine production under state socialism, the simultaneous high cost of quality fodder and the fall in procurement prices for swine led to the reduction of output. Retreating to the closed-cycle production implied radically scaling back animal production, proportional to the arable land size of their crop output. Thus, eight peasants I interviewed had reduced their output to merely 10 percent of their production level in the mid-1980s. This involution of production was further compounded by a forced reduction in land.[38]

For peasants previously involved in other lines of specialized production, the very process of switching to closed-cycle production was equally riddled with difficulties and instabilities. Those who had established multiyear contracts with the state trading agency to develop genetically improved seed, based on specialized equipment and seasonal employment of hired labor, faced few alternatives once their production contracts were eliminated due to drastic cuts in state funds. The specialized profile of their farms left these peasants without ownership of even the most rudimentary machinery or utility buildings necessary for multiculture crop and animal production. Thus, previously specialized and commercially oriented peasants who attempted the shift to a closed-cycle production had to generate substantial funds. Fearful of commercial loans, peasants in the studied community pursued two venues—they sold portions of their land and they searched for supplemental employment outside of agricultural production. While state socialism had created a unique stratum of peasant-workers, drawn primarily from the ranks of small agricultural landowners (1/2 to 2 hectares), the post-socialist environment pushed *middle*-size agricultural owners (7 to 15 hectares) with specialized, commodified production profiles into this stratum.[39]

Although the Balcerowicz program granted a formal, unprecedented liberalization of land transactions, the land sales within Rolnicy were limited in number and scope for the first three years of the transition. The middle-sized agricultural producers were the most active group in land sales, which were the last way to generate cash for the renewal of the production cycle and thus the survival of the farm. These survival strategies were reflected in local statistics. In the studied area, the first four years of transition were marked by a decline in the number of agricultural farms within the range of seven to ten hectares (from 110 to 99). Parallel to the decrease in the number of farms was a reduction in land area within this category, from 888 hectares to 800. Simultaneously, smaller farms—those within the range of five to seven hectares—grew both in number (from forty to fifty-three) and in share of land under this category (from 266 to 328 hectares).[40] Hence, the processes observed within the studied community were reflected in the national-level statistics. They thus point to a trend of the continued fragmentation of the private landholding structure rather than its rationalization as foreseen by reformers.[41]

In short, the reform initiatives led to an overall involution of agricultural production. The shift to a closed-cycle production system implied an extensive type of production that resulted in the lowering of production yields and the withdrawal from market exchanges.[42] All these measures implied a rapid 25 percent decline in peasants' income as compared to the year of initiation of the reforms, 1990, and a 50 percent reduction compared with the 1985 income level under socialism (Gorlach 1999; Forys 2008). For already specialized peasants, this shift forced them to reduce their farm sizes and to take on second jobs.

The Evolution of Peasants' Political Resistance to Reforms

In addition to these economic responses, peasants also engaged in collective protest against the post-socialist agrarian policy. In order to preserve the integrity of their plan (that is, the comprehensive introduction of the market as an exclusive regulator of economic transactions), the post-socialist government insisted on withholding any direct state support for individual agricultural producers and the agricultural sector as a whole (Balcerowicz 1992: 92, 1995: 423). Yet, peasants perceived the subsequent results of the reform not as an outcome of the invisible hand of the market, but rather as antipeasant measures deliberately inflicted on them by the government or as the government reneging on its obligation of protecting peasants from market harms. Those perceptions proved to be potent in mobilizing peasants against the terms of state-imposed economic transactions.[43] The network of *preexisting* peasant political organizations,[44] formed in the 1980s to challenge state socialism, facilitated their efforts to thrust economic negotiations into the political arena (Friszke 1990). Those efforts coincided with the political opposition to the Balcerowicz program articulated in the presidential campaign of 1990.[45] In effect, the post-socialist state was pushed away from its long-term goals and toward damage control and the pursuit of short-term political and economic stability.[46]

The peasants' collective action underwent three stages within the first three years of the transition. In the first phase, the contestation was regional, centered on specific economic transactions and led to corporate concessions. In early 1992, with the rise of the Self-Defense (Samoobrona), a splinter group of Rural Solidarity, the collective resistance reached a national level and became highly politicized (Kubik and Ekiert 1999; Forys 2008).[47] No longer focused on the terms of specific transactions, their contestation challenged the overall market logic of the economic transactions imposed on them. In the third stage, peasants successfully reformulated their class-based economic demands into national and societal grievances against the post-socialist state and its program.

An early incident in a local procurement center near Warsaw in June 1990 precipitated a wave of collective peasant actions. The incident was started by a group of peasants who blocked an international highway near the Polish capital to protest the policies and practices of a local procurement center and to demand the government's attention to the grievances, an action without precedent since World War II (Gorlach 1995). Instead of turning a sympathetic ear, the Solidarity-based post-socialist government forcefully removed the protesting peasants from the highway. The government action, in turn, prompted authorities of Rural Solidarity to support the protestors, thus escalating the incident into the first clash between Solidarity-led protestors and the first post-socialist government regime formed out of the members of the

Solidarity movement after the 1989 elections. The incident signified a critical rupture—putting the Solidarity-based government and the Solidarity-based peasant movement at odds in the first year of the reform implementation. This renewed the sense of an "us versus them" divide, bringing with it the damaging perception of a continuity between the present regime's practices and ones from the previous era. Thus, the incident set the government on a defensive path of damage control during the subsequent peasant protests, forcing it to depart from the neoliberal tenets of its reform program, such as no governmental economic intervention, and leading it to a pattern of short-term government measures in response to subsequent peasant collective actions, producing no consistent social policy.

Further episodes of peasant collective protests took place in the fall of 1990. The acute uncertainty experienced by the private agricultural subsector over the demand for their grain harvested in the summer of 1990 was renewed in the fall during the harvest of the two most important agricultural crops in Poland—sugar beets and potatoes. Across the country, the production contracts between the sugar processing plants and sugar beets producers were signed in the spring of 1990. At the time of sugar beet procurements, some sugar processing plants reneged on the price levels stipulated in the contracts, and thus precipitated a blockade of the individual sugar beet processing plants in the affected regions. This then induced national-level negotiations between the central committee of Rural Solidarity and the representatives of the sugar industry. The post-socialist government was drawn into the conflict early on, initially as a mediating party in the negotiations. As a series of multilevel talks continued, the blockade of selected roads and individual sugar processing plants spread. To avert national-level social unrest the government agreed to purchase the excess sugar beets not procured by the sugar plants.

This precedent of direct governmental involvement in the resolution of the sugar beet crisis was soon repeated in a regional conflict between the peasants and local milk procurement centers. The local units of Rural Solidarity organized a prompt and efficient peasant strike. This was met by an equally prompt intervention by the Ministry of Agriculture. The ministry advanced government-guaranteed preferential loans to the procurement centers, hence covering delinquent payments to the milk producers. The government also made available preferential loans to stimulate high-quality milk production within the individual sector. Petitions for the preferential loans were to be sponsored by the local boards of milk procurement cooperatives, as well as by chapters of the Cattle Breeders and Producers. The peasants in the studied *gmina* found those loans totally unavailable. Given the antagonistic relations with the cooperatives, they also considered the loan application procedure as misguided and unfair to peasants.[48]

Although the state was implicated in the sugar beets and milk crises, these conflicts were played out primarily between representatives of industrial buyers and agricultural producers. Yet, the potato crisis of 1990 brought the state directly into the center of agricultural conflict. In 1990, the processing industries in potato flour, starch, and cereal reduced their input demands by one-third. The most significant factor causing the drop in potato demand was a depression in domestic alcohol production prompted by cheap imported alcohol. The liberalization of government regulations relating to international trade resulted in a massive influx of alcohol from Germany in the second half of 1989 through early 1990. An investigation conducted by an independent governmental accounting agency (Najwyzsza Izba Controli (NIK)) estimated that state-owned and private enterprises together imported over eighteen million liters of alcohol at the end of 1989.[49] In early 1990, the import of alcohol expanded further, with private enterprises at the forefront. The comprehensive and swift liberalization of trade resulted in insufficient guidelines and controls over tariffs and licensing. Alcohol was smuggled into Poland at great profit and without limit.

"Alcohol-gate" became a major liability for the Balcerowicz program. The program became linked to the promotion of "shady trades" and the undermining of legitimate private agriculture. Instead of having an anti-monopolistic effect on the domestic alcohol industry, it narrowed the scale of domestic production within the alcohol plants and shrunk the suppliers' base, by that time almost exclusively drawn from the state farms. Further, it inflicted significant losses (estimated to be billions in Polish currency) on the state budget when it was intended as part of a stabilization package to alleviate the staggering budget deficit.[50] The massive flood of imported alcohol not only cast a shadow over the credibility of the Balcerowicz economic program, but it also violated the objectives of a social program to combat rampant alcoholism in Polish society inherited from the socialistic regime, still supported by law as well as in the public consciousness.[51]

In the fall of 1990, to protest the government's role in the potato crisis, peasants, organized by the National Committee of Protesting Farmers, marched on the capital. They dropped loads of potatoes in front of the Ministry of Agriculture and occupied government buildings. Trade liberalization policies were cast not simply as antipeasant but also as anti-Polish. Peasants saw these policies as destroying the domestic economy and undermining societal values.[52]

Hence, by the fall of 1990, the sugar beet and potato crises had produced a collective antigovernment reaction that went beyond a question of private ownership rights. By incorporating nationalistic and social accents into their protests, peasants gained the support of the wider society.[53] Political organizations representing agricultural producers, recruited mostly from members of the NSZZ RI Solidarnosc (Rural Solidarity), then articulated three basic demands for the reformulation of agrarian policy: to guarantee minimum prices for agricultural goods; to aid agricultural production through preferential credits; and to protect domestic agricultural production by erecting steep tariffs for foreign agricultural products (Kocik 1996; Wilczynski 1996). These three demands set the stage for numerous negotiations between peasants' representatives from different political organizations and the representatives of the government over the scope and nature of state intervention to ensure the genuine protection of peasants' ownership rights. These negotiations were bogged down by conflicting demands for sector-specific versus general intervention.[54] Participants also clashed over the precise locus of state intervention—that is, whether it should occur at the point of agricultural production or at the points of distribution and processing. The neoliberal premises guiding the reform program, reinforced by the immediate pressures of the potato and sugar beet crises, had inclined the government to gear its interventionist measures primarily toward stabilizing the processes of distribution and agricultural processing. It avoided financially assisting individual producers since such intervention was considered a form of state subsidy obstructing market regulation of production. In handling the negotiations with peasants, government officials emphasized a necessity to help financially existing procurement centers and processing plants to sustain their operations in order to help peasants preserve a demand base for their output and to expand it.

Dismayed by their inability to realize their demands, on March 16, 1991, Rural Solidarity called for a national strike. One week later, there were over five hundred road blockades organized in forty-seven provinces throughout Poland. To justify this form of protest, one of the peasant's leaders stated: "This is our type of strike because we cannot simply stop to work" (Gorlach 1999: 14).[55] Peasants renewed their key demands on the government: the restoration of profits through minimal price setting, the provision of preferential credits, and the imposition of effective tariffs for imported food (Kocik 1996; Wilczynski 1996).[56]

In the beginning of 1992 the Olszewski government was further challenged by a previously unknown political organization, the Committee for Peasant Self-Defense or "Samoobrona," a radical-populist peasant union organization (Gorlach 1999). Samoobrona was a splinter group of NSZZ RI Solidarnosc, newly formed by A. Lepper, an individual agricultural producer with 120 hectares from the northeastern province of Poland who amassed interest arrears close to 1 billion zloty on a loan of 280 million zloty.

The group initially attracted commercially oriented agricultural producers with high-debt liabilities. Yet it quickly broadened its membership to an estimated quarter of a million, including a segment of its former parent organization, RI Solidarity.[57] The Samoobrona showed its strongest presence in *voivodships* with long traditions of commercialized agricultural production.[58] By the end of 1991, when a growing number of enterprises with tax and loan arrears were testing the government's commitment to the program, it was Samoobrona that made a *political platform* out of the payments of loan debts.[59] Under the motto "that is not what we agreed with Balcerowicz," Samoobrona rejected responsibility for loan repayments. They branded the interest rates "criminal" and demanded that the government stop the liquidation of defaulting farms and sponsor the creation of a new debt restructuring fund. In response, the government agreed to infuse the banks with more money in order to postpone the foreclosure of indebted farms (Gorlach 1999:15). Moreover, Samoobrona also promulgated a conspiracy theory as its ideological platform. It branded all reformers and officials implementing agricultural policies as "criminals and thieves" who were acting on the directives of "foreign interests," particularly those of the IMF and World Bank. Based on this denunciation of post-socialist reforms as "anti-Polish" and "antipeasant," Samoobrona resorted to paramilitary, law-breaking activities. They disrupted numerous liquidation sales of indebted agricultural enterprises in the name of preserving individual peasant work stations and preserving domestic production endangered by the influx of foreign foods. They engaged in a campaign of physical and mental intimidation of those government officials who were implementing reforms on local and regional levels.[60] To exert pressure on the central government, in mid-1992, the Samoobrona occupied the agricultural ministry building (Gorlach 1999). It further mobilized its members from six *voivodships*, staging a highly publicized blockade of the roads and a "tractor march on the capital."

The main political parties appealing to the agricultural constituency (PSL, SL, and Solidarnosc RI) quickly distanced themselves from the Samoobrona, particularly from its tactics. Its methods of operation did not find approval among the wider society or the peasants. Further, the majority of peasants I interviewed did not condone the taking of, and then defaulting on, loans, even though they did not challenge Samoobrona's negative assessment of the agricultural and monetary post-socialist policies. With pride, they contrasted their own responses to those of Samoobrona's indebted members. Instead of irresponsibly accepting loans that could not be repaid, they preserved their farms by restraining from such loans. With concern, they also expressed a view that Samoobrona created a backlash against peasants' image in the wider society, portraying them as conservative and promoters of lawlessness.

Yet, although its formulations and tactics were radical, the Samoobrona did reverberate with the broader demands of a majority of peasants and their political parties for protection from reforms that turned out to advance "oppressive freedom."[61] In particular, its demand for preferential credits for agriculture and for governmental protection of domestic food production received approval. Further, in its characterization of government officials of all levels as highly opportunistic and involved in illegal activity, Samoobrona echoed and reinforced the growing perception among the peasantry that their hardships were not inevitable but were deliberately imposed on them by incompetent and corrupt officials of the government that vowed to instill the "rule of law." This potentially sympathetic perception of Samoobrona, combined with its growing numbers, caused government officials, police, and courts to confront Samoobrona's illegal activities in a very cautious, protracted, and inconsistent manner.[62] As Samoobrona praised itself for breaking unjust laws, the government grew hesitant to enforce the "rule of law."

Since the beginning of 1993, the political platform of Samoobrona shifted from the defense of indebted peasants and embattled agriculture. Envisioning themselves as a future electoral bloc, a newly formed offshoot of Samoobrona, the Committee for the National Self-Defense (Komitet Samoobrony Narodu), spoke for the preservation not only of peasant individual farms but also of all individual work stations. On a more global level, it also proclaimed opposition to the post-socialist reform program and its social consequences. Its leadership included heroes of World War II, the literary intelligentsia, labor union activists, and the former socialist satellite party activists. Its ranks were enlarged to all social groups experiencing the adverse social consequences of the new economic program: the homeless, unemployed, pensioners, and veterans. Their particularistic grievances broadened into a contestation between the dispossessed and the state. Thus, as its membership diversified, there was a growing generalization of collective opposition to the post-socialist state, evident in the increased usage of general identities such as "nation" and "society" (Halamska 2000b). As Gorlach puts it, Samoobrona transformed the language of protests into "those who suffer," "those who are cheated by those from above" (1999: 20). The fight for survival, unlike under socialism against the threat of collectivization, acquired new content following the impact of the post-socialist reforms; it became a defense "of the interest of domestic (Polish) agrarian producers facing all the threats caused by a globalizing market economy" (Gorlach 1999: 20).

Conclusion: The Polish "Advantage" Becomes the Downfall of the Transition

For the architects of the post-socialist reform program, the vision of a future affluent society engendered the perception of socialism as a shortage economy and an overemphasis on the economic failures of previous efforts at reforming it. The critical assessment of past efforts led to an assumption that a comprehensive and swift removal of all state intervention was synonymous with a spontaneous release of economic initiatives on the part of private property owners. This narrow preoccupation with the removal of past barriers then obstructed the reformers' vision; they failed to anticipate how the withering of the state-erected insurmountable barriers to market entry for newly "liberalized" private property owners would also leave the post-socialist state without the proper institutional and technical capacity to guide the transition. This left individual private owners in an economic and legislative environment that constrained their ownership rights. Despite formal liberalization, peasants experienced more restricted access to production resources than during the socialist period (Beskid 1995). The scope of their control over production became severely restricted, pushing even previously specialized peasants into an involuted, extensive agricultural production. They endured the systematic, and transparent to them, siphoning off of their profits. Their high transition costs compared unfavorably with their position under late socialism and with that of other agricultural subsectors.

Some scholars have argued that the involution of production and the instability of markets were unavoidable yet *passing* elements of any transition of this scale (Winiecki 1991; Berg and Sachs 1992). I would argue that these economic and political outcomes constitute more *fundamental* and *lasting* effects on the overall course of the post-socialist change. The post-socialist liberalization measures stood in stark contrast to the progressive consolidation of peasants' ownership rights in the late phase of state socialism. By reversing the agrarian price structure favorable to peasants, the post-socialist stabilization package immediately took away individual benefits won at the end of state socialism. In addition to reducing their economic gains, the post-socialist liberalization of prices and trade undermined future economic development. Once subjected to *arbitrary* state encroachment on their ownership rights, peasants fought hard (through Rural Solidarity and through their daily individual quiet resistance) for constitutional guarantees for their civil and property rights (Kocik 1996; Gorlach and Serega 1993). In dismantling authoritarianism and state regulation, the stabilization package of the post-socialist reform did not establish a "rule of law" (Litwack 1991; Cooter 1992; Comisso 1991). Litwack (1991) finds an economic legality as a prerequisite for creating incentives that could support a healthy market, and defines it as a mutually consistent set of economic laws *and* belief by the population in the stability and enforcement of these laws. Both elements were undermined in the early stages of Polish agrarian transition. Rather, the stabilization package subjected peasants to heightened uncertainty in accessing markets. Accordingly, it increased the arbitrariness and instability in their economic transactions.

In the conclusion of his analysis of the transition from capitalism to socialism, Przeworski posits that, given the alternatives existing within capitalism for the improvement of workers' economic welfare and the inevitable valley of transition, workers cannot be expected to opt for socialism based merely on their narrow economic interests. Workers' withdrawal from one system to another could not be guided by their belief in the *economic* superiority of socialism, but rather by its promise of *social* superiority. They will embark on this historical progression only if it leads to a society that promises higher production capacity as well as more egalitarian principles of redistribution (Przeworski 1985: 235–238).[63] The post-socialist reformers' quest for increased economic efficiency rested on the assumption that allocation decisions could be separated from redistributive ones (Murrell 1991; Przeworski 1991; Gorlach 1999). In their self-definition and in their vision of the future affluent society, they engendered an unconditional rejection of socialism as a shortage economy marked by economic wastefulness and arbitrariness. The early reality of the post-socialist transition challenged that vision. The stabilization package not only pushed peasants into a deep valley of high individual transition costs, but it also undermined their confidence in the *system's* capacity to bring about its intended objective of increased economic efficiency. Based on their economic transactions with monopsonistic centers and opportunist private companies, peasants viewed the emerging post-socialist system as promoting the mismanagement of resources and shady opportunities for the enrichment of old political and economic elites.

Moreover, peasants evaluated their present position and projected the future based on a different assessment of state socialism. For the general society, state socialism engendered critique of itself based not on its principles themselves, but rather on the disjuncture of these principles and reality (Burawoy and Lukacs 1992). Yet Polish peasants did not experience this disjuncture as acutely. The unique historical possibility opened up for peasants within the last period of state socialism and allowed them to consolidate their private ownership rights. This provided them with *individual economic gains* that benefited *society* and integrally advanced the central redistributive promises of socialism—economic equality and economic security. Through this prism, peasants saw themselves in the post-socialist transition as separated from the far side of the valley (capitalism) by unavoidable transitional costs. Moreover, in their eyes, the far side also failed to *rise higher* than state socialism and hence did not legitimate these individual and collective costs.[64]

The consolidation of private property owners' exclusive rights that took place within late state socialism engendered distinct ideological connotations for the owners that carried on into the post-socialist transition. A historical experience under state socialism in which peasants' individual gains were integrally connected to the advancement of collective benefits became their ethical imperative to reject a historical alternative aimed at narrow individual economic benefits. The peasants' early rejection of the post-socialist reforms was not merely an attempt to avoid temporary material deprivation. It was also a challenge to the foundation of the neoliberal program. Thus, the ascendant Polish peasant bourgeoisie were unlike their counterparts in the Western capitalist transition. They were not advancing *potentially* universal individual economic interests that inevitably spill into an actual differentiation of economic actors.[65] Rather, the ascendant Polish peasant bourgeoisie were promoting *actual* "people's capitalism." This implied placing a burden on the state to abate the unavoidable hardships associated with the economic transition to market economy and to regulate the spread of the benefits of the transition throughout the society. From the onset of the program, this ideology set a low threshold for their acceptance of the costs of transition and an impatience for receiving tangible benefits. Hence, the first "freed private owners" denounced the post-socialist system by effectively translating their particularistic economic demands into the language of collective contestation that united all those dispossessed by the reform.

In this chapter, I showed how the liberalization measures undercut peasants' earlier steady advancements in asserting their ownership rights in the areas of production control, residual income, and asset transfers. I also revealed how the post-socialist reform program confronted the specific, historically formed connotation of the collective value of private property that emerged under state socialism. Challenging the assumption shared by both neoclassical and evolutionary economics that asserts the universal validity of private property advancing economic efficacy, these historically constructed exclusive private owners exhibited political and economic responses to the post-socialist program that amounted to the involution of production rather than economic growth.

In the next chapter, I will analyze how the socialist past mediated the dynamics of articulating cooperative ownership rights under the post-socialist reform program. Furthermore, by analyzing the organization of local agricultural circles, I will examine the intersection of cooperative and private ownerships and the interplay of exercising cooperative and individual property rights.

Notes

1. In 1990, 76 percent of the farmland in Poland was in private hands, 18.7 percent was owned by the state, 3.7 percent by cooperatives, and 1.6 percent by so-called "agricultural circles" (Pilichowski 1994: 165–166; Maurel 2000: 99, cited in Buchowski 2003: 2). In 1998, more than 83 percent of agricultural land area was owned by close to two million private farms bigger than one hectare (GUS, *Rocznik Statystyczny* [Statistical Yearbook] 2000: 335, 337).

2. The private sector of Polish agriculture remained almost unchanged in the excessive fragmentation of landholdings at the onset of state socialism and throughout its duration. It resulted from a continuous abrogation of the peasants' rights in the areas of access to production resources and in their right to exchange, acquire, or transfer land. See Korbonski (1965); Magyar (1984); Duczkowska-Piasecka (1993); and Halamska (2000a).

3. Nagengast (1991) found in the Polish populism what Weber found in Protestantism in relation to the rise of capitalism. As she pointed out, the populism, which dated back to the nineteenth century and centered on the values of freedom, independence of the private producer, and economic individualism, condoned the allocation of a disproportional share of economic resources among the top layer of the peasantry and cast moral disapproval on the impoverished bottom. Thus, it provided a basis for legitimating economic polarization within peasantry.

In the context of earlier state socialist policies abrogating individual property rights of peasants, the same brand of populism, with its value placed on the independence of individual enterprises, served to oppose socialism and to unite peasantry and society vis-à-vis the state.

4. In this chapter, I will refer to peasants as a social category distinguishable from farmers in developed capitalist economies or from rural dwellers partially involved in agricultural production and incorporated into the national labor market of a socialist state. Many definitions identify peasants by reference to three general characteristics: sociopolitical, economic, and psychological. The definitions of cultural anthropologists accentuate sociopolitical characteristics—the inherent traditionalism of peasants. Sociologists point to the economic distinctiveness of the peasantry based on the identity of the household unit and the enterprise. Others point to the psychological dimension of peasantry as its central defining feature. See Kroeber (1948), Redfield (1956), Chayanov (1986), Wolf (1966), Scott (1976), and Shanin (1971). Although the socialist agrarian policy promoted some internal economic differentiation within the peasantry (seen by some as a "farmerization" of peasantry), it also generated peasants' resistance to socialist state interferences and cemented peasants' loyalty to traditional ideals and thus preserved their homogeneity. Hann (1985: 13) very eloquently articulates the point of preserved homogeneity of peasants when he states: "peasantry survives *in spite of* certain objective economic possibilities—concessions by the authorities, necessary to avoid shortfalls but taken up only by small numbers of well-placed individuals. The majority has resisted, not because of any inherent peasant opposition to progress and commercialisation . . . , but because this was a natural response to discriminatory policies against the private sector and agriculture as a whole." See also Fedyszak-Radziejowska (1993 and 1995) on the self-perception of peasantry as a cohesive social entity and on the collective orientation of peasants' responses to the post-socialist reform program—including their understanding of economic entrepreneurship as containing collective solidarity.

5. In 1988, during the second phase of Jaruzelski's reform, the average peasant's income exceeded that of urban workers by 17 percent. See World Bank (1990).

6. For more data on these increases, see Joanna Solska, Andrzej Mozolowski, and Pawel Tarnowski 1990, "Sceny z zycia gospodarczego." *Polityka* 2 (1706): 6; Jagienka Wilczak 1990, "Wielkie czekanie." *Polityka* 3 (1707): 1; Dzun 1993. On the drastic rise of inflation between 1989 and 1990 see World Bank (1995): 8.

7. For more on this, see Wieslaw Krencik 1991, "Nowy koszyk "Polityki." *Polityka* 5 (1761): 8.

8. Walerian Dziczkiewicz 1991, "Kto górą ?" *Polityka* 5 (1761): 11.

9. In an attempt to curtail the food demands that consistently and increasingly outpaced the food production capacity of the domestic agricultural sector, the Jaruzelski-led government then freed agricultural product prices while holding the agricultural input prices at their low, state-subsidized levels. This partial price reform allowed peasants a windfall in profits. See chapter 2 for more details.

10. At the end of state socialism, Polish peasants enjoyed a uniquely good economic standing relative to urban groups. By comparison, Hungarian and Yugoslavian peasants' income was below that of urban workers by 4 percent and 20 percent, respectively. See World Bank (1990).

11. For example, while prices for dairy products increased significantly in 1990 (especially for butter and cheeses), the milk procurement prices remained practically unchanged at the level of 500 to 600 zloty per liter. See "Pomoc Zachodu w roku przyszlym." *Tygodnik Rolnikow* 51–52 (December 23–30, 1990): 6; "Ceny swiatowe wciaz o wiele wyzsze." *Tygodnik Rolnikow* 43–44 (October 28–November 4, 1990): 8.

12. In the governmental estimates, the needs of capital investment in agriculture were at the level of 612 billion zloty at the start of transition. The investment needs in rural infrastructure amounted to 178 billion; food processing industry investment costs were estimated at 158 billion; creating small businesses in the countryside to absorb the superfluous labor from the restructured agricultural production units was projected at about 240 billion. Restructuralization of the small family-based agricultural enterprises had financial needs estimated at the level of 60 billion zloty (Ministerstwo Rolnictwa i Gospodarki Zywnosciowej 1993).

13. Hence, financial investments in the agricultural sector in the second year of the transition amounted to 30 billion zloty, a fraction of an estimated need of 610 billion zloty. Almost

50 percent came out of the financial self-resources of the economic subjects. Only approximately one-fifth of the sum was covered by the state budget. The state expenditures in agriculture were on a steady decrease. In 1990 the budget spending in agriculture amounted only to one-half of the proceeding year. In 1991 the investments were only equivalent to 20 percent of the 1989 level, and 1992 represented only 16 percent of the 1989 budget spending (Ministerstwo Rolnictwa i Gospodarki Zywnosciowej 1993: table 4).

14. In 1989, the proportion of credits allocated to the private sector of agriculture was only 1.6 percent. In 1990, it rose to 2.2 percent, in 1991 to 3.3 percent, and in 1992 to 3.7 percent. See statistical data of Prof. J. Weclawski (Ministerstwo Rolnictwa i Gospodarki Zywnosciowej 1993: table 6).

15. Ministerstwo Rolnictwa i Gospodarki Zywnosciowej 1993: table 6

16. Two times in 1990, the bank received funds for preferential fertilizer and pesticides credits in the amount of 250 million zloty each. The following years the amount was doubled. The loans for processing plants were channeled to the local bank by the regional cooperative bank, which administered the modernization funds of the European Foundation for the Development of Polish Agriculture.

17. Compared to 1985, when credits designated for investments constituted over 75 percent of all credits advanced for agricultural purposes, the ratio decreased in 1989 to 62 percent and further dropped to 20 percent in 1991 and 1992 (GUS, *Roczniki Statystyczne* [Statistical Yearbooks] 1992, 1993). In direct correspondence to this declining ratio of investment credits, there was a dramatic decline in construction of new utility buildings in agriculture, especially in its private sector. Construction of buildings for fattening swine, for milk and meat cattle production, and for grain storage was cut by half (from thirty thousand to fifteen thousand) between 1989 and 1992. By comparison, in 1985, 38,655 new units were constructed (GUS, *Rocznik Statystyczny* [Statistical Yearbook] 1993: 342).

18. Nostalgic and bitter, many peasants compared these post-socialist credit policies with those from the golden times of the 1970s and the 1980s under Gierek's and Jaruzelski's regimes. Then investment credits were loaned at single-digit interest rates. Additionally, significant portions of the investment credits were customarily forgiven, provided that a credit recipient maintained his/her production on a specified level (Gorlach 2000).

19. From 1980 to 1992, the number of tractors within the individual peasants' subsector tripled. Already in 1985 the private agricultural subsector outpaced the state farm sector in terms of the units of mechanical drafting power per 100 hectares of arable land. In 1980 the private subsector was trailing both cooperative and state farm subsectors with 21.6 units of draught power/100 hectares as compared with 30.7 and 25.7 units/100 hectares respectively. A decade later the trend had reversed. By 1990 private peasants had 48.9 units/100 hectares, while the cooperative sector had 36/100 hectares and the state sector only 27/100 hectares. The next two years produced only a widening gap between the sectors in mechanized draught power: the private subsector continuously rose to the level of 49.1/100 hectares, while the cooperative and state subsectors declined to 32/100 hectares and 23.9/100 hectares, respectively (See GUS, *Rocznik Statystyczny* 1993).

20. The practices observed in the villages under study reflect more general trends. 1990 did not reverse the course of aging machinery stock in Polish agriculture, but rather deepened it. By 1990, the coefficient of agricultural machinery renewal fell to 3.8 percent from the preceding year of 5.2 percent. By 1992, it further dropped to 1.4 percent (GUS, *Rocznik Statystyczny* 1993: 342).

21. With the opening of Polish-German borders, old, undocumented agricultural machinery from Germany found its way in large numbers to the Polish countryside. There were no available spare parts for these machines. New foreign machinery far exceeded the purchasing power of Polish peasants.

22. Under state socialism, the local agricultural trade cooperatives had secondary and tertiary cooperative structures that were integrated into a command economy. The delivery of foods was based on directives and subject to the manipulation of input and output prices by a complex system of state subsidies. The price for agricultural outputs was determined by administratively balancing the subsidies on agricultural production, distribution, processing, and consumption. Although a small private market for agricultural goods existed, it was residual to

the state-controlled cooperative system and only for selected produce such as vegetables, fruits, flowers, and eggs. In light of the persistent and growing gap between the demand for food and the agricultural sector's production capacity throughout state socialism, systems of subsidies were set to maximize the procurement of agricultural output by the state. The monopolistic procurement position of the state-controlled trade cooperative system was ensured by making access to agricultural inputs and services for individual agricultural producers contingent on the channeling of their agricultural outputs through these procurement cooperatives.

23. In the 1980s, milk and meats were subsidized between 60 and 80 percent. In the aftermath of the macrostabilization program and the reduction of state expenditures, the post-socialistic state budgeted 0.2 percent of GDP for agricultural input subsidies, down from 3.4 percent to 4.8 percent of GDP in the period from 1986 to 1989 and 1.3 percent in 1989 (World Bank 1990: 32–33).

24. Initially, the drop in the consumer aggregate and relative demand for food led to a build up in procurement center inventories. Yet, very quickly, the centers geared their efforts into decreasing their reserves by purchasing from agricultural producers below the level of their sales to retail redistributors. As a result, they maintained inventories proportional to the level of reduced sales.

25. While overall procurement of all grains in 1990 stood at 6,385 thousand tons, it was slashed to 4,598 thousand tons in 1991 and further reduced to 3,769 thousand tons in 1992 (GUS, *Rocznik Statystyczny* 1993: 387).

26. The preferential access to output markets by the state farm and the agricultural production cooperatives as compared with the peasants within the studied community were reflected in national statistics. Thus, in 1990, the grain purchased from state farms increased by 13 percent. In the same time, the purchase from individual producers decreased by almost 10 percent. It further dropped in the subsequent year to only a 75 percent level. Although, the decline was slowed in 1992, the recovery of demand for grain output was faster for the agricultural state farms and cooperatives than for the individual producers. The latter recovered 90 percent of sales in 1992 compared to sales from the prior year. The disparity in the rates of procurement of specific agricultural output by agricultural subsector becomes more visible once reference is made to the rate of the agricultural output by respective subsectors. Thus, the above mentioned 13 percent increase in grain procurement rates between 1990 and 1991 from the state farm sector coincided with a slight decline in grain production. (GUS, *Rocznik Statystyczny* 1994: table 44 at 446, 385, table 45 at 447, 386, table 47 at 449, and 387; also GUS, *Rocznik Statystyczny* 1993: table 1 at 413, and 319.)

27. In the case of grain humidity tests, peasants did not have the means for retesting or the facilities to reduce the grain water content, if requested by the centers.

28. In 1980, there were over 5 million milk cattle in Poland. The number was reduced to 4.8 million in 1985. At the time of the inauguration of post-socialistic reforms in 1990, the amount dropped to 4.3 million. Within the following three years, in the period from 1990 to 1993, there was a subsequent dramatic drop by another 0.7 million to 3.6 million cattle. The decreasing size of the milk cattle herd corresponded with the decline in global milk production for the period. In 1980, it was at the level of 16,000 million liters, and in 1990 it was a little over 15,300 million liters. Within the first three years of the post-socialist economy, production declined to 12,200 million liters (GUS, *Rocznik Statystyczny* 1994: table 30 at 432, 380, table 22 at 424, and 376).

29. The peasants' battles with the milk procurement center in Rolnicy were very representative of the relations between peasants and milk centers nationwide. See Walerian Dziczkiewicz 1991, "Kto górą?" *Polityka* 5 (1761): 11; Gorlach 1999.

30. This was the equivalent of $110,000. He generated this money from cashed savings, and from selling his car and specialized equipment.

31. The type of chicken raised in Poland (Astra) was very expensive in production. For every 1 kilogram of chicken weight, 2.6 kilograms of feed were required. Also, the Polish chicken had relatively low meat-to-bone ratio as compared with its Dutch counterpart.

32. The situation was exacerbated by the administrative reform of 1993, which eliminated the administrative layer above the local level of *gmina*—that of *powiat*—while, with respect to the role of *wojewoda*, the head of the administrative unit above *powiat*, it became unclear

whether the individual was a representative of central government or representative of the region. See also Starzynski (1993) on the drastic reductions (approximately 50 percent) in general employment within institutions servicing individual agricultural producers and the peasants' perception of the vacuum in the institutional agricultural infrastructure.

33. Applicants for a foreign credit were charged with a fee of 2.5 percent of the value of a foreign loan. There was an additional requirement of collateral equal in size to the amount of the credit plus 20 percent.

34. Unlike the majority of other foreign financial aid, the 1990 funds available from the World Bank were uniquely designated for the development of agriculture, in general, and the food-processing industry, in particular. The funds were allocated through Polish commercial banks. The loans were much underutilized due to the processing fees and the unattractive interest rates for the original loans.

35. Cuts in fertilizer use in the studied villages reflected more general tendencies in Polish agriculture. From 1989 to 1990, there was already a 20 percent reduction in fertilizer use. Yet, the drastic cut occurred after the Balcerowicz price liberalization. For 1990 to 1991, the use of fertilizers dropped by half, and further sank by 80 percent in 1991 to 1992. However, the reduction rates varied across agricultural subsectors, with deeper cuts in fertilizer application by individual peasants as compared with the agricultural production cooperatives or state farms subsectors; see GUS, *Rocznik Statystyczny* 1993: 343, table 37 at 449. In her article, K. Brooks (1991) pointed out already low fertilization rates for Poland at the onset of the reforms as compared with more advanced countries.

36. The studied *gmina* reflected national trends in the above aspect. In 1990, approximately 11,000 new facilities were built for animal production, only half the number built in 1985. This number further decreased between 1991 and 1993 from 8,500 to 5,500, respectively. The three-fold decrease in the construction of new facilities for swine production was still slower than the six-fold reduction in new facilities for cattle production (GUS, *Rocznik Statystyczny* 1994: 381, tables 32 at 434 and 33 at 435).

37. All the scrupulous calculations the peasant was making regarding his transactions with the duck company did not include the cost of his advanced labor.

38. Throughout the 1980s, state preferential credits (at a 3 percent interest rate) supported the extensive modernization of their farms in terms of utility buildings, machinery, and an expansion of production. Fearful that the unpaid remainder of those loans would be refinanced to post-liberalization interest levels, many peasants who took those loans sold small portions of their lands as a way to generate the desperately needed cash for the quick and full repayment of those loans.

39. For further discussion of peasant-workers, see I. Szelenyi (1988), as well as Szemberg (1980) and Turski (1965).

40. This is reflected in data compiled by the assessor's office of the *gmina* local government. There was an increase in agricultural farms in the range of five to seven hectares. Even more rapidly grew the agricultural plots of two to five hectares (both in number and in the overall land share within that category), thus solidifying the existence of peasant-workers in the post-socialist period.

41. On the national level, the slow process of the consolidation of lands by bigger peasants (farms between ten and fifteen hectares and those beyond fifteen hectares) with a corresponding decrease in small farms (five to seven hectares), which took place within the last decade of state socialism, halted or actually reversed during the early post-socialist period. Thus the shares of farms within the ranges of 7 to 9.9, 10 to 14.9, and beyond 15 hectares all slightly decreased while the percentage of small farms (2 to 4.9 and 5 to 6.7 hectares) increased. While the average private farm in 1989 was 7.2 hectares, by 1993 it dropped to 7.1 hectares (GUS, *Rocznik Statystyczny* 1994: 361, table 6).

42. The average yields in crop production during the last five years of state socialism were at the level of approximately 31 dt/hectare. Within the first four years of the post-socialist transition, they decreased to the average level of approximately 25 dt/hectare. Within the same time frame, there was a parallel decrease in the average number of cattle produced per hectare of agricultural land: from 56 down to 46. (GUS, *Maly Rocznik Statystyczny* 1995, 228, 232, and tables 8 and 11.)

43. The early manifestation of peasants' rejection of the Balcerowicz economic program was evident in their clash with the police in Mlawa, near Warsaw in the spring of 1990.

44. For a detailed analysis of various peasant organizations, see Gorlach and Mooney (1998).

45. Walesa with the Union of the Centrum, a political party that broke away from the Solidarity coalition, had proposed an alternative to the Balcerowicz plan. In what he called a "war at the top," Walesa attacked Mazowiecki's government for declines in employment, demand, output, and real incomes. Although Walesa affirmed a modern market capitalist economy "as the only economic order assuring civilized development," he pointed to the necessity of "including a system of social security appropriate to the level of our economic development." His proposed remedy was the acceleration of reforms (*przyspieszenie*) to shorten the transition costs. Further, to reactivate the economy, he called for the elimination of wage restrictions, reduction of taxes, and an introduction of guaranteed prices in agriculture. See Balcerowicz 1990; Mack 1994; Przeworski 1993.

46. In early summer of 1990, the Mazowiecki government showed visible signs of deviating from its original program and of inner government factions. In May, the Economic Council within the Council of Ministers proposed loosening fiscal discipline and some state intervention. Particularly, it proposed preferential loans and minimum prices in agriculture. Those changes provoked the resignation of the first vice-minister in the Balcerowicz team, Marek Dabrowski. For more details on the economic program debates see Balcerowicz 1990; Przeworski 1993; and Mack 1994.

47. For a more comprehensive analysis of the evolution of rural protests and their nature in the context of other social groups' opposition to the reforms, see Kubik and Ekiert (1999) and Forys (2008).

48. See Janusz Bylinski 1990, "Zachmurzenie trwale, Straj trwa," *Tygodnik Rolnikow* 43–44 (October 28–November 4): 6.

49. See Pawel Tarnowski 1990, "W oparach spritytusu" ["In the fumes of alcohol], *Polityka* 32 (1736): 3.

50. See Wojciech Markiewicz 1991, "Export wewnetrzny" *Polityka* 20 (1776): 11; Pawel Tarnowski 1990, "W oparach spritytusu" ["In the fumes of alcohol"], *Polityka* 32 (1736): 3.

51. The 1982 Bill on Alcoholic Abstinence aimed to preserve and enforce the state monopoly over the production, sale, and consumption of alcohol as a means to combat rampant alcoholism in Polish society.

52. In principle, the corporate resolution of the sugar beet crisis also included a demand for the government to immediately establish trade tariffs in order to prevent the sugar damping practices by the West, which was perceived by both otherwise opposing sides as effectively destroying the domestic sugar beets production and sugar industry.

53. The survey conducted in the aftermath of road blockades and occupation of governmental buildings by Centrum Badan Opinii Publicznej, CBOS (the Public Opinion Research Center), in 1990 found that one-third of society saw the demands of the peasants as fully justifiable, another 38 percent of respondents recognized the majority of the demands as justifiable. Only 5.5 percent responded negatively to the peasants' demands, while 16.7 percent, although supporting some of their demands, generally found the peasants' stands unjustifiable. Over 66.6 percent of respondents proposed that the government change its economic plan along the lines of peasant demands. See Jerzy Gluszynski 1990, "Za I przeciw rolnikom" *Polityka* 31 (1735): 6.

54. As peasants pointed to the specific nature of agriculture to justify a sectorial state intervention, the issue provoked deep division within the governmental ministries. The Financial Ministry and Ministry of Cooperation with Abroad fought against the Ministry of Agriculture on the issue of the curtailing of the liberalization of trade to protect domestic food production (Mack 1994).

55. Results of a survey of one thousand individuals conducted by CBOS in February 1992 entitled "Public opinion toward different forms of social protests and responses toward them," as well as a survey of 984 individuals conducted by CBOS in August 1992 (during the intense strike period) entitled "Opinion toward strikes, strikers and pressing national concerns," point toward public acceptance of an overall freedom to express opinions and employ various means

(even radical) that would affect political decisions. Even though the most popularly accepted form of protest was the collection of petition signatures, the survey indicated people felt stronger than in 1991 that the public should have more room in expressing dissatisfaction, while the government should have less authority to restrain public expression (CBOS February 1992: Graphic 2, 4). Furthermore, a majority of those surveyed thought that strikes were not only a result of compensation issues (thus, reflecting narrow group interests), but reflected the societal response to the overall economic program of the government. Similar results were reported by Lidia Beskid (1995).

56. The national survey conducted by CBOS shows that the demand for setting minimum prices was supported by 85 percent of peasants regardless of the size of their landholding. A similar percentage of peasants and of the general population expressed powerlessness—very little influence over local affairs or the direction of national-level development, seen as leading to "capitalism," which they opposed (Starzynski 1993: 23–25; Glowacki 1993: 57–59; Fedyszak-Radziejowska 1993: 131).

57. Out of 2.5 million individual agricultural enterprises, 183,000 took loans; 23,000 of them had loan indebtedness; and 4,000 were facing liquidation. People closely associated with Lepper in Samoobrona claimed to be peasants "burnt" in their efforts to take economic initiative in the new post-socialist system. See Ewa Czaczkowska 1992, "Bojownicy" ["Warriors"], *Rzeczpospolita* 157: 3.

58. The strongest centers of Samoobrona were in "agricultural regions"—in Poznanskie, as well as Koszalinskie (where Samoobrona originated), Leszczynskie, Kaliskie, and Bydgoskie *voivodships*. Only three *voivodships* did not have regional representation by Samoobrona: Krakowskie, Nowosadeckie, and Bialostockie. See Mariusz Janicki and Miroslaw Peczak 1993, "Kosynierzy nowej generacji" *Polityka* 14, April 3, 1993: 3; Janina Paradowska, "Czas Samoobrony" *Polityka* 34, August 21, 1993: 3.

59. By the end of 1991, about one-third of the loans made by commercial banks were nonperforming. Interest arrears were up by 35 percent in nominal terms within the second half of 1991 and interest payments were increasingly capitalized. In addition, enterprises were accumulating tax arrears. At the end of 1991, 12 percent of total tax revenues for 1991 constituted tax arrears. For specific taxes, like penalty tax for exceeding the level of wages beyond the level allowable by the government, arrears were substantially higher, reaching almost one-half of tax payments. See Blanchard and Dabrowski (1993: 109–149).

60. For details on the Samoobrona campaign of forcefully removing officials from their posts, see Miroslaw Peczak and Mariusz Janicki 1993, "Kosynierzy nowej generacji" *Polityka* 14 (1874): 3.

61. The term of "oppressive freedom" was coined by one of the leading rural sociologists in Poland, Krzysztof Gorlach, to depict the impact of post-socialist reforms on peasants and contrast them with the reforms of the 1970s and 1980s, which were denoted as "repressive tolerance" agrarian reforms. See Gorlach and Serega (1993).

62. Miroslaw Peczak and Mariusz Janicki 1993, "Kosynierzy nowej generacji" *Polityka* 14 (1874): 3.

63. Przeworski concludes that an "ethical imperative" will have to guide workers in the transition from capitalism to socialism. "I am now prepared to claim that socialism would be superior because it would permit the society as a whole, by which I mean all individuals through democratic process, to decide collectively which needs should be satisfied in the process of accumulation. This choice is not available under capitalism, where the economic mechanism can only maximize the production of commodities independently of anyone's will" (1985: 237–238).

64. Reflective of this perception are the outcomes of the presidential elections within the community I studied. Consistently, peasants casted votes against Walesa and for the new Social Democratic candidate Kwasniewski, a former member of the state socialist regime.

65. In Gramsci's (2011 [1992]: 260) words, the bourgeois class, an agent of capitalistic revolution, represented itself as a universal class in that it "pose(d) itself as an organism in continuous movement, capable of absorbing the entire society, assimilating it to its own cultural and economic level." The bourgeois claim of universality had rested on a *potentiality* of absorbing the whole of society.

References

Balcerowicz, Leszek. 1995. *Wolnosc i Rozwoj. Ekonomia Wolnego Rynku*. Krakow: Znak.

———. 1992. *800 Dni. Szok Kontrolowany*. Warsaw: Polska Oficyna Wydawnicza "BGW."

———. 1990. "The Price of Polish Economic Reform." In *Without Force or Lies: Voices from the Revolution of Central Europe in 1989–1990*, edited by W. Brinton and A. Rinzler, 223–238. San Francisco: Mercury House Books. U.K. Ltd.

Berg, Andrew, and Jeffrey Sachs. 1992. "Structural International Trade in Eastern Europe: The Case of Poland." *Economic Policy* 14: 117–173.

Beskid, Lidia. 1995. *Polacy a Nowa Rzeczywistosc Ekonomiczna—Procesy Przystosowywania sie w Microskali*. Warsaw. IFiS PAN.

Blanchard, Olivier, and Marek Dabrowski. 1993. "The Progress of Restructuring in Poland." In *Post-Communist Reform: Pain and Progress*, edited by O. Blanchard et al., 109–150. Cambridge, MA: MIT Press.

Brooks, Karen M. 1991. "Decollectivization and the Agricultural Transition in Eastern and Central Europe." Washington, DC: World Bank. Policy, Research and External Affairs Working Papers, October.

Buchowski, M. 2003. "Redefining Social Relations through Work in a Rural Community in Poland." *Max Planck Institute for Social Anthropology Working Papers*. Working Paper no. 58.

Burawoy, Michael, and Janos Lukacs. 1992. *The Radiant Past: Ideology and Reality in Hungary's Road to Capitalism*. Chicago: University of Chicago Press.

Chayanov, A. V. 1986. *The Theory of Peasant Economy*. Madison: University of Wisconsin Press.

Comisso, Ellen. 1991. "Property Rights, Liberalism, and the Transition from 'Actually Existing' Socialism." *East European Politics and Societies* 5 (1): 162–188.

Cooter, Robert. 1992. "Organization as Property: Economic Analysis of Property Law Applied to Privatization." In *The Emergence of Market Economies in Eastern Europe*, edited by R. Clague, 77–98. Cambridge: Blackwell.

Czaczkowska, Ewa. 1992. "Bojownicy." *Rzeczpospolita* 157: 3.

Duczkowska-Piasecka, Malgorzata. 1993. "Tendencje w zakresie zmian obszarowych." In *Rolnicy '92: Rolnicy wobec zmian systemowych*, edited by Andrzej Rosner, 98–106. Warsaw: CBOS.

Dziczkiewicz, Walerian. 1991. "Kto górą ?" *Polityka* 5 (1761): 11.

Dzun, W. 1993. "Spoleczno-Ekonomiczne Aspekty Rozwoju Rolnictwa w Warunkach Gospodarki Rynkowej." In *Wies I Rolnictwo na Rozdrozu*, edited by Izabella Bukraby-Rylska, Janusz Stacewicz, and Maria Wieruszewska, 38–56. Warsaw: PAN, IRWiR.

Ekiert, Grzegorz. 1990. "Democratisation Processes in East Central Europe: A Theoretical Consideration." *British Journal of Political Science* 21 (3): 285–313.

Fedyszak-Radziejowska, Barbara. 1995. "Rolnicy, przedsiebiorcy, mieszkancy wsi wobec wymagan gospodarki rynkowej." In *Wies i Rolnictwo w Okresie Transformacji Systemowej*, edited by Leszek Klank, 138–155. Warsaw: Polska Akademia Nauk—Instytut Rowoju Wsi i Rolnictwa.

———.1993. "Rolnicy o sobie na tle innych group spolecznych." In Rolnicy '92: *Rolnicy wobec zmian systemowych*. edited by Andrzej Rosner, 31–39. Warsaw: CBOS.

Forys, Grzegorz. 2008. *Dynamika Sporow. Protesty Rolnikow w III Rzeczpospolitej*. Warsaw: Wydawnictwo Naukowe Scholar.

Friszke, Andrzej. 1990. "The Polish Political Scene (1989)." *East European Politics and Societies* 4 (2): 305–341.

Glowacki, Marcin. 1993. "Rolnicy o Polityce Rolnej." In *Rolnicy '92: Rolnicy wobec zmian systemowych*, edited by Andrzej Rosner, 52–66. Warsaw: CBOS.

Gluszynski, Jerzy. 1990. "Za I przeciw rolnikom." *Polityka* 31 (1735): 6.

Gorlach, Krzysztof. 2000. "Post-Traditional Family Farm in the Post-Communist Modernity: The Case of Poland." Paper delivered at the Working Group 22 on Family Farming. *International Rural Sociological Association X World Congress*, July 30–August 2, Rio De Janeiro, Brazil.

———. 1999. "Presenting 'New Face': Polish Peasants' Protests in the Era of Post-Communism." Paper delivered at the Working Group 1: Social Movements in Rural Areas: Sources, Rationalities and Identities in the Process of Change." XVIII Congress of the European Society for Rural Sociology, August 24–28, Lund, Sweden.

———. 1995. *Chlopi, Rolnicy, Przedsiebiorcy: Klopotliwa Klasa w Polsce Post-komunistycznej*. Krakow. Uniwersytet Jagiellonski.

Gorlach, K., and P. Mooney. 1998. "Defending Class Interests: Polish Peasants in the First Years of Transformation." In *Theorizing Transition. The Political Economy of Post-Communist Transformations*, edited by J. Pickles and A. Smith, 262–283. London: Routledge.

Gorlach, Krzysztof, and Zygmunt Serega. 1993. "From 'Repressive Tolerance' to 'Oppressive Freedom': Polish Family Farms in Transition." In *Post-Communist Poland: From Totalitarianism to Democracy?*, 109–118, edited by Jaques Coenen Huther and Brunon Synak. Commack, NY: Nova Science.

Gramsci, Antonio. 2011 [1992]. *Prison Notebooks*. New York: Columbia University Press.

GUS (Główny Urząd Statystyczny). 1995. *Maly Rocznik Statystyczny*. Warszawa.

———. 1985, 1990, 1991, 1992, 1993, 1994, 1995, 2000, 2011. *Roczniki Statystyczne* Warszawa. GUS (http://www.stat.gov.pl/gus).

Halamska, Maria. 2000a. "Zróżnicowanie polskich gospodarstw rolnych i sposobów ich funkcjonowania ." In *Chłop, rolnik, farmer? Przystąpienie Polski do Unii Europejskiej—nadzieje i obawy polskiej wsi*, edited by X. Dolinska, 65–79. Warsaw: Instytut Spraw Publicznych.

———. 2000b. "Rolnicy '99 a Ziemia: od Mitu do Rzeczywistosci." In *Chłop, rolnik, farmer? Przystąpienie Polski do Unii Europejskiej—nadzieje i obawy polskiej wsi*, edited by X. Dolinska, 122–139. Warsaw: Instytut Spraw Publicznych.

———. 1991. "Polish Peasant at the edge of XXI century." *Wies I Rolnictwo* (4): 42–58.

Hann, C. 1985. *A Village without Solidarity: Polish Peasants in Years of Crisis*. New Haven, CT: Yale University Press.

Janicki, Mariusz, and Miroslaw Peczak. 1993. "Kosynierzy nowej generacji." *Polityka* 14, April 3: 3.

Kocik, Lucjan. 1996. "The Privatization and Market Transformation of Polish Agriculture." In *After Socialism: Land Reform and Social Change in Eastern Europe*, edited by Ray Abrahams, 115–133. Providence, RI: Berghan Books.

Korbonski, Andrzej. 1965. *Politics of Socialist Agriculture in Poland*. New York: Columbia University Press.

Krencik, Wieslaw. 1991. "Nowy koszyk 'Polityki.'" *Polityka* 5 (1761): 8.

Kroeber, A. L. 1948. *Anthropology*. New York: Harcourt, Brace & Co.

Kubik, Jan, and Grzegorz Ekiert. 1999. *Rebellious Civil Society and the Consolidation of Democracy in Poland, 1989–1993*. Ann Arbor: University of Michigan Press.

Kulesz, M. 1994. "Centralizm Rzadowy," *Wprost* 28: 6.

Lewandowski, J., and J. Szomburg. 1990. "Strategia prywatizacji." *Transformacja Gospdarki* 7. Gdansk: Instytut Badan nad Gospodarka Rynkowa.

Litwack, J. 1991. "Discretionary Behavior and Soviet Economic Reform." *Soviet Studies* 43 (2): 255–279.

Mack, Wales. 1994. *Rethinking the Market, Reconfiguring Institutions: The Case of Polish Agriculture*. Berkeley: University of California Press.

Magyar, Balint. 1984. "Peasantry and Agrarian Policy in Poland, 1944–1982." Manuscript.

Markiewicz, Wojciech. 1991. "Export wewnetrzny." *Polityka* 20 (1776): 11.

Maurel, Marie-Claude. 2000. "Patterns of Post-Socialist Transformation in the Rural Areas of Central Europe." In *Regions and Cities in the Global World*, edited by Gyuala Horvath, 141–158. Pécs, Hungary: Centre for Regional Studies, HAS.

Ministerstwo Rolnictwa i Gospodarki Zywnosciowej. 1993. *Raport o stanie rolnictwa i gospodarki zywnosciowej*. Warsaw: Ministerstwo Rolnictwa i Gospodarki Zywnosciowej.

Murrell, Peter. 1991. "Can Neoclassical Economics Underpin the Reform of Centrally Planned Economies?" *Journal of Economic Perspectives* 5 (4): 59–76.

Nagengast, Carole. 1991. *Reluctant Socialists, Rural Entrepreneurs: Class, Culture, and the Polish State*. Boulder, CO: Westview.

———. 1990. "Populism and the Polish State." *Socialist Review* 90 (2): 80–101.

Paradowska, Janina. 1993. "Czas Samoobrony." *Polityka* 34, (1894): 3.

Peczak, Miroslaw, and Mariusz Janicki. 1993. "Kosynierzy nowej generacji." *Polityka* 14 (1874): 3.

Pilichowski, Andrzej. 1994. "Chłopi w perspektywie strukturalnego przystosowania." *Kultura i Społeczeństwo* 38 (1): 163–173.

Podemski, Krzysztof, ed. 2011. *Spoleczenstwa Europy Srodkowo-Wschodniej: Projekt Eurequal*. Poznan: Wydawnictwo Naukowe UAM.

Przeworski, Adam. 1993. "Economic Reforms, Public Opinion and Political Institutions: Poland in the Eastern European Perspective." In *Economic Reforms in New Democracies: A Social-Democratic Approach*, edited by L. C. B. Pereira, J. M. Maravall, and A. Przeworski, 132–198. Cambridge, UK: Cambridge University Press.

———. 1991. *Democracy and the Market: Political and Economic Reforms in Eastern Europe and Latin America*. Cambridge, UK: Cambridge University Press.

———. 1985. *Capitalism and Social Democracy*. Cambridge, UK: Cambridge University Press.

Redfield, Robert. 1956. "Peasant Society and Culture." In *The Little Community and Peasant Society and Culture*. Chicago: University of Chicago Press.

Scott, James C. 1976. *The Moral Economy of the Peasant: Subsistence and Rebellion in Southeast Asia*. New Haven, CT: Yale University Press.

Shanin, Teodor. 1971. "Introduction." In *Peasants and Peasant Societies*, edited by T. Shanin, 11–20. Harmondsworth: Penguin.

Solska, Joanna. 1990. "Gorzki kredyt." *Polityka* 3 (1706): 4.

Solska, Joanna, Andrzej Mozolowski, and Pawel Tarnowski. 1990. "Sceny z zycia gospodarczego." *Polityka* 2 (1706): 6.

Staniszkis, Jadwiga. 1991. *The Dynamics of the Breakthrough in Eastern Europe*. Berkeley: University of California Press.

Starzynski, Piotr. 1993. "Rolnicy o instytucjach zycia spolecznego I politycznego." In *Rolnicy '92: Rolnicy wobec zmian systemowych*, edited by Andrzej Rosner, 22–30. Warsaw: CBOS.

Szelenyi, Ivan. 1988. *Socialist Entrepreneurs: Embourgeoisement in Rural Hungary*. Madison: University of Wisconsin Press.

Szemberg, Anna. 1980. *Przeobrazenia Spoleczno-Ekonomiczne Indywidualnych Gospodarstw Rolnych*. Warsaw: Zaklad Wydawnictw CZSR.

Tarnowski, Pawel. 1990. "W oparach spirytusu." *Polityka* 32 (1736): 3.

Turski, Ryszard. 1965. *Miedzy miastem a wsia. Strukura spoleczno-zawodowa chlopow-robotnikow w Polsce*. Warsaw: Panstwowe Wydawnictwo Naukowe.

Wilczak, Jagienka. 1990. "Wielkie czekanie." *Polityka* 3 (1707): 1.

Wilczynski, Waclaw. 1996. *Ekonomia i Polityka Gospodarcza Okresu Transformacjii. Wybor Prac z Lat 1991–1995*. Poznan: Wydawnictwo Wyszej Szkoly Bankowej.

Wilkin, Jerzy. 1988. "Reakcja chłopów na politykę rolną państwa w perspektywie historycznej." *Kultura i Społeczeństwo* 4: 30–47.

Winiecki, Jan. 1991. "The Inevitability of a Fall in Output in the Early Stages of Transition to the Market: Theoretical Underpinnings." *Soviet Studies* 43 (3): 669–676.

Wolf, E. R. 1966. *Peasants*. Englewood Cliffs, NJ: Prentice-Hall.

World Bank. 1995. *Farm Restructuring and Land Tenure in Reforming Socialist Economies: A Comparative Analysis of Eastern and Central Europe*. Washington, DC: World Bank Discussion Papers #268.

———. 1990. *An Agricultural Strategy for Poland. Report of the Polish European Community World Bank Task Force*. Washington, DC: World Bank.

Chapter Four

Cooperatives in the Vise of Information Constraints and Ownership Ambiguity

The previous chapter concluded with the argument that the strategy of destatization, or the comprehensive removal of all state ownership claims and state-imposed constraints on formal private property owners, did not lead to the effective exercise of ownership rights among the private agricultural sector. The insufficiently developed legal and organizational infrastructure of the transition period imposed new constraints on the exercise of agricultural private ownership in all of its dimensions.

This chapter will analyze the actual transition trajectory of agricultural cooperative ownership. The cooperative sector in Poland by the end of 1989 consisted of over fifteen thousand primary cooperatives and was comprised of over fifteen million cooperative members. Membership in the cooperatives was formally equated with ownership and formally distinguished from salaried employment in the cooperatives. Overall, cooperatives employed over 1.8 million people. Approximately seven thousand cooperatives existed in urban areas (such as cooperatives of housing and trading cooperatives). Another eight thousand cooperatives existed in rural areas. Within rural cooperatives the most important categories were: agricultural production cooperatives, cooperatives of agricultural circles, and cooperative banks. In over two thousand agricultural production cooperatives, members collectively cultivated 750,000 hectares of land, about 4.5 percent of the arable area. Some two thousand cooperatives of agricultural circles, based on hired labor, provided plowing, harvesting, and machinery services to individual agricultural producers, who were the circles' main members. Approximately sixteen hundred cooperative banks were the only institutions in rural areas offering small-scale credit and saving services. Therefore, cooperatives existed as a parallel form of agricultural production as well as, by way of agricultural circles and cooperative banks, an institutional system aiding private agricultural production (World Bank 1990, annex 6; Turowski 1995).

The actual transition trajectory of agricultural cooperative ownership confronted both the objectives outlined in the official post-socialist program for reconstitution of the existing cooperatives and the expectations of the "real" subjects of cooperative ownership. Both sides expressed the desire to reclaim cooperative ownership from the "deformation" instilled by state socialism and thus to revive the past genuine collective system in general and the cooperative agricultural subsystem in particular. The members of agricultural cooperatives and the post-socialist reformers both attempted to revive past critical components of *voluntarism* and of *self-governance* into the post-socialist future of the cooperative organizations. In the instances of service and trade cooperative rural associations (cooperatives of agricultural circles, cooperative banks, and trade associations), they also projected their *self-aid* characteristics as organizations supporting the private property owners in agriculture.

As both sides aimed to construct the future by reclaiming the past, they increasingly tended to invoke divergent points in the long history of cooperative organizations in Polish agriculture. On the one hand, post-socialist reformers referenced the Gomulka agricultural plan of 1956 (Korbonski 1965; Gorlach 2000), the *early* socialist legacy of cooperative local associations, before their subsequent subjugation to the centrally imposed economic directives, in their attempt to induce cooperative members to perform better economically. On the other hand, cooperative members, progressively disillusioned with the post-socialist agrarian program's tenets and its result, drew on the nineteenth-century cooperative legacy as a network of organizations in order to enhance economic performance, to articulate agrarian political interests, and to stage active resistance to adverse reform policies.[1]

For post-socialist reformers, the spontaneous revival of the cooperative sector and the firm reassertion of cooperative ownership rights rested on the rapid lifting and dismantling of the superimposed state socialist institutional superstructure—a structure that had engulfed ground-level cooperative organizations and which allowed the socialist state as an actor to assert its claims to cooperative property. Predicating their notion of property, and consequently their reform strategies, on the assumption of constant behavioral characteristics that promote economic efficiency narrowed the post-socialist reformers' basis for assessing the lasting effects of joint cooperative ownership and its institutional representation on the local cooperatives. Their specific conceptualization of property also limited their ability to fully scrutinize the effects of the institutional environment on the behavior of economic agents and on the development of cooperative organizations in the transition period.

Scholarship within an evolutionary economic framework (Arrow 1963; Coase 1960; North 1991; Murrell 1992) and within a neoinstitutional perspective in sociology (Meyer and Rowan 1991; DiMaggio 1991, 1988; Oliver 1991; DiMaggio and Powell 1991; Pfeffer and Salancik 2003 [1978]; Scott 2008) provides a challenge to the neoclassically oriented reformers for not according enough attention to the negative effects that the rapid destruction of system-specific institutional infrastructure brought on the performance of the economic organizations. Giving prime importance to the complex problems of decision making and organization under conditions of uncertainty, evolutionary economics and neoinstitutionalism operate under the premise of bounded rationality and tie the performance of economic agents and their organizations to the effects of the external institutional environment and to the internal processes of the information spread among organization members. Within this perspective, economic agents operate under constant information constraints and information asymmetry between them—the organization of specific knowledge is the most essential organizational asset and can be acquired only through experience and "routines." This perspective thus emphasizes the persistence of routines, of organizational behavior, and of the limited organizational capacity for innovation. The policy implication of this intellectual framework holds that, unless reform efforts include some continuity with the previous system's institutional capital, and thus avoid subjecting economic agents and organizations to overwhelming uncertainty, they will directly contribute to undermining the organizations' economic efficacy.

Because neoliberal reformers focus on the transformation of the ownership structure as a means to enhance economic performance and also assume the homogenization of economic behavior within one property form (i.e., cooperatives), they do not fully theorize the unevenness in organizational responses. Evolutionary economists, on the other hand, do account theoretically for variability in the economic performance of organizations within a given ownership form. Yet, by rejecting the language of property relations and privatization strategy, evolutionary economics cannot fully theorize the consistent differences of economic behavior across ownership forms.

Diverging from the post-socialist reformers' assumptions of the unidirectionality of change in organizational structure—a change into self-management and economic actions positively related to the market forces—my analysis will document the real multidirectional and uneven evolution of the ownership and governance of the cooperative associations. I will argue that the post-socialist reform architects, guided by political expediency to radically distance themselves from the socialist past, underestimated the lingering consequences of the organizational control of the socialist state over ownership rights. Without sufficiently acknowledging the role of *institutions* in shaping the transformation of the property structure, they obscured the fact that organizational control under state socialism not only suppressed the exercise of specific ownership rights of members, but also profoundly undermined cooperative ownership as such. In the post-socialist transition, this heightened the ambiguity about what constituted cooperative ownership and about who were the legitimate subjects of cooperative ownership.

In this way, my empirical analysis will be informed by the intellectual framework of evolutionary economics and neoinstitutionalism. However, I will also argue for the need to theorize the behavior of economic agents and organizations by synthesizing the emphasis on organizational forms *and* property forms. Thus I will illustrate that the heightened uncertainty in primary cooperatives, produced by rapid changes in their institutional and legislative environment, locked individual cooperatives within the legacies of their profiles of production and so radically reduced their options for production changes in the transition. This acute uncertainty then led to managerial centralization in place of the expected revival of genuine cooperative self-governance. As cooperatives exhibited an overall tendency toward management centralization, individual cooperatives followed *divergent* routes toward the consolidation of managerial power. These routes reflected an interplay between positive and negative claims to the exercise of ownership rights by the cooperative members and management's monopolization of scarce resources. The divergent routes of managerial centralization then had distinct consequences for the survival of their organizations as such and their ability to act as *cooperative* organizations.

To chart the transition in the cooperative sector, I will trace the divergent trajectories of two kinds of agricultural cooperative associations in the new post-socialist economic environment. In the first part of the chapter, I will analyze three primary agricultural *production* cooperatives, in which members collectively cultivate the land. The second part of the chapter will be devoted to an analysis of a *service cooperative*—a cooperative of agricultural circles in which collective ownership refers to production resources (such as agricultural machines) other than individually owned land. Based on hired labor, agricultural circles performed mechanical plowing, planting, and crop harvesting services for their cooperative members and agricultural producers. The evolution of agricultural circles will be traced through analysis of the behavior of their members in their dual role as owners: cooperative owners in their agricultural circles and individual owners of their private agricultural farms. In their latter role, peasants were the dominant client base for the cooperative of agricultural circles.

The Transition of Agricultural Production Cooperatives

At the onset of the post-socialist transition, agricultural production cooperatives that existed within the boundaries of the studied community were among the 2,000 cooperatives across Poland cultivating approximately 750,000 hectares of land. The number and landholdings of agricultural cooperatives radically fluctuated throughout state socialism in direct relation to changing agrarian policy directives regarding the cooperative subsector.

The first agricultural cooperatives appeared in socialist Poland in 1948, at the beginning of the official collectivization campaign. The state stipulated the creation of three types of "producer cooperatives" to socialize the agricultural sector. In cooperatives of type I, which represented the lowest form of socialized production, the members were to participate in some collective cultivation of their landholdings (for example, sowing or harvesting). Livestock and equipment were to remain in private hands. The output was to be divided based on individual contribution of land, labor, and capital. Type II, called producers associations, represented a more advanced form of socialized production. In cooperatives of type II, the members were supposed to conduct all productive activities collectively, with land and capital becoming a common property. In the most advanced cooperatives, type III, called producers unions, members were to cultivate land collectively and divide the income based on labor only, regardless of the contribution of land and capital (Magyar 1984; Korbonski 1965). In the first wave of collectivization, between 1950 and 1951, over three thousand cooperatives were formed. By 1952, the number had climbed to 4,500. In the third wave of collectivization ending in 1956, it reached its peak at 10,000 agricultural collectives predominantly of type I and II (Magyar 1984; Korbonski 1965). In overwhelming proportions, cooperative members were middle-size peasants residing in the western provinces of Poland. Although collectivization was to be based on the voluntary accession of peasants into cooperative production, most joined the ranks of cooperatives out of a mixture of economic incentives and coercion. Under the slogan "collectivization equals large-scale farming equals mechanization," peasants were enticed to join by the state's promise of better access to agricultural resources, such as machinery. In addition, they were threatened as private owners with the confiscation of their farms and higher taxes if they resisted bringing their landholdings into cooperatives (Gorlach 2000).

In 1956 there was a rapid and drastic drop in the number of agricultural production cooperatives in Poland. The slogan that equated collectivization with mechanization and increased agricultural production had proven to be a myth for both participants and policy makers. The creation of cooperatives coincided with a sharp decline in the share of agricultural investment expenditures in the state's total investment expenditures. Hence, this translated into a meager economic performance of the cooperative subsector.[2] During the Polish "thaw" of 1956, the state reassessed its collectivization program and presented a choice to existing cooperatives: they could dissolve or persist. Over 80 percent of the agricultural production cooperatives dismantled soon after (Korbonski 1965; Gorlach 2000).

The 1960s began the long trend of the changing social composition and institutional structure of cooperatives, which would bear a direct impact on the attempts to clarify cooperative ownership rights in the subsequent post-socialist period. Thus, in light of the earlier failed campaign of voluntary accession of landed peasants to cooperative organization, the radically reduced number of cooperatives of the 1960s and 1970s increasingly drew their members from landless agricultural laborers while the state as a property coclaimant provided productive assets for cooperative property. Already by the mid-1960s, almost half of the cooperative land was not collectivized by individual members, but rather was allotted by the state from the state land fund. By the mid-1970s, the land originating from the state land fund accounted for nearly 70 percent of all cooperative farmland, while their nationwide number stagnated at the level of 1500 cooperatives (Magyar 1984).

In the 1980s cooperative membership increased, although the rise was of a specific character. In order to broaden the cooperative subsector, state policy stipulated that landed peasants could bring only a portion of their land to qualify for a cooperative membership. Hence, in the early 1980s the number of cooperatives did in fact rise to over two thousand nationwide. By committing a fraction of their land to cooperatives, peasants used the measure to gain access to those production resources (fertilizers, fodder, and so on) controlled by the redistributive monopoly and made disproportionally scarce for the private agricultural sector. Thus, the membership entry requirements (no or an insignificant land contribution), combined with substantial state financial capital to subsidize cooperative production on a continuous basis, meant that the members' cooperative ownership became disassociated from the cooperative capital assets. Their assets became indivisible as a "cooperative" property.

In addition, the state, as a co-claiming property subject, imposed upon primary agricultural cooperatives a growing institutional centralization by the 1960s. After a 1961 decree, the cooperatives were vertically integrated with the central and regional cooperative organizations. With compulsory integration into an organizational superstructure of regional and national cooperative unions, and the imposition of institutional links to party units, local-level cooperatives were subjected to management and personnel selection directives from above. They were also obliged to work out economic and financial plans in compliance with the guidelines of the central cooperative unions and the central economic plan targets (Turowski 1995). In the 1970s, the vertical channels through which the agricultural cooperatives were subsumed into a redistributive economy were strengthened by the lateral integration of individual cooperatives, thus creating conglomerates of agricultural cooperatives (*Kombinats*).

The Organizational Reconfiguration of Cooperatives: Planned Deinstitutionalization and Spontaneous Fragmentation

From the post-socialist reformers' perspective, the tactics of organizational control employed progressively by state socialism effectively suspended the exercise of cooperative rights. The cooperative rights of individual members, reflected in the principles of self-aid, self-governance, and the voluntarism of cooperative associations, effectively were preempted.[3] In the context of organizational control by the state of all property forms, the factual distinction between the cooperative and state sectors in terms of property types became generally *perceived* as almost meaningless. Thus, with the inauguration of the post-socialistic era, the cooperatives were initially counted in official data as in the state sector. Following the liquidation of the unions of cooperatives, they became classified as part of the private sector. This chapter highlights the shortcomings of this dichotomous classification and the unreliability of data suggesting a rapid growth of the private sector and the appropriation of cooperative ownership by individual agricultural producers.

To undo the organizational tactics employed under state socialism, the post-socialist reformers viewed the dismantling of the institutional environment of cooperatives as a *necessary* and *sufficient* condition for the reclamation of genuine cooperative agricultural organizations. With it, they assumed there would be a spontaneous revival of cooperative membership/ownership. The removal of organizational control over cooperative ownership rights became synonymous with the privatization of cooperatives. This, in turn, became equated with the *deinstitutionalization* of primary cooperatives. The Cooperative Law Amendment of January 20, 1990 to the 1982 cooperative law was intended to swiftly and comprehensively dismantle the effects of organizational control of state socialism in the cooperative sector. As agriculture became the testing ground for privatization and restructuring in other sectors of the economy, the agricultural cooperative subsector was singled out as appearing easier to privatize than the usually larger-scale state agricultural farms. The amendment stipulated two measures to remove past constraints and to re-create genuine collective ownership. First, it imposed an immediate, mandatory liquidation of cooperative unions on the central and regional levels, including the transfer and sale of union assets to the new owners. It also established a two-year ban on forming new cooperative associations as a preemptive measure to avoid the re-creation of monopolies. Second, it called for the democratic election of new member representatives at the level of primary cooperatives in order to involve the membership in their governance.

Although the Cooperative Law Amendment of January 1990 explicitly stipulated the mandatory dismantling of the *vertical* organizational superstructure of the secondary and tertiary cooperative unions, it also provided a legal venue for further spontaneous fragmentation of the primary cooperative conglomerates into autonomous individual cooperatives. Such a conglomerate (the *Kombinat*) existed within the boundaries of the studied community until 1990. It consisted of four local agricultural production cooperatives and two service units, each operating in a distinct village of the studied *gmina*. The cooperatives were autonomous as production units, but were organizationally and financially integrated. Apart from some smaller mechanical and transportation equipment owned and operated by the individual agricultural production cooperatives, the machinery park was the common property of the conglomerate.

Each cooperative was involved in animal husbandry that was supported by its own crop production. In addition, each agricultural cooperative was involved in some processing (meat processing, dairy processing, or fodder mixing). Apart from agricultural production the cooperative performed various social functions for its members (for example, housing, cafeterias, restaurants, and daycare centers). The three cooperatives I studied had an arable land size of six hundred to seven hundred hectares.[4] The cooperatives differed in terms of their membership size at the beginning of 1990. Cooperative A had sixty-four members when it broke from the *Kombinat* and this number was lowered to thirty-eight by the middle of 1992. In 1990, Cooperative B started with 112 members and progressively moved down to sixty-one persons, with the remaining overemployment of approximately twelve people. Cooperative C began with 180 members. By 1992 it had been reduced to 120 with persisting overemployment of thirty members. Unlike cooperatives A and B which were predominantly involved in grain production and animal husbandry, Cooperative C was unique in that vegetable and fruit processing and canning had constituted a significant portion of its production activities since the cooperative's beginning in the Kombinat in the early 1970s.

Shortly after the 1990 Cooperative Law Amendment was issued, Cooperative A initiated a motion to break up the conglomerate. The cooperative acted on a recommendation of an accountant who formerly had a joint position in the *Kombinat* and Cooperative A, and who followed closely the legislation on the cooperative sector. The general assembly of the cooperative conglomerate voted on the petition and rejected it by a narrow margin.[5] Following an unsuccessful attempt to gather a majority vote for a breakup, Cooperative A filed a petition in court in February 1990. Cooperatives B and C then joined Cooperative A in the petition for secession from the *Kombinat*. In June 1990, the court issued a decision granting the petitioners legal secession from the *Kombinat*. After losing three cooperatives, the *Kombinat* continued to exist as a legal entity that consisted of one remaining cooperative and the building and construction units. In November 1990 it was liquidated.

The court ruling on the secession of the member cooperatives reflected an unevenness of state regulation in the redefining and restructuring of cooperative property rights. The Cooperative Law Amendment fell short of providing specific guidelines as to the division of assets between the member cooperatives or as to supervision of the breakup of the *Kombinat* by appointed personnel. Thus, the machinery park, and the housing facilities for administrative personnel located on the premises of Cooperative A, became a focus of contention among member cooperatives. Immediately following the court permission to abort the conglomerate, Cooperative A unilaterally assumed property rights to the conglomerate's administrative building that stood on Cooperative A's premises. Acting as the sole owner of the building, Cooperative A's management sold it on the market and kept the proceeds, generating much-needed financial resources for the cooperative. In addition, Cooperative A appropriated a major share of the conglomerate machinery stationed on its premises.

The sale generated very negative relations among the separating cooperatives, as other members disputed Cooperative A's ownership rights to the *Kombinat's* assets. In the hostile atmosphere that ensued, it became impossible to reach any agreement about how to distribute financial responsibility for the 500 million zloty debt, amassed by the *Kombinat*. The *Kombinat* attempted to impose one-fifth of the debt payment on the newly independent Cooperative A. The cooperative rejected the claim and sought a court ruling on the issue. The court decision was still pending in late summer of 1993, while the personnel and paper trail of the property rights has been mostly lost with passing time. The petition for a court ruling was withdrawn before the court deliberated on the claim, right after Cooperative B signed a debt restructuring program and during the succession of managers at Cooperative C.

By allowing Cooperative A to appropriate a disproportional share, and lacking clear guidelines as to the redistributive principle, the Cooperative Law Amendment of 1990 created *differential entry* by the individual cooperatives into the new economic environment. However, it also instilled a profound sense of uncertainty, shared by all departing cooperatives, over the distribution of the *Kombinat* assets as well as the overall future of the cooperative form of organization.[6]

The Cooperative Strategies for Economic Transition

Polish agriculture in general, and its cooperative subsector in particular, were subjected to early distress caused by the stabilization and liberalization measures of the shock therapy program. As interest rates rose sharply and agricultural domestic markets were opened to competition from foreign producers almost overnight, the demand for agricultural goods fell. In addition, the input prices more rapidly approached world levels, while producer prices showed much slower adjustment. While all cooperatives faced unfavorable price structures for agricultural producers, their *conditions of entry* varied substantially. This contributed to a pursuit of distinctive strategies of adjustment by each cooperative.

Cooperative A: The Maintenance of Existing Agricultural Markets and Improvement of Trade Terms

Cooperative A gained an advantageous start in the new economic environment by breaking away from the *Kombinat* early on and by selling the conglomerate building. Secession from the conglomerate allowed Cooperative A to be reclassified into a more favorable tax bracket. The cooperative was involved in production activities classified within the new tax laws as "strictly agricultural in nature" and thus subjected to lower taxation. By contrast, agricultural processing (meat, dairy, fruit, or vegetable processing) performed at other cooperatives in the conglomerate carried higher taxes ("special sector" taxation). At the level of the agricultural cooperative, this tax structure provided a powerful incentive for agriculturally oriented individual cooperatives to legally break away from those within the "special sector" and to avoid subsidizing them. Such tax considerations became an initial impetus for Cooperative A to seek independence.[7]

Secession and the sale of the administrative facilities brought cash to the cooperative, which cash was partially diverted to the renewal and expansion of machinery. Additional funds were secured by auctioning the old machines to individual buyers. During the transition, when other cooperatives of the former *Kombinat* did not have amortization funds, Cooperative A was able to modernize and expand its machinery. It sold used and outdated machines to individual peasants and replaced them with new ones.

As a result, Cooperative A avoided taking out loans with high interest rates for immediate production needs (fertilizers, pesticides, and seeds) and therefore eliminated the risk of defaulting on loan payments. Furthermore, a portion of the building sale revenues was used for the cooperative's most important investment project. In summer 1992, the cooperative completed the construction of three grain silos that completely covered the cooperative's storage needs. The silos provided better control of the grain humidity level, thus commanding better prices for the producer. More importantly, they allowed the cooperative flexibility in putting grain on the market. Instead of being forced to sell immediately, the storage silos allowed Cooperative A to withhold the grain from the market and await more favorable prices. The investment in silos was a conscious attempt to strengthen the cooperative's position vis-à-vis distribution centers. By comparison, the individual grain producers with inadequate storage or drying facilities could not negotiate the same kind of price levels in their dealings with the distribution centers.

In addition to bringing in scarce financial capital, the sale of the administrative building led to the closing of a few unprofitable economic services housed in that facility, such as wash-and-dry cleaning services. This justified a reduction in personnel. Apart from voluntary early retirement, disciplinary firing, and quitting, the elimination of specific economic activity was the only viable way of reducing overemployment. Closing the dry cleaning facilities allowed for a 10 percent reduction in employment.

In its response to the market-oriented reform program, Cooperative A retained its overall agricultural production profile, thus qualifying for a lower taxation bracket. Unlike the two other cooperatives under study, Cooperative A did not venture into agricultural processing. Since the introduction of the reform program, the cooperative stayed within its customary areas of production (grain and cereal, swine, and dairy and beef cattle) but *modified the levels of production.* The cooperative lowered its dairy production by 25 percent from 1990 to 1992.[8] The reduction was prompted by a request from a monopolistic milk processing center for a twenty-five million zloty membership fee from its milk suppliers. Failure to pay the membership fee implied either a 50 percent reduction in milk producer prices or a total inability to sell milk to the center. On the other hand, the cooperative increased its number of beef cattle. Confident that the four-year decline of cattle production would cause the price of beef to rise, the general manager acquired one hundred cattle from a state farm undergoing liquidation. By purchasing the cattle at a bargain price, the cooperative expanded its herd from 450 to 550. Further expansion would have required an investment in new facilities. The prohibitive cost of investment loans prevented the cooperative from expanding its swine production.[9]

The changes prompted by the reform program occurred primarily in the *method of production.* In the face of falling produce prices and a generally unfavorable price structure for agricultural producers, Cooperative A followed the path of other agricultural producers (both state farms and individual producers) and moved toward a *closed-circle production system.* The cooperative reduced its reliance on the market for maintaining and reproducing its resource base. With the exception of the commodity production of wheat, rapeseed, and sugar beets, the majority of its grain production was diverted from the market and into animal husbandry. For example, to reduce its production costs, in mid-1992, the cooperative cut by half its purchasing of high-protein fodder from a state farm supplier. The strategy of relying almost exclusively on its own crops for livestock fodder seriously reduced or altogether eliminated the purchase of mineral and high protein feed supplements on the open market. However, by the manager's own admission, this strategy of lowering the cost of production resulted in decreased technical productivity, lags in breeding, and lengthening the production cycle by 10 to 15 percent, with a corresponding increase in labor expenditures. Similarly, reliance on the cooperative's own grain seed or customary exchanges of grain seeds led to lower grain yields.[10]

In addition to the financial resources available to Cooperative A after the sale of the *Kombinat* building, the cooperative general manager sought other methods of generating finance capital for renewing the production cycle. He refrained from taking out loans due to the high interest rates.[11] Instead, he turned to raising capital through the sale of some of the collective's productive assets. In 1991 he sold one thousand sheep and two hectares of the collective land. In the same year, he sold an additional ten hectares of land for forestation purposes. In a separate transaction, he liquidated a similar plot of cooperative land adjacent to the international highway, for nonagricultural purposes. Land sold for nonagricultural conversion brought significantly higher prices than sales for agricultural purposes. For instance, land along the highway increased in value even more dramatically from 1991 to 1993. In the subsequent year, he sold yet another piece of cooperative land with housing buildings on it. Members of the cooperative repeatedly (albeit secretly) complained that neither the specific amount of revenues generated by these sales nor the precise allocation of funds obtained from the sales was disclosed to the general cooperative membership. Furthermore, Cooperative A created for itself a new source of revenue by constructing an additional silo in 1993. For a storage fee, the cooperative stored the grain of local (mostly individual) grain producers.

Cooperative B: Fluctuating between Old and New Markets

In contrast to Cooperative A, which remained within its traditional profile of agricultural production, Cooperative B initially responded to the market reforms by introducing and subsequently expanding its production of poultry (geese, ducks, and chickens) for export purposes. In 1990, the cooperative's production of ducks and geese was at the level of two thousand per year. The targeted amount for 1991 was twice as high. However, the cooperative abruptly withdrew from this line of production in early 1991 following a failed attempt by the general manager to identify and secure markets for its poultry. The general manager was subsequently charged with negligence. The total losses incurred by the cooperative exceeded thirty million zloty. This additional financial liability of the cooperative came after an earlier loss of credit eligibility in the summer of 1991.

Unlike Cooperative A, Cooperative B had a tradition of semi-processing that dated back to its integration within the *Kombinat* in the 1970s. The nutria processing shop was the most profitable sector of the whole cooperative. At the beginning of the reform program it worked at capacity, processing four to five thousand nutria monthly, supplied by individual growers. Indeed, the capacity of these processing operations was projected to triple in size by 1991. After the slaughtering and the meat and fur semi-processing, the boneless nutria meat was sold by the cooperative to privately run and state-owned meat processing plants as an additive for sausages. The bones were sold as animal feed, while the fur was in demand throughout Poland by various enterprises within the fur industry. However, by the end of 1991, the nutria shop staff was charged with embezzling funds from the general cooperative membership and was subsequently dismissed. The shop was then liquidated. The incumbent general manager was held ultimately responsible and discharged from his duties by a general membership vote.

Thus, in the fall of 1991, the cooperative found itself not only with failed production lines, but also with mounting debts. In the aftermath of the production crisis, the cooperative experienced management crises and went through a succession of general managers. The first candidate, hired from the outside in a national search, was quickly dismissed by the general assembly as inexperienced and incompetent. He was replaced by a manager selected from the ranks of the cooperative production unit supervisors. The new general manager reversed his predecessor's production approach. Instead of searching for new markets, the general manager attempted to stay within the "proven" markets and to concentrate on the overall "agricultural" profile of production. Thus, his main emphasis was on expanding swine production within the confines of the existing utility buildings and based on a closed-cycle production method. As in the case of Cooperative A, the general manager refrained from purchasing fodder, with the exception of a special fodder for hogs and piglets. In dairy cattle production the new general manager followed the steady trend of decline. In 1990 dairy cattle were reduced by nearly 50 percent from 180 to 92. In 1992 the number was lowered further to 58. The managers of both Cooperatives A and B justified their decisions by the unfair policies of the monopolistic dairy distribution centers in setting prices and classifying milk quality.

Apart from expanding swine production, the other major component of Cooperative B's new economic plan was adaptation of a utility building. By insulating the building, the general manager wanted to create a major facility for drying and storing grain. Just as in Cooperative A's case, his strategy for adapting to the new economic environment was centered around redefining and negotiating the terms of exchange with the monopolistic grain procurement centers.

Yet unlike Cooperative A, which cashed in early by appropriating the *Kombinat's* building and machinery, Cooperative B entered the new economic period without any financial reserves. Thus, it was forced to take high-percentage loans to reproduce the production cycle. To supplement the extremely scarce financial capital, in 1990 and 1991, the general manager of

Cooperative B and a director of the neighboring private dairy processing farm regularly exchanged informal short-term loans to meet payroll or other expedient expenditures. By the summer of 1991, the cooperative lost credit eligibility. The newly elected general manager then found it necessary to liquidate some of the cooperative assets to finance production needs. He put part of the cooperative buildings and eight hectares of agricultural lands up for sale. After a few months, the best offer he received was half the asking price, scheduled for payment in ten installments. One year later, the manager reduced the size of his cooperative's land by selling another piece to generate resources for the renewed production.

The major break, however, came with an application for the debt restructuring program. The refinancing of the cooperative's massive debt entailed a drastic lowering of the loan's interest rate and the rescheduling of loan payments. It further restored the cooperative's credit-worthiness. In 1994, eligibility for the debt restructuring application was restricted to a specific time frame. In contrast to many other cooperatives, the manager of Cooperative B took advantage of the program.[12] The manager of Cooperative B was then fully credited by the membership for securing the financial stability of the cooperative. On my visit in 1995, he solidified his power over the cooperative and pursued the same profile of production and markets.

Cooperative C: Expansion into Agricultural Processing

Cooperative C was the largest of the three cooperatives in this study, in terms of both land and membership. More importantly, unlike Cooperatives A and B, the most substantial and fastest growing part of Cooperative C's production involved semi- or full agricultural processing.

In spite of the imposition of special sector taxation, Cooperative C continued to expand its processing activities, which started in the early 1970s. Out of Cooperative C's five productive units, three were involved in agricultural processing. In addition to its cereal and grain production, and its livestock husbandry units, Cooperative C had a meat processing facility, feed-mixing units, and vegetable and fruit canning facilities. The latter facilities were the most prominent and profitable units.

Like Cooperative B, Cooperative C expanded its swine production based on a closed-cycle production method. In 1991 and 1992, to be self-sufficient in producing fodder for its expanded swine operations, the general manager modified his grain and cereal production profile by increasing the share of potatoes, rapeseed, corn, and grain used for feed. He intended to increase his current stock of 100 sows to 150 in order to breed approximately 2000 piglets in one breeding cycle. This, in turn, led to a capacity of approximately 1800 animals in one pig-fattening production cycle.

However, unlike the case of Cooperative B, the general manager at Cooperative C saw long-term prospects for dairy cattle production. He was convinced that reestablishing cattle production following a period of continual decline involved a lengthy process that was difficult for individual agricultural owners to undertake, thus favoring cooperative producers. He concluded that the current unfavorable price structure for cattle should not be a deterrent to sustaining production at an unchanged level. In 1990, while Cooperative C was separating from the *Kombinat* and starting independent production activity, the general manager selected 120 high-quality dairy cattle from the existing herd of 180. These high-quality dairy cows produced high-grade milk, which commanded a 15 percent higher price than regular milk. He continued to maintain this stock level, awaiting better times for enlarging the herd.

While his long-term plan on cattle production was a promising area of future production, vegetable and fruit canning remained the most profitable activity in Cooperative C. The cooperative maintained canning operations for a wide assortment of marinated vegetables including red cabbage, red beets, cucumber, mixed vegetable salads, and cucumber salads. It also produced various fruit compotes of apples and cherries for the domestic market.

The vegetable and fruit canning and processing unit had been operating since the early 1970s. Its production profile had remained relatively unchanged since that time. In order to keep the production profile and volume stable in the drastically changed economic environment, the general manager instituted several measures aimed at organizing capital for continued production and a demand for his goods. Even though the prices for vegetables and fruits collapsed after 1990, the costs of production in the processing industry (glass jars, metal jar covers, labels, and processing machines) spiraled. At the same time, credit became increasingly in short supply, while the market demand for processed produce remained quite low. As a result, the general manager entered into contracts with several private and state wholesalers that required them to advance 30 percent of the cost of input for the contracted processed output.

The cooperative also reacted to the uncertainties of the new economic environment and to the state-established preferential loans for purchasing domestic fruit and vegetables for processing by trying to minimize costs and by contracting with individual cooperative members to supply a portion of the produce used in vegetable and fruit processing. The members of the cooperative received small, individual plots as a part of their cooperative membership social entitlement. The cooperative management offered a guaranteed demand from the processing unit for the purchase of produce grown on these plots. It also offered slightly higher prices than members could get on the open market. These incentives provided the cooperative with a guaranteed source of produce and eliminated the transportation costs connected with obtaining supplies from outside growers. Participating cooperative members received a supplemental income greater than what they could obtain in the marketplace. Apart from the mutual economic benefits, this subcontracting system brought social benefits by linking the members' interests with those of the cooperative as a whole.

The above measure partially eased the tension between the cooperative and a part of its membership hurt by lay-offs. To reduce overemployment, the general manager shut down one production line in the vegetable and fruit processing unit. This move legally justified the elimination of the corresponding work stations and terminated one out of two fifteen-member permanent shifts. In its place, the general manager later reopened the same line as a seasonal one and staffed it with retired cooperative members. The manager thus economized by reducing the employment level, and by eliminating the high cost of insurance (45 percent of the wage level) tied to permanent employment status. This employment reduction precipitated a lawsuit against the cooperative by the displaced members. The matter was pending in the labor relations court for over a year, when the general manager got a verdict in his favor.

Restricted by cooperative laws that prevented him from freely hiring and firing workers, the general manager found a new way of utilizing excess labor. Between 1990 and 1992, the cooperative reduced employment from 180 to 125 members through an early retirement system and the liquidation of work stations. Despite these measures, approximately thirty "excess" workers remained. The general manager contracted with a private investor outside the cooperative to open a new line of bottled fruit juices. The investor provided the equipment for this venture, while the cooperative supplied the labor and the produce. The investor was responsible for distributing the product under the investor's label. In this cooperation, the manager was able to utilize excess labor without increasing capitalization or the cooperative's output.

By 1993 the cooperative's fortunes had shifted. Encouraged by the successful production of bottled fruit juices, the manager took a more aggressive approach to the expansion of the food-processing line. Through his personal contacts with the regional commercial banks, he secured production loans for the project. However, the cooperative's private trade partner (a limited liability joint-stock company), which had contracted to distribute the cooperative's product, defaulted on payments for the received products and then dissolved its company. This left the cooperative with a noncollectible account.

This case reflected a more general situation. While private competitors to the monopolistic distribution centers appeared, they proved to be quite unreliable in business relations and economically unstable. All three cooperatives reported several unpaid and noncollectible accounts from their trade relations with private partners. They complained of the high opportunism displayed by newly emerging private trade partners. As a result, after briefly entering into relationships with these private competitors to the monopolistic distribution centers, the general managers expressed a loss of faith in the emerging private sector. Although the most critical evaluation of exchange relations with private partners came from Cooperative C, they all reported returning to the market transactions with the monopolistic centers as more stable and predictable, if not more profitable, partners in exchange relations.

The financial problems faced by the cooperative were compounded by the manager's decision to modernize the cooperative's machinery park. Through a local dealer, he replaced the existing five domestic older grain combines for a more advanced German model. The exchange transaction was completed in the midst of the harvest. It therefore disrupted the schedule, leading to delay and substantial losses in the volume of harvested grain and in revenues. Members rebelled over the decision—questioning the rationality of the decision, its overall cost, its ultimate efficacy, and the sheer timing of it. They resented the fact that the manager made the decision unilaterally, without any prior consultation with the membership. The resentment was further fueled by the membership's growing suspicion that the manager was embezzling cooperative funds and preparing for relocation to another region of Poland for early retirement. Voting in the annual membership meeting, the members rejected the renewal of the manager's tenure. They also ousted four of the cooperative's bookkeepers hired from the outside. The manager was replaced by a local member of the cooperative who did not have the same college qualifications, but who was seen as a trustworthy, long-time member of the cooperative and local community. Thus, at the conclusion of my study, Cooperative C experienced quite a radical discontinuity in its management, accounting personnel, and production practices. Furthermore, it incurred substantial financial losses through failed trade relations and the manager's miscalculations. In contrast to Cooperative B, the management crisis within Cooperative C prevented it from meeting the deadline for the debt restructuring program application, perpetuating its financial instability.

Between Ownership-Based and Expertise-Based Control: Routes to Managerial Centralization and Imperfect Exclusive Cooperative Ownership

The common element underlying the cooperatives' divergent strategies of adaptation was the rampant *uncertainty* surrounding their entry into the new economic environment. By rapidly dismantling the secondary and tertiary cooperative unions and banning the creation of new ones during the most volatile initial period of their transition, the state deprived primary cooperatives of their information-transmitting institutions. Given the scarcity of properly trained staff, all cooperatives shared profound limits on their information-processing capabilities. The case of Cooperative A demonstrated the significance of the legal expertise of the general bookkeeper: it allowed the cooperative to proceed quickly with the secession and to gain advantageous terms of that secession relative to other cooperatives. Without the capability to process information about the rapidly changing legal, economic, and organizational issues, and without the skills, assistance, and training in establishing internal control and management procedures, cooperatives had a difficult time identifying new market opportunities. They also had difficulties calculating the profit and loss necessary to determine whether a particular effort was worth the risk.

Thus these information constraints prompted economic responses based on previously learned channels of action. Cooperatives adhered to the production lines that originated prior to the introduction of the reform program. Cooperative B's short-lived attempt to identify new opportunities and to move into new, foreign poultry markets also illustrates this point. This heightened its financial uncertainty and precipitated a retreat to old profiles of production. The constraints on the information-processing capabilities of the cooperative in identifying new markets led it to adopt strategies of adaptation to the new economic environment by *imitation*. Cooperatives, as well as individual producers, often focused on specific markets by imitating the production profiles of their counterparts. These approaches resulted in shallow markets, rapid fluctuations in the supply, and the recurrent erosion of producer prices. This process was most evident in the swine market.

As Cooperatives A and C showed, the degree of financial uncertainty shaped the strategies adopted. Relatively less constrained by a scarcity of financial capital, Cooperatives A and C concentrated on a strategy of adjustment with longer terms of return in focus. Thus they rebuilt dairy cattle production, with calculated larger market demands but a much longer production cycle than that of swine production. The combined impact of the informational and financial uncertainty resulted in a shift on the part of all agricultural producers into closed-cycle production technology.

Financial uncertainty made the reduction of production costs the fundamental objective of the agricultural cooperatives. However, a shift to closed-cycle production, a rational strategy of adaptation on the level of individual economic units, had the cumulative effect of moving away from commercial and specialized production on the macroeconomic level. It also reduced productivity. The adaptation strategy of producing "on the cheap," practiced by all agricultural production cooperatives, also implied expanding production only within the physical confines of the existing production means and facilities. The few investments undertaken by Cooperative A and Cooperative B were intended to change the *terms of exchange* on the market rather than to change the nature of production. Cooperative C appears to present a contrasting case, as it entered into a new production line of fruit juices. Yet this strategy was dictated by the need to reduce costs and the persistent overemployment within the cooperative. This was also undertaken in order to spread the risk connected with a new market orientation, by entering a partnership with an individual private entrepreneur.

The perpetuation of routine production lines became a protection against the prevalent uncertainties in the new economic environment. The resulting *patterns of divergent development* were tied to the production profiles inherited from the past. This can be interpreted as an effect of the rampant uncertainties of the new economic environment on organizational behavior, which severely limited the range of alternatives available to each cooperative in its individual strategies of adjustment. The empirical results revealed that all three agricultural cooperatives exhibited *less flexibility* and *less responsiveness* in their production organization, their profile, and their market orientation than the reform program anticipated. Thus, as Murrell (1992: 38) put it, "the search for alternatives should be characterized, not as wide-ranging choice over a universe of alternatives, but rather as a history-bound process of discovery within a neighborhood of existing operations."

Yet, despite their divergent developmental paths, all three agricultural cooperatives changed their governance structure in similar ways, undermining the consolidation of ownership rights on the part of their cooperative members. In a situation of increased uncertainty, the value of access to scarce information sources and information processing capabilities increased (Hess 1982). This increased demand on expertise and the need to accurately and expediently identify economically viable strategies of adaptation to a very volatile economic and legal environment led to *managerial centralization* in all of the cooperatives. Thus, the process of increasing managerial control was underway in all cooperatives under study, in spite of the preserved formal democratic distribution of control.

By referring to the *uncertainty* of the economic future, general managers gained the upper hand in the decision-making process over the other managerial board members, as well as the general assembly. Since the job security of cooperative members directly depended on the cooperative's economic viability, especially when they had few prospects for alternative employment, members were unable to question the rise of managerial authority as a way of protecting their livelihood.

At the same time, the specific character of the emergent managerial centralization varied across cooperatives. This variation depended on (1) the nature of resources available to the managers, (2) the character of their economic activities, and (3) the constraints of the formal structure of cooperative control stipulated by each cooperative's statutory regulations. The specific combination of these factors gave rise to *patrimonial* managerial power within Cooperative A. This type of managerial centralization is built on the loyalty of cooperative members to the individual manager and on the non-exercise of ownership rights by cooperative members. An *imperfect professional* managerial centralization developed within Cooperative B. In this case, members delegated decision making to a manager on the basis that he demonstrated the competence to promote microeconomic efficiency. In case of a disappointing record, cooperative membership manifested its disapproval by exercising their ownership right by default—by firing the general manager. Cooperative C represents an emergence of *consent-based* managerial power. In this case, members vested their manager with power for supervision and decision making based on his competence to bring microeconomic efficiency. Yet they positively claimed their cooperative ownership rights not only by firing the underperforming manager but also by participating in the process of decision making by disputing specific managerial decisions and policies.

The general manager of Cooperative A had financial resources unmatched by other cooperatives. Access to updated accounting and legal expert knowledge, via the trusted bookkeeper, enabled the manager of Cooperative A to secure vital financial resources at the early stages of the transition. Furthermore, he was able to replenish the scarce financial capital, on an as-needed basis, through the repeated sale of the cooperative's land parcels, unchallenged by the general membership. He was able to do this because member-vested land was almost nonexistent in Cooperative A, as contrasted with Cooperative C. The overall agricultural nature of Cooperative A did not call for any special expertise on the part of cooperative members. Their low skill level and general shortage of alternative employment implied that their cooperative presented their only realistic source of livelihood. The low skill level, combined with the relatively small size of the cooperative membership, enabled the manager to maintain direct supervision over their work activities. In addition, his wife, a zoologist, who headed animal husbandry for the cooperative, reinforced his ability to effectively supervise the membership.

The specific statute of Cooperative A did not allow for members' dissension. The statute of Cooperative A obliged the general manager to share executive power with a smaller management board than was the case in the two other agricultural cooperatives.[13] The statutory regulations of Cooperative A also made sanctions for inappropriate individual conduct (monetary sanctions, disciplinary firing) more readily available to the cooperative's general manager than to the managers of Cooperatives B and C, respectively. In addition to the stricter sanctions available to him, the manager installed a reward system to elicit compliance from his members. He diverted part of his financial reserves to increase the wages of his members beyond the salary levels of Cooperatives B and C. The fear of disciplinary firing and the threat of the elimination of specific work stations followed by unemployment, combined with the steady and relatively high income, prevented members of the general assembly from challenging the manager. Although the cooperative members widely questioned the efficiency of the resources used by the general manager and suspected him of substantial misappropriation of cooperative assets, they did not challenge him openly. This specific set of factors allowed the manager to manage the cooperative in an arbitrary, personalistic, and despotic style and to elicit grudging compliance on the part of the members.

Cooperative B presented the path to managerial centralization marked by the negative exercise of ownership rights by the general assembly over managerial power. Initially, the most critical resource the manager of Cooperative B possessed was his expertise in identifying markets for the cooperative's established and new production. The meager financial capital of Cooperative B made this resource all the more valuable. Cooperative B's more diversified agricultural production and processing did not allow the general manger to directly oversee work activities or the internal distribution of production proceeds. This opened up possibilities for economically opportunistic behavior. The broader managerial board, composed of members with some degree of specialized skills, proved harder for the general manager to head. The issuance of decisions and policies was more protracted. In addition, the statutory regulations made the sanctions for improper work conduct quite ineffective. Once highly unstable markets and internally opportunistic activities of the membership's faction threatened the cooperative's very economic viability, the general manager's competence became challenged. The general assembly remained effective in exercising control *by default*. It asserted veto power to dismiss the manager.

The very difficult financial situation of the cooperative only facilitated the subsequent centralization of control by the new general manager. He was given a broad mandate to lead the cooperative out of its economic crisis. The mandate from the general assembly was extended on the basis of competence to restore the cooperative's economic viability. However, the notion of the competence sought by the general membership in its new manager got redefined. The national search for a candidate with high credentials in agricultural management was replaced by a search within its internal ranks. They sought a *trustworthy* individual living locally who was thus accountable to the local community and capable of safeguarding it against internal and external economic opportunism. The recurrent financial shortages led to repeated uncertainty in making the payroll and in meeting other financial obligations, thus prompting potential revolt of the general membership. In 1994, the manager was able to stabilize his control over the cooperative when he successfully applied for governmental debt-restructuring credits.

The consolidation of managerial power in Cooperative C was marked by the general assembly's active exercise of ownership rights. Its diversified character of production, its relative scarcity of financial resources, its more formal statutory restrictions on the use of workers' sanctions, and its relatively high level of member-vested land in proportion to the overall cooperative land, led to centralization based on some measure of consent.[14] The partial dependence of the cooperative processing units on inputs from the private plots of its cooperative members lowered the overall costs of production. It also called for authority relations based more on voluntary compliance from the cooperative members. As the specific policies and decisions were initiated by the general manager, the managerial board and general assembly were able to open them up for discussion. Ultimately, the manager's decision to modernize the cooperative's machinery park precipitated the general assembly's questioning of the economic and ethical soundness of his decision. The members exercised their veto power as cooperative owners to oust the incumbent manager. They elevated to that position one of their own members, who had no formal professional credentials. Instead, his main assets were employment in the cooperative throughout his adult life and his residence in the local community since his childhood. As in the case of Cooperative B, the qualifications for the general manager sought by the membership were trustworthiness and accountability based on local ties rather than formal skills.

As the three case studies of Rolnicy *gmina* cooperatives show, the deinstitutionalization measures did not facilitate the articulation of property ownership in the agricultural production cooperatives. Rather, they only deepened the sense of uncertainty regarding legitimate owners in the post-socialist period. They further weakened the capacities of local cooperative organizations to articulate an effective strategy of adaptation to the new economic environment created by the reform program. Against the policy objectives, and the wishes of the general cooperative membership, the deinstitutionalization of the primary cooperatives pushed those organizations to evolve more consistently with an imperfect model of professional management rather than with the pursued model of self-management.

Cooperative of Agricultural Circles and the Articulation of Cooperative Ownership

The second part of this chapter analyzes the effects of deinstitutionalization on the organization of a service cooperative of agricultural circles, in which membership is of the intersection of collective and private ownership. Members of cooperative agricultural circles were almost exclusively peasants. Their aim was to reclaim the self-governance and self-aid character of their cooperative organization in the post-socialist period. This coincided with their simultaneous efforts to survive as owners of private agricultural farms. As a result, both types of ownership rights were often in direct tension.

The socialist past of cooperatives of agricultural circles dates back to 1956. Under the Gomulka agricultural plan, agricultural circles were envisioned as the organizational vehicle to provide the private agricultural subsector with access to machinery and agricultural equipment and to bring it closer into socialism. As the collective ownership of machinery, agricultural circles were a practical solution to overcome the financial constraints individual peasants had in acquiring agricultural implements on their own. Since very few peasants could afford to purchase, individually, agricultural equipment, the agricultural circles were designed to entice peasants to join these organizations. By advancing the mechanization of private farms, the agricultural circles were expected to contribute to the growth of private agricultural production output. In addition, agricultural circles were to become the foundation of a socialistic transformation of agriculture. In contrast to the agricultural production cooperatives, based on the collective cultivation of lands, the agricultural circles, as trade and service cooperatives, represented a primitive form of socialization of agriculture. Yet they did represent the first element of socialism—collective ownership of the production resources other than individually owned land. Furthermore, they provided the socialistic state with an organizational vehicle to control the production of individual farms. Thus, soon after an initial spontaneous growth of local agricultural circles, various party resolutions emphasized the importance of the participation of party members in the circles. This was justified in terms of the need to establish the lateral links between agricultural circles and the commune heads, the party-appointed leaders of a local *gmina*'s councils.[15] Equally, party resolutions sought control of the network of agricultural circles by coordinating their activities and tying them to obligatory regional associations. Those lateral and vertical organizational connections allowed the state to maintain a powerful say in drafting plans and inspecting the work of agricultural circles—thus eroding the principles of self-government and the voluntarism of cooperative machinery associations.

The progressive subjugation of cooperative machinery associations to state control reached its new stage during Gierek's economic program. In 1973, as part of a general trend in pursuing economies of scale, local agricultural circles were centralized to form cooperatives of agricultural circles. A cooperative of agricultural circles was set up for each group of fifteen to twenty villages. This move first reduced their number from thirty-five thousand to about three thousand and then to fewer than nine hundred. In the course of centralization, the machine stock of agricultural circles was removed from villages to newly formed communal centers. It became highly cumbersome for private peasants to have access to mechanized land cultivating services (Magyar 1984). Furthermore, by new governmental guidelines, significant portions of the farmland from the state land fund got reallocated to cooperatives of agricultural circles for direct cultivation. This process of "collectivization without peasants," undertaken through the better part of the 1970s, increased the land at the disposal of the cooperatives of agricultural circles by over 50 percent. This resulted in the allocation of over a quarter of the machinery capabilities for the cooperatives' land cultivation, thus further curtailing services provided to individual peasants.

By the end of the 1980s the cooperatives were organized in a highly contracted, three-tiered network. The seventeen existing central unions controlled the two hundred regional unions, which were comprised of approximately nine thousand primary cooperatives. The leaders of the primary cooperatives were, almost without exception, under the control of state and regional cooperative organizations.

In the post-socialist period, the cooperative of agricultural circles remained the only institutional network providing machinery services to smaller and mid-sized individual producers who were unable to obtain their own equipment. Almost as an immediate consequence of the reform program, the cooperative of agricultural circles in the studied community, as in some two thousand other such local cooperatives in rural Poland, experienced a decline in the demand base for its agricultural services and an even faster decline in its financial revenues (Dzun 1993; Kulawik and Tkaczyk 1993). Within the first three years of the transition, the cooperative faced more than a 30 percent decline in demand for its aggregate machinery services from its regular service patrons, despite set prices for machinery services at cost or below cost. This was associated with drastic cuts in applying fertilizers and some reduction in pesticides and herbicides by individual agricultural producers.

The overall decline in the client base was not offset by an increased demand for selected services from specific subsections of individual peasants. In the context of rapidly increased prices, some of the bigger individual agricultural producers who had their own machinery opted to be serviced by the cooperatives of agricultural circles (especially services of grain, potato, and sugar beet combines). This was more cost effective as compared to the cost of operation and amortization of their own equipment. On the other hand, with the introduction of market reforms, agricultural circles found themselves in direct competition with some of their members. Larger individual producers who owned machinery equipment often serviced other peasants and engaged in nonmonetary exchanges of labor for other machinery services as a way to use their own machinery more efficiently and to reduce the overall cost of their agricultural production.

However, the shrinking patronage base was outpaced by a decline in revenues. The cooperative faced a growing number of defaults on payments from its patrons for the performed services. The uncollected fees from the 1990 and 1991 harvesting services amounted to over 300 million zloty ($30,000). This constituted about 40 percent of the services performed. The effective demand base for the following summer was projected to shrink even further, given that those who defaulted were to be considered ineligible for future machinery services regardless of their machinery needs. Despite the adoption of formal sanctioning measures for the nonpayment of fees, the membership had difficulties implementing them consistently. During sessions of the financial committees that I observed, committee members always accommodated the delinquent members on a case-by-case basis without uniformly enforcing the sanctions. The exclusion of services for the following season as a sanction for nonpayment was viewed as counterproductive for the agricultural circles because it implied further reduction of the client base. Furthermore, the committee members felt uncomfortable imposing and enforcing sanctions against fellow village members with whom they felt solidarity in economic times perceived as adverse to peasants (Fedyszak-Radziejowska 1995: 142, 152). In one meeting, members of the financial committee particularly forgave the debt of a small landowner and structured his delinquent payment without imposing any interest penalties. This was proposed in appreciation for his unique show of goodwill, expressed in a written formal request to the committee for a postponement of his fees. For other peasants who failed to meet their financial obligations and showed no initiative in settling them, the committee considered collecting payments in kind. Yet since the agricultural circles did not have the capacity to handle such payments, in the end this option was not adopted. The 1992 harvest approached without any clear policy about how to handle the potential request for services by delinquent members.

In addition to this significant shortage of revenues, the agricultural circles were dealing with a growing problem of enforcing legal contracts for machinery services. These difficulties were directly tied to the organizational structure of the cooperative of the agricultural circles. The cooperative had its administrative headquarters and some service facilities (such as a gasoline station and car diagnostic station) in one location. However, its ten machinery stations were spread throughout sixteen villages and serviced their respective geographically adjacent agricultural clientele. The administrative staff, as well as the machinery operators and their local stations' supervisors, were paid employees of the cooperative. As was frequently debated in the membership meetings, the headquarters could not adequately monitor the local machinery stations. There were numerous informal reports of illegal, direct service agreements between machine operators and individual agricultural producers (both members and nonmembers of the cooperatives) that bypassed the cooperative's official work orders. Given that nonmembers had to pay higher fees for services, the cooperative machine operators had stronger economic incentives to give service priority to nonmembers. This was in direct opposition to the cooperative's official policy. The bypassing of the agricultural circle's formal channels in job orders not only resulted in lost revenues to the organization, it also led to a very unreliable schedule of services for those patrons of agricultural circles who requested services through formal channels. The unreliability of scheduled services, for which agricultural circles were notorious during state socialism, seemed to be well-cultivated also in the days of the post-socialist transition. In the preharvest meetings, many individual peasants complained of the production losses incurred due to delayed machinery servicing.

The unreliability of services related to the frequent work stoppages also stemmed from the progressive dismantling of the machinery park of agricultural circles. In the context of high prices for machinery parts, the employees of the machinery stations allegedly were destroying machinery equipment by replacing new parts with the old ones in order to sell them on the open market. In addition, the inadequate use of machinery oil was frequently reported. All of these improprieties cost the cooperative approximately 25 percent of their total revenues from the machinery services, as estimated by the general manager and the chair of the supervisory council. In particular, the intense "cannibalism" of the machinery park by the employees within one machinery station resulted in the closing down of the site in early 1992.

Alternative forms of labor organization and monitoring practices were not readily available. A proposal by the chairman of the agricultural circles, designed to provide economic incentive for the machinery operators, called for the creation of independent labor-machine teams that would not be on the cooperative payroll. The labor-machine teams that subcontracted with the cooperative for the machinery services would legally require massive layoffs and advances of three months' severance pay. This alternative was clearly too costly for the financially strapped cooperative.

A less tangible, yet more pervasive, barrier to the tightening of the control of the work contracts was members' unwillingness to move to a more active involvement in the monitoring of the work contracts within the stations. By the statutory rules of the cooperative, disciplinary actions against employees or local supervisors who entered into illegal contracts with clients could be undertaken only if a written complaint was submitted by two cooperative members. In the eyes of the agricultural circles' membership, the measures, although necessary in order to ensure increased efficiency of machinery services, were unacceptable. They were equated with the disdained state socialist practice of surveilling local agricultural circles and their members. Thus, they were unenforceable. Applauded by the others, one member proclaimed in a preharvest meeting, "Nobody would want to be involved in the 'spying' activities against their neighbors and fellow peasants. For precisely that reason we have left socialism."

Clearly, peasants were facing a conflict between their roles as individual agricultural owners and as owners of the cooperative with an interest to protect its economic viability. In the former role, they attempted to lower the cost of their individual production; in the latter role, they sought to protect the cooperative's economic viability. This conflict was also reflected in the practices of labor/machinery service exchanges between individual peasants who were members of the cooperative. Although the practice of reducing the cost of individual production was not widely reported, it also contributed to the narrowing of the demand base for their cooperative services.

Charting a New Economic Profile of Organization

Recognizing that the demand base for the traditional services had been eroded and that the costs associated with continued performance of those services had increased, all members agreed that the continuation of the agricultural circles in the new economic conditions required expansion into different areas of activities. However, the agreement over the need to change the economic profile did not generate any specific program. The chair and his newly appointed general manager proposed an alternative for future economic activities and channeled their energy into selling their revitalization plan to the circles' general assembly.[16] As the revitalization plan was unveiled, the general reaction from the membership consisted of a mixture of admiration, contempt, and insecurity. Ultimately, the plan was accepted as the only articulated alternative of adaptation to the new environment.

In unison with the general manager, the chair pressed for expanding the economic activity of the cooperative into nonagricultural areas. With some existing financial reserves and bank and private loans, the cooperative began venturing into new economic activities. The cooperative invested eighty-one million zloty in 1990 and quadrupled this level of investment in 1991. The investment efforts went into loosely connected directions. Under the new economic revitalization plan, the cooperative committed financial resources to complete a gasoline station that had not been completed by the previous managerial board. From the start, the gasoline station had not been fully operational in 1991, due to the uneven supplies of gasoline from the wholesalers.[17] Nevertheless, as the chair of the supervisory council assured the membership, the station had produced a twenty-three million zloty surplus in the first year of its operation. Recurrent supply problems prompted the cooperative to lease the gasoline station. The best bid came at the 70 percent level of the income received from operating the station. Thus, the lease option was temporarily withdrawn.

A car diagnostic center was another investment project of the cooperative. Contingent on obtaining more financial resources for its expansion, it represented a first step in a planned car repair facility. As the chair of the supervisory council explained to the general meeting, the diagnostic center was not fully operational due to weak demand. In the chair's opinion, the center's distant location from the main roads resulted in its low-level operation. To improve the center's standing would have required a costly advertising campaign for which there were no sufficient funds. Several individual agricultural producers and members of the cooperatives countered the chair's assessment with a divergent explanation for the center's poor financial performance. They complained about very inefficiently run services, untrained and tardy personnel at the center, and noncompetitive prices for car parts (as compared with the private agricultural parts distributor in the area). They claimed that this discouraged clients even among the circles' members. Thus, to improve the demand would require allocating funds mainly for training and restructuring the operations, rather than for advertising.

The pet project of the supervisory board's chair was the excavation of gravel. The cooperative advanced over one hundred million zloty for geological surveys, the licensing for excavation, land leasing fees, and machine leasing fees.[18] As claimed by the chair, the project showed early signs of success—it managed to secure a stable demand for gravel among six independent wholesalers. Yet the future of the project remained uncertain since the land lease for gravel excavation was short term (three years) and subject to revocation by its owner, an individual peasant. The chair attempted to extend the exclusive rights of excavation with no term limits. At the same time, a battle was going on between the cooperative and the village council over the level of local fees for the excavation concession and tax rates on the excavated gravel.

During the annual meeting, the chair informed the general membership that the circles had already committed over thirty million zloty to the production of ceramic tiles. The investment decision was made by the chair and the board without consulting the general membership, thus violating the statutes of the circles. The chair argued that the economic opportunity appeared great and thus required swift action. Subsequently, the project was quickly phased out due to lack of any substantial demand for its output.

Furthermore, in its overall plan of economic adjustment and diversification, the cooperative entered into an agreement with a local army unit (itself under growing budgetary constraints) to obtain and adapt a military truck for purposes of transporting fuel and coal. By providing the gasoline station's own fuel transportation, the cooperative's chair projected a substantial lowering of its operational costs. He also claimed that the direct transportation of coal from the mines of southern Poland would bring new revenue to the cooperative and provide the local population with cheaper coal than supplied by any intermediary outlets. All of these economic revitalization projects were either at the conception stage or at some level of completion and operation by the end of my research and they required further substantial investment funds.

The Evolution of the Governance Structure

The statute of agricultural circles allocated formal authority to articulate organizational goals to the general assembly and supervisory board. One of the critical aims of the 1990 Amendment to the Cooperative Law was to replace the de facto distribution of power with a system of formal authority within the cooperative organizations. It was to empower the general membership to take part in the decision-making process. The reformers envisioned that the passage of the January 1990 Amendment to the Cooperative Law, which required new elections within local cooperative organizations, would lead to the ousting of the old cadre and major personnel changes within the cooperative management. Yet, in spite of his clear ties to the previous regime, the incumbent chairman of the supervisory board of the Rolnicy agricultural circles was reelected in the first post-socialist local cooperative elections for another term. Moreover, from my observations of the Rolnicy's agricultural circles meetings, it was clear that the chairman of the supervisory board wielded power over the circle and its members that was not proportional to the formal allocation of authority to his position.

The local circle's membership was well aware of the chair's involvement in various economic organizations as well as in regional and national politics. Prior to the introduction of post-socialist reform, he was very involved in the United Peasant Party (Zjednoczone Stronnictwo Ludowe ZSL). After the reforms, he unsuccessfully ran for parliament deputy within the Peasant Party, and was also involved in the Supreme Cooperative Council—the central organ of cooperatives. In the circle's meetings, he frequently alluded to his multiple business connections as a successful individual owner of a local multimillion zloty private agribusiness that specialized in mustard production. His Mercedes sedan was a tangible reminder of his elevated position vis-à-vis the circle's membership. There were persistent, albeit unconfirmed, rumors among the circle's members that, among the personal loans advanced in 1991 and 1992 for the financing of the circle's economic activities, the chair's portion was the most significant. At delicate moments when he attempted to persuade the general membership of specific arguments, the chair repeatedly pointed to his Mercedes and his overall financial standing to underscore that his involvement in the circle's adjustment to the new environment was not dictated by economic opportunism, but rather stemmed from a heightened sense of community duty.

Yet the membership became increasingly ambivalent toward the chair. The initially hesitant approval of his proposed economic revitalization plan gave way to growing suspicions about the rationale behind the plan. As the chair of the supervisory council and the general manager of the cooperative presented a semiannual preharvest report on the cooperative's economic activities, the revitalization plan met sharp and vocal criticism from its members. In response to the chair's boosting of a new capital-intensive, dynamic development and diversification of the agricultural circles, several members charged that the plan shifted the whole profile of the agricultural circles haphazardly, without careful prior analysis, into dubious activities, and away from servicing the agricultural production of its members. During the circle's meetings and in conversations with me, individual peasants emphasized the importance of reviving an original, pre-socialist profile of local agricultural circles—as institutions devoted to the support of the agricultural production of individual peasants that also reflected their cultural and political traditions. The members also attacked the aggressive pursuit of credits for proposed new activities. For example, to avert the proposed purchase of a heavy truck from an army unit for several million zloty, one member offered his own truck for the transportation needs of the cooperative, free of charge.

Just as the members criticized the very economic soundness and direction of the proposed or already started investment projects, they also opposed the nonstatutory, undemocratic method of developing them. In the annual meeting, one member of the three-member supervisory council fervently charged that, in spite of having a well-functioning private telephone and post office in his village, he had not been notified about the supervisory council meetings for a year, as prescribed by the circle's statutes. He claimed that this deliberately prevented him from having input into the elaboration of the economic revitalization plan. As the membership was alerted to the practices of circumventing the formal authority structure in developing the plan, they also realized that they did not have the means to effectively monitor the plan's implementation. In the heated exchange, they demanded from the chair and the general manager more concrete financial reports on the investment funds and the performance of particular investments. The chair admitted that such reports were unattainable. He pointed out that the former general manager's resignation from his post in the midst of the development of the circle's economic plan coincided with the departure of his four-member administrative staff. This included his bookkeeper with all the bookkeeping records.[19] As a result, there was no continuity in financial records on the economic performance of the cooperative from 1991 to 1992, to which the general membership could refer.

Like their counterparts in agricultural production cooperatives, members of agricultural circles faced a severe scarcity of information, which became detrimental to their ability to participate in decision making regarding their cooperative. Moreover, the physical dispersion related to the individual agricultural production carried out by the members of agricultural circles further attenuated their ability to control their cooperative. Thus, in the absence of systematic financial records, members had no solid grounds to independently assess the economic soundness of new projects. The evaluation of the gas station located on the premises of the circles basically rested on the members' personal and sporadic evaluations of services. Most of them complained about its inefficient personnel and noncompetitive prices. Other projects, like the gravel excavation or the ceramic tile production, were unrelated to the economic activities of agricultural producers and the circle's members. In addition, they were located in distant sites. Thus, they were not subjected even to such rudimentary and fragmented independent experiential scrutiny from the general membership as was the gas station. Such projects gave the chair and his manager close to free rein vis-à-vis the cooperative membership.

The ongoing, highly pronounced discord between the cooperative circle's members, its chair, and the general manager over the direction of activities and the governance of agricultural circles prompted the chairman of the community council to only half-jokingly observe that a proposed loan allocation from the community council to the circles might be a politically and economically very unsound decision.

However, despite an intensifying internal conflict over the heterogeneity of goals projected for the circles, the general membership did not show any indication of voting the chair of the supervisory board out of his position. He clearly possessed scarce resources indispensable to sustaining the operations of agricultural circles in the new economic environment—resources that none of the other local cooperative members wielded. Although they criticized the specific content of his economic plan, none of the individual peasants was capable of articulating an alternative plan. Nor were they able to obtain institutional assistance to effectively ascertain their organizational needs and develop such a plan. Numerous enterprises previously operated by the regional level cooperative unions, which provided various financial, technical, auditing, and other services to the primary cooperatives, got scrapped during the rapid liquidation of regional and national unions, and a re-creation of comparable institutional structures was suspended for two years under the Amendment of Cooperative Law guidelines.

In the context of disrupted institutional arrangements and missing institutional links, the cooperative members developed a personal dependence on the chair. His role as chair of the supervisory board prior to the post-socialist reforms gave him an advantage in the post-socialist local elections, since he could provide a much-needed continuity in the context of the profound uncertainty on the level of day-to-day operations. More specifically, with the tightened credits and disrupted financial arrangement previously handled by the regional and national cooperative unions, he was able to provide continued access to funds to sustain the operation of the circles from his personal reserves, as well as from well-established contacts with the management of several commercial banks in the city and in the local cooperative bank.[20] He also promised personal access to foreign capital. Thus, in his capacity as an individual *independent* of the cooperatives, the chair had access (or claimed to have access) to technical and organizational knowledge, as well as legal, financial, and institutional resources critical to the economic survival of the cooperative organization as such.

Hence, the chair's power derived from his unparalleled access to, and his ability to mobilize, resources deemed by the membership necessary for the survival of the local agricultural circles in the new economic environment. Yet, as he mobilized resources for agricultural circles, he formulated goals for the local agricultural circles that were increasingly in tension with those broadly and tacitly defined by the general membership. The peasants expected to reconstitute the agricultural circles as bodies that would genuinely assist the individual peasants in their struggles to survive in the new economic realities of the post-socialist transition. Instead, the chair's new economic investments steadily led the cooperative into nonagricultural-oriented operations.

The contestation between the general membership and the chair over decision making regarding the circle's economic profile progressed directly into a battle over the overall cooperative ownership. This was prompted by the chair's campaign to change the agricultural circles into a joint stock company. During the summer of 1992, he attempted to convince the cooperative members of the necessity of transforming itself into a stock company to secure further financial loans for their economic activities. He introduced the notion of a joint stock company to a fragmented membership, in a series of preharvest meetings with ten local chapters constituting the cooperative. The chair was explaining the recent credit denial to the cooperative with reference to the pervasive ideological antipathy toward cooperatives by the governmental agencies and the leading private lending institutions. He claimed they saw cooperatives as remnants of the socialist economic past. As he alleged, the cooperative form of property was viewed as suspect, given the mass privatization objective of the reform program. He also recited cases of foreign funds designated for the development of Polish agriculture that were misappropriated and/or mishandled by the central bureaucracy and never reached their rightful recipients. Further, he referred to his personal contacts with the foreign lenders, claiming that they would make possible the direct acquisition of funds without the governmental intermediaries. The chair concluded each meeting by pressuring the local chapters to accept his solution of reconstituting the cooperative into a private stock company as the only viable way to obtain financial resources.

In the first local chapter of the cooperative agricultural circles, the members did not spend any time deliberating the issue. The proposal was voted on and passed unanimously. However, in subsequent meetings of the local agricultural circles, the reaction of peasants was much more reserved. The members requested a more detailed analysis of the consequences of a change to a joint stock company, as well as a vote on the issue at the general assembly of the cooperative, with all members present from all of the local agricultural circles' sites. During the semiannual cooperative general assembly, the issue of the joint stock company was conveniently not placed on the agenda. However, members forced the issue of the stock company into the meeting agenda and expressed deep suspicion that the proposed transformation would give the chair and the manager an unchallenged controlling voice. The members of the cooperative realized that the potential transformation of the cooperative would unavoidably raise the issue of the cooperative shareholding. In Rolnicy's circles, as in most cooperatives, the total amount of equity held by members constituted a marginal part of the net assets.

This outcome resulted from a combination of the initial conditions for creation of agricultural circles and the co-claims of the socialist state to cooperative ownership rights. From the conception of agricultural circles, their initial investment funds came only marginally from the actual financial contributions of peasants entering the agricultural circles. In line with overall policy objectives to raise farm outputs by 30 percent in the period from 1959 to 1965, the objective of the Gomulka plan to speed up the mechanization of farming had led to the creation of a special fund for agricultural development, which financed the purchases of tractors or tractor-driven machines (Szurek 1987). The fund was set to finance the purchases of machinery for circles and for cooperatives. In stipulating conditions for actual machinery purchases, the fund expected the peasants within specific circles to advance between 15 percent and 25 percent in order to qualify for matching state money from the fund.

The initial gap between the peasants' membership investments and the assets of their agricultural circles only grew wider with the years of subsequent integration of the primary agricultural circles into the regional and national union, as well as state funding of subsidies and state-regulated internal redistribution of surpluses generated in the primary circles. Under socialism, the state subjected cooperative unions to a prescribed system of internal redistribution, which aimed to transfer surpluses away from their membership. Thus about one-quarter or one-third of the surpluses was paid in taxes, and 10 to 20 percent was allocated into a development fund administered by the central and regional unions. Another 30 to 55 percent of the surpluses was allocated into reserve funds of primary cooperatives as an indivisible property owned by the entire group of cooperative members. The remaining 20 percent was allocated for social funds within the cooperatives. Thus, the union's considerable net assets of the circles was not matched by an equivalent amount of member equity. The total amount of equity held by members in a majority of cooperatives amounted to roughly 1 percent of the cooperative property.[21]

Given the members' marginal share in the cooperative assets, a precise delineation of the membership would be a complex task. The cooperative members could have dual claims to the cooperative assets, as shareholders and as providers of business. However, considering the symbolic fees required to become a member, nonmember users of the cooperative of agricultural circles could lay claim to the cooperative assets on the basis of their substantial patronage payments. Peasants also knew that membership claims to cooperative assets could be made by the cooperative employees. Although the cooperative staff was paid as regular employees, the chair of the supervisory council, in preparation for the attempted conversion into a joint stock company, further diluted the peasant members' shares. In 1991, he proposed and passed a statutory regulation that allowed employees of the cooperative to become cooperative members after six months of employment and the payment of nominal membership fees. Irrespective of the precise guidelines for the restructuring of ownership of cooperative assets, the most plausible outcome of the transformation of the cooperative into a stock company appeared to be an ownership structure that would have formally removed altogether the small and mid-sized individual agricultural producers from control of the agricultural circles.[22] By the end of 1992, tacitly knowing this, the peasants resisted the chair's preparations to transform the cooperative into a joint stock company.

The contestation over the reconfiguration of the cooperative into a joint stock company was cut short by legal proceedings against the chair. In court proceedings, it was proven that he obtained massive loans as a representative of the cooperative and then diverted these funds for the expansion of his private food processing company. When the chair was unable to refinance the loans, he defaulted on their payments and signed the ownership of his company over to his immediate relatives. Legally, the cooperative became liable for the defaulted loans. In 1994, the cooperative underwent liquidation. The state and the commercial creditors sold the machinery and equipment to cover the debts. The remaining machines were auctioned in the *gmina* to peasants. Four years into an attempted revival of the genuine cooperative organization, the agricultural circles, as a service organization to peasants and as the institutional representation of their interests, ceased to exist.

Local Agricultural Circles and National Level Politics

What complicates the picture of the relations between the membership of the agricultural circles and the chair of the supervisory board is that the intensifying tensions over the formulation of goals for agricultural circles within their local arena was kept in check by the seeming coalescence of the chair's and the membership's objectives as they related to national politics. Thus, as a person with long-established ties to regional and national political and cooperative organizations, the chair projected to peasant members that their local agricultural circles would be an organizational vehicle necessary in a concerted effort with other circles and collective peasant protest to induce changes in agricultural policies (Gorlach 1999).[23] Those changes were to be consistent with members' interests as both cooperative owners/members of agricultural circles and also as individual agricultural owners. Hence, by collecting signatures and writing petitions, he involved the members in a campaign to challenge the *legality* of the government policies relating to the full monetarization of the economy, which led to high interest rates. At the time when interest rates on credits were 50 to 60 percent, the agricultural circles petitioned the government to forgive the defaulted loans and restructure the new ones at 12 percent. Also, the financial difficulties experienced by the cooperatives were presented to the general membership not as an inevitable cost of government anti-inflationary policies, but as a function of rampant corruption within the ranks of the state bureaucracies administrating the funds specifically designated for agriculture. He claimed to have personal knowledge of specific individuals who took advantage of high interest rates and made fortunes by merely postponing the granting of the loans to the rightful recipients and temporarily depositing the funds into their personal accounts.

Furthermore, by capitalizing on the particularly potent historical experiences of Germanic influences in the Wielkopolska region in general, and the Rolnicy *gmina* in particular,[24] the chair skillfully used the local agricultural circles as a forum to channel members' growing resentment of the one-sided policy of trade liberalization and to use them as a vehicle to articulate demands for erecting protectionist measures, and thus to deny the German agricultural counterparts renewed opportunity for economic domination of Polish markets.[25] In each meeting that I observed in the summer of 1992, the chair updated the cooperative members on progress in the battle with the post-socialist government to reduce interest rates on credits and to revise the policy of the liberalization of trade.

The increasing discord over the governance structure of the circles was being neutralized on and off by building cohesion within local agricultural circles based on the articulation of economic grievances of the agricultural producers in the language of national interests. This served a dual purpose—to pacify conflict within the agricultural circles and to translate it into societal opposition to the state and its policy.

Conclusion: The Intersection of Management and Ownership Control: Agricultural Production Cooperatives and Service Cooperatives

This chapter has revealed how the policy of deinstitutionalization of the cooperative sector (liquidation of the state-imposed organizational superstructure over the primary cooperative associations) did not bring about the expected results. Instead of self-governance, the primary cooperative organizations exhibited the managerial centralization of power. In the case of the agricultural circles, the contestation between the membership and the chair over the internal control of the cooperative ultimately led to the dissolution of the cooperative.

Within agricultural production cooperatives, managers consolidated their power in the context of the attempted reconstitution of property rights inherent to exclusively one type of property subjects—the cooperative owners. The manager of Cooperative A ruled unopposed by members who were unable to claim their ownership rights. Members of Cooperative B claimed their ownership rights only to select candidates, but not to effectively influence managerial decision making. The managerial power in Cooperative C was constrained by ownership control at the point of the manager hire and fire, as well as in the process of executive decision making.

Despite variations in the consolidation and articulation of managerial control in the three agricultural production cooperatives, over time there was a progressive convergence in management control across these agricultural production cooperatives. Members of Cooperatives B and C reverted from the delegation of managerial power based on formal professional expertise to that based on shared local cooperative experiences. In the aftermath of managerial crises in Cooperatives B and C, the members relied on localism; they found that, in the context of increased economic uncertainty and the absence of institutional control from above, recruitment of cooperative managers from within their locality and their organization's ranks created a better safeguard for maintaining the viability of their cooperatives and the accountability of managers to the membership.

In comparison with the agricultural production cooperatives, the case of the cooperative agricultural circles presents yet another way of consolidating managerial power while undermining consolidation of the exclusive property rights of cooperative owners. The chairman of the supervisory council pursued the centralization of control in the context of agricultural circles members' attempted articulation of ownership rights that were tied to two types of property—cooperative and individual. As the case of the agricultural circles showed, the new economic environment made the rights and obligations tied to cooperative and to individual ownership often in conflict with one another. Thus, instead of building stronger private ownership of individual agricultural producers based on asserting their cooperative ownership rights and on recreating the self-aid character of their cooperative organization, the new economic environment further alienated the individual peasants from their cooperative association.[26] In their efforts to preserve their individual farms, peasants resorted to practices that undermined the economic viability of their cooperative service organization as such, and lowered their chances of resuming effective control of those institutions as cooperative owners. Their efforts to lower the costs of agricultural production prompted them to sharply reduce their demand for machinery services from the agricultural circles. Their conflicting responsibilities as members of the cooperative organization and as individual farmers led to a situation where the adversity facing agricultural circles (a shrinking demand base for services) further removed the possibility of simply continuing, expanding, or modifying past economic activities—as was the case with the agricultural production cooperatives. Rather, in the longer run, it called for more drastic changes in resource allocations, behavioral patterns, and expectations. Most critically, it also opened room for a change in the principle based on which control of resources would be vested—from cooperative to joint stock company.[27] Broadening the scope of the necessary changes in order to adjust to the new economic environment implied a greater volatility of the agricultural circles as compared to the agricultural production cooperatives.

The powerful resources available to the chairman of the supervisory council were his exclusive access to informational sources, together with control of substantial private financial reserves. Combined, they were critical in securing the chairman a dominant voice within the cooperative and in sustaining the economic viability of the organization in the short run. However, the issue of transition to a joint stock company precipitated an internal governance crisis in terms of deep conflict and a stalemate between management and the members over the distribution of cooperative assets. Due to the fact that the economic viability of the cooperative was not directly tied to the source of the members' livelihood, the members had some autonomy vis-à-vis management and thus could openly challenge the pressures for the centralization of control. On the other hand, the physical dispersion of the members of the agricultural circles and their split interests between the preservation of their farms and their agricultural circles limited their ability to effectively challenge the chair.

The routes to the managerial centralization of agricultural production cooperatives and agricultural circles clearly point to the limitation of conceptualizing the post-socialist transition strictly in terms of judicial ownership transformation. The reformers' assumption, that formal assignment of property rights by decree would instantly create owners who positively respond to the market, had obscured understanding of the conjoint nature of cooperative property under socialism and thus had underestimated the effect of organizational control of cooperative ownership under socialism. The progressive, vertical institutional integration of primary cooperatives not only imposed restrictions on specific cooperative ownership rights, but it altogether diluted the base upon which ownership rights could be claimed. The legacy of organizational control of the cooperative sector left a distinction between the cooperative members, the patrons of cooperatives, and the employees. Rapidly lifting up the institutional superstructure as a tactic to release genuine cooperative ownership could not possibly have produced the intended results.

The reformers' position also underestimated the effects of the insufficiently developed institutional infrastructure in the time of transition. The swift dismantling of the only institutional framework for assistance to the primary cooperatives, without creating a new one, negatively impacted implementation of the intended changes in property structure and, specifically, precipitated the processes in the primary cooperatives' struggle to survive the new environment that made the weak cooperative membership even weaker. The rapid deinstitutionalization of local cooperatives gave the management of local cooperatives more autonomy, and made it impossible to create any effective control of managerial decisions from within.

In congruence with evolutionary economics, the data here suggests that, in the context of an underdeveloped institutional infrastructure and heightened economic uncertainty, the options for change in ways that are similar to previous economic behavior are narrowed (Murrell 1992). The results of this study are in congruence with the findings from a complex national survey conducted among peasants by the Public Opinion Research Center (CBOS). The predominant reaction to post-socialist reforms was avoidance and awaiting, stemming from a profound sense of uncertainty and lending the peasants the label "awaiting society" (Lapinska-Tyszka 1993: 127). The process of change in the cooperative subsector was marked by the diversification of responses at the individual cooperative level—responses which depended on the preexisting organizational and production profiles. As the data presented here suggest, the *unevenness of transformations* referred to by Stark (1996) on the *societal* level, and by Burawoy (1995) on the *industry* level, seems to reveal itself on the level of *individual enterprises* within one subsector of the economy.

As divergent as the individual strategies of the cooperatives were, they shared common characteristics: they aimed at reducing the workforce within existing legal constraints; they attempted to eliminate unprofitable plants and lines of production; and they tried to reduce the cost of production. They also located their limited investment funds to improve their share in trade relations and redistribution, rather than production. However, neither of these characteristics appears central to the capitalist development understood as promoting production or dynamic efficiency. In fact, my data suggests that the underdeveloped institutional framework undermined the rationalization of resource allocation and the responsibility to obey budget constraints in a dual way. Apart from creating institutional discontinuity in external monitoring and auditing functions, it undermined internal democratic governance structure and removed management decisions from those views asserted by the membership. Thus, paradoxically, yet consistent with the neoinstitutional approach (Pfeffer 1972; Pfeffer and Salancik 2003 [1978]; Scott 2008), the discontinuities in information and limited financial and legal resources connected with decentralization appeared to preserve the inertia of the economic organizations rather than to induce competitive behavior. The rapid stabilization and liberalization measures and the resultant decentralization may prolong and ultimately impede the development of the new private and cooperative sectors. They also lengthen the transition. This runs contrary to the neoclassical model, which assumes that unrestrained market force has disciplining effects on economic behavior.

Contrary to the suggestions of other scholars like Stark, that ambiguous ownership rights enhance the flexibility of the economic organizations in the transition period, results presented here point to the opposite conclusion: policies that were detrimental to the clarification of ownership in the cooperative sector seemed to narrow the organizations' capacity to positively adjust to the economic environment and to bring about economic growth. As the case with agricultural circles revealed, such policies critically undermined cooperative ownership altogether, leading to the demise of the cooperative organization.[28]

In congruence with the neoliberals' emphasis on property transformation, this chapter shows that ownership *does* count—members do attempt to revive their ownership. However, this chapter shows that reform-stipulated deinstitutionalization of cooperatives left a fragmented, conflicting institutional context that attenuated, rather than consolidated, cooperative ownership rights. Furthermore, by examining the managerial centralization of power within cooperatives that emerged out of strategic responses to the external pressures of cooperative members (with differential access to information and resources), the chapter shows interest and agency impacting the claim and exercise of cooperative ownership rights. This study's findings regarding the process of structuration of ownership—nascent "corrupted" cooperative ownership—illustrate the neoinstitutionalists' emphasis on agency and interest, best articulated by DiMaggio when he states that: "Institutionalization is a product of the political efforts of actors to accomplish their ends and that the success of an institutionalization project and *the form that the resulting institutions takes* depend on the relative power of the actors who support, oppose, or otherwise strive to influence it" (1988: 13, emphasis added). Furthermore, my study shows that ownership has wider and often conflicting connotations than that imputed by neoliberals (Radin 1993; Singer 2000). The preservation of the agricultural circles was not only viewed by the members in strictly economic terms, as an organization meeting its production needs, but also as an institutional expression of social, cultural, and political aspirations. With the liquidation of the organization, they felt muted and violated in their self-knowledge.

Notes

1. The first local cooperative organizations in Wielkopolska—agricultural circles—were established over a century ago, when these territories were annexed by the Prussian Empire. Under Prussian law, Poles were prohibited from forming any political associations in the

occupied territories. Agricultural circles composed of individual peasants were created as associations strictly of an economic nature, formally aiming at advancing rationalization of agricultural production among individual property holders. In their multiprofile activities, agricultural circles organized training to promote modern methods of farming including the application of fertilizers and pesticides and bookkeeping. Agricultural circles disseminated modern technological information, as well as acquired machinery and equipment, which the members could share. In the later part of the nineteenth century through the early twentieth century, the agricultural circles became an umbrella organization of various self-governing institutions such as cooperative banks and agricultural, supply, and servicing cooperatives, as well as of a network of educational institutions disseminating specialized agricultural and general knowledge among the rural population. In defiance of the Prussian strict prohibition of political activities, agricultural circles' multiprofile economic activities carried political and nationalistic overtones. Their objective of enlarging the size of individual landholdings as a means of production rationalization equally aimed to preserve and expand land proprietorship in Polish hands in the territories under Prussian domination. Dissemination of technological information among the circles' members simultaneously served the function of promoting Polish manufacturers of agricultural machinery over the Prussian ones (Turowski 1995; Brodowska 2001).

2. In his speech to Parliament (*Sejm*) in 1956, the first secretary of the Polish United Workers' Party, W. Gomulka, acknowledged that the per hectare output of cooperative farms and state farms accounted for only 83.3 percent of that of privately owned holdings, despite government preferences for the socialized sector.

3. On this issue see Blanchard 1994: 51–91.

4. The fourth cooperative, which together with the *Kombinat's* transportation and construction units had opposed the motion to break up the *Kombinat*, made itself unavailable for the study despite several attempts on my part.

5. The system of formal authority of agricultural production cooperatives is as follows: the general assembly, which encompasses all members and meets twice a year, is formally the supreme governing body of the cooperatives. (In principle, the governance structure of the agricultural production cooperative resembles the governance structure of the cooperatives of agricultural circles, which will be discussed in the later part of the chapter.) The general assembly elects the supervisory board, which consists of a specific number of members stipulated by the individual cooperative's statute and, in turn, appoints a general manager. The supervisory board has the authority to make decisions regarding production profile, finances, etc., and requires approval by the general assembly.

The governance structure of the cooperative conglomerate, similar to the one of the agricultural circles, was as follows: the highest organ, the general assembly, encompasses all members of the conglomerate and elects the supervisory board, which in turn oversees the board of general management.

6. At the end of 1992, cooperatives were still waiting for a new cooperative law, which would specifically address these issues.

7. Under the tax law, from 1990 to 1992 individual agricultural units encountered higher "special sector" taxes when they ventured into processing activity *above a specific level.* If an enterprise's processing activities exceeded 40 percent of its overall production value, a 40 percent income tax was imposed. If processing activity accounted for less than 40 percent of production, the cooperative was exempt from the special sector income tax and paid a lower agricultural tax. Until the end of 1991, the agricultural tax was 14 percent; in April 1992 it was raised to 30 percent, retroactive to January 1, 1992. The special sector taxes included such agricultural activities as mixing fodder and processing meats, vegetables, and fruits. Poultry production was also subsumed under the special sector category. Furthermore, the compulsory insurance rate paid by agricultural cooperatives for workers employed within special sector industries was set at 45 percent of a worker's wage, as compared with 35 percent for non-special sector workers within the enterprise. Divergent tax implications for different types of economic activities and investment decisions within an enterprise point to how governmental tax policies, which on the macrolevel were to give an advantage to a specific sector, on the microlevel locked economic organizations within a narrow range of adaptive strategies.

8. Reduction in dairy cows for that period was from 120 to 90 cattle.

9. According to the general manager's calculations, it would have taken thirty years at 1991 prices to recover the investment cost (four billion zloty) required to construct a building housing eight hundred swine. With this projection in mind, the general manager abandoned the plan of increasing swine production.

10. Yields were consistently lower for 1991 across all specific grain categories as compared with the preceding year. The yields for 1992 dropped dramatically, as a result of the agricultural reforms at work compounded by severe drought. See *Rocznik Statystyczny* [*Statistical Yearbook*] 1994: 372 and table 18 at 420.

11. The only exceptions were the fertilizer loans with the preferential rate of 27 percent.

12. Others financially indebted (among them Cooperative C) learned of this opportunity after the program was phased out in 1994.

13. Cooperative A had a three-member managerial board, while both the other cooperatives had five-member boards.

14. Cooperative C had 40 percent of its cooperative land out of the membership's land and the rest came from the state land fund. In Cooperatives A and B, the membership land amounted to less than 5 percent of the cooperative land.

15. Only nine thousand members of agricultural circles were registered in 1956, the year of their inauguration. Within a year, the membership swelled to 325,000 and climbed the following year, 1957, to 454,000 peasants, and in 1959 further to over 550,000 members. See Turowski 1995.

16. In early 1991, the former general manager resigned, after, as it was rumored, a conflict with the chair over the revitalization plan.

17. Imports from two major suppliers were interrupted due to the Gulf War and to political instability in the former Soviet Union.

18. Thirty-five million zloty was paid as a down payment and sixty-five million zloty in loan payments.

19. In my personal conversations with the peasants/members of the circles, I heard that the former manager, who voiced objections to the direction of the revitalization plan, was pushed by the chair to resign.

20. The initial phase of the revitalization plan had been financed by commercial and cooperative bank funds. Several times, unable to pay the loan on time, the cooperative's chair successfully negotiated refinancing agreements with the lenders. However, in 1991, the cooperative lost its credit eligibility. The continuing investment projects were financed by loans in the amount of 590 million zloty (roughly sixty thousand dollars) from individual private lenders, among them the chair of the supervisory council.

At the end of 1994 the local cooperative bank announced its insolvency. It became common knowledge among the members of the Rolnicy community that the default of three credit takers on their huge loans (exact figures unknown) primarily brought the bank down. Among them was the chair of the agricultural circles. See Tittenbrun (2007) regarding numerous cases of fraud and corruption in the process of privatization profoundly shaping public distrust of privatization and its participants.

21. Thus, on the level of primary cooperatives, the nominal membership fees that carried an entitlement to a discount for received machinery services and formal priority in getting those services separated those individual peasants who were judicial owners of the cooperatives of agricultural circles from nonmember individual peasants who were providers of business to the agricultural circles. Often, as was the case in the Rolnicy *gmina*, the formal distinction between the members and nonmembers did not hold in reality either. Above and beyond the machinery services, the agricultural circles provided other services, such as technical services, agricultural information, educational courses for individual agricultural producers, and so on. Thus the membership included a majority of the individual agricultural producers irrespective of their machinery needs. The Rolnicy *gmina's* agricultural circles reflected the general structure of circles membership—it comprised all peasant strata: small, medium, and large peasants. See World Bank 1990, annex 6, for more on the impact of state socialist financial policies on ownership claims. On the history of agricultural circles, see Jakobczyk 1982.

22. The amendment to the cooperative law of 1990 provided an outdated legal framework as far as the issues of ownership, division, liquidation, or transformation of cooperatives were concerned.

23. By then a newly formed national association of agricultural circles was to coordinate the campaign.

24. The written documents place the existence of the studied community back in the thirteenth century as part of the cradle of Slavic origins and of Polish statehood. See Stanislaw D. Kozierowski 1935: 417–418. The long past as a Slavic community was interrupted in the aftermath of the partition of Poland. As a result of the aggressive colonization policies of Prussia, in the mid-nineteenth century, a majority of the inhabitants of Rolnicy were German. Germany began taking over the ownership of land, and the German language started to replace Polish as a formal language. The aggressive implementation of colonization and cultural domination by Prussia, and, in more recent history, during World War II, provoked active participation in the resistance movements of the Polish sections of the community. See an unpublished manuscript "Z Tysiaclecia Kroniki Regionu Tarnowa Podgornego" by Stanislaw Zbierski.

25. Western European economies mounted tariffs against agricultural products from Poland, while Poland pursued the liberalization of trade (Wilczynski 1996).

26. Yet, as strong empirical evidence indicates (Fedyszak-Radziejowska 1993: 36; Rosner 1993: 83), peasants were aware of the value of cooperatives in protecting their private ownership rights under the adverse conditions and expressed a need to create cooperatives in the future as the most important strategy to counteract the neoliberal post-socialist reforms.

27. See Dzun (1993), reporting on a broader trend of joint ventures emerging out of the intended creation of primary cooperatives in the process of deinstitutionalization of socialist cooperatives.

28. During my annual visits to Poland I have observed the gradual decline of the cooperative ownership form. By 2006 the agricultural production cooperatives that had existed in the Rolnicy community all were dissolved. In his broad study of rural transition in post-socialist Central Europe, Nigel Swain (2000) draws similar conclusions, pointing to a general trend of decline in agricultural cooperatives.

References

Arrow, Kenneth. 1963. "Uncertainty and the Welfare Economics of Medical Care." *The American Economics Review* 53 (5): 141–149.

Blanchard, Olivier. 1994. "Transition in Poland." *Royal Economic Society* 104 (426): 1169–1677.

Brodowska, Helena. 2001. *Chlopi o sobie I Polsce: Rozwoj swiadomosci spoleczno-narodowej.* Lodz: Ludowa Spoldzielnia Wydawnicza.

Burawoy, Michael. 1995 "Industrial Involution: The Russian Road to Capitalism." In *A La Recherche des Certitudes Perdues*, edited by Burgit Müller, 11–57. Berlin: Centre Marc Bloch.

———. 1982. "The Written and the Repressed in Gouldner's Industrial Sociology." *Theory and Society* 11 (6): 831–851.

Coase, R.H. 1960. "The Problem of Social Cost." *Journal of Law and Economics*, 3: 1–44.

DiMaggio, Paul. 1991. "Social Structure, Institutions, and Cultural Goods: The Case of the U.S." In *Social Theory for a Changing Society*, edited by P. Bourdieu and J. S. Coleman, 135–155. Boulder, CO: Westview Press.

———. 1988. "Interest and Agency in Institutional Theory." In *Institutional Patterns and Organizations: Culture and Environment*, edited by L. G. Zucker, 3–21. Cambridge, MA: Ballinger.

DiMaggio, P. J., and Powell, W. W. 1991. "Introduction." In *The New Institutionalism in Organizational Analysis*, edited by W. W. Powell and P. J. DiMaggio, 1–38. Chicago: University of Chicago Press.

Dzun, W. 1993. "Spoleczno-Ekonomiczne Aspekty Rozwoju Rolnictwa w Warunkach Gospodarki Rynkowej." In *Wies I Rolnictwo na Rozdrozu*, edited by Izabella Bukraby-Rylska, Janusz Stacewicz, and Maria Wieruszewska, 38–58. Warsaw: PAN, IRWiR.

Fedyszak-Radziejowska, Barbara. 1995. "Rolnicy, Przedsiebiorcy, Mieszkancy Wsi Wobec Wymagan Gospodarki Rynkowej." In *Wies i Rolnictwo w Okresie Transformacji Systemowej*, edited by Leszek Klank, 138–155. Warsaw: PAN, IRWiR.

———. 1993. "Rolnicy o sobie na tle innych group spolecznych." In *Rolnicy '92: Rolnicy wobec zmian systemowych*, edited by Andrzej Rosner, 30–41. Warsaw: Centrum Badania Opinii Spolecznej (CBOS).

Główny Urząd Statystyczny (GUS). 1985, 1990, 1991, 1992, 1993, 1994, 1995. *Roczniki Statystyczne*. Warsaw: Główny Urząd Statystyczny.

Gorlach, Krzysztof. 2000. "Post-traditional Family Farm in the Post-Communist Modernity: The Case of Poland." Paper delivered at the Working Group 22 on Family Farming. International Rural Sociological Association X World Congress, July 30–August 2, Rio De Janeiro, Brazil.

———. 1999. "Presenting 'New Face': Polish Peasants' Protests in the Era of Post-Communism." Paper delivered at the Working Group 1: Social Movements in Rural Areas: Sources, Rationalities and Identities in the Process of Change." XVIII *Congress of the European Society for Rural Sociology*, August 24–28, Lund, Sweden.

Hess, James. 1982. "Risk and the Gain from Information." *Journal of Economic Theory* 27: 231–238.

Jakóbczyk, Witold. 1982. *Wielkopolskie kólka Rolnicze 1866–1939*. Białystok: Krajowa Agencja Wydawn.

Korbonski, Andrzej. 1965. *Politics of Socialist Agriculture in Poland*. New York: Columbia University Press.

Kozierowski, Stanisław. 1935. *Atlas Nazw Geograficznych Słowiańszczyzny Zachodniej*. Poznan: Nauka i Praca.

Kulawik, J., and E. Tkaczyk. 1993. "Ocena kredytowania rolnictwa I przemyslu spozywczego w 1992 r. In *Komunikaty, Raporty, Ekspertyzy* Nr. 329. Warsaw: IERiGZ, Pp. 3–9.

Łapińska-Tyszka, K. 1993. "Kraj I Rolnictwo a Moje Gospodarstwo I Rodzina." In *Rolnicy '92: Rolnicy wobec zmian systemowych*, edited by Andrzej Rosner, 123–130. Warsaw: Centrum Badania Opinii Spolecznej (CBOS).

Magyar, Balint. 1984. "Peasantry and Agrarian Policy in Poland, 1944–1982." Manuscript.

Meyer, J. W, and Brian Rowan. 1991. "Institutionalized Organizations: Formal Structure as Myth and Ceremony." In *The New Institutionalism in Organizational Analysis*, edited byW. W. Powell and P. DiMaggio, 41–62. Chicago: University of Chicago Press.

Murrell, Peter. 1992. "Evolution in Economics and the Economic Reform of the Centrally Planned Economies." In *The Emergence of Market Economies in Eastern Europe*, edited by C. Clague and G. C. Rausser, 35–53. Oxford: Basil Blackwell.

North, Douglass. 1991. "Institutions." *Journal of Economic Perspectives* 5: 97–112.

Oliver, C. 1991. "Strategic Responses to Institutional Processes." *Academic Management Review* (16): 145–179.

Pfeffer, Jeffrey. 1972. "Merger as a Response to Organizational Interdependence" *Administrative Science Quarterly*. 17: 382–394.

Pfeffer, J., and G. R. Salancik. 2003 [1978]. *The External Control of Organizations*. New York, Stanford, CA: Harper & Row and Stanford University Press.

Radin, Margaret J. 1993. *Reinterpreting Property*. Chicago: University of Chicago Press.

Rosner, Andrzej. 1993. "Trudnosci rolnikow w gospodarowaniu I mozliwosci ich przezwyciezania." In *Rolnicy '92: Rolnicy wobec zmian systemowych*, edited by Andrzej Rosner, 80–86. Warsaw: Centrum Badania Opinii Spolecznej (CBOS).

Scott, W. R. 2008. *Institutions and Organizations: Ideas and Interests*. (3rd ed.). Thousand Oaks, CA: Sage.

Singer, Joseph W. 2000. *Entitlement: The Paradoxes of Property*. New Haven: Yale University Press.

Stark, David. 1996. "Recombinant Property in East European Capitalism." *American Journal of Sociology* 101 (4): 993–1027.

———. 1992. "Path Dependence and Privatization Strategies in East Central Europe." *East European Societies and Politics* 6 (1): 17–54.

Swain, Nigel. 2000. "The Rural Transition in Post-Socialist Central Europe and the Balkans." *Max Planck Institute for Social Anthropology Working Papers* 9.

Szurek, Jean-Charles. 1987. "Family Farms in Polish Agricultural Policy: 1945–1985." *East European Politics and Societies* (1): 225–254.

Tittenbrun, Jacek. 2007. *Z deszczu pod rynnę. Meandry Polskiej Prywatyzacji.* Poznan: Zysk I S-ka Wydawnictwo.

Turowski, Jan. 1995. *Sociologia Wsi i Rolnictwa.* Lublin: Towarzystwo Naukowe KUL.

Wilczynski, Waclaw. 1996. *Ekonomia i Polityka Gospodarcza Okresu Transformacji. Wybor Prac z Lat 1991–1995.* Poznan: Wydawnictwo Wyzszej Szkoly Bankowej.

World Bank. 1990. *An Agricultural Strategy for Poland.* Washington, DC: World Bank.

Zbierski, Stanislaw. 1986. "Z Tysiaclecia Kroniki Regiony Tarnowa Podgornego." Manuscript.

Chapter Five

The Privatization of State Farms: Slow or Illusory?

Several years into the post-socialist transition, observers generally agree that the intended rapid transfer of state enterprises into private ownership has not been successful. In 2004, thirteen years into the creation of the Agency of the State Agricultural Property (*Agencja Wlasnosci Rolnej Skarbu Panstwa* [AWRSP]), an agency appointed by the state to administer the process of privatization of state-owned agricultural assets, only 31.4 percent of the state farms' land has been sold, while a majority of it (49.1 percent) has been leased. The remaining approximately 20 percent of land has been returned to the previous private owners, the Church, or allocated to local communities or to the state forests enterprises for forestation (Buchowski 2009: 57).

Divestment of state assets has progressed at a very slow pace not only in Poland, but also in other Eastern European countries.[1] Even the conversion of Polish state enterprises into joint-stock companies has been limited. Despite general agreement that the results of privatization programs have been disappointing, there is little consensus about the causes of this outcome or about a solution to the problems of privatizing the state sector.

For neoclassical proponents of the "big bang" reform approach, the ineffective post-socialist political system was the principal factor inhibiting the implementation of rapid privatization. Others explain it in relation to the self-perpetuation interest of the officials within the agency created to oversee privatization (Buchowski 2009), or those officials charged with implementation of the reforms (Kornai 1990; Murrell 1991). The outcomes of privatization programs were, the latter argued, dependent on the responses of state-owned or formerly state-owned enterprises to reform measures. In a view advanced by Janos Kornai, state managers were too sclerotic to react positively to the radical introduction of market forces. This inflexibility then accounted for their poor market responsiveness and effectively destroyed the enterprises before privatization had occurred.[2]

Early empirical evidence of state firms' reactions appeared to reaffirm the latter approach. Because this argument assumes a uniform economic response, however, it is challenged by studies pointing to the *unevenness* of state-sector responses. Estrin's international comparison of state firms' responses indicates that portions of state firms *did* make significant adjustments to changing economic conditions (Estrin, Gelb, and Singh 1993). The study also shows great intracountry variation among responses. Although 30 percent of Polish managers showed poor motivation, a lack of authority, and an inability to develop or implement a long-term strategic plan for operations within the new market environment, fully 20 percent demonstrated high managerial motivation and successful strategic adjustments to the new environment.

Estrin relates these variations to actual or anticipated privatization. He contends that the emphasis on pending privatization explains much of the considerable progress toward enterprise adjustment. Estrin's approach emphasizes socialism's effects on property rights rather than on behavioral traits. Legacies of the past surface not in the inflexible behavioral traits of state managers, he argues, but rather in the ambiguity of property rights. Because state ownership implies "nobody's" ownership, rather than respond rationally to market signals, managers tend to make operating decisions that serve their own interests. For Estrin, the privatization program mediates the outcomes of socialist legacies through its actual execution and through individual firms' anticipation of its implementation. The privatization program thus establishes property rights and stimulates increased responsiveness to the new environment. These research conclusions translate into a policy recommendation that the privatization program be accelerated (Estrin, Gelb, and Singh 1993; Brada 1993).

Poznanski (1992) advances an alternative approach. His argument diverges from Estrin's by emphasizing that the slow implementation of the privatization strategy is critical. The actual transfer of assets has been slow, Poznanski argues, because the privatization process is inherently complex. Given the complexity of the process, post-socialist policies that presume a rapid asset transfer *contribute* to the crisis instead of effectively adapting them to the new economic climate. As Poznanski puts it, "Radical privatization programs declared at the outset of transition, rather than being neutral, have undermined the property structure in the state sector. A peculiar property vacuum was created as enterprises were left without any firm deadlines or even clear-cut ideas on the exact form of privatization" (1995: 10). Thus, state-directed privatization programs that were proclaimed imminent but remained unrealized, and that were touted as firm while remaining fluid, increased uncertainty about payoffs at the enterprise level. From Poznanski's perspective, this uncertainty was directly responsible for output decline and high rates of inflation.[3] Counter to the argument that privatization reform would clarify property rights, Poznanski posits a property vacuum as an unintended product of radical privatization. According to Poznanski, then, post-socialism does not mediate the legacies of the past, but instead breeds microlevel outcomes unintended by macrolevel programs. The contradictory characteristics of the transition reveal themselves between the macro- and microlevels.

In this chapter, I will trace the transition trajectory—from early adjustment strategies through liquidation in 1994—of one agricultural state farm located within the study area. A larger analysis of the asset transfer of all state farms in the Wielkopolska region will augment the study's scope. Theoretically, the approach advanced by Poznanski informs my empirical analysis. While I concur with Poznanski that we should conceptualize specific domestic policy choices as conditioning intended or unintended microeconomic responses of state enterprises, I enlist a three-pronged argument to strengthen his claims.

Firstly, I will further analyze Poznanski's cryptic notion of how the *complexity of privatization* necessarily prevents its fast implementation. As I argued in chapter two, the specific post-socialist choices are path-dependent and are thus positioned on the trajectory of the successive reformers' attempts, with each policy approach and its outcome constraining the choices available in the following reform stage.

The former socialist government's practices had demonstrated to post-socialist reformers an *ineffective* approach to policy implementation. Seeking to break from the socialist government's tradition of prolonged and fragmentary reform efforts, reformers attempted to gain credibility for their reforms by firmly rejecting past practices. I argue, however, that this rejection, though signifying a repudiation of past procedures, also forced post-socialist reformers to make only short-term changes, even as they strove for a comprehensive restructuring of the economy and society.

Thirdly, I argue that an adequate analysis of the policies' effects must extend beyond state enterprises' microeconomic responses. The impacts of privatization practices surface not only through specific reactions within the state sector, but also through specific responses within the private sector. In particular, analysis of the private sector's capacity to receive state assets reveals the policies' effects. I argue that the post-socialist policies produced a vacuum of property rights within state enterprises and a weakening of property rights in the private sector. The sluggishness and fragmentation apparent in the shift from state ownership to private property is not responsible for the alleged failure of state-sector privatization. Rather, privatization's failure stems from the *restatization* of property and the second *embourgeoisment of the nomenklatura* precipitated by reform efforts.[4]

Initial Transition of State Farms to a Market Economy

The Wysoki state farm conglomerate (PGR), located in the northern edge of the *gmina's* administrative borders, was founded in early 1966. Its founding occurred alongside renewed attempts by the socialist policy makers to concentrate agricultural production. In the period immediately preceding the conglomerate's establishment—that is, from 1956 to the early 1960s—in line with the general trend of downward assignment of rights within state property, several organizational changes were made in the structure of state farms to grant them more autonomy from the center in drawing their own production plans. State farms' decentralization involved the dismantling of state farm "groups" (*zespoly*) formed earlier and resulted in the stabilization of independent state farms of approximately four hundred hectares on average. Production growth was expected to derive from allowing workers' councils to participate with the management of the PGR in delineating production plans on the level of the individual state farms and from creating "bonus funds" to tie compensation level more closely with the level of production performance.

Wysoki PGR was created shortly after the state farm concentration began again full-scale in 1965. With an assumption of the production efficiency benefits stemming from economies of scale, concentration of land and production, and specialization and coordination, agricultural state-farm conglomerates (*kombinaty*) were reinvented similarly to earlier existing state farm groups (*zespoly*). A conglomerate developed several separate service units for transportation, machinery service, storage and grain drying, fodder mixing, fertilizer application, and so forth. The service units were designed to assist and intensify the modernization of agricultural production in all of a conglomerate's farms. As the size of an individual state farm was previously approximately four hundred hectares, the state farm conglomerates oscillated in size between two thousand and six thousand hectares and consisted of four to nine individual agricultural farms/production units. Growth in production was attributed mainly to the intensified mechanization of agricultural production rather than to increased labor efficiency. The conglomerate's administrative structure remained largely unaltered until post-socialist reforms precipitated considerable changes in its organization. At the advent of the transition period, the general manager (*Naczelnik*) had headed the state farm for twenty years.

From its inception, PGR played an important role in the local economy. It generated an average of five hundred employment positions, which were filled primarily by members of the local community. The conglomerate was the biggest agricultural output producer and provider of agricultural inputs (mainly fodder) to individual peasants in the immediate area. It also provided significant revenue to the *gmina's* budget through the payment of an agricultural tax based on the size of its land and buildings. In addition, PGR constituted a significant provider of social welfare services within the community. Apart from generating employment positions, it provided housing for the employees and their families. The Wysoki PGR entered the post-socialist transition with over seven hundred housing units, which were occupied by conglomerate employees, pensioners, and some nonemployees of the farm.[5] As well, it provided a daycare center for employees' children, a restaurant, a cultural center for villagers, and vacation facilities in a resort town for the exclusive use of the state farms' employees and their families. On a national scale, state farms housed in excess of one million people at the initiation of the post-socialist transition. Therefore, efforts to privatize state farms entangled the issues of production efficiency with those of social welfare.

The Wysoki conglomerate, which numbered among twenty-nine other state farms in the *voivodship*, belonged to a group of larger PGRs. The conglomerate employed 490 people at the beginning of the transition period and operated on over 5,200 hectares of land, 5,000 hectares of which were arable. Unlike many individual farms or PGRs that had acquired their land over time and thus had fragmented land parcels, the relatively late establishment of the Wysoki conglomerate had enabled its land and production facilities to remain almost in one piece. This consolidation had significant implications for the efficiency of the conglomerate's land cultivation. Overall, in terms of good fertility, the PGR's arable lands were classified predominantly as second- and third-class.[6]

Indeed, with respect to agricultural performance, all economic indicators designated the PGR as one of the leading conglomerates in the *voivodship*. Less than a year before the inauguration of post-socialist reforms, the Wysoki conglomerate boasted one of the highest levels of gross outputs per employee and per unit of cultivated land in the area.[7] The conglomerate positioned itself equally well among other PGR conglomerates in the *voivodship* with respect to commodified production per hectare of cultivated land, in net animal production output per hectare, and in grain yields.[8]

More significantly, the Wysoki conglomerate ended 1990 with its balance sheet in black, whereas, for the same period, all conglomerates in the *voivodship* reported average losses of 2.8 billion zloty. Amounting to over 32 billion zloty, the combined value of production reserves and commodified production exceeded total production costs by the comfortable margin of 3 billion zloty.[9] Also in 1990, the Wysoki PGR was in a minority of PGRs with low debts and a specific debt structure. Its outstanding financial obligations fell to below 5 billion zloty at a time when many other conglomerates had debts two or three times as high. At the close of the first transition year, the combined debt of the *voivodship's* PGRs topped 175 billion zloty. Furthermore, while turnover credits constituted major portions of debts for all other PGRs in the *voivodship*, the Wysoki conglomerate carried out its agricultural production in the first transition year without taking any turnover credit. Its debt consisted mainly of investment credits that had been taken to finance the construction of facilities, including a small animal slaughterhouse, a meat-processing facility based on internal animal production, and a retail meat-product store that supplied goods to residents in the surrounding area. This construction project began before the advent of the transition era. The PGR utilized a second investment loan for the development of a forty-eight-unit housing complex for employees' families. With the inauguration of stabilization measures, the construction, then 70 percent complete, drew to an abrupt halt. During the second year of adjustment to the early post-socialist economic environment, the conglomerate's economic standing deteriorated rapidly. In order to understand the decline of a conglomerate whose operations had flourished before the transition period, we must first examine the PGR's organizational and administrative structures.

State Farms' Proprietorship and Adjustment Strategies in the New Market Environment

The Wysoki conglomerate consisted of six agricultural enterprises that, though formally autonomous as production units, were neither legally nor financially independent of the conglomerate. As a whole, the PGR produced livestock—swine, sheep, and cattle (for milk and meat)—and grains; its grain production centered specifically on cereals, rapeseed, and sugar beets. Each of the six individual enterprises specialized in a specific line of animal husbandry supported by its own crop production. All enterprises were functionally dependent on five auxiliary servicing units, centrally located within the conglomerate. The unit for machinery and transportation provided mechanized land cultivation services, transport of agricultural products, machine repair, and conservation. The second unit was responsible for preparing, drying, and mixing fodder for animal husbandry. The conglomerate, which produced enough fodder to exceed internal needs by 50 percent, was self-sufficient in fodder production with the exception of imported mineral-fodder components. The third shop specialized in breeding animals, which were mainly for the conglomerate's own use. The fourth, a construction unit, was in charge of building, maintaining, and renovating the utility buildings and living quarters. The conglomerate's lab facilities represented a fifth unit and pretested meat, grains, and milk. The testing facilities secured the PGR with a markedly better bargaining position than individual peasants would have vis-à-vis the procurement centers that set prices for procured agricultural goods.[10]

Among the Wysoki conglomerate's numerous facilities were two alcohol plants with a combined capacity of 600,000 liters. Despite the abundance of internally produced resources for alcohol production, within the first two years of transition, the conglomerate's alcohol production was only 20 percent of capacity. The low alcohol output was due to centrally imposed restrictions on production and sale of alcohol.[11]

At the time of the introduction of the post-socialist reforms, the PGR's administrative structure had remained virtually unchanged since the conglomerate's founding in the mid-1960s. Before the transition, managers of the individual agricultural enterprises exercised relative autonomy over production decisions. Within each enterprise, however, the general manager (*Naczelnik*), assisted by his central administrative staff, made decisions regarding employment, capital investment, and modernization outlays. In addition, grain harvesting, the harvesting and processing of sugar beets, and the organization of labor within each production enterprise were subject to central directives from the *Naczelnik*. With the introduction of the post-socialist reform program, the *Naczelnik*'s subordination to the head of the Wielkopolska *voivodship*—the conglomerate's founding body—almost completely dissipated. The *Naczelnik* was left to self-finance and to make independent economic decisions for the conglomerate. Although the PGR's self-financing principle had been established (yet rarely exercised) in the early 1980s, in the context of the post-socialist market, price structure tensions arose among the conglomerate's agricultural units. Functionally separate but financially and legally bound, the more profitable enterprises became increasingly resistant to subsidizing other, less profitable production units. For example, swine production enterprises were reluctant to subsidize cattle and sheep husbandry or milk units. Such tensions led to the dissolution of one PGR in Wielkopolska at the beginning of 1991.

With growing internal pressures and a rapidly changing external economic environment, the general director searched for organizational and production solutions. One proposed solution called for the phasing out of the labor- and capital-intensive cultivation of sugar beets, which had become marginally profitable due to the new price structure. This solution would have saved a substantial portion of the conglomerate's spending on salaries. It also would have amortized the cost of the expensive, specialized machinery and thus allowed the conglomerate to turn to cheaper cereal cultivation. The alternative proposal also called for a 20 percent employment reduction to eliminate excessive labor in the conglomerate. This microeconomic adjustment to macroeconomic stabilization measures proved infeasible, however. The impact of the comprehensive post-socialist price reform could not be isolated at the enterprise level from the effects of labor policies carried over from state socialism. The Solidarity movement's lasting impact at the state-enterprise level surfaced particularly in the areas of hiring and firing. All management decisions on the termination of employment were subject to approval by the conglomerate workers' council and by a local chapter of the workers' union. Thus, the *Naczelnik* was unable to implement the alternative line of production since he could not lay off one hundred employees, a prerequisite for changing the production profile.

At the time of my first series of interviews in 1991, the PGR had reduced its employees by twenty, from 490 to 470. All were voluntary early retirements. Retirement payments, often higher than previous salaries, were an incentive for volunteers. The 1990 retirement bill allowed the PGR to use this method of overemployment reduction. The bill reflected political sensitivity, yet presented an enormous expense to the state, which desperately sought to reduce the huge budget deficit. This avenue of labor reduction quickly became self-liquidating. On the one hand, the state could not afford these retirements and thus altered the retirement provisions within a year.[12] On the other hand, the list of employees eligible for early retirement was limited. Consequently, within two years of post-socialist reforms, the Wysoki conglomerate reduced its employment by only 10 percent. By the *Naczelnik*'s estimates, an additional 15 to 20 percent of his conglomerate's labor force remained superfluous.[13]

In mid-1991, the *Naczelnik* told me that the second line of adjustment was the elimination of subsidized housing, water, and utilities for employees. Employees were to be charged market value for those services, while their salaries were to be raised proportionally. The *Naczelnik* reasoned that this solution would ensure more efficient use of these resources and services, and thus motivate employees to eliminate waste. However, this solution also encountered legal constraints. In 1990, the government introduced a confiscatory tax (*popiwek*), levied at state employees whose salaries rose above state-established levels. This law effectively preempted the second solution. The *popiwek* was designed as a central countermeasure to control the inflationary spiral of rising salaries. While critically important at the macrolevel, the *popiwek* curtailed attempts to rationalize the distribution of employment and productive resources within the PGR. It not only preempted the realization of this specific adjustment strategy, but it also made it difficult for management to tie any monetary remuneration to individual productivity results. The imposition of the *popiwek* precipitated stormy debates about its effectiveness within legislative circles and at the local level. It was considered a temporary measure, to be revoked within a year. Yet the date of its termination was repeatedly extended. As the *Naczelnik* told me, "*Popiwek* might eventually help to resolve the problem of inflation, but the patient might just bleed to death by then."

Poznanski's work on the real effects of the privatization reform implicitly addresses the area of *future* ownership rights. An analysis of the economic adjustments of the Wysoki conglomerate, however, requires the application of Poznanski's notion of privatization-induced "uncertainty" to the retroactive settling of *past* ownership claims. Two years passed between the explicit, yet ambiguous promise of state-farm privatization and the enactment of a new bill regulating the privatization path.[14] Immediately following the inception of the reform program, however, state farms were required to deliver on obligations stemming from their past ownership status. The state-imposed dividend tax burdened the Wysoki PGR, like all other state enterprises. Introduced in 1989, the tax derived from a judicial claim that the state laid against state farms. This claim was based on the state's contribution to the initial assets for the state farms' creation and on its subsidies throughout state socialism. The tax level was assessed in relation to the capitalization rate of a given state farm; the more modernized the state farm, the higher its dividend tax. Thus, the post-socialist reforms, which were premised on invalidating the previous socialist regime and its property relations, and on drawing a thick line between the socialist and post-socialist regime, paradoxically, through the imposition of the dividend tax, legitimized the past ownership claims of the socialist state to the assets of the state farms by implying a continuity of state governance.

The dividend tax evoked deep resentment on the part of state farms. Though run and financed by the state at their inception, state farms had been granted financial autonomy in 1982 in an attempt to reform state socialism. As was the case with the Wysoki conglomerate, a substantial part of their machinery, equipment, and maintenance costs came from their own budget rather than from the state. The dividend tax did not recognize this distinction. Rather, the tax was levied against all constant assets of state farms. This was perceived as deeply unjust and soon became a point of contention between state farms and the state. As the *Naczelnik* reasoned to me, the dividend tax forced him to cut amortization spending and to stand for progressive devastation and devaluation of his constant capital. This allowed him to decrease the value of the conglomerate and, consequently, to lower the amount of the dividend tax owed to the state. Thus, the dividend tax hit the most economically viable state farms the hardest and produced an incentive to decrease the enterprise's capital systematically.

On the supply side of the state farms' microeconomic adjustment, the effects of the dividend tax and the *popiwek* tax, in combination with the prolonged uncertainty relating to the exact formula of privatization and the PGR's legal status, caused the *Naczelnik* to adopt a very short time horizon. Prevented from making production-profile changes, reducing employment, or bringing about effective organizational restructuring, the *Naczelnik* approached the renewal of production with the short-term objective of keeping production going extensively. With little consideration for long-term economic viability or for production-efficiency results, he covered the necessary costs of production through sustained borrowing. For example, he planned to eliminate chemical fertilizers completely and to reduce pesticide use by at least 50 percent. Furthermore, due to his inability to advance the funds or to afford investment credits at an annual rate of 60 percent, he refrained from the amortization of machinery and buildings for the first three years of the transition. As the *Naczelnik* declared to me in mid-1991, "We need to produce; we don't have a choice in that. But now, they teach us how to produce extensively."

Faced with all of these new constraints, the *Naczelnik* joined other general directors in steadily increasing his conglomerate's debt in order to keep production going. By the beginning of 1991, the conglomerate's balance sheet had slipped into red: the total costs exceeded the conglomerate's total income by over 6 billion zloty. The conglomerate then took a 6-billion-zloty turnover credit to cover its production expenditures, particularly those incurred by energy and fuel costs (over 30 percent of its total production bill). The conglomerate was also left with an outstanding investment credit for the unfinished construction of apartment buildings and an animal slaughter facility. In an interview published in a local paper, the *Naczelnik* stated that, at their inception, the slaughter facilities were estimated to bring a full return on investment within seven years.[15] Under the price structure established with the economy's full monetarization, however, the pursuit of such investments became economically nonviable. Housing, as a subsidized project, was never expected to pay for itself. Although the conglomerate amassed interest payments on the unfinished housing project (reaching over 1 billion zloty by the time of its privatization in mid-1992), the *Naczelnik* pointed out to me that the only available option was to have the building completed and occupied. This would only have deepened expenditures due to the enormous energy bills. Thus, the conglomerate refrained from completing the two investment sites. Furthermore, in 1991 and 1992, the Wysoki conglomerate defaulted on its dividend tax and agricultural tax payments.

Thus, on the supply side, by virtue of their legal status as state enterprises with unclear past and future economic obligations, state farms were subjected to extensive state intervention in the allocation of their productive resources. Restrictions placed on the general managers' ability to hire and fire, and the imposition of dividend and tip taxes, effectively eroded the resource base of state farms. This undermined their incentives and their ability to respond positively to market forces. Legal restraints placed on the general directors narrowed their room to maneuver, locked them in unchanged lines of production, and forced them into short-term horizons. As a result, they were pushed more quickly into debt than were the other agricultural subsectors.

On the demand side, the Wysoki conglomerate, like other agricultural producers, was squeezed through increases in the price of inputs, high credit costs, and persistently low product prices. While the irrational price structure derived largely from preexisting monopolistic agricultural procurement centers, state farms' ability to function within this monopolistic market seemed to be better than that of other agricultural subsectors. State farms were more effective than their cooperative and individual agricultural counterparts in reducing the uncertainty over demand for their products and exerting control over procurement prices. In his twenty-year career, the general manager established formal and informal relations with the heads of monopolistic procurement centers. Therefore, he had a much better chance of effectively locating demand for his crops and animal husbandry as compared to individual peasants. The large size of state farms ensured them an advantageous position in finding demand for their agricultural goods.

In addition to relying on preestablished contacts to find demand for output, the *Naczelnik* had the means for effective communication: he had access to telephones, which were unavailable to the majority of peasants as they searched for markets. The *Naczelnik* had to make a few phone calls to secure a transaction with a specific procurement site. For peasants, however, often the only option was to stand in long lines at procurement centers without any certainty of outcome.[16]

The situation observed within the studied community was reflected in national statistics. While the volume of grain procured from state farms rose by 13 percent from 1989 to 1990, the corresponding private sector's procurement rate dropped by 9 percent. Although grain procurement in 1991 and 1992 decreased across all agricultural sectors, the decline was faster within the private sector.[17] This uneven procurement of grain output becomes more apparent once we examine the rate of total grain production output in these sectors. In 1991, the monetary value of purchased grains from the state sector was 1.27 million zloty per hectare of cultivated land but, for individual producers, was approximately 800 thousand zloty per hectare.[18]

In addition, with price liberalization, the procurement centers were better able to mask their monopolistic profits through production classifications from individual peasants than from employees of state farms. Various classification systems of procured agricultural products (especially milk and grain) were not open to verification by individual peasants.[19] Allegedly, the systems were used by procurement centers to transfer profits from individual producers. Since the PGRs were equipped with testing facilities, the conglomerates could pretest their procurement goods and thus lower their transaction costs with the procurement centers. Thus, in this respect, the PGRs had stronger bargaining power over the setting of procurement prices.

Finally, differential treatment between state and private agricultural producers became evident in the scheduling of payments for output. While peasants experienced high transaction costs with procurement centers due to the centers' continual delays in payments or payments in kind, the conglomerate found steady demand for its outputs and also received full payments on time. As the *Naczelnik* informed me, his long-established personal ties with the heads of the local procurement centers were especially valuable in times of scarce money supply: he made sure that he was paid off promptly, before any other suppliers.

The Effective Interests of PGRs: The Capacity to Shape the New Political Environment

While the state farms' adjustment to reform played out within the market settings and carried differential transaction costs for state farms and individual agricultural producers, it also occurred within the setting of political institutions. Although the post-socialist agrarian program targeted state farms for elimination, these farms quickly became a formidable force in actively shaping agrarian policy. By the beginning of 1991, the Wysoki conglomerate's deteriorating financial standing resulted in several payment delays of employees' monthly salaries. Growing concerns about the uncertain future of their own state farms and rumors that other PGRs hovered at the brink of economic ruin mobilized employees.

Across Poland, the liquidation of PGRs precipitated massive unemployment. Privatization of PGR state farms has remained a central cause of widespread agricultural unemployment.[20] Levels of unemployment were highest in Poland's northern and western regions, which had had the largest number of state farms under socialism. As numerous subsequent studies show, those early transition levels of unemployment generated not temporary but persistent and regionalized poverty concentrated in the rural areas with former state farms, and, thus, twenty years into state farm privatization reform, such areas are referred to as "postPGR" (post-state farm) zones of poverty or as "inna" Polska ("other" Poland) (Tarkowska 2009). In January 1991, the conglomerate's strike committee organized, compiled a list of demands, and threatened the conglomerate with a strike.

As reflected in the list of demands, the strike committee viewed its enterprise's difficult economic situation as the result of specific reform policies and thus called for these policies' prompt revision. The strike committee demanded the removal of the *double bias* inherent in agricultural reform policies targeting state farms. Referring to the alleged bias on the economic *intersectorial* level, the committee insisted on the legal differentiation of state enterprises and state farms. Farms, it argued, were purely *agricultural* enterprises with a specific, season-bound cycle of production distinct from that of industries. The committee demanded that credit terms and measures of productivity and profit be distinct for agricultural and industrial enterprises. It suggested 12 percent as the maximum acceptable level of production credit for agricultural enterprises and requested state intervention to guarantee minimal prices for agricultural output. On an *intrasectorial* level, the committee called for the creation of formally *equal* conditions for economic adjustment across agricultural subsectors. It demanded an immediate abandonment of the dividend and *popiwek* tax applicable only to the state agricultural enterprises, which it viewed as detrimental to the conglomerate's positive responsiveness to the new economic environment.[21] To the committee's members, it was akin to the political and ideological discrimination experienced by the agricultural private sector under state socialism.

Furthermore, the committee deemed state reform policies directly responsible for the adverse economic outcomes within the Wysoki conglomerate. First, it pointed to conflicting state policy objectives, claiming that trade liberalization and the influx of foreign alcohol were direct causes of the profound economic losses within the conglomerates' two alcohol plants (which were restricted by the state in their production levels).[22] The conglomerate then demanded that the state acknowledge its accountability by compensating it for incurred revenue shortages. Second, with respect to the suspended housing construction burdened by heavy credit payments, the committee asked for an administrative resolution making the facility available for employees' use.

The *Naczelnik* very skillfully conveyed the committees' demands to the founding body of the conglomerate: the *voivodship* leaders. In his personal talks with the head of the *voivodship*, he emphasized the unity among his farm's managers and employees in formulating the demands. He also alluded to the potential political costs to the new regime if this unity extended to other state farms. In this way, he warned of social unrest and a wave of mass unemployment. As he pointed out, there was an even higher risk associated with uniting the private, cooperative, and state agricultural subsectors to push for protectionist measures for agriculture, a particularly vulnerable sector of the economy in the time of transition. As an outcome of his negotiations, he received emergency funds (of an undisclosed amount) "to ease up hardship within the enterprises while awaiting more complex policy resolutions on the central level."

The formation of strike committees on the conglomerate level was not isolated to Wysoki. In contrast to protest actions in the Wysoki conglomerate, however, those in the numerous other PGRs affected by deepening economic difficulties did not secure funds that produced such a quick (though temporary) diffusion of internal pressures.[23] Many strike committees accused their directors of blocking the articulation of their grievances to higher administrative levels.[24] Unable to resolve their demands through the conglomerate or at a regional level and often with the encouragement of state farm managers, strike committees made a coordinated effort to advance their demands to the central state authorities in February 1991. The massive national strike that engaged 1,300 state farms lasted several weeks and threatened the newly formed government of Prime Minister Bielecki.[25] With the ongoing strike in the background, representatives of state farm managers and employees demanded emergency funds for the current payroll as well as a guarantee to purchase their production inputs. Furthermore, they proposed policy changes that affected the agricultural sector in general and the state farm subsector in particular. They called for immediate dividend tax relief for state farms, the establishment of guaranteed agricultural prices based on production costs, heightened tariffs on agricultural imports, and the reduction of credits to an annual rate of 12 percent.[26] The threat of political unrest posed by the PGR strikes resulted in the release of some emergency funds.[27] More importantly, a year and a half after the initiation of the post-socialist reform program, it substantially weakened the government's resolve in preserving the original stabilization plan and prodded it to embrace some state intervention.

Restatization of State Farms: The Second Embourgeoisment of the *Nomenklatura*

In the context of the state farms' deteriorating economic and political situation, on October 19, 1991, the Polish parliament passed a law establishing an agency to exercise, on behalf of the state, ownership rights to state farms' agricultural property. By January 1, 1992, the state had created the Agency of the State Agricultural Property to head the process of privatizing the state agricultural sector. On the day the agency was created, 1,576 of the existing state farms had accumulated a bank debt totaling 7.447 billion zloty. The debt owed to other entities, such as suppliers of production inputs, was 8.349 billion zloty.[28] The agency's budget for the takeover of these state farms amounted to 30 billion zloty. The parliament allotted the agency one year to accomplish this mammoth task. Six months into the privatization process, however, only two hundred state farms were under the agency's administration. Therefore, the deadline was revised to two years from the agency's inception.

The first task confronting the agency was the development of nonbank emergency funds to sustain current production activities in those state farms that had lost, or were about to lose, credit eligibility. According to the BGZ, the biggest commercial bank and credit lender to state farms, close to 400 of approximately 1500 existing state farms had lost their credit eligibility, and a further 700 were in an unstable financial standing as of April 1992.[29] Second, in the short term, the mixture of prolonged uncertainty about the exact future of state farms and the constraints on their immediate adjustment strategies reinforced soft budget constraints and thus led to massive debt for individual PGRs.[30] These constraints, in turn, had far more lasting implications for the direction and pace of the privatization procedures adopted by the Agency of the State Agricultural Property. In effect, the state farms' debt gave priority in the transfer of assets to groups (such as lender to the PGRs) that were not identified in the policy guidelines as the intended recipients of the state farms' assets. Given that lenders would advance immediate claims to their uncollected credits when the agency took over the administration of a state farm, the agency, with its meager budget, had to pursue the most solvent firms first and leave the highly leveraged ones for an unspecified, later date. This practice of first privatizing economically strong state farms left the weak ones in a state of continual uncertainty and thus perpetuated further the cycle of soft budget constraints among the latter. State farm debt not only imposed on the agency the specific sequencing of privatization procedures, but also pressed a complicated task of debt restructuring into the agency's agenda as a prerequisite for farms' subsequent privatization.

A combination of remaining socialist constraints *and* post-socialist goals for privatization shaped the trajectory of the agency's privatization of the state agricultural sector. With regard to the former, the intended privatization of the state farms raised issues of restitution such as the reinstatement of ownership and the restructuring of landholdings. First, the privatization proposal precipitated claims by the alleged pre-collectivization landowners. Six months after its creation, the agency received over 16,000 petitions statewide disputing the lawful ownership of over 900,000 hectares of state farmland.[31] The claimants warned the state not to proceed hastily with any privatization program without first rectifying injustices committed under state socialism.[32] At the time of this avalanche of reprivatization claims, only a proposed reprivatization bill circulating among state agencies was subject to further input and revision.[33] The specter of reprivatization, raised by prolonged debate over the reprivatization bill, hovered over state farms and frightened potential buyers. In northern and western Poland (an area including the Poznan *voivodship*), where there was the highest concentration of state farms and a high proportion of economically strong ones, the wide selection and availability of state farms for sale or lease met with very weak interest.[34] Land that could be reclaimed later by former owners was not considered a good investment.[35]

Contention over ownership claims in the reprivatization debate pertained to land for which state farms held formally documented ownership titles. The debate revolved around the issue of the legality of land title transfers carried out under the socialist state's land nationalization program. In addition, land confiscated from peasants without a formal ownership title change and "given" by the state land fund to individual state farms for cultivation became the subject of ownership disputes. Those lands were to be returned to their legal owners once the agency had taken over the state farms' administration. In the Wysoki conglomerate, eighty hectares of land were of the latter category and therefore returned to peasants in 1994.

The privatization of formerly state-owned farmland triggered further debate with regard to foreign investment. While, in late 1998, some 33 percent of Poles favored an increase of foreign investment in the Polish economy, by December 2000, CBOS reported that only 14 percent subscribed to this view. Opposition to foreign investment in Polish enterprises had risen threefold, although the strength of respondents' opposition differed according to the particular enterprise in question.[36]

Second, restitution for the past confronted the agency from its inception and involved the issue of agricultural land consolidation. Due to the effects of both pre-socialist history and socialist agrarian policies, land tenure in Poland's agricultural sector was highly fragmented.[37] Individual peasants petitioned the agency to administer land exchange and to regulate formally the land-parcel borders prior to state farms' actual privatization. Twelve individual peasants whose farms neighbored the Wysoki state farms petitioned the agency's local chapter for land exchanges in order to consolidate their fragmented land parcels. Statewide, 1.5 million hectares of land remained the subject of a complicated and ongoing campaign of land exchange and regulation aimed at land consolidation and the rationalization of a previously very fragmented structure of land ownership.[38] Although the process of land consolidation affected state farmland, the agency was not formally authorized to settle those issues. These requests had to be handled instead by the appropriate chapters of the state bureaucratic system *prior to* the agency's privatization of the land in question.

In an effort to rationalize the distribution of landholdings, the Agency of the State Agricultural Property initiated a program providing an incentive for private farmers who agreed to move their farms from south-central Poland, where demand for farmland was high, to the less-populated regions of northern Poland. Because the state had owned less land in areas of central and southern Poland than in the northern provinces, less land in the central and southern areas was available for distribution among private farmers. In 1997, the Polish government proposed a plan offering private farmers with land in central areas of Poland the opportunity to trade their farmland for leases on land in the northern and western provinces. Under the proposed arrangement, each hectare of farmland in the central provinces would enable the lease of several hectares in northern or western regions. In spite of the fact that the terms of the trade were favorable to farmers willing to resettle, developers of the program reported that, as of July 1997, fewer than one hundred farmers had signed up to participate in the land trade.[39]

Intensifying tensions surrounded the agency's future goals for its privatization efforts. Particularly contentious were the agency's stated program objectives, specifically with regard to the intended social and landholding structures in post-socialist agriculture. In a substantial revision of the earlier post-socialist agrarian program entitled "The Chances for the Countryside and Agriculture" (*Szanse dla wsi i rolnictwa*), Gabriel Janowski, the minister of agriculture and a former leader of the Agricultural Solidarity of Individual

Peasants, proposed a new 1992 agrarian program, "Principles of Agrarian Policy" (*Zalozenia Polityki Rolnej*). The plan proposed a wide range of state measures aimed at protecting and advancing the interests of family farms; it offered preferential credits to peasants, guaranteed minimal prices for agricultural products, and protected the domestic agricultural market. With respect to the privatization of the state agricultural sector, the program proposed giving preference to peasants in the privatization of agricultural farms and industrial enterprises supporting agriculture (such as food-processing enterprises). It proposed doing this by offering peasants shares at preferential rates and priority in sale offers (*pierwszenstwo wykupu*).[40]

Although, in the revised agricultural program, the minister of agriculture proposed measures designed to assist the development of the private agricultural sector, he simultaneously announced strong opposition to the creation of large farms with *hired* labor. Guided by the explicitly stated social objectives of social justice and egalitarianism—of preempting the creation of hired agricultural labor and a large landowner stratum—he proclaimed the optimal size of family farms to be ten to fifteen hectares.[41] As measures for deterrence, he proposed steep increases in taxes and the denial of credits to private farms exceeding twenty hectares of land. At the time of these proclamations, the law allowed individual farms to reach fifty hectares in eastern and central Poland and one hundred hectares in the country's northern and western regions. The minister's stand on the socially optimal size of landholding was found quite inflexible and arbitrary. In the public debates, many critics of the minister's stand on the future structure of landholdings pointed out that the requirement of family labor on the private farms correlated with the high variability in farm size (up to several hundred hectares), depending on the type of agricultural production and method of land cultivation (manual versus mechanized).

The agriculture minister's pronouncements about the future of family farms implied an approach to privatization that involved the subdivision of PGR land into small parcels for purchase by individual peasants. Thus, the intended social outcome of the state agricultural sector's privatization conflicted with the production performance objectives of privatization. Supported by many agricultural experts, the agency's director, Adam Tanski, described state farms as large, inseparable agricultural enterprises. He argued that the agriculture minister's proposed subdivision or fragmentation of agricultural enterprises would have lead to disastrous economic results from the standpoint of production efficiency.

Although all of these policy pronouncements regarding specific approaches to agricultural privatization and their projected outcomes were tentative, their public articulation produced tangible microeconomic results. The small minority of peasants whose interest in acquiring state farmland had not been shattered by credit constraints withdrew their interest in light of the legal uncertainties involved with attempted farm enlargement.[42] Although individual peasants' farms that had a long tradition of commodified and specialized agricultural production surrounded the Wysoki conglomerate, these peasants expressed a collective demand for merely two hundred hectares of the conglomerate's land. Only one hundred and seventy hectares of the Wysoki PGR were turned over to peasants.

In legal contrast to a transfer or partial liquidation of state farm assets, the agency's privatization of state farms entailed a *full* transfer of farm assets based on a submitted business plan specifying the future productive deployment of those assets, coinciding with the organizational and legal liquidation of the state farms as legal entities.[43] The founding body (the head of the *voivodship*) or the employee council was to initiate liquidation. After the founding body evaluated the PGR's assets, established an auction price, and notified the PGR's employees, permission for the farm's liquidation could be secured from the Ministry of Property Restructuralization. With the preparatory actions completed, the designated PGR was marketed in an auction.

Policy guidelines granted a PGR's employees priority in the formation of joint-stock companies. In its broad guidelines, the policy also stipulated that peasants had preferential status in state farms privatization. In the actual privatization processes, however, neither of these groups received preferential access to the asset transfer. In the summer of 1992, the Wysoki PGR's employees complained that they were not properly informed about their eligibility to participate in the privatization of their farm. At the same time, their *Naczelnik* insisted that the employees showed no interest in actively participating in privatization. Their actual nonparticipation was very much representative of the situation in other state farms. In many of them, the formal creation of employee joint-stock companies camouflaged the long-term lease of state property to a narrow managerial group, which formerly had governed the farms. These groups simply had recruited a few employees in order to appear to meet criteria for preferential status in asset acquisition. Even employees who were well informed about the privatization procedures of their farms encountered financial barriers to their participation in the asset transfer. They were unable to pay an advance that, even at a preferential price, amounted to 2 million zloty: the employees' average monthly salary. Furthermore, the Agency of State Agriculture Property imposed a condition of prior privatization of housing facilities on state farms that petitioned for the privatization of the farmland and related production assets. Thus, employees at the time of state farms' privatization were faced with buying out their living quarters. Although the financial terms of the flat buyouts were very convenient, state farm employees' meager financial resources did not allow for multiple financial advances.

Similarly, financial constraints effectively shut peasants out of the privatization process.[44] The few who did not face that constraint met legal barriers.

The policy provided for their preferential status only in the case of state farm capital privatization, and not in connection with a liquidation privatization.[45] Since state farm privatization was conducted primarily based on liquidation, the process prevented individual peasant participation. Finally, beyond the financial and legal constraints, cultural and ideological barriers kept peasants from pursuing the state farm land. On the one hand, decades of the socialist agrarian policy, what Gorlach (1999) called "economic growth without development," had firmly formed a perception in over 90 percent of peasants about an optimal form and size of a private agricultural farm as based on family labor and land size not exceeding 10 hectares (Rosner 1993: 68; Gorlach 1999). This vision of an optimal private agricultural farm has not conformed to a model of capitalist agricultural enterprise based on hired labor and expanding land acquisition. On the other hand, nearly half of the peasants believed that the rightful recipients of the state farm privatized land and assets should be not them but the state farms' employees (Rosner 1993: 70).

In the summer of 1992, only half a year after the agency's formation, the *Naczelnik* of the Wysoki conglomerate took the initiative to prepare a business plan to liquidate the state farm and transfer its assets.[46] The plan fit the general agricultural policy objectives in that it called for the elimination of large, state farm landholdings; the proposal split them into smaller, individual agricultural enterprises. It then proposed to lease them to the employee stock company, which, as the plan specified, would consist of the general manager, several members of his former administrative and production management team, and a few employees.

The *Naczelnik* never submitted his plan to the agency, however. When the manager formulated the business plan, he had one main goal in mind: to secure the transfer of his power. However, his observations of the privatization processes and outcomes for other state farms led him to see the risks accompanying such a proposal. In an interview, he cited the case of one manager of a state farm who, in his yearly preparations, staged "favorable conditions" to secure a lease of over two thousand hectares of land for himself and an additional twelve hundred hectares for his deputy manager. He mobilized sufficient funds to control shares in an employee stock company and persuaded the state farm's employees to support the project as beneficial to all of them. To his surprise, at the last moment, he was outbid by a trade and food-processing joint-stock company that offered a leasing fee far higher than even the most optimistic projections of the farm's profitability. The incident exposed the general manager's opportunistic intentions to the employees of his conglomerate.

In addition to closely following other state farms' privatization procedures, the general manager of the Wysoki state farm probed the "local climate" to assess the chances for the realization of his initial business plan. He started a rumor about his intention to bid as a private investor for agricultural lands offered for sale in his area. His name as a potential buyer instantly attracted five competitive bids, indicating to him strong potential resistance to his original plan for the restructuring of the state farms.

In early 1994, the *Naczelnik* proposed a new business plan. He was short of the personal funds necessary to form an employee stock company with the controlling shareholding for himself. He was uncertain of the level of support he could generate for the employee stock company proposal. He had also gained wisdom from observing other general managers' experiences. His plan called for an asset transfer that would preserve the conglomerate's organization. It would have left all six production enterprises intact. All the machinery, the production resources, and the animal stock were to become the assets of a new legal entity—a stock company. The Agency of State Agricultural Property would become the sole shareholder of this company. Its land and existing buildings would be separated and deemed "state assets" leased to the stock company for sixteen years at 5 billion zloty per year.

The new proposal drew diverse responses from various interested parties. Upon a close inspection of the conglomerate, a representative of the Ministry of Restructuration acknowledged the conglomerate's maintenance of high production standards relative to other state farms operating in an equally adverse economic environment. Yet he found the conglomerate's proposal for preservation unviable on political grounds: he claimed it was in conflict with the social objectives of the agrarian policy. Support from the conglomerate's employees counterbalanced the ministry's negative recommendation of the plan. They saw the preservation of the conglomerate as the best way to ensure their uninterrupted employment. Furthermore, the *Naczelnik's* strong interest in preserving his managerial position was aided by his personal contacts within the agency's regional chapter, giving him a powerful advantage to secure his proposal's approval. A former bookkeeper who had become a member of the agency's executive committee counseled the *Naczelnik* as he prepared his new business plan and submitted it to hearing. Support for the specific asset transfer proposed by the *Naczelnik* was not devoid of personal incentives for this former bookkeeper. While the strict transfer of state farm assets into private hands would have made his position and the whole agency obsolete, the formation of a joint-stock company owned by the agency spelled the preservation of his own position—as a periodic examiner of the performance of the joint-stock company's managerial board.[47] In addition, the *gmina's* leadership had a vested interest in supporting this legal asset transfer. The creation of a stock company with the agency as the sole shareholder implied revenue of 2.5 billion zloty per year from the agricultural tax. The creation of a private stock company would lead to a tax exemption for the first three years.

After a series of hearings at the regional chapter of the agency, the asset transfer had been officially conducted and legally registered. The general manager, appointed to a one-member management board, acquired full autonomy in production decisions. His only constraint was that the agency imposed a 15 billion zloty credit limit. The agency induced him to amortize the leased buildings by receiving up to a 50 percent discount on the lease fee compensating his investment expenditures. The newly issued state regulation called for the potential removal of 20 percent of the leased lands from the contract, contingent on demand for the land from individual peasants.[48] In his recent legal maneuvering, the manager attempted to transfer a further 20 percent of the leased land into legal assets of the stock company.[49] In the event of their sale to peasants, the profits would go to the company instead of to the state treasury. The manager intends to invest the proceeds into purchases of new machinery.

The process of the formal privatization of Wysoki signifies the *restatization* of state farms and *the circulation of the economic nomenklatura.* The specific legal form of asset transfer represented a strong form of a more general trend: the state's retention of the ownership of farms and its allocation of management control to the old managerial cadre. The Wysoki state farm's assets were effectively allocated to two legal state entities: the agency and the treasury. Although this strong form of restatization occurred in only a limited number of cases, a weaker form of restatization was a common outcome of the privatization of state farms.[50]

By January 1994, the agency had assumed control over assets of 1600 state farms; the area of the appropriated land encompassed some 3.3 million hectares.[51] A particularly high percentage of state farms in areas of northern Poland had been privatized; in the Elblag *voivodship*, for instance, 67 percent of land belonging to state farms in the socialist era was under private ownership. Privatization processes occurred less frequently in central Poland. For instance, in early 1994, only 30 percent of formerly state-owned farmland in Lodz, Suwalki, and Skierniewcie *voivodships* had private owners.[52] Nationwide, over 60 percent of state farms administered by this state agency were leased predominantly to the former managerial and administrative groups of the state farms, often under the guise of employee joint-stock companies. Individuals (mostly former managers) without a distinct legal identity administered an additional 10 percent. By contrast, for only 4 percent of state farms did privatization occur in the narrow sense—as an asset transfer into private hands. The restatization trend was even more pronounced in the territories administered by the agency's Poznan chapter. Despite these areas' higher economic viability, the restatization of state farmland in the region exceeded 80 percent. Of this, 55 percent was in the form of leasing and 27 percent was in the form of administrating by individual persons rather than legal entities.

Conclusion

Contrary to the explanation advanced by evolutionist economists, the observed failure of state farms' economic restructuring was not the result of their managers' inflexibility in the face of new economic demands. Rather, the stabilization package itself had contradictory effects at the microlevel and constrained state farms' capacity to change.

As Poznanski argues (1993, 1996), because the government promised to eliminate state farms but did not specify the specific steps involved with the privatization process, state farms, forced into a state of uncertainty, adopted short-term survival strategies. As they waited for the government to establish new property rights, state farms, as state enterprises, were subject to proprietary claims and governmental intervention with regard to their income and allocation of production resources. This intervention directly affected the farms' adjustment abilities. Restricting general directors' ability to hire and fire and imposing dividend and excessive wage taxes (*popiwek*) effectively eroded state farms' resource base. The state's interventionist measures undermined state farms' incentives and their ability to respond positively to market forces. Legal restraints on general directors' operations locked the PGRs into unchanged lines of production and pushed them into deeper debt. Thus, rather than impose hard budget constraints on state farms, stabilization measures compelled enterprises to liquidate their assets partially and to accrue a heavy debt.

The unintended microeconomic outcomes elicited specific political behavior from state-farm employees. Employees' political action, in turn, shaped the political process and policy formulation. By threatening with strikes and mass unemployment, state farms exerted political pressure so that their economic interests trumped those of the private and cooperative agricultural subsectors. The threats quite effectively gained the government's immediate attention and triggered ad-hoc governmental bailouts, thereby directly contradicting the macrolevel objectives of the stabilization package.

The contradiction between macroeconomic programs and microeconomic actions in the initial phase of stabilization shaped the dynamics of privatization at later stages and primarily affected the sequencing of state farms' privatization. Instead of quickly transferring the assets of the most indebted farms in order to avert further strain on economic resources and on the state budget, by default, the agency privatized the poorest state farms last.

In addition, the inherent complexity of privatization reform, in both aspects of policy formulation and implementation, bred its own contradictory outcomes that were revealed in the pace and direction of ownership changes. In its articulation, the privatization reform was driven by a dual goal: to establish property rights that would yield efficient economic *and* social outcomes. On the one hand, the failure of repeated and protracted reformist endeavors to enhance the economic efficiency of state property seemed to unambiguously advance the conclusion that the *rapid* establishment of *any* form of private property remained the only relevant tool to yield economically efficient outcomes. Privatization appeared as the only means to maximize economic output and in that it stood as an unequivocal rejection of socialist nationalization. At the same time, privatization was understood as a way to actively mediate the effects of the socialist nationalization of property—by amending the unjustly denied private ownership rights and by producing a future distribution of economic benefits that stands as a social advancement toward, rather than a regression from, state socialism. In that context, not any form of private property but only a *specific* form of private property became relevant.

On the level of the formulation of the privatization program, the conflicting connotation of privatization as means and goals revealed itself in the contest between policy makers who promoted two distinct systems of private property in agriculture, thus leading to different developmental outcomes. Advocates of agriculture based on specializing and economically differentiated private farms were challenged by those who promoted private property based on family farming devoid of the exploitation of hired labor. The prominence of the agricultural minister's vision of family-farm agriculture at the time that the program was launched effectively discouraged individual agricultural producers interested in the future expansion and intensification of their production. The ministry's projections of heavy taxation and preferential credit withdrawal for "excessively sized" private farms threatened peasants' ownership right to exchange and transfer assets and scared them off. Furthermore, these pronouncements heightened the ambivalence about what strategies of the state farm asset transfer should be pursued.

The privatization of state farms revealed its complexity and an inherent tension in its objectives at the implementation level as well. From its inception, the agency was faced with complex issues that required resolution *prior* to undertaking privatization proper. It was necessary to deal with the ambiguity of the socialist ownership structure by settling the unclear legal status of some state farmland. Furthermore, it required the consolidation of agricultural lands, which involved complicated exchanges of land, to be coordinated with the transfer of ownership titles. The complexity of these tasks was compounded by their assignment to distinct, uncoordinated state agencies. Finally, the privatization of state farm housing, expected to be conducted independently from and completed prior to the privatization of the state farms as agricultural production enterprises, forced delays in implementation of the objective, despite its political exigency.

By design, the liquidation path of state farm privatization allowed individual state farms to initiate the processes of their own privatization. However, in these privatization processes, management gained the unintended powerful advantage of instigating and controlling asset transfers due to the necessarily extended nature of the process. The grossly inadequate financial and information resources and the limited legal powers vested in the agency exacerbated the situation. Thus, the privatization of state farms simultaneously bred two parallel processes: it eliminated private peasants from contending for these assets and put managerial insiders in an advantageous position. The pronouncements of future family-based agriculture, combined with the underdeveloped and underfinanced institutional framework, gave local managers excess room to maneuver in transferring assets. Through various leasing scenarios, managers from the former state farms preserved their positions and managed to remain the heads of joint ventures that combined private and state assets. As the Wysoki case illustrates, they searched for ways to appropriate profits generated by state assets. This process closely resembled the late 1980s *nomenklatura* privatization (Berg 1994; Staniszkis 1991). This earlier *nomenklatura* privatization resulted from the reforms of late state socialism designed to establish the economic and financial independence of state enterprises. It quickly became perceived not as a strategy for more efficient allocation of production assets, but rather as a vehicle for the *nomenklatura* to convert their political capital into economic power—by privatizing profits while squandering social assets. Amidst wide public condemnation of the *nomenklatura* privatization, the 1990 reforms of the post-socialist regime indirectly aimed to curb this sort of asset transfer. Yet three years into the process of the legal liquidation of state farms, similar results were produced.

My analysis of the initial economic adjustment and privatization process of the Wysoki state farm allows us to deepen Poznanski's account. The variability in the outcomes of the stabilization and privatization measures within individual state farms could not be explained by reference to behavioral characteristics of the state managers. Rather, property rights were the key. Privatization reform was caught among three issues: the push to bring about a rapid change in the property structure; an ambivalence about the wider social objectives the property structure was to serve; and institutional and procedural nonreadiness for successful ownership transfers. Ultimately, it created a specific vacuum of property rights not only within the state sector as Poznanski asserts, but also within the individual sector. The actual defining of the system of emerging property rights became a function of the economic interests and political contestation of various local players—managers, local and regional governments, and state farm workers. In this contest, state farms' managers seized the initiative to redefine the system of property rights culminating in the effective restatization of state farms.

Notes

1. Some analysts suggest that Hungary and Romania outpaced other post-socialist countries in privatization, while others, such as Stark, find Hungary equally slow in privatization endeavors.
In Poland, AWRSP expected to reprivatize the state farms within a year of its operation. However, as World Bank (1995) and Dzun (1993: 46) pointed out, by the first quarter of 1993, the agency managed to privatize only 10.6 percent of the land under its administration.

2. In this view, the state manager invariably wants to "invest more, obtain an even greater amount of hard currency, import more machinery and equipment from a hard currency market, travel more, and let his colleagues do the same. . . . He wants to pay more wages, since this can boost his popularity among employees and ease the tensions around him. It is time to abandon hope that the budget constraint can be hardened" (Kornai 1990: 62).

3. Burawoy (1996) has advanced a similar argument. In his thesis on production involution, Burawoy asserts that radical economic reforms instill ever shorter time horizons on the enterprise level, which gives rise to little concern for the future repercussions of current financial decisions and thus to the rationalization of soft budget constraints rather than to their abolition (1996: 43).

4. For a detailed analysis of the process of the first embourgeoisment of *nomenclatura* and the phenomenon of political capitalism in the aftermath of late state socialism, see J. Staniszkis (1991).

5. On a national scale, state farms housed in excess of one million people at the initiation of the post-socialist transition. Therefore, efforts to privatize state farms entangled the issues of production efficiency with those of social welfare.
The value of the Wysoki conglomerate's housing facilities, excluding those utilized in agricultural production, amounted to 60 billion zloty. Thus, housing represented over one-fifth of the conglomerate's total worth, estimated at approximately 240 billion zloty, and far exceeded the 38 billion-zloty value of all machines, technical equipment, and transportation. The high value of the farm's housing relative to that of its other assets was representative of the *voivodship's* other state-farm conglomerates. In some conglomerates, however, the value of housing for employees exceeded 30 percent of total assets (Source: Unpublished internal report on the production and financial results of PGRs in the *voivodship* of Poznan). As will be discussed later in some detail, housing and its financing became critical issues in the Wysoki state farm's privatization process.

6. Agricultural lands within the classification levels of 1 to 3 allow for the cultivation of high-quality crops (mainly high-priced wheat for human consumption), while lands within the fourth and fifth class are of poorer soil quality, more costly in cultivation, and restrict agricultural production to the lesser grains used mainly for animal fodder.

7. While, in the Wysoki conglomerate, the gross output per employee was 35 million zloty (4.5 million zloty per hectare of cultivated land), the figures for the majority of PGRs in the *voivodship* were within the range of low to mid-20s and 2 to 3 million zloty. (Association of the State Agricultural Farms 1991).

8. For the same period, all conglomerates in the *voivodship* reported average losses of 2.8 billion zloty. The Wysoki conglomerate's commodified production amounted to over 50 grain units per hectare of cultivated land, while that of the majority of PGRs fell within the wide range of low 30s to high 40s. Wysoki's animal output was 483 kg/hectare; average animal output for twenty-nine conglomerates in the *voivodship* was 448 kg/hectare. Wysoki achieved grain yields of 48q/hectare, while the average for the remaining state farms was 41q/hectare (Association of the State Agricultural Farms 1991).

9. Only three other PGRs reported higher profits than Wysoki; five PGRs closed the first post-socialist transition year breaking even; and fully fifteen of twenty-nine were already deeply in the red.

10. For more information on the activities of procurement centers, see chapter 3.

11. "Ankieta Przedsiebiorstw Przejmowanych przez Agencje Wlasnosci Rolnej Skarbu Panstwa" [Survey of the State Farms privatized by the Agency of the State Agricultural Policy], Internal document of a local Wielkopolska chapter of AWRSP.

12. On my return in 1995, early retirement had been reinstated and was available (among three other options) to people whose work stations were eliminated as an outcome of the work restructuring.

13. The total employment in May 1992 stood at 457 employees, down from 490 at the reforms' introduction, with 364 blue-collar positions and 93(!) administrative and managerial positions. (*Ankieta Przedsiebiorstwa Przejmowanego przez Agencje Wlasnosci Rolnej Skarbu Panstwa* 1993, Survey of the State Farms privatized by the Agency of the State Agricultural Property. Attachment no 7.)

14. Until 1992, the state farms remained legally subject to state regulation as state enterprises.

15. "Ziemi sie nie oszuka" ["You can't cheat the land"] 1991, *Glos Wielkopolski, 25 lipiec*, 5.

16. See chapter 3.

17. Due to severe drought, 1992 marks an especially dramatic drop in the production and procurement of agricultural output.

18. See GUS 1993, *Rocznik Statystyczny* [*Statistical Yearbook*]: table 44 (456), 345.

19. The process is described in chapter 3.

20. As of June 1994, fully one-half of newly unemployed workers in Poland's agricultural sector had lost their jobs because of state farms' liquidation. On unemployment in the aftermath of the liquidation of state farms, see Wilkin 1997: 72; Halamska 1999; Frenkel 1997; and Tarkowska 2000, 2009.

21. Jerzy Baczynski 1991, "Gorzki popiwek" ["Bitter Anti-inflation Tax"]. *Polityka* 7 (1763): 1; Joanna Solska 1991, "W imieniu zalogi: Panstwowe Przedsiebiorstwo istnieje po to aby placic" ["Representing the Employees: State Farms Exist to Make (Tax) Payments"], *Polityka* 7 (1763): 1.

22. For a more detailed discussion of alcohol-gate, see chapter 3.

23. In early 1991, out of 1200 state farms, 406 had low creditworthiness, 92 lost their creditworthiness, and 21 were facing bankruptcy. See "Informacja o realizacji uchwaly Sejmu RP z dnia 9 maja 1991r w sprawie programu dzialan doraznych i systemowych dla panstwowych gospodarstw rolnych," discussing implementation of a Parliament Bill of May 9, 1991, regarding the short-term and long-term actions on behalf of the state farms. Ministry of Agriculture, Warsaw, June 1991. Unpublished material.

24. Report of the Meeting of the Striking Committees of PGR of May 3, 1991 in Iwno. Unpublished material.

25. See Witold Pasek 1991b, "Flagi w 1300 PGR-ach" ["Flags in 1300 State Farms"]. *Gazeta Wyborcza*, February 14, 3; Ewa Czaczkowska 1991, "Strajkuja PGR-y. Prywatyzacja to nie parcelacja." *Rzeczpospolita*, February 12, 1.

26. Then, the ongoing rate was over 60 percent. See Witold Pasek 1991a, "W Zoruchowie strajk," *Gazeta Wyborcza*, February 18, 3; Edmund Szott 1991, "Manifestacja zakonczona rozmowami," ["Protest Ended by Negotiations"], *Rzeczpospolita*, March 9: 4.

27. The government was under heightened pressure not only from PGR strikes but also from the parliament. In bitter debates, many parliamentary members accused the government of strangling the state farm sector and of failing to resolve the PGR economic crises. By August 1991, there were persistent rumors of a no-confidence vote for the government. See Halina Flis-Kuczynska 1991, "O Sabotazu przy pustej sali: w Sejmie o rolnictwie," ["About the Sabotage of Agriculture within the Empty Halls of the Parliament"], *Gazeta Wyborcza*, August 22: 6.

28. See Edmund Szott 1992, "*Niecierpliwosc. Prywatyzowanie PGR*" ("Impatience. Privatization of the PGR), *Rzeczypospolita* 172 (3210): 2.

29. "Ankieta Przedsiebiorstw Przejmowanych przez Agencje Wlasnosci Rolnej Skarbu Panstwa" ["Survey of the State Farms Privatized by the Agency of the State Agricultural Policy"], Internal document of a local Wielkopolska chapter of AWRSP.

30. See also Burawoy's (1996) analysis of the adjustment strategies in Russia.

31. Regarding the complexity of considerations and the complicated procedures related to restitution for unfair expropriation in the past, during the process of transferring, or creating a

new basis for, ownership of agricultural assets in pursuit of efficiency in the agricultural sector, see Tomczak 1994; Swain 1996; and Halamska 1998.

32. Development of the specific formula for how to address former owners' claims took a long time. Only in May 1995 was the formula for compensation elaborated. The state considered only indirect compensation for land instead of its return. The lands formerly within Poland's eastern border and granted to the Soviet Union after World War II in exchange for gained territories on the western front were designated legally ineligible for compensation claims. The reprivatization bill cited the Nationalization Act as a violation of the ownership rights of former owners, whose land was taken to the state farms and thus subject to property claims.

33. Edmund Szott 1992, "Rada Ministrow dyskutuje o prywatyzacji," *Rzeczpospolita* 76 (3114), 1.

34. Krystyna Naszkowska 1992, "Nie szli na Zachod Obszarnicy," *Gazeta Wyborcza* 275 (1048): 13.

35. Apart from reprivatization issues, farms that were functioning well were priced too highly to attract buyers.

36. Centrum Badan Opinii Spolecznych [Research Center of Public Opinion] (CBOS) 2000, *Opinions on Privatisation and the Presence of Foreign Capital in Poland*, 1.

37. See chapter 2.

38. See "Scalanie i wymiana gruntow" ["Consolidation and Exchange of Land"] 1993, *Gazeta Rolnicza* 18 (192/68), 15.

39. Polish farmers showed an unwillingness to accept the offer for resettlement, particularly among relatively young Poles who lived on farms with their families. These young Poles, who were typically better educated than their older family members, recognized that their labor was superfluous to farm operations but, unlike their counterparts from previous years, resisted migrating to urban centers. Instead, they tended to search for employment opportunities in rural areas so that they could continue to live on their families' farms. (Halamska 1998; Frenkel 1997). Rosner (1993) asserts that the attachment to land and the local community had both emotional and pragmatic motivation. Family and land presented the means for reducing uncertainty and devising survival strategies in the trying times.

40. See World Bank 1990; also Dorota Pilot 1992, "Rolne sprawy do poprawy" ["Agricultural Matters Subject for Correction"], *Gazeta Wyborcza* 267 (1040), 14.

41. See Flis-Kuczynska 1992, "Bat na dziedzica," *Gazeta Wyborcza* 243 (1025): 18.

42. See chapter 3 on the strategies of adjustment by individual peasants; also Krystyna Naszkowska 1992, "PGR-y w Chlopskie rece" ("State Farms into Peasants' Hands"), *Gazeta Wyborcza* 218 (990): 5. Many peasants who were already involved in the process of purchasing land from the liquidated state farms withdrew their applications after Janowski's statements about the family farms.

43. Partial liquidation, which entailed a spontaneous, progressive decapitalization of individual state farms, was practiced earlier as a means of obtaining much-needed production resources for renewing production cycles.

44. See chapter 3 for more on these constraints.

45. The Law on Privatization of State Enterprises of August 1, 1990, envisaged two paths for an enterprise's privatization. *Capital* privatization, intended predominantly for large enterprises, was based on a top-down approach. The initial process of capital privatization involved commercialization, whereby the representative of the Treasury appointed two-thirds of the board of directors and workers appointed the remaining one-third. Following commercialization, the Ministry of Privatization became responsible for the enterprise's privatization. The second path of privatization intended for smaller enterprises, *liquidation* privatization, reflected a bottom-up approach. Thus, the enterprise took the initiative to privatize and received permission from the branch ministry responsible for the enterprise and from the Ministry of Privatization. The branch ministry implemented the liquidation. The state enterprise ceased to exist legally. In the outcome of liquidation, the state assets were sold piece by piece by the responsible ministry. Alternatively, a new company could be created by the Treasury and a private investor. Finally, the management and employees could create a private firm and lease the

assets and the liabilities from the Treasury. For more details see Dabrowski 1991: 317–25; Berg 1994.

46. See Jerzy Kleer 1991, "Albo szybko, albo dobrze: Prywatyzacja jest trudniejsza niz sadzimy" ["Either Fast or Well: Privatization Is More Difficult than We Assume"]. *Polityka* 8 (1764): 4.

47. In fact, the former bookkeeper drew substantial payments (equivalent to one-quarter of the *Naczelnik*'s monthly salary) for his bimonthly visits to the new joint-stock company to assess its performance.

48. To stimulate such demand, preferential land credits became available at a 10 percent interest rate.

49. Based on yet another personal contact within the legal system, the *Naczelnik* expected to complete the procedure within a few months of what formally was to take five years.

50. Twenty-eight thousand hectares out of over four million hectares of state farmland nationwide were within this form of asset transfer.

51. Polish Press Agency 1994, "Agency Privatizes Property of Former State Farms," *PAP News Wire*, January 17.

52. Zbigniew Grzegorzewski 1995, "Four Years of Privatisation," *Polish News Bulletin*, April 4.

References

Association of the State Agricultural Farms. 1991. *Wyniki Gospodarczo-Finansowe Za Rok 1990 Zwiazek Panstwowych Gospodarstw Rolnych w Poznaniu*. Unpublished internal statistical report.

Baczynski, Jerzy. 1991. "Gorzki popiwek" ["Bitter Anti-inflation Tax"]. *Polityka* 7 (1763): 1.

Berg, Andrew. 1994. "The Logistics of Privatization in Poland." In *The Transition in Eastern Europe*, edited by O. J. Blanchard, K. A. Froot, and J. D. Sachs, 165–88. Chicago: University of Chicago Press.

Brada, Josef C. 1993. "The Comparative Economics of Bankruptcy: Dealing with Loss-Making Firms in Capitalist, Socialist, and Transitional Economies." *Eastern European Economics* 31 (4): 82–96.

Buchowski, Michal. 2009. "Property Relations, Class, and Labour in Rural Poland." In *Postsocialist Europe: Anthropological Perspectives from Home*, vol. 10, edited by L. Kurti, P. Skalnik, EASA Series, 51–75. New York: Berghahn Books.

Burawoy, Michael. 1996. "Industrial Involution: The Russian Road to Capitalism." In *A La Recherche des Certitudes Perdues*, edited by Burgit Müller, 11–57. Berlin: Centre Marc Bloch.

Centrum Badan Opinii Spolecznych [Research Center of Public Opinion] (CBOS). 2000. *Opinions on Privatisation and the Presence of Foreign Capital in Poland*. Warsaw: CBOS.

Czaczkowska, Ewa. 1991. "Strajkuja PGR-y. Prywatyzacja to nie parcelacja." *Rzeczpospolita*. February 12, 1.

Dabrowski, M. 1991. "Privatization in Poland." *Communist Economies and Economic Transformation* 3: 317–325.

Dzun, W. 1993. "Spoleczno-Ekonomiczne Aspekty Rozwoju Rolnictwa w Warunkach Gospodarki Rynkowej." In *Wies I Rolnictwo na Rozdrozu*, edited by Izabella Bukraby-Rylska, Janusz Stacewicz, and Maria Wieruszewska, 38–56. Warsaw: PAN, IRWiR.

Estrin, S., A. Gelb, and I. Singh. 1993. "Restructuring, Viability and Privatisation: A Comparative Study of Enterprise Adjustment in Transition." Mimeo, London: London Business School.

Flis-Kuczynska, Halina. 1992. "Bat na dziedzica," *Gazeta Wyborcza*, November 15, 18.

———. 1991. "O Sabotazu przy pustej sali: w Sejmie o rolnictwie" ["About the Sabotage of Agriculture within the Empty Halls of the Parliament"], *Gazeta Wyborcza*, August 22, 6.

Frenkel, Izaslaw. 1997. *Ludnosc, Zatrudnienie i Bezrobocie na Wsi w latach 1988–1995*. Warsaw: PAN, IRWiR.

Główny Urząd Statystyczny (GUS). 1993. *Rocznik Statystyczny* [*Statistical Yearbook*] Warsaw: Główny Urząd Statystyczny.
Gorlach, Krzysztof. 1999. "Presenting 'New' Face: Polish Peasants' Protests in the Era of Post-Communism." Paper delivered at the Working Group 1: Social Movements in Rural Areas: Sources, Rationalities and Identities in the Process of Change. XVIII Congress of the European Society for Rural Sociology, August 24–28, Lund, Sweden.
Grzegorzewski, Zbigniew, 1995. "Four Years of Privatisation." *Polish News Bulletin*, April 4, 4–9.
Halamska, Maria. 1999. "Procesy marginalizacji na wsi popegeerowskiej." *Wieś i Rolnictwo* 2: 37–49.
———. 1998. *Dekolektywizacja Rolnictwa w Europie Srodkoweji i jej Spoleczne Konsekwencje*. Warsaw: PAN IRWiR.
Kleer, Jerzy. 1991. "Albo szybko, albo dobrze: Prywatyzacja jest trudniejsza niz sadzimy" ["Either Fast or Well: Privatization Is More Difficult than We Assume"]. *Polityka* 8 (1764): 4.
Kornai, Janos. 1990. *The Road to a Free Market Economy*. New York: Norton.
Ministry of Agriculture. 1991. *Informacja o Realizacji Uchwaly Sejmu RP z Dnia 9 Maja 1991r w Sprawie Programu Dzialan Doraznych i Systemowych Dla Panstwowych Gospodarstw Rolnych*. Warsaw.
Murrell, Peter. 1991. "Can Neoclassical Economics Underpin the Reform of Centrally Planned Economies?" *Journal of Economic Perspectives* 5 (4): 59–76.
Naszkowska, Krystyna. 1992. "Nie szli na Zachod Obszarnicy." *Gazeta Wyborcza*, 273: 13.
———. 1992. "PGRy w Chlopskie rece" *Gazeta Wyborcza*, 218: 5
Pasek, Witold. 1991a. "W Zoruchowie strajk." *Gazeta Wyborcza*, 510: 7.
———. 1991b. "Flagi w 1300 PGR-ach." *Gazeta Wyborcza*, 507: 3.
Poznanski, Kazimierz. 1996. *Poland's Protracted Transition: Institutional Change and Economic Growth, 1970–1994*. Cambridge: Cambridge University Press.
———. 1995. *The Evolutionary Transition to Capitalism*. Boulder, CO: Westview.
———. 1993. "Restructuring of Property Rights in Poland: A Study in Evolutionary Politics." *East European Politics and Societies* 7 (3): 395–421.
———. 1992. "Privatization of the Polish Economy: Problems of Transition." *Soviet Studies* 44 (4): 641–664.
Rosner, Andrzej. 1993. "Opinie o strukturze rolnictwa." In *Rolnicy '92: Rolnicy Wobec Zmian Systemowych*, edited by Andrzej Rosner, 66–79. Warsaw: PAN IRWiR.
Solska, Joanna. 1991. "W imieniu zalogi: Panstwowe Przedsiebiorstwo istnieje po to aby placic." *Polityka* 7 (1763): 1.
Staniszkis, Jadwiga. 1991. *The Dynamics of the Breakthrough in Eastern Europe*. Berkeley: University of California Press.
Swain, Nigel. 1996. "Getting Land in Central Europe." In *After Socialism: Land Reform and Social Change in Eastern Europe*, edited by Ray Abrahams, 193–215. Providence: Berghahn Books.
Szott, Edmund. 1992a. "Niecierpliwosc. Prywatyzowanie PGR" ["Impatience. Privatization of the PGR"]. *Rzeczypospolita* 172 (3210): 2.
———. 1992b. "Rada Ministrow dyskutuje o prywatyzacji." *Rzeczpospolita* 76 (3114): 1.
———. 1991. "Manifestacja zakonczona rozmowami" ["Protest Ended by Negotiations"]. *Rzeczpospolita* 59 (2794): 4.
Tarkowska, Elżbieta. 2009. "Oblicza Polskiej Biedy." *Laboratorium Wiezi* 2, Kwiecien.
———. 2000. *Zrozumieć biednego*. Warsaw: Wydawnictwo IFIS PAN.
Tomczak, F. 1994. *Legislative Framework for Agricultural Transition in Poland*. Liverpool: Centre for Central and Eastern European Studies, Rural Transition Series. Working Paper 16, Spring.
World Bank. 1995. *Farm Restructuring and Land Tenure in Reforming Socialist Economies: A Comparative Analysis of Eastern and Central Europe*. Washington, DC: World Bank Discussion Papers #268.
———. 1990. *An Agricultural Strategy for Poland. Report of the Polish European Community World Bank Task Force*. Washington, DC: World Bank.

Conclusion

Property change during the post-socialist transition is unproblematically assumed, yet still theoretically and historically unexplored (Kowalik 2009). Over twenty years after 1989, we are, as Falk (2011) pointed out, "in an Arendtian conundrum; we are between the past and the future." For Arendt, between past and future is "a productive place to be, given that such intervals present the possibility for 'moments of truth' . . . stripped of all masks of understanding and interpretations" (Falk 2011). In my empirical account, I seek this "moment of truth," examining often overlooked social agents of change, agrarian producers, and their impact on the scope and type of political, social, and economic change. With my new approach to property change—my introduction of the notion of conjoint property evolving into incomplete exclusive property—this book aims to conceptually reconcile this reality between the past and future.

Post-Socialist Property Change: Economic Outcomes Confront Policy Intentions

From the standpoint of the architects of the post-socialist program in Poland, the transition was to be about privatization of state property and about the consolidation of private owners' property rights, free from the state and its intervention. This was to be accomplished by radically and swiftly separating the economy from the withering state. The clarification of property rights was expected to create at least one fundamental outcome—production efficiency that in its aggregate results would translate into sustainable economic growth. From the perspective of evolutionist economists, as well, the transition was to be about the consolidation of property rights in order to realize a growth-oriented economy based on higher production performance from entrepreneurial agents. However, in both cases, this outcome was projected in the context of a temporal (although unspecified in duration) coexistence between the nascent private sector and the previously dominant state sector. The consolidation of private property rights and enhanced economic efficiency was forecasted under the conditions of the state's active institutional and financial protection of private owners against economic actions of the state sector. Although the evolutionist economists emphasized the importance of the state and the institutional infrastructure for the outcome of individual economic action, their analysis left unarticulated what trajectory the transition would take if these conditions were not met.

I agree that the transformation of property ownership was central to the post-socialist transition. Yet, it was not a unilinear transition from state to private property. In this book, I show the early transition that *was*—in its multiple trajectories of reconfigured forms of conjoint property that were prompted by the post-socialist privatization drive. I delineate interdependent trajectories of coexisting properties and their outcomes under the absence of the conditions that the evolutionist economists pronounced indispensable for the outcome of enhanced economic efficiency. Thus I show how the Polish post-socialist shock therapy rapidly subjected private, state, and cooperative agricultural property forms to conditions of unprofitable agricultural production, financial scarcity, and institutional discontinuity. Furthermore, these three forms of property were faced with the post-socialist regime's programmatic comprehensive withdrawal of state protectionism of any economic agents, and its exclusive reliance on market coordination of economic actions. I show that the reform program adversely affected all three properties in their capacities to adjust production activities to the new economic environment, leading to decreased economic output and production efficiency. Yet, it exerted differential constraints on each property form, and prompted changes in relations between these coexisting agricultural subsectors that contradicted the explicitly pronounced reform objectives.

The post-socialist program undermined peasants' capacities to exercise effectively their property rights over production control, residual income, and exchange of assets by imposing severe constraints on both the supply and the demand side of their production activities. Thus, beyond the sharp increases in all agricultural resource costs and the overall scarcity of financial resources, as stipulated by post-socialist price liberalization and fiscal policies, peasants also faced national-level and local-level credit allocation practices that effectively shut them off from production or investment credits and gave credit preferences to the cooperative and state sectors. On the other hand, beyond the effects of wage control policies that constricted aggregate food demand, peasants endured disproportional high uncertainty in disposing of their output as compared with state farms and cooperatives. If they found demand for their output, they were subjected to systemic and unsanctioned siphoning off of their profit by the economic institutions inherited from the socialist past (monopsonistic procurement centers) as well as the organizations created in the post-socialist period (limited liability joint ventures).

For cooperative enterprises, their capacity to exercise effectively their rights to self-governance and self-aid were undermined by restrictions that predominantly surfaced on the supply side of production activities. The most pronounced constraint on the exercise of their ownership rights was information discontinuity, resulting from the reform program's rapid dismantling of the institutional superstructure surrounding local cooperatives. Acute uncertainty about how to access potential markets severely limited the cooperatives' range of production alternatives, thus inflicting inertia and locking the cooperatives in the lines of production from the past. Furthermore, informational and institutional discontinuity undermined the cooperative ownership principle of self-management. It removed effective control by cooperative members over managerial decisions and enhanced opportunism in the cooperative managers' decision making. The policy-stipulated dramatic increase in the costs of production resources and the scarcity of financial capital posed as serious a threat to a renewal of cooperative production as it did to that of individual agricultural owners. However, in contrast to peasants, cooperative enterprises were able to circumvent these constraints by relying on long-established informal relations with other agricultural cooperatives and/or local lending institutions to engage in interenterprise borrowing or the taking of bank loans. Over time, they were able to push the costs of financial credits onto the state by applying for government-sponsored restructuring of their debts. On the demand side, the general constriction of demand for food did not translate into equally tight and unpredictable demand for cooperative production output as it did for that of private owners. Although cooperatives had narrowed abilities to venture into new production markets, they relied on preexisting contacts to secure demand for their established production lines.

The adaptive capacity of state farms to the new and changing environment was severely restricted in some aspects of the supply side, while they enjoyed favorable standing relative to other agricultural subsectors on the demand side. On the supply side, the attenuated exercise of control over allocation of resources derived in large measure from the reform policies' differential and inconsistent impact on macro- and local levels. Thus, microeconomic adjustment to post-socialist macrostabilization measures proved infeasible under labor policies carried over from state socialism, which subjected management decisions regarding the reduction of employment to the approval of workers' councils and local chapters of the workers' union. Equally, the introduction of anti-inflationary macrolevel measures preempted local efforts to rationalize housing and utilities spending for state farm employees. There were also privatization-induced constraints on state farms over future ownership rights, as well as retroactive settling of past ownership claims. The imposition of a dividend tax represented a judicial reparation claim laid by the post-socialist state against state farms for the socialist state's contributions to the initial assets at the state farms' creation.

On the demand side, however, state farms enjoyed a favorable standing relative to other agricultural ownership forms, significantly affecting not only the state farms' privatization results but also the outcome of private property rearrangements. Although the state farms were squeezed through increases in the prices of inputs, high credit costs, and persistent low product prices, within the monopolistic market, their large size and their utilization of established market networks or interenterprise transactions[1] gave them an advantage over individual peasants and cooperatives in securing procurement of their output, negotiating prices, and scheduling payments. The state farms as a collective actor also proved to be formidable in exerting political pressure on the post-socialist state to advance emergency funds for renewing the farms' production cycles, thus deterring the state from achieving its programmatic long-term objective of liquidating state farms.

I show that the attempted divestment by the state of its co-claims to state farm ownership and the transfer of production assets to private exclusive owners was inhibited. The Agricultural Agency, the institutional embodiment of the post-socialist state as an owner, had very partial and slow success in transferring assets to individual agricultural owners, despite the post-socialist state's pronounced programmatic commitment to unfettering and strengthening private ownership rights, including the right to preferential acquisition of state farm production assets. The Agricultural Agency was equally unsuccessful in vesting the state farm employees with exclusive ownership rights of state farm assets, leading to their de facto restatization, with the state retaining ownership of state farms and creating a hybrid property form through lease options or joint ventures with the farms' former managers.

Tracing empirically the early trajectories of the adjustment strategies to post-socialist reform, this book points to the rapid privatization program itself as contributing to the unintended outcome of restatization of state farm assets. Due to the complexity of the property rearrangement that entailed both settling the complicated past ownership co-claims to state farm assets and implementing their forward transfer, the process required an extended period of time for completion.[2] The privatization of state farms that was proclaimed imminent could only remain unrealized because, rather than being a neutral, radical privatization program, it heightened uncertainty and generated a property vacuum, thus preventing the articulation of meaningful adjustment strategies within the state farms and undermining the confidence of potential private buyers of the assets.

Gouldner (1954) points to the Janus-faced nature of organizations that are designed to solve one problem and instead give rise to others. His point equally pertains to the historically formed post-socialist reforms, which exhibited the dilemma of unintended consequences. The post-socialist privatization reforms were designed to remove the state as a subject from any ownership claims on productive assets and to eliminate any constraints upon the effective exercise of property rights by exclusive owners imposed by the state's institutional superstructure. In doing so, however, the reforms failed to safeguard against barriers that appeared as a result of insufficient state regulation and underdeveloped institutional infrastructure.[3] This programmatic emphasis on the minimal state bred constraints on building the post-socialist state's capabilities as an agent and as an institutional structure that would support the emerging exclusive owners. Thus, from the start, the post-socialist program created conditions that undermined capacities to exercise exclusive ownership rights and steered rationally acting economic agents toward production activities that amounted to a regressive transformation in agriculture—toward the economic involution.

From Economic to Social Connotation of Historically Specific Property

My analysis of these differentiated yet disappointing economic outcomes in all three distinct property trajectories of the post-socialist privatization program presents an empirical challenge to the neoliberal assertion that private property is an economic category generating universally stable and predictable outcomes of advanced economic efficiency and thus superior to other economic approaches.

In contrast to the prevailing notion of the post-socialist privatization program as guiding homogenous change from state to private property, I show that privatization policy engendered new and differential contexts for the distinct property forms, producing varied outcomes. Adjustment strategies by social actors within each ownership form generated unexpected property rearrangements. In examining them and their origins, consistent with the neoinstitutional perspective, I posit the institutional underpinnings of property, in that economic performance and outcomes are not simply a reflection of individual universal and stable propensities to advance one's economic interest. I further refocus attention on the critical importance of formal and informal social institutional infrastructure on economic performance. I show how institutional context delineated boundaries for actors' exercise of property rights in that it defined a limited scope of options available to them in making ownership decisions regarding allocation of production resources, deriving residual profits, and transferring assets.[4] In addition to emphasizing the formal institutional undergirding of the exercise of property rights, I show how, in search of the best adjustment strategy to the changed environment, the actors on the ground made context-bound rational and purposeful decisions that often led to the spontaneous creation of, and involvement in, various informal structures and horizontal networks. I not only show that institutions—formal and informal—played a key role in the exercise of property rights and economic performance, but I further ascertain what elements in that institutional context were at play at a given point. Specifically, I demonstrate that the intertwined trajectories of the three different forms of property showed how the ability to exercise one's property rights had a relational quality and was contingent on the other owners' differential capacity to impinge on one's ownership entitlement.

Empirical results in this book, in tension with the neoliberal atomistic connotation of property, support the assertion that property is not an individual entitlement but is a social institution involving many owners. Thus, I show how the collective responses of the agents on the ground plotted often conflicting and interlocking trajectories of multiproperty rearrangements. Although Kornai (1991) theoretically conceives the post-socialist property rearrangements as an interdependent process where some potential impediments to the exercise of private property rights could stem from the adjustment responses coming from the state ownership form, I examine the actual, complex interdependencies between the trajectories of the three property forms and identify concrete mechanisms through which adjustment responses detrimentally impacted economic outcomes.

Analysis of the reconfiguration of property arrangements during the transition from socialism to post-socialism reveals the socialist property to be a social institution of historically specific design and content. It was organizationally designed to carry out in tandem production and redistribution objectives. Yet, the significance of this particular feature had not been sufficiently acknowledged in the design of the post-socialist reforms, precipitating necessary subsequent reformulations of the reform policies. Thus, the post-socialist privatization reforms put the preeminent focus on liquidating the socialist state's imposed organizational superstructure as a way to separate the economy from the political sphere on the macrolevel, and to unfetter economic actions of the agents on the microlevel. This prism accorded scant attention to the actual relations between political and economic domains (Pfeffer and Salancik 2003 [1978]), and to the distributional consequences of ownership rights (Kantor 1998; Knight 1992). Such focus obscured the unique and complex organizational fusion of economic production and social care under socialism (Haney 2002) and prevented adequate recognition of how narrowly targeting economic change in one domain produced real and compounded consequences in both domains, subjecting in turn the newly implemented policy to social pressures for its reformulation.

Social welfare under socialism was characterized by pluralism (Walder 1986; Gu 2001), where social entitlements were differentiated by, and provided within, each property form's organization system, rather than dispensed through central government agencies. This property-based system embodied the broader social contract between the state and its citizens, ascribing to state, cooperative, and private property forms a differential social standing and corresponding levels of "deservedness" with respect to social entitlements. Dismantling the organizational systems within which private owners, cooperatives, and state farms carried out their respective production activities concurrently unraveled the system of social welfare consolidated within socialism, inadvertently breeding uncertainty over how and whether social needs would be met within the new social context and whether social entitlements allotted earlier to these distinct property forms would be protected. Thus the strategy to separate the economic and political spheres by dismantling the state as an institutional structure inadvertently impacted property owners in their status as citizens and, equally integrally, it affected the state as an agent. The individuals entered the contestation with the state not as economic agents, but as *social* agents collectively bargaining over the norms and values of distributional fairness and advancing social welfare and ultimately over the transformation of the old implicit social contract into a new one. Thus, regardless of how narrowly the privatization reform was characterized by its architects, it could not be conceived distinctly from the debate over social entitlements and broader social objectives. Thus, the strategic economic behavior of the actors on the ground was informed by social and ideological concerns, underscoring that norms and values undergird property. Referencing the Western context, J. Singer cited Joseph Weintraub in order to point out the ultimate normative basis of property: "Property rights serve human values. They are recognized to that end and are limited by it" (Singer 2000: 37).[5] The specific organizational structure of property rearrangements in the post-socialist context further cemented the connection between economic entitlements and ideological values and norms.

Internal Agency and Path Dependency of Post-Socialist Property Change

One of the central and fiercely debated issues in transition theory, albeit, as Szelényi (1996) points out,[6] not fully articulated and resolved, focused on whether the trajectory of changes was of a teleological character, reflecting the well-defined intentions of post-socialist reformers to construct market capitalism. With his category of recombinant property, Stark (1992) countered the dominant teleological thesis with the evolutionary one, where the impetus for the trajectory of change came from the bottom up. The empirical analysis presented here reverberates with this theoretical question. The *interactive* approach in this book takes issue with the teleological thesis and views the trajectory of change in property arrangements as charted by the aggregate of intended actions on the part of the planners and those affected by their reforms. It conceives of the post-socialist reform program as both the product of, and the context for, action. Reforms provided context for action of the actors on the ground, who, by pursuing strategic choices rooted in their local knowledge and experiences, in significant ways translated the meaning of reformers' intentions and, through their responses, changed them.[7] Equally, the interactive perspective in this book views the neoliberally oriented reform program in Poland as itself a product of actions unfolding within socialism, rather than being diffused from the West and rapidly adopted in the aftermath of socialism by the new, passive post-socialist regime, as the predominant view holds. Consistently with the accounts of Bockman and Eyal (2002) and Kowalik (2009), I argue in this book that the reform program was constructed in a long discourse between East and West, by actively engaged Eastern European intellectuals in search of a strategy to mount an effective challenge and an alternative to the socialist regime.

This interactive perspective emphasizes then the endogenous impetus for the post-socialist changes, where not only the responses to, but the intentions of, post-socialist reformers were historically conditioned. The post-socialist reforms were path-dependent in that the past delineated the policy options conceivable and feasible to the post-socialist government. Post-socialist reformers sought to avoid the political liability of being associated in the public perception with the former discredited regime and its reforms, specifically the unsuccessful economic and budget deficit reforms led by the socialist state, and the specific, negotiated exit from socialism. This path dependency required reformers to manifest a clear differentiation of the post-socialist reforms from the ones pursued by their predecessors.[8] This channeled their policy options to the narrow emphasis on playing economic catch-up with the West and on minimizing the state in the project of building market capitalism. Accordingly, the post-socialist reforms were not an expression of an emancipated refutation of the past, even though they were articulated as such, but were conditioned by, and bore an imprint of, the past.

Thus, as I contend, it was the dynamics of socialism that conditioned the onset of the post-socialist reforms, yet different "founding events" (Powers and Cox 1997: 618) in those dynamics became particularly formative moments for the distinct social actors' cumulative experiences and their specific interpretations of history, which in turn provided a contextualizing framework for them to construct divergent meanings of property and to interpret their current circumstances. Those founding events became "prior understandings" of the contested past and guided these actors' actions as stakeholders in the subsequent post-socialist property rearrangements. These "prior understandings" and "different maps of meaning" (Watts 1992) of property implied different and conflicting expectations of the post-socialist privatization process and its outcomes, producing not its smooth implementation, but the *crisis of interaction* at the initial stage of the reforms, concluded three years later when the first post-socialist regime was voted out of office.

For private agricultural producers, as owners and as citizens, the quiet revolution of Polish agricultural property relations in the early 1980s became such a formative event. It marked the relinquishing by the socialist state of co-claims to their land and productive resources, bringing to a close the long contestation over the constant threat of collectivization of private owner's lands. Winning the state's concession of full unalienable ownership rights constituted them as exclusive owners. The recognition by the socialist state of private owners as a legitimate and permanent element of socialist property structure elevated their status to "worthy" citizens in the socialist welfare system, entitling them to earlier-denied pension provisions, thereby fostering equality between them and state farm and cooperative members. For private property owners, these events of the 1980s constituted a radical shift in socialist property relations amounting to privatization, and imparting a context-bound meaning of private ownership.

From the prism of post-socialist reformers, also focused on property relations, a series of formative moments of property rearrangements punctuated the contested socialist past. Yet these founding events were not understood as unfolding power contestations over property rights. Instead, they took the form of a series of debates between economists and government planners on the socialist and capitalist economic calculation models and the principles of resource distribution under a socialist property structure compared to a competitive system of private property. The progression of these discursive activities and power struggles surrounded a sequence of distinct property reform designs under socialism, which repeatedly yielded unsatisfactory macroeconomic performance and political instability and, cumulatively, led to the conclusion that socialist-state coordination of economy and property arrangements was nonviable. The negotiated extrication of the socialist regime in 1989 served as the pivotal event that cemented the prior understanding of the economic and political necessity, in drafting the blueprints for the post-socialist transition, for a radical shift in property design from those pursued in the past.[9]

Early Transition Interaction Crisis: Historically Produced Divergent Notions of Property

The historically constructed and inconsistent meanings of property informed the conflict-ridden post-socialist property rearrangements. Thus, the reform program narrowly committed itself to the consolidation of exclusive property rights as a vehicle for promoting individual economic benefits, without specifically committing itself to any broader social agenda. This individualistic connotation of the outcomes of exclusive property clashed with the historically formed expectations of the collective value of exclusive private property that had emerged under state socialism. Peasants formed these expectations in the long process of consolidating the exclusive ownership rights that were achieved in late socialism. Through a passive resistance and an active collective political challenge to the state, agricultural private property owners dislodged all remaining state claims to their property, and thus caused the shift from conjoint to exclusive property, but further obliged the state to intervene in their economic transactions in order to secure favorable collective economic outcomes from their exclusive ownership through a system of guaranteed minimum prices. The demands for favorable outcomes for exclusive owners grew out of, and resonated well with, a broader social agenda of state socialism—the elevation of peasants' economic standing to match that of the other population segments. These individual and collective peasants' gains also integrally advanced the central redistributive promises of socialism—economic equality and economic security. This historically specific process engendered distinct ideological connotations for the owners that carried on into the post-socialist transition. A historical experience under state socialism, in which peasants' individual gains were integrally connected to the advancement of collective benefits, became their ethical imperative to reject a post-socialist program that aimed at narrow individual benefits.

The historically formed connotation of exclusive private property, and the way in which exclusive ownership was won under state socialism, engendered expectations not only of the individual and social outcomes of the further consolidation of such ownership in the post-socialism period, but also of the state's role in this process. It placed a burden on the state to abate the unavoidable hardships connected with the economic transition and to steer the spread of the benefits throughout society. Thus, contrary to the reformers' insistence on the separation of the political and economic domains, inherent in the notion of exclusive property constructed under state socialism was an expectation of the state's integral involvement in the economic transition. The state was expected to delineate clearly substantive goals to which the enhanced economic capacity was to be subsumed, and to provide institutional infrastructure that would facilitate enhancement of the economic system.

Thus, in the context of the early adverse results of the shock therapy, these historically constructed exclusive private owners posed a specific challenge to the reform architects, as well as marked the uniqueness of the East European transition to capitalism. As historically formed political actors, they rejected mediation by the parliamentary democracy's institutional channels of the multitude of emerging interests vis-à-vis the post-socialist economic program. Instead, they viewed the post-socialist government as the political heir to the opposition staged against the state socialist regime. Therefore, they saw the post-socialist government as obliged to uphold concessions already won under the socialist regime. They saw the basis of the post-socialist government's legitimacy not merely in enhancing production capacity of the economic system, but also in subsuming this instrumental goal to the broad social objectives spelled out in the terms of the Round Table—the negotiated extrication from state socialism. Hence, the exclusive agricultural owners obliged the post-socialist government to follow historical systemic progression—to shelter the gains already won from the late state socialist regime, and to advance those universal socioeconomic objectives that were set out, yet unfulfilled, under state socialism. Thus, whereas the post-socialist regime's formative moments led it to seek radical discontinuity from the system in place at the advent of post-socialism, the pivotal experiences of agricultural producers under socialism led them to insist on continuity in order to reflect the historical progression to a better future. As Verdery perceptively points out, the normative premise of socialism was not to eliminate private property altogether but to eliminate a bourgeois property that imposes human exploitation. Accordingly, from the vantage point of agricultural producers exiting socialism, to achieve a better society required, if not preserving the economic and social wins from socialism, at the minimum establishing property arrangements representative of advanced capitalism, with its progressively built-in social entitlements attenuating the negative social consequences of bourgeois property, as chronicled by T. H. Marshall. The neoliberal goal of unfettered private property was in the agricultural producers' perception tantamount to historical regression.[10]

Thus, early on, they engaged in nonparliamentary political actions and successfully placed the state under pressure not to compromise the substantive social objectives inherited from state socialism, and to compensate economic agents for the early transition costs. These demands required the state to maintain or even increase state expenditures, whereas one of the main goals of the post-socialist stabilization and liberalization measures was to reduce the staggering state budget deficit by radically decreasing the state's expenditures. At the same time, exclusive private agricultural owners contributed to the contracting revenue base for the state expenditures by virtue of their individual microeconomic responses that involuted agricultural production, which was compounded by the state and cooperative subsectors' reduced agricultural output, the growing indebtedness, and preservation of soft budget constraints.

The trend established in the early transition became of lasting trajectory. Writing several years after the inauguration of the post-socialist reforms, M. Kramer (1996) pointed to the incongruent transformation of the post-socialist system, where the changes to the social welfare system have deviated from changes in the production sector. In the former, the expenditures, despite the official proclamations about the necessity of their reduction, have expanded—mainly for pensions and unemployment benefits,[11] reaching 30 percent of the GDP for social services and exceeding one-half of GDP for the overall state budget. J. Kornai (1997), examining social welfare systems of post-socialist societies, came to the similar and startling conclusion that socialism, with all its characteristic features, continues in Eastern Europe within the social welfare system. It has been retained by effective social pressures on the government to issue ad hoc measures, preempting formulation of any coherent social program (Podemski 2011; Kochanowicz 1999).

The foregoing supports Przeworski's (1991) assertion that the construction of capitalism is a project that inherently involves both the political and the economic systems. As such, it is a problematic project for contemporary societies. For East European societies exiting state socialism, however, the problematic validity of this project does not stem from what Przeworski perceives as the challenge of the simultaneous creation of a democratic electoral system and a market economy. Rather, I suggest that, not only in regard to the early post-socialist transition trajectory in Polish agriculture, but extending into its subsequent period, the problematic validity of the transition to capitalism from state socialism stems from reconciling the building of substantive democracy along with a growth-oriented economy.[12]

The Exception that Matters and Also Confirms the Rule

As acknowledged at the outset of this study, Polish agriculture has been customarily approached with an emphasis on its uniqueness, and therefore its unsuitability for forming any generalizations about the dynamics of socialist societies. Yet, from my perspective this very uniqueness provided a valuable base for drawing broader conclusions regarding the property change and process of the post-socialist transformation. Joseph Stiglitz (1999), in his assessment of the first decade of the privatization reforms, remarks on the absence of initial private capital, or real ownership interests, which posed a great challenge for their architects, limiting their formal options from the standpoint of clarification and strengthening of private property rights to a few imperfect alternatives—voucher privatization, selling assets to foreign investors, or regulating "spontaneous" privatization. These options entailed a separation of ownership and control, resulting in a problematic alignment of owners' and managers' interests, referred to by a vast literature as an "agency problem" (Keynes 1963; Berle and Means 1932; March and Simon 1958; Sah and Stiglitz 1987). Those privatization alternatives were problematic because the separation of ownership and control weakened natural ownership incentives for the maximization of profits and undermined the clarification and strengthening of property rights. Given this presupposition, in order for post-socialist privatization reform to succeed, Kornai (1990) explicitly posits the necessity of owner-controlled private property to generate natural incentives for enhanced economic efficiency after a long absence of entrepreneurial experience under socialism. The neoliberal model assumed that Polish agriculture dominated by private ownership was the most fertile ground for a successful neoliberally oriented privatization reform—it had real existing social agents with owner-controlled property, invested and experienced in the protection and advancement of private property rights.

As the privatization program's objectives were expected to best reverberate with the preexisting private individual agricultural producers, the actual resistance staged to the reforms—passive and active, individual and collective—on the part of the private agricultural producers proved the reforms' strongest test and challenge. Although many critics explain away the unexpected outcomes as a debased form of the reforms' realization or the result of the attributes of the agricultural producers, I argue that the program's conceptualization bred such contradictory and unexpected results. One might then argue that the responses generated within Polish agriculture reflected broader outcomes of the reforms and thus can shed light on the dynamic of post-socialist change. More so, my empirical analysis, and studies done by many other scholars (including Heyns and Bialecki 1991; Gorlach 1999), point to economic and political actions of agricultural producers that were vital in bringing about the electoral victory of the post-socialist regime in 1989, in dramatically affecting its reforms, and in bringing about its defeat in 1993.

The behaviors of social actors in the agricultural sector within all three property forms, where the reforms were introduced ahead of any other in the economy, can be viewed as not only reflecting but also affecting the responses elsewhere, thus making them a crucial collective co-architect of the post-socialist change.

With that assertion, this approach deviates from the predominant current in transition debate, intent on identifying and examining "winners" of the transition (past or emerging elites, managers, intellectuals, and so forth), while failing to consider other social groups that are, even if less influential, active participants in interweaving the trajectory of change and the overall outcomes.[13] In her recent article, "Resistance and Dissent in Central and Eastern Europe: An Emerging Historiography," Barbara Falk asserts that "in many accounts the 'people power' of mass demonstration and protest is unproblematically assumed yet theoretically and historically underexplored." She points toward "the tendency . . . to fall into a 'heroes versus villains' narrative" and the "regrettable tendency toward hero-worship—especially among Western scholars . . . and an unfounded drive to identify 'leaders' in a situation that may not in fact have conformed to a hierarchical 'leader-follower' model" (2011: 342). She emphasizes that "against this fixation on the 'peaks' rather than the 'valleys' of dissent, . . . there is a pressing need to examine the many actors who were not household names, and who are too often cast as the passive recipients of history rather than as subjects possessing agency of singular or collective importance" (342). Falk further asserts that "focus on the internationally known dissident 'stars' has unfortunately resulted in near-complete 'ignorance' of the actual diversity of dissent—divergent economic backgrounds, societal representation, social embeddedness, relationships, and conflicts are sidelined or not addressed" (342). In my empirical analysis, I concentrate on these "valleys." I lift from analytical obscurity social groups that are commonly relegated to the category of powerless "losers." By drawing a distinction between benefiting from, and impacting, the dynamics of socialism and post-socialist transition, I find their individual and collective responses significant in charting the direction of change.

The Lasting Shadow of the Initial Phase of Privatization

I show in my empirical analysis that, although in its initial phase the privatization reform undermined private and cooperative ownership rights and created for the former employees of state farms conditions of a systemic poverty and unemployment (Tarkowska 2000, 2009; Buchowski 2003), those relative losers influenced the direction of post-socialist change by coining a new meaning of property, thus providing a contextualizing framework for their assessment of the unfolding circumstances and for shaping the pattern of discourse. Out of the early outcomes of the reforms, private property acquired a lasting and converse connotation to the one explicitly propagated by the post-socialist government. Instead of being viewed as a reliable instrument for enhancing efficiency and undoing the socialist state's intrusion and arbitrariness in the name of advancing individual freedom, private property became perceived as embedded in criminality—associated with a disregard of the letter of law by breeding opaque procedures and corruption, an allocation of production resources that was wasteful from the production standpoint and questionable on moral grounds, the production of social dislocations and inequality, and the promotion of selfish individualism (Tittenbrun 2007). The new connotation sharply contrasted with the still pervasive language of "public good" and national interest, thus diffusing easily into, and resonating within, a broader social domain.

The social ambivalence toward private property articulated in the early phase of the transition impacted the sustainability of further post-socialist reforms. It impaired the feasibility of privatization as the core economic policy's instrument. More importantly, by bringing into the forefront the social stratification consequences of private property, it enmeshed the narrow formulation of the economic neoliberal reform program in a broader debate over inequality in the emerging society. Consequently, it gave rise to growing pressures on the post-socialist regime to bear the social costs of privatization and to remedy the social consequences of private property by increased state redistribution. This set the post-socialist regime on a protracted course of internally contradictory reforms, where neoliberal policies designed to shrink the state and reduce budget deficits were amended on an ad hoc basis to provide for de facto expansions of welfare provisions, state building, and increased fiscal spending. A decade into the post-socialist change, Polish surveys showed that rejecting socialism was not in tandem with rebuffing collectivist and statist solutions. To the contrary, it coincided with social expectations for the expansion of welfare protection and the social safety net (Pascall and Kwak 2005). Redistributive concerns have become dominant over macroeconomic policies not only in Poland, but also in almost all post-socialist countries (Podemski 2011; Csaba 2006).

Formulated under immediate political pressures and without clearly articulated normative principles guiding them, these internally conflicting policies created an ambiguous basis of legitimacy for the post-socialist regime from the onset of the reforms, which in turn detrimentally impacted prospects for building a formal democracy. An initial engagement of agricultural agents in noninstitutional forms of contesting the privatization reform—strikes, boycotts, occupations of governmental buildings, and road blockades—gained, with time, a growing support from the general population as legitimate, if radical, strategies to affect political decision making. The agricultural agents' lack of confidence in the governmental reform programs was equally expressed in, and set a pattern of, low participation in election voting, little differentiation among distinct parties in their election programs, and a short lifespan for such parties.

Polish agriculture based predominantly on peasant production, which, due to its unsuccessful collectivization, is commonly thought of as an exceptional case when compared with other Eastern European socialist countries where agricultural state property was successfully established, confirms the general rule in yet another dimension. It uncovers and represents the general direction of changing socialist property arrangements and the more general dynamics of socialism. My study traces the downwards assignment of property rights under the growing pressure of a domestic food production deficit relative to societal needs, threatening the political stability of the Polish socialist regime. For other socialist regimes, as well, the systemic limitations of food production stemming from inefficient state farms posed the same, recurrent, vital threat to the system's reproduction. In Poland, the state's ownership rights to expropriate income and resources from the direct producers were progressively limited in exchange for the promise of increased food production in response to state-created incentives. The system evolved from the state's "repressive tolerance" of peasants (Gorlach 2006) and the policy of "economic growth without development" (Kuczynski 1981), in which a contained growth in productivity was sought in the narrow segment of peasant agriculture without stimulating development of private agriculture as a whole, to the establishment of peasants as exclusive subjects of private property. In other socialist regimes, the same pressure of insufficient domestic food production led to the pursuit of a parallel strategy of "economic growth through contained diffusion," that is, within state farms and industrial state enterprises, creating conditions for intensified food production by granting partial, yet growing ownership rights to income and resources (such as family land plots) for family-based food production. Thus, by tracing across the socialist regimes the different forms of attenuating socialist state ownership rights and their downward assignments in specific bundles in exchange for intensified food production (Swain 2000; Gorlach 2006; Lampland 1995; Szelényi 1988), we see the dynamics of socialism as a system and the vital importance of agriculture for the preservation of its rule, which are often overlooked in the scholarly depictions. While the alternative modernization project emphasized industrialization through heavy industry, an analysis of its dynamics points to the advancement of *agrarianism* as the essential component of this industrialization project. And at the heart of this advancement was the state's creation of ownership incentives for a growing share of the population—both in the state farms and in other nonagricultural sectors—to be actively involved and increasingly self-sufficient in food production.

Historical Production of Property Relations and Systemic Change

My account of the evolution of property relations under socialism and postsocialism deviates in its implications from the general rendition of the nature of the 1989 Eastern European revolutions. They are traditionally viewed as sudden and abrupt political revolutions, starting in Poland and spreading throughout Eastern Europe, that created an opening for the subsequent radical economic changes. I suggest a different periodization and succession in the systemic change, echoing Tocqueville's (1955) words depicting the French Revolution of 1979: "Though it took the world by surprise, it was the inevitable outcome of a long period of gestation, an abrupt . . . conclusion of a process . . . in which . . . generations had played an intermittent part." I posit the systemic change not as an event but as a long process with an asynchronic collapse of socialism once a gradual transformation of Poland's economic system reached the pivotal point of a quiet revolution that established exclusive private ownership for Polish peasants. Although such property rearrangement was irreconcilable with the fundamental principle of legitimacy of the socialist political regime, it did not precipitate the system's immediate political collapse but instead led to the delayed end of the system with an extrication of its political regime a decade later.

Rather than representing the post-socialist changes as radically opposite in their course to the preceding period, I integrally situate these initial four years of post-socialist changes within the far longer, gradual changes of state socialism. The post-socialist transition was firmly and deeply anchored within state socialism and its trajectory of gradually transformed ownership in the direction of exclusive property. The asynchronic extrication from socialism generated an incomplete exclusive property, in which antistatist connotations in the post-socialist reform design clashed with specific expectations on the ground of state paternalism of centrally sponsored opportunities for all. As such, the initial years of the post-socialist trajectory represented only a specific, yet distinctive phase in the socialist transition. Although rooted in the past, the brief phase and its distinctive dynamics dictated the path for the transition's future, out of which emerged a new and negative connotation of private property, generating lasting effects for the subsequent post-socialist development.

This initial phase clearly demonstrated that, contrary to the assumptions of the reform architects, property is not a self-validating category that can be transplanted from the West and that the state is not the source of property rights. Instead, property embodies a broad and continually contested concept. The affirmation of specific property arrangements is a complex and ambiguous process. To achieve the respect of citizens and thus a stable property regime, they must be rooted in a preexisting consensus on the guiding hierarchy of societal values. Such consensus, as I show, had not emerged by Poland's exit from socialism, and its absence produced shaky grounds for the rule of the post-socialist regime and was manifested in the interaction crisis that followed the inauguration of the post-socialist privatization program. As Stiglitz (1999) points out at the ten-year observance of the transition, the transition dynamics were far more important for its trajectory than the pace or sequencing of the reforms, which occupied prime attention of the reform architects and many scholars of the transition.

My thesis that the path of the transition was dependent on the contradictory dynamics in the early phase of post-socialism between the historical transformation of property under socialism and the neoliberal assumptions underlying the reforms relates to the prominent current in the present discourse on the unexpected outcomes of the transition. Rather than blaming socialism and its inherent flaws or the debased form of realization of post-socialist reforms, the new critique blames first-wave reformers. David Ost (2005), Tadeusz Kowalik (2009), and other accounts suggest that the working class was betrayed by opposition leaders who later introduced post-socialist reforms that compromised the early 1980s goals of Solidarity or hijacked the political agenda by a small elite. These prescriptive accounts delineate what should be done to recapture the missed "window of opportunity" in order to advance strong democracy in post-socialism, while ascribing to the early reform architects unconstrained options for actions. Although I risk the misguided accusation of being guilty of socialist sympathies, my descriptive and dispassionate analysis presents the transition as a series of socially and historically bound actions, with limited policy options available to the opposition leaders, turned reform architects at the naissance of post-socialism.

Analytical Considerations

The post-socialist transition often viewed through the prism of an artificial state property-private property dualism presumes capitalism based on exclusive property as its destination and end point. In my new approach to property, however, I resist analytical categories that presume the course and outcome of post-socialist change as unproblematic. Following the institutional theorists I show property to be far more than an economic category. It is a layered social construct containing a complex combination of regulatory, normative, and cultural-cognitive elements that together shape the allocation of production assets and economic action. Scholars of the Eastern European transition, starting with Stark's analysis of recombinant property emerging in post-socialism, emphasize the impact of property's regulative, institutional features on production behavior and on the actual trajectory of the transition. In my notion of property change from conjoint ownership to incomplete exclusive property I echo the neoinstitutionalists in that I identify, in addition to regulatory elements, normative and cultural components of property as salient factors shaping economic behavior and the course of transition.[14] These deeper layers of property, far more difficult to manipulate externally, prevent the Arendtian past from staying in the past. Instead the past carries forward, into the interval between the past and future, mediating interpretations and expectations of the future. These normative cultural factors were the forces behind the demand that the post-socialist state continue social welfare provisions, as well as the ongoing association of private property with the promotion of selfish ends and unjust social outcomes. It is mostly these factors that render exclusive property incomplete, creating a lasting ambiguous basis for both the post-socialist state and for private property and thereby eroding the fragile foundation for a sustainable future of capitalism in Eastern Europe.

Instead of the dichotomous concept of property that derives from comparisons between social systems—socialism and capitalism—I construct a positive content of socialist property and pursue an endogenous comparison of a system across time—state socialism transforming into post-socialism. In doing so, my analysis captures the dynamics of the advanced socialist societies and their lasting impact on the future more accurately than the "modernization" approach, which centers on gradual market diffusion in redistributive economies. Its debates on market penetrations impose a false duality between the spheres of economy and polity and the coordinating mechanisms within the economic system, clouding the intricate and evolving interconnections between them. My category of conjoint property, as an evolving system of rights and obligations reflecting an implicit social contract between the two co-claiming property subjects, instead incorporates the theory of the socialist state in the notion of ownership and points to the fusion of political and economic domains. Furthermore, in contrast to the emphasis of the modernization approach on the replacement of socialist ideology by pragmatic, non-ideological orientations indispensible in all advanced industrial societies and market economies, my property relations analysis incorporates what the modernization perspective misses—the underlying ideological, political, and normative ramifications in which these practical orientations and actions were embedded, and by which they were constrained and carried over to the post-socialist period.

Echoing the assertion of influential institutional and neoinstitutional scholars (Giddens 1979; DiMaggio 1991; Oliver 1991; Granovetter 1992; Friedland and Robertson 1990; Swedberg 1993) that the organization of a macroeconomy reflects the social organization of participants, this property approach further provides a mezzolevel bridge between micro- and macro-level analyses in that it speaks not of generalized normative systems engulfing and directing social actors on the ground; instead, it shows that the macrolevel trajectory of post-socialist changes was generated by socially and historically bounded coclaimants engaged in ongoing bargaining and contestation over property rights. Finally, my analysis of the evolution from conjoint to incomplete exclusive property draws attention to *time* and *timing* as salient variables in the formation of property arrangements and accentuates the distinction between the naissance and reproduction of property that the neoliberal model conflates. It shows property not as an act, but instead depicts the emergence of exclusive property owners as a historically specific process. In the process of applying my analytical prism to property relations in post-socialism, we can also gain insight into social action in Western societies by examining the limits of its universality and the feasibility of replicating Western institutions in other contexts, as was attempted in Eastern Europe.

Contrary to the expectation of homogeneity of outcomes across the former Socialist bloc, my analysis reemphasizes the historical complexity and specificity of outcomes that prevents easy generalizations. It shows a diversity of outcomes between the property forms but also within them, and thus implies a multiplicity of patterns far beyond national levels—at sector and enterprise levels. I further point to future areas of study in order to advance understanding of these processes. Unlike neoliberally oriented scholars who forecasted the shrinking of the state in the face of the introduction of a market-regulated economy, this study, following Evans et al. (1985), and others, brings the state back in but points to a paradoxical position of the post-socialist state from its inception—its critical and lasting importance for post-socialist development in contrast to its diminishing capacity due to its weak and ambiguous basis of legitimacy.[15] Further, I underscore the importance of reexamining the validity of the conceptual arsenal with which we approach post-socialist reality and the need to acknowledge dispassionately the lasting impact of both socialism and the early stage of post-socialism on present development. By reemphasizing the endogenous impetus of post-socialist change, we should not perceive the present dynamics as simply shifting to reflect the play of external forces of global capitalism associated with the integration to the European Union of the post-socialist Eastern European societies, but as a result of what Watts (1992) terms as a contradiction between powerless places and placeless power—dynamics stemming from the interplay between the local and the global.

Notes

1. The importance of the utilization of networks on economic outcomes has been emphasized by neoinstitutionalists (Granovetter 1974; DiMaggio and Louch 1998; Uzzi 1996).
2. See Poznanski 1996.
3. Grzegorz Kolodko (2001), an economist and two-time Polish finance minister, and others (Kolodko and Nuti 1997; Stiglitz 1998) emphasize that the formulation of successful policy to liberalize owners and to stimulate sustainable economic growth does not hinge on the question of "too fast versus too slow" (2001: 289) but instead on the question of institution building.
4. As Murrell (1992: 38) puts it, "The search for alternatives should be characterized, not as wide-ranging choice over a universe of alternatives, but rather as a history-bound process of discovery within a neighborhood of existing operations."
5. Arrow (1972), Hirschman (1992), Putnam (1993), Fukuyama (1995), and many others point out that narrow *economic* incentives are insufficient for a successful market economy: norms, social institutions, social capital, and trust are of critical importance. Stiglitz (1999) states that "reformers" simply destroy the old norms and constraints in order to "clean the slate" without allowing for the time-consuming processes of reconstructing new norms, as well as the new legislated institutions, to take hold. Then the reforms will be discredited and the "reformers" will blame the victims for not correctly implementing their ill-considered designs.
6. Szelényi and Kostello (1996) in "The Market Transition Debate; Toward a Synthesis?"

7. Michael Burawoy, commenting on Gouldner's (1954) *Patterns of Industrial Bureaucracy*, writes: "Can we conceive of individuals simultaneously producing and being produced? Can social structure be grasped as both constraining and enabling social action? This would involve a conception of human agency that . . . go(es) beyond individuals both as carriers of social relations, transmission belts of external, inexorable forces, and as centers of consciousness, violating or conforming to expectations, executors of norms that are somehow given. It would, above all, treat social structure as a complex of practices." (1982: 847)

8. Stiglitz (1999: 22–23) addresses the path dependency of post-socialist policy when he states: "One deeper origin of what became known as the 'shock therapy' approach to the transition was moral fervor and triumphalism left over from the Cold War. Some economic cold-warriors seem to have seen themselves on a mission to level the 'evil' institutions of communism and to socially engineer in their place . . . the new, clean, and pure 'textbook institutions' of a private property market economy. From this cold-war perspective, those who showed any sympathy to transitional forms that had evolved out of the communist past and still bore traces of that evolution must themselves be guilty of 'communist sympathies.' Only a blitzkrieg approach during the 'window of opportunity' provided by the 'fog of transition' would get the changes made before the population had a chance to organize to protect its previous vested interests."

9. Many accounts of the 1989 Round Table negotiations report the shift in the outlook of Solidarity intellectuals at the point when they were to become the members of the first post-socialist government (Ost 1993; Kowalik 2009; Wozniak 2009; Balcerowicz 1990). In the early 1980s, when the intellectuals associated with Solidarity comprised the opposition, their position was encapsulated in the motto "no economic reform [of socialism) without political reform," which called for radical democratization of the political sphere and, with it, the assignment of rights to economic decision making downward and away from the economic center; the negotiated exit from socialism in 1989 led them to a reversed stand of "no political reform without economic reform" and a strategy of radical privatization and marketization that drew a thick political line separating them from the failed reform efforts of their socialist predecessors.

10. The salience of time and timing, evident in my analysis of agricultural producers who, in the name of historical progress, were pressing the reformers for the preservation in post-socialist times of socioeconomic gains from socialism, also is shown in Michal Buchowski's ethnographic work on an agricultural community located in the same Wielkopolska region as the community I studied. Buchowski (2003) documents widespread fears among former state farm employees of regressing to pre-socialist agrarian relations as the outcome of post-socialist privatization. He cites one unemployed state farm worker, who abhorred seeking work among local private farm owners and exclaimed: "It is preposterous! What does it mean that he has to work there? Are pre-war times coming back?" (2003: 11). Buchowski captures the dual sense of historical regression in the perception of unemployed former state farm workers, who viewed peasants as representatives of a bygone era of agrarian economy and, simultaneously, as capitalist employers engaged in labor exploitation.

A large, longitudinal, and cross-national Euroequal study, carried out in Poland by a research team led by K. Podemski (2011) almost twenty years into constructing a post-socialist society, among many other studies, attests to the widespread and deeply entrenched negative connotation of capitalism associated with labor exploitation and therefore as a social system (more or less consciously viewed) on a lower stage of historical progression than the socialism they exited. When asked to identify with one of the presented class categories that included high class, capitalist class, *or* bourgeois class (an interesting classification in itself), none of the respondents self-assigned to the bourgeois category, only 0.6 percent of the respondents perceived themselves as belonging to the high class, and 0.1 percent viewed themselves as capitalists, while the majority saw themselves within the middle class. Significantly, there was a strong preference voiced for the further development of society toward a greater economic and social equality.

11. Analyzing the system of pension benefits, Tadeusz Szumlicz (2000: 36) asserts: "The cost of this system was very high. In the 1990s spending on old age and disability pensions amounted to 16% of the GNP (in countries with a comparable level of development, spending on social security does not exceed 8%, while in Western Europe spending amounts to 11% on

average). Old age and disability pensions accounted for 50% of all public spending, while other countries spend an average of 33% or 40% at the most." Further Szumlicz points out that "the actual retirement age is decreasing, which is unheard of in other countries. Currently, despite the official retirement age being set at 60 for women and 65 for men, women actually retire at the age of 55 while men retire at 59 years of age" (36).

12. David Ost (1993) draws similar conclusions when attempting to account for the political behavior of the working class during early post-socialism. For him, the weak development of parliamentary democracy, and the impending "politics of uncertainty and electoral chaos," stem from the difficulty of shifting from the socialist legacy of the working class's commitment to communitarian values and substantive democracy into an articulation of its particularistic economic interests in the post-socialist society, rather than from the challenges of the concurrent construction of a market-based economy.

13. A growing number of scholars draw attention to the still prevalent homogeneity paradigm categorizing Eastern European societies under socialism and in transition, in which people are viewed as either part of the masses or the elites or as winners or losers.
Among others, Linda Fuller's (2000) critique of the homogeneity paradigm centers on the scholars' tendency to present these societies as an undifferentiated mass, with everyone belonging to it, or, alternatively, as comprised of the small groups confronting the regime. Sometimes, as Fuller asserts, "authors simply redefine inclusive terms like "people" to be synonymous with the much narrower social category of intellectuals" and, further, she points out that a "number of troubling, even contradictory practices accompany the paradigm-induced ease with which intellectuals assume the right to speak for every one else in analyses of East and Central Europe" (589).

14. See Elizabeth Dunn (2004) for an excellent case study of an acquisition of a Polish factory by an American corporation. She highlights the importance of cultural, normative factors in the process of transforming the factory's workers into "privatized persons" and in the contestation over the legitimacy of different privatization schemes in the wake of the factory's privatization.

15. See the very insightful analysis by Rafal Drozdowski (2011) of the post-socialist state's paradoxical position, reflected in its recent shifting into the role of need "interpreter" as opposed to its former role of need "satisfier" in order to deal with the growing state deficit and high societal welfare demands. For an excellent analysis of distinct welfare state regimes under socialism and early post-socialism in Hungary and the evolution of the state from need provider to need interpreter, see Haney (2002).

References

Arrow, Kenneth. 1972. "Gifts and Exchanges." *Philosophy and Public Affairs* 1 (4): 343–362.

Balcerowicz, Leszek. 1992. *800 dni. Szok kontrolowany*. Warsaw: Polska Oficyna Wydawnicza "BGW."

———. 1990. "The Price of Polish Economic Reform." In *Without Force or Lies: Voices from the Revolution of Central Europe in 1989–1990*, edited by W. Brinton and A. Rinzler. San Francisco: Mercury House Books. U.K. Ltd.

Berle, A., and G. Means. 1932. *The Modern Corporation and Private Property*. New York: MacMillan.

Bockman, Johanna, and Gil Eyal. 2002. "Eastern Europe as a Laboratory for Economic Knowledge: The Transnational Roots of Neoliberalism." *American Journal of Sociology* 108 (2): 310–352.

Buchowski, Michal. 2003. "Redefining Social Relations through Work in a Rural Community in Poland." *Max Planck Institute for Social Anthropology Working Papers*. Working Paper no. 58.

Burawoy, Michael. 1982. "The Written and the Repressed in Gouldner's Industrial Sociology." *Theory and Society* 11: 831–851.

Csaba, László. 2006. *Social Change in Central and Eastern Europe: General Trends and National Patterns*. Warsaw: Tiger. Working Paper no 98.

DiMaggio, Paul. 1991. "Social Structure, Institutions, and Cultural Goods: The Case of the U.S." In *Social Theory for a Changing Society*, edited by Pierre Bourdieu and James S. Coleman, 133–155. Boulder, CO: Westview.

DiMaggio, Paul, and Hugh Louch. 1998. "Socially Embedded Consumer Transactions: For What Kinds of Purchases Do People Most Often Use Networks?" *American Sociological Review* 63 (5): 619–637.

Drozdowski, Rafal. 2011. "W jaki sposob kryzys finansow publicznych moze sie okazac oplacalny dla wladzy panstwowej—czyli o tym, ze z punktu widzenia wladzy nigdy nie ma tego zlego co by na dobre nie wyszlo." *Ruch Prawniczy, Ekonomiczny i Socjologiczny* 3: 125–136.

Dunn, Elizabeth C. 2004. *Privatizing Poland: Baby Food, Big Business, and the Remaking of Labor*. Ithaca, NY: Cornell University Press.

Evans, Peter, Dietrich Rueschemeyer, and Theda Skocpol, eds. 1985. *Bringing the State Back In*. Cambridge, UK: Cambridge University Press.

Falk, Barbara J. 2011. "Resistance and Dissent in Central and Eastern Europe. An Emerging Historiography." *East European Politics and Societies* 25 (2): 318–360.

Friedland, R., and A. J. Robertson, eds. 1990. *Beyond the Market-Place: Rethinking Economy and Society*. New York: Aldine de Gruyter.

Fukuyama, Francis. 1995. *Trust: Social Virtues and the Creation of Prosperity*. New York: Free Press.

Fuller, Linda. 2000. "Socialism and the Transition in East and Central Europe: The Homogeneity Paradigm, Class, and Economic Inefficiency." *American Review of Sociology* 26 (1): 585–609.

Giddens, Anthony. 1979. *Central Problems in Social Theory: Action, Structure, and Contradiction in Social Analysis*. Berkeley: University of California Press.

Gorlach, Krzysztof. 2006. "Between Hopes and Fears: Rural Eastern Europe in Its Way to Europe." *Eastern European Countryside* (12): 5–30.

———. 1999. "Presenting 'New Face': Polish Peasants' Protests in the Era of Post-Communism." Paper delivered at the Working Group 1: Social Movements in Rural Areas: Sources, Rationalities and Identities in the Process of Change. XVIII Congress of the European Society for Rural Sociology, August 24–28, Lund, Sweden.

Gouldner, Alvin W. 1954. *Wildcat Strike: A Study in Worker-Management Relationships*. Antioch Press.

———. 1954. *Patterns of Industrial Bureaucracy*. New York: Free Press.

Granovetter, Mark. 1974. *Getting a Job. A Study of Contacts and Careers*. Cambridge, MA: Harvard University Press.

Gu, Edward X. 2001. "Dismantling the Chinese Mini-Welfare State? Marketization and the Politics of Institutional Transformation, 1979–1999." *Communist and Post-Communist Studies* 34: 91–111.

Haney, Lynne. 2002. *Inventing the Needy: Gender and the Politics of Welfare in Hungary*. Berkeley: University of California Press.

Heyns, Barbara, and Ireneusz Bialecki. 1991. "Solidarność: Reluctant Vanguard or Makeshift Coalition?" *American Political Science Review* 85 (2): 351–370.

Hirschman, Elizabeth C. 1992. "The Consciousness of Addiction: Toward a General Theory of Compulsive Consumption." *Journal of Consumer Research* 19 (September): 155–179.

Kantor, S. E. 1998. *Politics and Property Rights: The Closing of the Open Range in the Postbellum South*. Chicago: University of Chicago Press.

Keynes, J. M. 1963. *Essays in Persuasion*. New York: Norton.

Knight, J. 1992. *Institutions and Social Conflict*. Cambridge: Cambridge University Press.

Kochanowicz, Jacek. 1999. *Raporty CASE*. Warszawa. Centrum Analiz Spoleczno-Ekonomicznych.

Kolodko, Grzegorz W. 2001. "Globalization and Catching-Up: From Recession to Growth in Transition Economies." *Communist and Post-Communist Studies* 34: 279–322.

Kolodko, Grzegorz W., and D. M. Nuti. 1997. "The Polish Alternative: Old Myths, Hard Facts, and New Strategies in the Successful Transformation of the Polish Economy." *Research for Action* 33.

Kornai, Janos. 1997. "Reform of the Welfare Sector in the Post-Socialist Countries: A Normative Approach." In *Transforming Post-Communist Political Economies*, edited by J. M. Nelson, C. Tilly, and L. Walker, 272–298. Washington, DC: National Academies Press.

———. 1991. "Privatization: The Great Problem of Transition in Eastern Europe." *Bulletin of the American Academy of Arts and Sciences* 44 (8): 32–40.

———. 1990. *The Road to a Free Market Economy*. New York: Norton.

Kowalik, Tadeusz. 2009. *www.PolskaTransformacja.pl*. Warsaw: Muza SA.

Kramer, M. 1996. "Social Protection Policies and Safety Nets in East-Central Europe: Dilemmas of the Post-Communist Transformation." In *Sustaining the Transition: The Social Safety Nets in Post-communist Europe*, edited by E.B. Kapstein and M. Madelbaum. New York: Council on Foreign Relations.

Kuczynski, Waldemar. 1981. *Po wielkim skoku*. [*After a Great Leap*]. Warsaw: PWE

Lampland, Martha. 1995. *The Object of Labor: Commodification in Socialist Hungary*. Chicago: University of Chicago Press.

March, J. G., and H. A. Simon. 1958. *Organizations*. New York: Wiley.

Marshall, T. H. 1998. "Citizenship and Social Class." In *The Citizenship Debates*, edited by Gershon Shafir, 93–111. Minneapolis: University of Minnesota Press.

Murrell, Peter. 1992. "Evolution in Economics and the Economic Reform of the Centrally Planned Economies." In *The Emergence of Market Economies in Eastern Europe*, edited by C. Clague and G. C. Rausser. Oxford: Basil Blackwell.

Oliver, C. 1991. "Strategic Responses to Institutional Processes." *Academic Management Review* (16): 145–179.

Ost, David. 2005. *The Defeat of Solidarity: Anger and Politics in Postcommunist Europe*. Ithaca, NY: Cornell University Press.

———. 1993. "The Politics of Interest in Post-Communist Eastern Europe." *Theory and Society* 22 (4): 453–485.

Pascall, G., and A. Kwak. 2005. *Gender Regimes in Transition in Central and Eastern Europe*. Bristol: Polity Press.

Pfeffer, J., and G. R. Salancik. 2003 [1978]. *The External Control of Organizations*. New York, Stanford, CA: Harper & Row and Stanford University Press.

Podemski, Krzysztof, ed. 2011. *Spoleczenstwa Europy Rrodkowo-Wschodniej: Projekt Eurequal*. Poznan: Wydawnictwo Naukowe UAM.

Powers, Denise, and James H. Cox. 1997. "Echoes from the Past: The Relationship between Satisfaction with Economic Reforms and Voting Behavior in Poland." *American Political Science Review* 91: 617–33.

Poznanski, Kazimierz. 1996. *Poland's Protracted Transition: Institutional Change and Economic Growth, 1970–1994*. Cambridge: Cambridge University Press.

———. 1995. *The Evolutionary Transition to Capitalism*. Boulder, CO: Westview Press.

Przeworski, Adam. 1991. *Democracy and the Market: Political and Economic Reforms in Eastern Europe and Latin America*. Cambridge, UK: Cambridge University Press.

Putnam, Robert. 1993. *Making Democracy Work: Civic Tradition in Modern Italy*. Princeton, NJ: Princeton University Press.

Sah, Raaj Kumar, and Joseph Stiglitz. 1987. "The Architecture of Economic Systems: Hierarchies and Polyarchies." *American Economic Review* 76 (4): 716–727.

Singer, Joseph William. 2000. *Entitlement: The Paradoxes of Property*. New Haven, CT: Yale University Press.

Stark, David. 1992. "Path Dependence and Privatization Strategies in East Central Europe." *East European Societies and Politics* 6 (1): 17–54.

Stiglitz, Joseph. 1999. "Toward a General Theory of Wage and Price Rigidities and Economic Fluctuations." Papers and Proceedings of the One Hundred Eleventh Annual Meeting of the American Economic Association. *The American Economic Review* 89 (2): 75–80.

_______. 1998. "Whither Reform: Ten Years of the Transition." World Bank Annual Bank Conference of Development Economics.

Swain, Nigel. 2000. "Rurality in Modern Societies with a Particular Focus on the Countries of Central and Eastern Europe." In *Rural Development in Central and Eastern Europe*, edited by Davis Brown and Anna Bandlerowa, 21–34. Nitra: Slovak Agricultural University.

Swedberg, Richard, ed. 1993. *Explorations in Economic Sociology*. New York: Russell Sage Foundation.

Szelényi, Ivan. 1988. *Socialist Entrepreneurs: Embourgeoisement in Rural Hungary*. Madison: University of Wisconsin Press.

Szelényi, Ivan, and Eric Kostello. 1996. "The Market Transition Debate: Toward a Synthesis?" *American Journal of Sociology* 101 (4) (01): 1082–1096.

Szumlicz, Tadeusz. 2000. "Social Security Reform: Old Age and Disability Pensions." In *The Second Wave of Polish Reforms*, edited by Lena Kolarska-Bobinska, 35–45. Warsaw: Institute of Public Affairs.

Tarkowska, Elzbieta. 2009. "Oblicza polskiej biedy." *Laboratorium Wiezi*, April 2: 1–8.

———. 2000. *Zrozumieć biednego*. Warsaw: Wydawnictwo IFIS PAN.

Tittenbrun, Jacek. 2007. *Z deszczu pod rynnę. Meandry Polskiej Prywatyzacji*. Poznan: Zysk i S-ka Wydawnictwo.

Tocqueville, Alexis de. 1955. *The Old Regime and the French Revolution*. Garden City, NY: Doubleday.

Uzzi, Brian. 1996. "The Sources and Consequences of Embeddedness for the Economic Performance of Organizations: The Network Effect." *American Sociological Review* 61 (4): 674–698.

Walder, Andrew. 1986. *Communist Neo-Traditionalism: Work and Authority in Chinese Industry*. Berkeley: University of California Press.

Watts, Michael John. 1992. "Capitalisms, Crises, and Cultures: Notes toward a Totality of Fragments." In *Reworking Modernity: Capitalism and Symbolic Discontent*, edited by Allan Pred and Michael John Watts, 1–21. New Brunswick, NJ: Rutgers University Press.

Williamson, Oliver. 1991. "Economic Institutions: Spontaneous and Intentional Governance." *Journal of Law, Economics and Organization* 7: 159–187.

Wozniak, Zbigniew. 2009. "Poklosie Okraglego Stolu. Przeszlosc dla Przyszlosci." *Ruch Prawniczy, Ekonomiczny i Socjologiczny* 2: 349–379.

Index

About the Author

Suava (Slawomira) Zbierski-Salameh heads the Haverford Institute in Haverford, Pennsylvania, where she works for the advancement of exchanges between U.S. and East European academic communities. Previously, for several years she served at Haverford College on the steering committee for the Center for Peace and Global Citizenship, and on the advisory board for the study abroad program. Born in Poland, she received a PhD in sociology from the University of California, Berkeley. She has taught at UC–Berkeley and Haverford College. Her articles have appeared in numerous journals and books, including *Uncertain Transitions* (1999). She lives in Haverford, Pennsylvania, and Poznan, Poland.

www.ingramcontent.com/pod-product-compliance
Ingram Content Group UK Ltd.
Pitfield, Milton Keynes, MK11 3LW, UK
UKHW020126290926
15471UKWH00003B/318

9 780739 165140